CAMB[...]   [...]CS

General Editors: B. COMRIE, C. J. FILLMORE, R. HUDDLESTON,
R. LASS, D. LIGHTFOOT, J. LYONS, P. H. MATTHEWS,
R. POSNER, S. ROMAINE, N. V. SMITH, N. VINCENT

LEXICAL SEMANTICS

In this series:

P. H. MATTHEWS *Morphology*

B. COMRIE *Aspect*

R. M. KEMPSON *Semantic Theory*

T. BYNON *Historical Linguistics*

J. ALLWOOD, L.-G. ANDERSON, Ö. DAHL *Logic in Linguistics*

D. B. FRY *The Physics of Speech*

R. A. HUDSON *Sociolinguistics*

J. K. CHAMBERS and P. TRUDGILL *Dialectology*

A. J. ELLIOT *Child Language*

P. H. MATTHEWS *Syntax*

A. RADFORD *Transformational Syntax*

L. BAUER *English Word-formation*

S. C. LEVINSON *Pragmatics*

G. BROWN and G. YULE *Discourse Analysis*

R. HUDDLESTON *Introduction to the Grammar of English*

R. LASS *Phonology*

B. COMRIE *Tense*

W. KLEIN *Second Language Acquisition*

A. CRUTTENDEN *Intonation*

A. J. WOODS, P. FLETCHER and A. HUGHES *Statistics in Language Studies*

D. A. CRUSE *Lexical Semantics*

F. R. PALMER *Mood and Modality*

A. RADFORD **Transformational Grammar**

H. GARMAN *Psycholinguistics*

W. CROFT *Typology and Universals*

LEXICAL
SEMANTICS

D. A. CRUSE

DEPARTMENT OF GENERAL LINGUISTICS
UNIVERSITY OF MANCHESTER

CAMBRIDGE
UNIVERSITY PRESS

Published by the Press Syndicate of the University of Cambridge
The Pitt Building, Trumpington Street, Cambridge CB2 1RP
40 West 20th Street, New York, NY 10011–4211, USA
10 Stamford Road, Oakleigh, Melbourne 3166, Australia

First published 1986
Reprinted 1987, 1989, 1991, 1995, 1997

British Library cataloguing in publication data

Cruse, D. A.
Lexical semantics. –
(Cambridge textbooks in linguistics)
1. Semantics
I. Title
422 P325

Library of Congress cataloguing in publication data

Cruse, D. A.
Lexical semantics.
(Cambridge textbooks in linguistics)
Bibliography.
Includes index.
1. Semantics.   I. Title.   II. Series.
P325.C78 1986   412   86–917

ISBN 0 521 27643 8 paperback

Transferred to digital printing 2001

TO PAULE, PIERRE AND LISETTE

CONTENTS

Typographic conventions   *page*   xi

Preface   xiii

1   A contextual approach to lexical semantics   1
1.1   Introductory   1
1.2   Meaning and grammar   1
1.3   The data of semantics   8
1.4   Disciplining intuitions   10
1.5   The meaning of a word   15
     Notes   20

2   The syntagmatic delimitation of lexical units   23
2.1   Introductory   23
2.2   Semantic constituents   24
2.3   Semantic constituents which fail the test   29
2.4   Indicators, tallies and categorisers   32
2.5   Phonetic elicitors of semantic traits   34
2.6   Words   35
2.7   Idioms   37
2.8   Degrees of opacity   39
2.9   Idioms and collocations   40
2.10   Idiom and 'dead' metaphor   41
     Notes   45

3   The paradigmatic and syntactic delimitation of lexical units   49
3.1   Introductory   49
3.2   Selection and modulation of senses   50
3.3   'Indirect' tests for ambiguity   54

Contents

3.4 Direct criteria for ambiguity 58
3.5 Some difficult cases 62
3.6 Non-lexical sources of ambiguity 66
3.7 Establishment of senses 68
3.8 Sense-spectra 71
3.9 Syntactic delimitation 74
3.10 Lexemes 76
Notes 80

4 **Introducing lexical relations** 84
4.1 Preliminaries 84
4.2 Congruence 86
4.3 Cognitive synonymy 88
4.4 Hyponymy 88
4.5 Compatibility 92
4.6 Incompatibility 93
4.7 Congruence variants 95
4.8 Partial relations 96
4.9 Quasi-relations 97
4.10 Pseudo-relations 98
4.11 Para-relations 99
4.12 Syntagmatic relations of meaning between lexical units 100
Notes 109

5 **Lexical configurations** 112
5.1 Introductory 112
5.2 Hierarchies 112
5.3 Proportional series 118
Notes 134

6 **Taxonomies** 136
6.1 Hyponymy and incompatibility 136
6.2 Taxonymy 137
6.3 Characteristics of natural taxonomies 145
6.4 Over-specification, under-specification and the generic level 153
Notes 155

7 **Meronomies** 157
7.1 Introductory: parts and pieces 157

7.2	Defining meronymy	160
7.3	Aspects of transitivity: integral parts and attachments	165
7.4	Characteristics of meronomies	168
7.5	Close relatives of the part–whole relation	172
7.6	Meronomies and taxonomies	177
	Notes	180
8	**Non-branching hierarchies**	181
8.1	Introductory	181
8.2	From branching to non-branching	181
8.3	Chains, helices and cycles	187
8.4	Ranks, grades and degrees	192
	Notes	195
9	**Opposites I: complementaries and antonyms**	197
9.1	Oppositeness	197
9.2	Complementaries	198
9.3	Antonyms	204
9.4	Sub-classes of antonyms	206
9.5	Inherentness	214
9.6	Implicit superlatives	216
9.7	Stative verbs	217
9.8	Contrastive aspects	218
	Notes	220
10	**Opposites II: directional oppositions**	223
10.1	Directional opposites	223
10.2	Directions	223
10.3	Antipodals	224
10.4	Counterparts	225
10.5	Reversives	226
10.6	Relational opposites: converses	231
10.7	Indirect converses	233
10.8	Congruence variants and pseudo-opposites	240
	Notes	242
11	**Opposites III: general questions**	244
11.1	Impartiality	244
11.2	Polarity	246
11.3	Linguistic polarity and natural polarity	247

Contents

11.4	Logical polarity	252
11.5	Neutralisation and semantic markedness	255
11.6	The nature of opposition	257
11.7	What makes a 'good' opposition?	262
	Notes	262

12	**Synonymy**	**265**
12.1	Absolute synonyms and the scale of synonymity	265
12.2	Cognitive synonyms	270
12.3	Plesionyms	285
12.4	Congruence relations and synonymy	289
12.5	'Absolute', 'cognitive' and 'plesio-' relations outside synonymy	290
	Notes	291

References	295
Subject index	302
Author index	309

TYPOGRAPHIC CONVENTIONS

Small capitals
For names of scales associated with antonyms (e.g. LENGTH, COLDNESS: see 9.3)

Bold type
For technical terms when first introduced

Italics
For citation forms when not set on a different line

Obelisk
For technical terms not in current use elsewhere (when first introduced)

Single quotation marks
For quotations from other authors

Double quotation marks
For meanings (e.g. *stallion* = "male horse"), concepts and relations (e.g. the relation "– father of –")

Question marks
For semantic abnormality (e.g. ? *The cat barked*)

PREFACE

The title of this volume may lead some readers to expect a book about semantics. They will, I am afraid, be disappointed: the book is, in fact, about the meanings of words. It is not therefore *about* semantics; it is an exercise *in* semantics. My approach is descriptive, rather than formalistic. It will no doubt be seen as a fault by some that I have not tried to work within an explicit formal–theoretical framework. However, I do not believe that any currently available formal theory is capable of encompassing all the facts concerning word-meanings that have a prima facie claim on the attention of linguists. We have to choose, therefore, between theoretical rigour combined with descriptive poverty, and descriptive richness combined with a lower degree of theoretical control. The ultimate goal may well be an explicit theory with comprehensive explanatory power, but in the meantime it seems to me that research endeavour should continue on two parallel (but inter-connecting) fronts: theory constructions and theoretically uncommitted exploration of the field. This book exemplifies the latter approach.

The absence of a formal–theoretical framework does not mean, however, that I have attempted nothing more than semantic botanising: linguistics has certainly developed beyond the stage where a collection of pretty and curious semantic specimens, however attractively arranged and aptly and minutely described, would be an acceptable offering. My aim has been an exploration of the semantic behaviour of words which, methodologically, is located in the middle reaches of the continuum stretching from mere anecdotalism to fully integrated formal theory – an exploration disciplined by a consistent method of approach, and by a predilection for systematic, recurrent and generalisable facts rather than for particularity and idiosyncrasy. Although this is the spirit in which the vast majority of natural scientists – biologists, chemists, physicists, etc. – go about their research, I feel that work of this type is both undervalued by linguists and underrepresented in the linguistics literature.

Preface

In writing this book I have assumed very little in the way of a technical linguistics background on the part of the reader. Linguistically sophisticated readers may be irritated by the low level of discussion of technical linguistic – especially grammatical – matters. I hope such readers will be forbearing: I certainly hope they will find what I have to say on word-meaning interesting and worth while; but I would like the book to be accessible also to those with no formal training in linguistics (although I assume familiarity with traditional grammar). I have not attempted to give full bibliographical coverage of theoretical topics; for the sake of non-linguists I have tried to indicate a good general treatment of the topic in question; I assume that linguists will look elsewhere for full references.

I would like to thank all those who have helped, directly or indirectly, in bringing this book into being. Probably the person to whom I owe the greatest debt of gratitude is William Haas, under whom I first studied linguistics, and who inspired in me a particular interest in semantics. Over the years I have enjoyed innumerable lengthy discussions with him on virtually all the topics which appear in the book; his influence is so pervasive that I cannot properly detail his contribution. He also read and commented on the whole manuscript. The book developed from a course of lectures given to postgraduate and advanced undergraduate students in the General Linguistics Department at Manchester University. Many of my ideas changed considerably over this period as the scepticism of successive generations of students forced one re-think after another. I benefited greatly from comments on draft chapters by Tony Cowie (chapter 2) and David Allerton (chapters 1, 2 and 3). The person who has undoubtedly had the greatest direct influence on the final text is John Lyons, whose detailed comments – at the same time provocative and sympathetic – on virtually every page of the manuscript led to countless improvements. I shall probably live to regret the few instances where I decided not to follow his advice. Of course, the contents of the book do not necessarily reflect the views of any of those who have helped me, and responsibility for errors, misrepresentations and infelicities is entirely my own. The final manuscript was expertly typed by Irene Pickford, under considerable pressure, and in record time.

Finally I would like to thank my wife Paule for her love, patience and encouragement during the long gestation period, and for carrying an extra burden of family responsibility on many occasions so that I could work undisturbed.

I
A contextual approach to lexical semantics

1.1 Introductory

Before embarking on a study of lexical semantics, even one which is avowedly descriptive rather than theoretical in orientation, it is necessary to make explicit certain basic assumptions concerning meaning, and to establish, as far as possible, a consistent method of studying it. The approach which is adopted in this book, and which is described in this introductory chapter, is a variety of 'contextual' approach:[1] it is assumed that the semantic properties of a lexical item are fully reflected in appropriate aspects of the relations it contracts with actual and potential contexts. The full implications of this will become clearer as the exposition proceeds. In theory, the relevant contexts could include extra-linguistic situational contexts. But there are good reasons for a principled limitation to linguistic contexts: first, the relation between a lexical item and extra-linguistic contexts is often crucially mediated by the purely linguistic contexts (consider the possible relations between *horse* and the extra-linguistic situation in *That's a horse* and *There are no horses here*); second, any aspect of an extra-linguistic context can in principle be mirrored linguistically; and, third, linguistic context is more easily controlled and manipulated. We shall therefore seek to derive information about a word's meaning from its relations with actual and potential linguistic contexts.

However, the combinatorial characteristics of words in utterances are constrained not only by their meanings, but also by their grammatical properties. Grammatical constraints may overlap and reinforce semantic ones, but they may also be semantically arbitrary. In order to be able to use contextual relations for semantic purposes, therefore, we need to be able to recognise and discount combinatorial peculiarities which are purely grammatical in nature.

1.2 Meaning and grammar

Drawing a clear-cut distinction between meaning and grammar

1

is not an easy task, because the two are so intimately interwoven (this is hardly surprising: ultimately, the only purpose of grammar is to serve the conveyance of meaning). However, they can be disentangled sufficiently to allow our study of lexical semantics to proceed.

The distinction between grammar and meaning has a strong intuitive basis (notwithstanding difficulties of characterisation, and regions of uncertainty). Few, I imagine, would dispute that 1 is odd by virtue of its meaning, and 2 by virtue of its deviant grammar:

    1.   He harvested a magnetic puff of amnesia.
    2.   Them yesterday goed to home.

However, while every effort will be made to found arguments on intuitively clear cases of semantic deviance, it is only prudent to have some notion of what is involved in distinguishing this from syntactic deviance. Let us then take the discussion a stage further. Consider the following sentences:

    3.   It's too light for me to lift.
    4.   I've nearly completed. – (in answer to *How are you getting on with those jobs I asked you to do?*)

Both are, of course, deviant. But in attempting to decide whether the deviance in either case is grammatical or semantic, we are not wholly dependent on unaided intuition: reasoned arguments can be deployed. In 3, for instance, the deviance disappears completely if *light* is substituted by the semantically distinct, but syntactically identical, *heavy*. There would seem, therefore, to be ample justification for describing the deviance of 3 as semantic. In the case of 4 the deviance can be cured by inserting *them* after *completed*. This alters the syntactic nature of the sentence, but is (almost) semantically empty. We can also point to the difference in degree of deviance between 4 and 5, which is out of all proportion to any difference of meaning between *complete* and *finish*.

    5.   I've nearly finished.

It would seem perverse, therefore, to see the deviance of 4 as anything other than syntactic. These examples suggest that there is a possible principled basis for the distinction between semantic and syntactic deviance.

A frequently mentioned, and as often criticised, criterion is that of 'corrigibility':[2] the idea is that syntactic deviances can be readily corrected, whereas semantic deviances cannot. Consider sentences 1 and 2, for example: it is perfectly obvious what 2 'should be' – *They went home yesterday*; but what is to be done with 1? So far, so good. However, it is not difficult to find semantically ill-formed sentences which are easy to straighten out.

We need look no further than 3 – it is obvious enough what it 'should be'. Moreover, the notion of corrigibility is itself suspect: strictly speaking, one can only correct an utterance when one knows what the speaker intended to say, and this is not the case with the specially constructed sentences used in semantic analysis.

A more promising strategy is to ask not how or whether a deviant sentence can be corrected, but what the minimal changes are that will render it normal; then we examine the nature of the changes. If a deviant sentence can be normalised by adjusting its grammatical structure – for instance, by changing the order or syntactic category of elements, or by adding, substituting or deleting one or more grammatical elements – then it would seem reasonable to suppose that its deviance is grammatical in nature. If, on the other hand, the minimal change required is one necessarily involving one or more full lexical items, then it would seem justifiable to diagnose the deviance as semantic.

This procedure would be more informative if we were able to characterise grammatical and lexical elements more explicitly. This is, in fact, possible in terms of what are called **closed set items** and **open set items**.[3] The closed set elements in a sentence are those belonging to classes whose membership is virtually constant during the lifetime of an individual speaker (on a longer time-scale they do, of course, change). Typically they have few or no possibilities of substitution in an actual sentence:

6. John's kind*ness* amazed Mary.

   -s

They comprise affixes (*dis*like, kind*ness*, John's, wait*ed*, com*ing*, black*en*, etc.) and independent words (sometimes called **markers**), such as articles, conjunctions, prepositions and so on, a major part of whose linguistic function is to signal the grammatical organisation of sentences. The open set elements, on the other hand, are those which belong to classes which are subject to a relatively rapid turnover in membership, as new terms are coined and others fall into obsolescence. They are the lexical roots – the principal meaning-bearing elements in a sentence. (The open set elements in 6 are *John*, *kind*, *amaze* and *Mary*.) They typically have numerous possibilities of substitution in a sentence:

John's	*kind*ness	*amaze*d	*Mary.*
Bill-	*cool-*	*amuse-*	*Sue*
Mary-	*rude-*	*disturb-*	*John*
Sue-	*sad-*	*shock-*	*Bill*
etc.	etc.	etc.	etc.

3

It is with words containing open set elements that lexical semantics is principally concerned.[4]

We can now formulate a provisional test to determine whether a deviance is grammatical or semantic ('provisional', because, as we shall see, things are not so simple): if the minimal change required to 'cure' an anomaly in a sentence involves one or more closed set items, then the deviance is grammatical; if, however, the sentence can most easily be normalised by replacing one or more open set elements, then the deviance is semantic. With this test, sentences 1 and 2 are correctly diagnosed (that is to say, in accordance with strong intuition) as semantically and grammatically deviant, respectively. To normalise 1, the lexical roots must be altered, as no adjustment of closed set items has a noticeable effect: *He exhaled a carcinogenic puff of smoke*. All the changes needed to normalise 2, on the other hand, involve closed set items. A correct diagnosis is also obtained for 3: since it can be normalised by a simple substitution of an open set item, the test diagnoses its deviance as semantic.

It is, of course, perfectly possible for a sentence to exhibit semantic and grammatical deviance simultaneously:

    7.   The green idea sleep.

Two separate operations are needed to normalise this sentence, one involving closed set items:

    8a.   The green idea is sleeping.

and the other an open set item:

    8b.   The green lizard is sleeping.

What is more disturbing if we wish to achieve a simple separation of grammar and semantics is that on occasions one and the same deviance may be cured either by adjustment of closed set items, or by the replacement of open set items. Sentence 9a, for instance, can be normalised either as in b or as in c:

    9a.   The table saw Arthur.
     b.   The table was seen by Arthur.
     c.   The rhinoceros saw Arthur.

Similarly, 10a can be normalised as in b or c:

    10a.   I visited Arthur next week.
     b.   I shall visit Arthur next week.
     c.   I visited Arthur last week.

Are 9a and 10a, then, grammatically or semantically deviant? It will be argued that basically these sentences are semantically deviant; however, it must also be recognised that it is not possible to disentangle semantics from grammar completely. One reason for this is that many grammatical elements are themselves bearers of meaning – this is true, for instance, of the past tense affix *-ed*, and the plural affix *-s*. Because grammatical elements typically need to have the capacity to combine normally with semantically very various roots, their meanings tend to be of a very general sort: the notion of past tense, for instance, can combine without anomaly with virtually any conceivable verbal notion. But otherwise the meaning they carry is not of a radically different sort from that carried by lexical roots, and grammatical and lexical elements frequently interact semantically.[5] This is what happens in 10a. Since the anomaly arises here from a clash between the meaning of a closed set item and the meaning of an open set item, it can be cured by changing either.

Sentence 9a illustrates another type of meeting point between grammar and semantics. Here we have a semantic clash between two open set items (*table* and *see*); however, this is mediated in a crucial way by grammar. The grammar of English provides the verb *see* with two points of interaction with noun phrases:

$$X - \text{see} - Y$$

A noun phrase in the X-position interacts semantically with *see* in a different way from a noun phrase in the Y-position (the exact nature of these interactions can be considered part of the meaning of *see*). Sentence 9a is odd because *table* does not combine normally with *see* if it occupies the X-slot; it does, however, function as a perfectly normal occupant of the Y-slot (*Arthur saw the table*). This is why changing the voice of the verb in 9a from active to passive – which has the effect of interchanging the valency slots that the noun phrases occupy – removes the anomaly as effectively as replacing *see* or *table*.

Does this mean that, whenever we encounter a deviance that can be cured either by adjustment of grammar or lexical content, we can take it that semantics is involved? Unfortunately, no: such a deviance may be purely grammatical. Sentence 11a, for instance, can be normalised either by grammatical adjustment (11b) or by lexical adjustment (11c):

11a. The cake was baken.
   b. The cake was baked.
   c. The cake was taken.

We are led to the conclusion that 11a is grammatically but not semantically deviant by the fact that substitutes for *bake* which normalise the sentence (e.g. *shake*, *forsake*), as a class, have no distinctive semantic attributes (that is to say, members of the class share no characteristic patterns of co-occurrence with other open set elements that differentiate them from non-members); however, they do share a grammatical peculiarity, which is that they form their past participles with *-en*. The deviance of 11a is thus different from that of 9a: the substitutes for *table* in the latter which remove the anomaly can be distinctively characterised in semantic terms. The point concerning 11a can be made with greater force in respect of 12a, which can also be rendered normal by changing either a closed set item (12b) or an open set item (12c). In this case it is clearer, because of the greater number of possibilities, that the substitutes for *table* which normalise the sentence (*lit*, *buffet*, *journal*, *balcon*, etc.) have no common semantic properties which distinguish them from items (such as *chaise*, *bibliothèque*, *revue*, *assiette*) which do not remove the oddness:

    12a.   Le livre est sur le table.
       b.   Le livre est sur la table.
       c.   Le livre est sur le lit.

It is also significant that the oddness of 9a can be reduced by modifying *table* semantically: *The table with the electronic eye saw Arthur* (we know that it is the meaning of the modifying phrase which is important because the reduction in oddness depends on the open set items the phrase contains – compare *The table with the melamine top saw Arthur*); no similar modification of *bake* in 11a, or *table* in 12a, can reduce the degree of deviance of these sentences.

    We are now in a position to re-formulate our criteria for deciding whether an anomalous sentence is semantically or grammatically deviant:

(i)   an anomaly which can only be removed by replacing one or more open set items is semantic;

(ii)   an anomaly which cannot be removed by replacing one or more open set items, but can be removed by changing one or more closed set items, is purely grammatical;

(iii) an anomaly which can be cured either by changing one or more closed set items or by replacing one or more open set items is semantic (albeit with grammatical implications) if the open set replacements are distinguished by the possession of certain semantic properties;[6] otherwise, it is purely grammatical.

The concept of normalisability also forms the basis of a rather different way of determining whether an anomaly has a grammatical or semantic origin. Without tampering with the deviant sentence itself, we can investigate the effects of placing it in variously elaborated discourse contexts. If, by contextual manipulation, we can reduce the apparent oddness, or at least cause it to be perceived as communicatively appropriate, then we can take it that we are dealing with a semantic deviance (although the involvement of grammatical elements cannot be ruled out).[7] A purely syntactically ill-formed sentence, on the other hand, is irredeemably deviant, and the only contexts which can accommodate it are those which induce a tolerance for grammatical incompetence or, at any rate, nonconformity:

> As my two-year-old son said the other day: '. . . . . .'
> As our Portuguese plumber remarked: '. . . . . .'

A poetic context can also condition the reader or hearer to accept grammatical deviance, especially if syntactic well-formedness is clearly being sacrificed to some higher aesthetic end, such as the maintenance of rhyme, or metre, or some other patterning. The difference is that whereas a syntactic deviance may be tolerated, only a semantic deviance can be directly interpreted. A syntactically deviant sentence can be interpreted only by reference to a non-deviant sentence: a speaker, in other words, is not free to create his own grammar. Another way of formulating this criterion is to say that only a semantic deviance can be taken as a 'figure of speech'.

By this test, sentence 2 is clearly grammatically odd – no context can improve it. Likewise, 13:

13.   The old peasant's only possessions were three goat.

Sentence 9, on the other hand, can be seen as a sort of ironic hyperbole:

Arthur is paranoiac. He believes all his accidents are due to a cosmic conspiracy. No doubt the table saw him, computed his path across the room, and placed itself just where he would trip over it!

This is therefore a semantic oddity, according to the test. (A fairy-tale or science-fiction context could also normalise it.) What of sentence 1? It can be construed figuratively. Imagine a newly discovered plant, whose leaves when dried and smoked cause a temporary loss of memory; imagine, too, that it is highly addictive . . . *I am irresistibly drawn to a magnetic puff of amnesia.* Even a sentence like *I finished mine tomorrow morning* can be contextualised so as to present itself in the guise of a jocular paradox:

A: Have you all finished the jobs you were assigned?

B: Er ... yes. Tom and Dick finished theirs yesterday; Bill and Arthur finished this morning; and I ... er ... well, I finished mine tomorrow morning, I promise!

Notice that the two tests agree pretty well in their diagnoses, except that the contextualisation test reveals only syntactic deviance in sentences like 7, since they resist normalisation.

Objections can be raised to both these tests, and trickier examples unearthed. What seems indisputable, however, is that there are good grounds for attempting a separation of meaning and grammar. Furthermore, enough insight has been achieved in mapping their respective domains to allow us henceforth to set the problem of demarcation to one side.

1.3   The data of semantics

Any empirical study (a category to which lexical semantics, as outlined in this book, undoubtedly belongs) must rest, at some point, on a body of primary data, whose factuality is not questioned, and which is not subjected to further analysis. For a study of lexical semantics, there would seem to be two principal sources of primary data; needless to say, the native language-user is central to both of them.

One source is the productive output, spoken or written, of native users of the language. Clearly much insight into word-meaning is to be gained by observing the ways in which words are strung together by competent practitioners of a language. However, the approach has its limitations. Semantics done this way has more of the character of an 'observational science', like geology, than that of an 'experimental science', such as physics or chemistry. Scientists of the former type are, in a sense, at the mercy of the phenomena they study; what happens, and when, and under what conditions is largely beyond their control. An experimental scientist, on the other hand, arranges matters so that what happens will give him the greatest possible amount of information. Not surprisingly, the experimental sciences advance more rapidly than observational sciences, and achieve more sophisticated hypotheses and, ultimately, theories within a shorter space of time. A good example of this imbalance can be seen in psycholinguistics, where the study of language comprehension, being more experimental, is markedly more advanced than the study of language production, in which the investigator has less control over what happens. Probably the most disadvantaged researchers in this respect in the field of linguistic semantics are those who study 'dead' languages. Often virtually the only direct evidence available to them is a corpus of written utterances, of somewhat fortuitous make-up, and now probably fixed for eternity.

Speakers' utterances can be made semantically more informative if the investigator is able to constrain their production in various ways – for instance, by elicitation in tightly controlled situational contexts. An example might be to show informants a series of drawings, models, or other stimuli, and ask them to name them. If the materials are properly prepared and used, the procedure can have all the advantages of an experimental study. It is not, however, ideal as a general methodology for lexical semantics: it is far too cumbersome, many areas of meaning do not lend themselves to illustration in this fashion and, in any case, production only taps active competence.

The second principal source of primary data on which a study of lexical semantics can be based is furnished by intuitive semantic judgements by native speakers of linguistic materials of one kind or another. The investigator can, of course, exercise full control over the nature of these materials, and is thus in a position to elicit whatever information he needs. In essence, this is the strategy we shall adopt (except that the reader will be invited to act as his own informant: we shall not be concerned with problems and methods of field investigation). Two important questions arise from this decision. The first is: what sort of linguistic items should native speakers be asked to pass judgement on? The second is: what sort of judgements should they be asked to make?

It might seem obvious that, if one is studying word-meanings, one ought to find native speakers' intuitions concerning the meanings of words the most informative. However, this is not so. We shall inquire presently whether we should ask informants what things mean; let us first consider whether words are the most appropriate items of language on which to elicit judgement. As a matter of fact, there is no reason why language-users should be specially attuned to the semantic properties of words. We do not communicate with isolated words; words are not the bearers of messages; they do not, of themselves, 'make sense'; they cannot, taken singly, be true or false, beautiful, appropriate, paradoxical or original. A linguistic item must in general have at least the complexity of a simple sentence to show such properties. Words contribute, via their own semantic properties, to the meanings of more complex units, but individually they do not occasion our most vivid and direct experiences of language. We communicate with utterances; it seems reasonable to suppose, therefore, that our intuitions concerning utterances will be sharper, clearer and more reliable than those concerning individual words. Consequently, in this book arguments about the meaning of a word will be made to rest, as far as possible, on facts concerning utterances which contain the words in question.

The intuitions most relevant to a study of meaning would seem at first sight to be intuitions about what things mean. However, the reader is invited to try to formulate an explanation of the differences in meaning between the members of the following pairs of sentences:

14a. He watched it with intense concentration for a few moments, then left the room.
  b. He looked at it with intense concentration for a few moments, then left the room.
15a. However, she got the job in the end.
  b. Nevertheless, she got the job in the end.

It is safe to predict that many will find this task quite difficult. The fact seems to be that the ability to 'explain' meanings is an uncommon skill. This is not to suggest that the average speaker of English does not understand the differences of meaning. But it does appear that asking people what things mean is not necessarily the best way of tapping their semantic knowledge. How, then, is this to be done? The answer is to elicit not intuitions OF meaning, but intuitions ABOUT meaning, which, although they are one step removed from the primary object of interest, can, if properly chosen, be clear and reliable. Not all 'secondary semantic intuitions' are equally suitable as a basis for semantic analysis. Suppose, for example, one asks whether 16a and b have precisely the same meaning:

16a. The reign of William V commenced in the year 1990.
  b. The reign of William V began in the year 1990.

In a typical class of linguistically innocent students, some will reply 'Yes,' some 'No,' and most of the rest will be unable to make up their minds. Whether two expressions do or do not mean the same is a matter of some importance, but, again, it is evidently not something we should expect informants to tell us directly. What the most appropriate intuitions are, and how they are best used, form the topics of the next section.

1.4 Disciplining intuitions

No empirical science can operate without human intuitive judgement intervening at some point. This may be no more than a judgement of which line on a graduated scale a movable needle is nearest to. Equally, science would be much less advanced than it is if the only available data were intuitive estimates of quantities. What would be the chances of arriving at the principle of a constant coefficient of expansion in metals (the notion that for a given metal there is a fixed relationship between amount of change of temperature and amount of change of length) if the only data to hand concerning temperature and length were estimates based on unaided touch and sight? Although we can judge and compare lengths and temperatures to some extent, our naked intuitions of these properties are simply not accurate or reliable enough. However, matters can be arranged so that the judgements required of human observers are only those which they can make reliably and accurately. In studying the expansion of metals when they are heated, it is more profitable to limit the role of observers' intuitions to, for instance, judgements of the position of the top of a column of mercury relative to a graduated scale.

A parallel strategy is open to the semanticist. The things we really want to know are too difficult for straightforward intuition; we must therefore ask our informants questions that they CAN answer reliably and accurately. Unreliable, complex intuitions must be reduced to reliable, simple ones.

There is, of course, no inventory of appropriate intuitive judgements given in advance: candidates have to prove themselves by their effectiveness in analysis. On the other hand, a fairly circumscribed set of possibilities suggest themselves. The list offered here is not a closed one; the items put forward are simply those which have been found useful.

One of the simplest and most basic semantic judgements one can make concerning an utterance in one's native language is whether it is to some degree odd or not. Extensive use will be made of normality judgements in the course of this book. Each of the following pairs of sentences illustrates a difference of normality:[8]

17a. ? This is a club exclusively for married bachelors.
  b. This is a club exclusively for married men.
18a. ? Kicking with the feet incurs a penalty of 25 points.
  b. Kicking with the left foot incurs a penalty of 25 points.
19a. ? Let's sit by the stream and have a drink of time.
  b. Let's sit by the stream and have a drink of tea.
20a. ? The ant devoured the buffalo.
  b. The ants devoured the buffalo.
21a. ? We took the door off its hinges then went through it.
  b. We smashed the window then climbed through it.

Informants cannot, of course, be expected to quantify degrees of abnormality; but what they can do is distinguish a fully normal sentence from one which is to some degree odd. They can also very often rank sentences in order of normality. The sentences in 22 and 23 are arranged in order of normality:

22a. It's tea-time for my pet rabbit.
  b. It's tea-time for my pet scorpion.
  c. It's tea-time for my pet amoeba.
23a. The harpsichord needs re-tuning.
  b. The jam-jars need re-tuning.
  c. The banana needs re-tuning.

It perhaps ought to be pointed out here that an odd sentence is not necessarily meaningless, or incapable of conveying a message; nor is it the case that such sentences never occur naturally. On the contrary, an oddness of one sort or another is frequently a signal that an expression is being used creatively, in a novel extension of its usual sense.

A great deal can be done using only an undifferentiated notion of abnormality, especially in conjunction with suitable 'diagnostic frames' (see below); but it will not have escaped the notice of the attentive reader that the (a) sentences in 17–21 above are all odd in different ways. Perhaps, therefore, a more delicate and sophisticated analysis would be possible if different types of oddness were recognised?

The following are the principal varieties of semantic anomaly which can be easily recognised by direct intuition. As potential primitive terms, not to be subjected to further analysis, they are here defined ostensively, that is to say by exemplification:

A. Pleonasm
    Kick it with one of your feet.
    A female mother.
    He was murdered illegally.

B. Dissonance
    Arthur is a married bachelor.
    Let us drink time.
    Pipe . . . ditties of no tone. (Keats: *Ode on a Grecian Urn*)
    Kate was very married. (Iris Murdoch: *The Nice and the Good*)

C. Improbability
   The kitten drank a bottle of claret.
   The throne was occupied by a pipe-smoking alligator.
   Arthur runs faster than the wind.

D. Zeugma
   They took the door off its hinges and went through it.
   Arthur and his driving licence expired last Thursday.
   He was wearing a scarf, a pair of boots, and a look of
   considerable embarrassment.[9]

Intuitive judgements of the kind listed above are undoubtedly more informative than gross judgements of abnormality. However, the more subtle the judgement, the greater the dangers inherent in reliance on unaided intuition. Many instances of abnormality fall clearly into one or other of the four types; but, equally, there are certain uncertainties of application. Prudence might suggest that we should dispense with subdivisions of oddness: they are not needed, for instance, in connection with most diagnostic frames (see below). However, it would be a pity to ignore a potentially valuable source of information, and, in fact, some use will be made of them.

It is a matter of normal practice in the natural sciences for the human judgement involved in a measurement to be only indirectly related to the variable property which is the primary focus of interest. In measuring temperature, for instance, one uses a thermometer, in which temperature is reflected in the length of a column of mercury in a glass tube; the length of the mercury column, in turn, is estimated by lining up the mercury meniscus with one of a set of lines engraved on the glass. It is this last operation which is performed by the human observer, using only the equipment he was born with. A transformation is carried out by the measuring instrument: it can be viewed as a device for converting properties that unaided human intuition cannot deal with into ones that it can. The use of litmus paper furnishes another example of such a transformation. Humans are not very sensitive to the acidity or alkalinity of liquids, but they are perfectly capable of deciding whether a piece of red paper has turned blue, or vice versa. There is a parallel to this process of transformation in semantic analysis. By the use of what will be called 'diagnostic frames', semantic properties we wish to diagnose, but cannot leave to naked intuition, are converted into properties concerning which straightforward intuitive judgements are relatively reliable. Consider the frame *Xs and other Ys*. This can be used, in the manner of litmus paper, for the diagnosis of a particular relation between X and Y (relations of this sort are discussed in chapter 4). The judgement required of the informant is one of normality:

> dogs and other cats (odd)
> animals and other dogs (odd)
> dogs and other animals (normal)

A very useful intuition for semantic analysis is that of **entailment**.[10] A proposition P is said to entail another proposition Q when the truth of Q is a logically necessary consequence of the truth of P (and the falsity of P is a logically necessary consequence of the falsity of Q). Although the fundamental relation of entailment holds between propositions, we shall use the term to refer to an analogous relation between sentences. A sentence like *That's a dog* can be used to express an indefinitely large number of propositions (every distinct referent for *that* creates a different proposition). When it is said (as we shall say) that the sentence *That's a dog* entails the sentence *That's an animal*, what is meant is that in any conceivable situation in which *That's a dog* can (with appropriate reference) express a true proposition, there exists a corresponding proposition (i.e. with no change in the referents of referring expressions) expressible by *That's an animal*, whose truth is a necessary consequence of the truth of the first proposition. The intuition of entailment can be used directly, and it will be so used in this book. But it is arguable that its deepest roots are to be sought in patterns of normality and abnormality in a family of ordinary language expressions (which could be formulated as a set of diagnostic frames).[11] Thus the statement that *That's a dog* entails *That's an animal* can be viewed as a kind of shorthand for a pattern of normality like the following:

> It can't possibly be a dog and not be an animal.
> It's a dog therefore it's an animal.
> If it's not an animal, then it follows that it's not a dog.
> ? It's a dog, so it must be a cat.
> ? It's not an animal, but it's just possible that it's a dog.
> ? It's a dog, so it might be an animal.
> etc.

The most interesting entailments from the point of view of lexical semantics are those which hold between sentences which differ only in respect of the lexical fillers of a particular syntactic slot (e.g. *It's a dog, It's a cat*; *It's a rose, It's a flower*). In appropriate cases, the logical relations between the sentences can be correlated with meaning relations between the differentiating lexical items.[12]

The intuition of entailment may be used to establish four logical relations between sentences:

1. Unilateral entailment:
   It's a dog unilaterally entails *It's an animal*
2. Mutual entailment, or logical equivalence:
   The meeting began at 10.00 a.m. entails and is entailed by
   The meeting commenced at 10.00 a.m.
3. Contrariety:
   It's a cat and *It's a dog* stand in a contrary relation: *It's a cat* unilaterally entails *It's not a dog*
4. Contradiction:
   It's dead and *It's alive* stand in a contradictory relation:
   It's dead entails and is entailed by *It's not alive* (and *It's alive* entails and is entailed by *It's not dead*).

Another useful and reliable intuition is that of recurrence of semantic contrast, or semantic proportion. For instance, speakers are well able to judge that the contrast between 24a and b is the same as that between 25a and b, but different from that between 26a and b, and 27a and b:

24a. I like him.
  b. I dislike him.
25a. They approved of the idea.
  b. They disapproved of the idea.
26a. We appointed her.
  b. We disappointed her.
27a. You must embark now.
  b. You must disembark now.

This, too, will be used as an elementary intuitive judgement (especially in chapters 2 and 5). But it is a relatively complex judgement, and, like entailment, will probably prove to be derivable from more elementary intuitions (e.g. from patterns of normality and abnormality), although it is not at present clear how this is to be done.

1.5 The meaning of a word

It is taken as axiomatic in this book that every aspect of the meaning of a word is reflected in a characteristic pattern of semantic normality (and abnormality) in grammatically appropriate contexts.[13] That which is not mirrored in this way is not, for us, a question of meaning; and, conversely, every difference in the semantic normality profile between two items betokens a difference of meaning. The full set of normality relations which a lexical item contracts with all conceivable contexts will be referred to as its †**contextual relations**. We shall say, then, that the meaning of a word is fully reflected in its contextual relations; in fact, we can go further, and say that, for present purposes, the meaning of a word is constituted by its contextual relations.[14]

In its basic form, this conception of the meaning of a word is of limited usefulness:[15] much important information concerning word-meaning remains, as it were, latent. The picture can be made more revealing and informative in various ways. For instance, we can picture the meaning of a word as a pattern of affinities and disaffinities with all the other words in the language with which it is capable of contrasting semantic relations in grammatical contexts. Affinities are of two kinds, syntagmatic and paradigmatic. A syntagmatic affinity is established by a capacity for normal association in an utterance: there is a syntagmatic affinity, for instance, between *dog* and *barked*, since *The dog barked* is normal (a syntagmatic affinity always presupposes a particular grammatical relationship). A syntagmatic disaffinity is revealed by a syntagmatic abnormality that does not infringe grammatical constraints, as in *? The lions are chirruping*. Paradigmatically, a semantic affinity between two grammatically identical words is the greater the more congruent their patterns of syntagmatic normality.[16] So, for instance, *dog* and *cat* share far more normal and abnormal contexts than, say, *dog* and *lamp-post*:

> Arthur fed the dog/cat/?lamp-post.
> The dog/cat/?lamp-post ran away.
> The ?dog/?cat/lamp-post got bent in the crash.
> We painted the ?dog/?cat/lamp-post red.

An extremely useful model of the meaning of a word, which can be extracted from the contextual relations, is one in which it is viewed as being made up, at least in part, of the meanings of other words. A particular word-meaning which participates in this way in the meaning of another word will be termed a †**semantic trait**[17] of the second word. To render this picture more informative, it is necessary to distinguish degrees and modes of participation. We shall do this initially by defining a number of †**statuses** (degrees of necessity) of semantic traits: **criterial**, †**expected**, †**possible**, †**unexpected** and †**excluded**.

Criterial and excluded traits can be diagnosed by means of entailment relations between sentences: for instance, "animal" is a criterial trait of *dog* because *It's a dog* entails *It's an animal*; "fish" is an excluded trait of *dog* because *It's a dog* entails *It's not a fish*.

For the diagnosis of expected, possible and unexpected traits, the *but*-test is extremely useful.[18] This utilises the normality or abnormality of sentences of the form *P, but Q*. Consider the status of "can bark" as a trait of *dog*. First of all, *It's a dog* does not entail *It can bark* (since a dog may have a congenital malformation of the larynx, or some such); hence, "can bark" is not a criterial trait. However, the following two sentences show it to be an expected trait:

28. It's a dog, but it can bark. (odd)
29. It's a dog, but it can't bark. (normal)

The sort of oddness exhibited by 28 may be termed †**expressive paradox**, since the expressive meaning[19] carried by *but* is inappropriately deployed. The pattern of oddness is reversed in 30 and 31, showing that "can sing" is an unexpected trait of *dog*:

30. It's a dog, but it can sing. (normal sentence, unusual dog)
31. It's a dog, but it can't sing. (expressive paradox)

(It is of course necessary to ascertain that "can sing" is not an excluded trait of *dog*; the fact that *It's a dog* does not entail *It can't sing* confirms this.) A possible trait is signalled when both test sentences exhibit expressive paradox, and *P and Q* is normal:

32. It's a dog, but it's brown. (Why shouldn't it be?)
33. It's a dog, but it isn't brown. (Why should it be?)
34. It's a dog and it's brown. (normal)

At first sight, the picture of word-meaning given by patterns of affinity and disaffinity is, at least in some respects, different from the picture given by semantic traits. For instance, *cat* and *dog* have a fairly high degree of paradigmatic affinity, as they are equi-normal in a wide range of contexts:

> I stroked the cat/dog.
> We have a cat/dog at home.
> The cat/dog died.
> The children love the cat/dog.

But "cat" is an excluded trait of *dog*, since *It's a dog* entails *It's not a cat*. The two pictures are not, however, incompatible, they merely highlight different aspects of meaning. The affinity between *dog* and *cat* reveals itself in the number of equi-status or near-equi-status traits they have in common; and the differences between *dog* and *cat* appear more sharply when the affinity patterns are articulated in greater detail by means of diagnostic frames.

Although we have distinguished five discrete statuses, it must be borne in mind that the reality being described is a continuum – any discreteness is an artefact of the definitions. This is true even within the statuses that we have chosen to define by means of entailment. Probably most speakers of English would accept both of the following entailments:

> *It's a triangle* entails *It has three angles*
> *Lesley is Arthur's mother* entails *Lesley is female*

Although we shall continue to regard "three-angled" as a criterial trait of *triangle* and "female" as a criterial trait of *mother*, it must be conceded that there is a palpable difference in the degree of necessity of these two traits. A four-angled triangle is totally inconceivable – but a male mother? Is it beyond imagination, in these days of biological engineering, to conceive of a time when embryos will be implanted in a man's body, and develop, and be born – perhaps by caesarian section? Surely not TOTALLY?[20] No systematic use will be made here of a 'more criterial'/'less criterial' distinction. However, there is a distinction that can be made within 'expected' status which is of some significance in lexical semantics. Consider the relation between "adapted for flight" as a semantic trait of *bird*, and "possesses four legs" as a trait of *dog*. They are alike in that neither is criterial, both are expected:

> *It's a bird* does not entail *It is adapted for flight*

(There are birds such as the ostrich and the kiwi which are not adapted for flight.)

> *It's a dog* does not entail *It has four legs*

(A dog may have a birth abnormality, or may lose a leg in an accident.)

> It's a bird, but it's adapted for flight. (odd)
> It's a bird, but it's not adapted for flight. (normal)
> It's a dog, but it has four legs. (odd)
> It's a dog, but it doesn't have four legs. (normal)

There is, however, a difference in the status of these two traits. There is a sense in which a dog ought to have four legs – if it does not, it is imperfect, ill-formed, not fully functional. There is no recognised sub-category of dogs for which the possession of a number of legs other than four is the norm (as there is a sub-category of cats for which the absence of a tail is the norm). Species of birds which are not adapted for flight, on the other hand, are not ill-formed – they are merely atypical. Semantic traits whose absence is regarded as a defect will be called †**canonical traits**.[21] Canonical traits can be distinguished from non-canonical expected traits in a number of ways:

> ? The typical dog has four legs.
> ? Dogs typically have four legs.
> The typical bird is adapted for flight.
> Birds are typically adapted for flight.
> ? A dog that does not have four legs is not necessarily defective.
> A bird that cannot fly is not necessarily defective.
> ? What kinds of dog have only three legs?
> What kinds of bird are not adapted for flight?

Canonical traits are not only to be found in words denoting living things. We could say, for instance, of *le table ronde* that it lacked a canonical trait of noun phrases in French, namely, concord in respect of gender. Likewise, a command enjoining some action which was logically impossible, or which had already been carried out, or a lie that through ignorance on the part of the perpetrator turned out to be objectively true, can both be considered defective through the lack of a canonical trait.

The adoption of the contextual approach to word-meaning outlined in this chapter has certain inescapable consequences that some might consider to be disadvantages. One is that any attempt to draw a line between the meaning of a word and 'encyclopaedic' facts concerning the extra-linguistic referents of the word would be quite arbitrary; another is that there is no motivation for isolating 'pragmatic meaning' as a separate domain of lexical meaning.[22] Perhaps most importantly, it would seem that we have no grounds for believing that the meaning of a word, when viewed in this fashion, is finitely describable – without severe circumscription it is an unpromising candidate for formalisation, or representation in terms of logical or quasi-mathematical formulae. However, our conception of word-meaning has the advantage of being intuitively plausible: its scope coincides well with the pre-theoretical notion of word-meaning that anyone with a practical interest in meaning – a lexicographer, translator, or language teacher, or even a novelist or poet – is likely to have. Unwieldy it may be in certain respects, but it is surely better for a model of meaning destined to serve a descriptive as opposed to a theoretical study to err on the side of generosity of scope, rather than on the side of austerity.

While the contextual method is well-suited to the exploration of the infinite subtlety and particularity of word-meanings, it is nonetheless more particularly the aim of this book to seek out and highlight anything which lends itself to generalisation, even of a limited sort, any tendency towards structure, system and recurrence, in the domain of word-meaning.

Notes

It will be obvious to anyone familiar with the thinking of W. Haas on semantic topics that this chapter and chapter 2 owe a heavy debt to his ideas. Unfortunately, there is no comprehensive exposition of these views.

1.1

1. The elements of the contextual approach described in this chapter can be found in Haas (1962 and 1964). See also the introduction to Allerton *et al.* (1979).

1.2

2. For discussion of the criterion of corrigibility (and different conclusions) see Lyons (1977: 379–86).
3. See Allerton (1979: 46–7).
4. The distinction between open and closed set elements is not an absolute one, although marginal cases are relatively uncommon. The temporal prepositions in English – *after, at, since, during*, etc. – may be cited as borderline instances: there is a relatively, but not absolutely, fixed inventory – a recent arrival is *pre* (see Howard (1985: 8)); the number of members in the set, and the semantic burden they carry, are both greater than is usual for closed set items. It should also be noted that semantic notions which are expressed in one language grammatically (i.e. by means of closed set items) may well be expressed in another language lexically (i.e. by means of open set items).
5. See Lyons (1968: 438).
6. Circularity is avoided by interpreting 'possession of common semantic properties' as "having similar patterns of normal co-occurrence with other open set items".
7. See Haas (1973: 82).

1.4

8. The property of normality was introduced earlier in connection with utterances – here it is used of sentences. There is no doubt that it is primarily a property of utterances (this term is used here to denote sentences put to particular communicative use in an actual context). For some sentences, however, because of their semantic make-up, it is extremely difficult to conceive of a context in which they could be used to form a normal utterance. We may describe these as abnormal sentences. Notice that a normal sentence (i.e. one for which it is easy to think of a situation in which it would constitute a normal utterance) might well constitute an abnormal utterance in some particular context: for instance, *I was born in Gateshead* is a normal sentence, but would be odd as an answer to *What time is it?*

9. *Pleonasm* and *zeugma* are traditional terms; *improbability* is, I hope, self-explanatory; *dissonance* is my own invention. The following points are worth noting here:

   (i) A pleonastic expression can be normalised by replacing one of its elements with something more specific: *a female mother* (odd), *a lesbian mother* (normal); *Kick it with one of your feet* (odd), *Kick it with your left foot* (normal). A dissonance, on the other hand, can only be cured, if at all, by replacing one element by something less specific: *The cat barked* (odd), *The animal barked* (normal). These points are developed more fully in 4.12.

   (ii) It is normal to express astonishment, or disbelief, on hearing an improbability:

   A: Our kitten drank a bottle of claret.
   B: No! Really?

   This is not true of the more extreme forms of dissonance:

   A: We went on falling upwards.
   B: Did you really?

   (iii) A zeugma can often be normalised by 'unyoking' the items that have been inappropriately linked: thus in *Arthur and his driving licence expired last Thursday*, *Arthur* and *his driving licence* should not be hitched simultaneously to a single occurrence of *expire*, as they involve different senses. Separating them out cures the oddness: *Arthur expired last Thursday; his driving licence expired that day, too.*

10. From the point of view of a logician or formal semanticist what I say under this heading is extremely superficial. However, my main aim here is to identify a particular semantic intuition. (It is possible that what I call entailment is better described by Lyon's expression 'pragmatic implication' (1977: 204).) More detailed and rigorous discussion of logical matters relevant to semantics can be found in Allwood, Anderson and Dahl (1977).

11. For the view that logical notions are a 'distillation' or 'refinement' of ordinary language notions see, for instance, Strawson (1952: ch. 1) and Haas (1975).

12. Such as cognitive synonymy (4.3 and 12.2), hyponymy (4.4), incompatibility (4.6), etc.

1.5

13. The distinction between semantic and grammatical deviance assumes crucial importance here.

14. This is not intended to be a philosophical statement concerning what Ross (1981: 14–15) calls 'absolute meaning': it is, in Ross's terms, a statement about what 'linguistic meaning' will be taken to be.

15. It is not, however, entirely uninformative: see the definition in 12.1 of 'absolute synonymy'.

16. Haas (1964) portrays the meaning of a word as a 'semantic field', which contains all possible (grammatical) sentential contexts of the word, and all possible (grammatical) substitutes within those contexts. The semantic field has a 'focal area' which consists of the word's most normal contexts, and the most normal substitutes in those contexts. The focal area shades off gradually to an indeterminate periphery. What is proposed here is very close to this. Both – to some extent at least – are Firthian in spirit: Firth (1957: 194–6) held that the meaning of a word (at one level) could be known by the company it keeps. (See also Mackin (1978).)

17. I have chosen to use this term rather than the more usual **semantic features** or **semantic components** as a deliberate act of distancing. Representing complex meanings in terms of simpler ones is as problem-ridden in theory as it is indispensable in practice. I would like my semantic traits to carry the lightest possible burden of theory. No claim is made, therefore, that they are primitive, functionally discrete, universal, or drawn from a finite inventory; nor is it assumed that the meaning of any word can be exhaustively characterised by any finite set of them. They are close to what logicians call **meaning postulates** (see Carnap (1952)). For various theoretical positions concerning semantic features see Hjelmslev (1961: 60–75), Katz and Fodor (1963), Bendix (1966), Coseriu (1967), Bierwisch (1969 and 1970a), Geckeler (1971), Pottier (1974), Leech (1974: ch. 6), Nida (1975), Wierzbicka (1980). For critical comment see Bolinger (1965), Lyons (1977: 317–35), Sampson (1979), Moore and Carling (1982: 126–39), Cruse (1983), Pulman (1983: 29–51).

18. See Bendix (1966: 23–31).

19. Expressive meaning is discussed in 12.2.

20. See Lyons (1981: 89).

21. A notion which is frequently invoked nowadays in discussion of word-meaning is that of **prototypical features**. The work of Rosch and her associates (summarised in Rosch (1978) has shown that informants judge some members of taxonomic categories to be 'better' or 'more central' than others. The most central examples are called **prototypes**. Those features which correlate with judgements of better category membership are called prototypical features. There is a detailed critical discussion of prototypicality in Pulman (1983: 83–106); see also Coleman and Kay (1981). I am still uncertain what the precise linguistic significance of this notion is, so I prefer not to work with it. My distinction between canonical and non-canonical expected traits seems to have some similarity with Coleman and Kay's distinction between prototypical and typical features; however, my impression is that the traits that are described here as canonical are not envisaged by Rosch as falling into the category of prototypical features.

22. In this book the domain of semantics is taken to be the whole realm of linguistic meaning. It is more usual nowadays, however, to draw a distinction between 'semantic meaning' and 'pragmatic meaning', although not everyone draws the line in the same place. See Levinson (1983: 5–35) for discussion of this issue.

2
The syntagmatic delimitation of lexical units

2.1 Introductory

Now that we have the outline of an approach to the study of the meanings of words, we can turn our attention to the task of providing a more exact characterisation of the linguistic units which will form the objects of our study. As a beginning, it may be said that the conception of a lexical unit which will be adopted here is not very different from that of a traditional lexicographer, although we shall try to be more explicit than lexicographers are wont to be.[1] An ordinary dictionary characterises a lexical item in three distinct, though intimately inter-connected, ways: first, its form (graphic and phonological); second, its grammatical function; and, third, its meaning. Correspondingly, we shall have to consider three aspects of the delimitation of a lexical item. First of all, we must delimit the form of a lexical item syntagmatically; that is to say, we must be able to state in any sentence where the boundaries between lexical items are (we shall assume that any well-formed sentence consists of a whole number of such units). Second, having set up syntagmatic units, we shall observe that many of them appear to operate in a variety of grammatical environments, and we shall have to ask ourselves whether some differences of grammatical usage of a particular form do not merit recognition as separate lexical items. Take, for instance, the word form *open*: *The Concise Oxford Dictionary* (*C.O.D.*) has two separate main entries for this, corresponding to its occurrence in *The sky-light was open* and *The duchess refused to open the safe*. Lest anyone should think that the matter is totally unproblematical, it is perhaps worth pointing out that the same dictionary gives no separate recognition to the parallel occurrences of *shut*. Finally, it is clear that besides having a variety of grammatical uses, a word form may well display a split semantic personality, too, even within a constant grammatical frame. Consider *bank* in *We finally reached the bank*. There is here a choice of readings which is in some ways not so very different from the sort of choice available in

> John saw the cat
>> carpet
>>
>> cushion
>>
>> etc.

There is, of course, one important difference, namely, that in the latter case the meaning options are paralleled by differences of form, and so it is easy to individuate and enumerate the elements from which the choice must be made. However, there is at least a prima facie case for believing that a word form like *bank* should be considered to represent more than one lexical unit. The criteria for deciding how many lexical units we are dealing with in cases like *open* and *bank* will be discussed in chapter 3. The principal concerns of the present chapter are the criteria for establishing lexical units syntagmatically, and to these we now turn.

The basic syntagmatic lexical units of a sentence will be defined as the smallest parts which satisfy the following two criteria;

> (i)   a lexical unit must be at least one semantic constituent
>
> (ii)   a lexical unit must be at least one word.

These criteria need careful elaboration, but the following will serve as a preliminary illustration of the points:

> – the prefix *dis-* of *disobey* is not a lexical unit because, although it is a semantic constituent, it is smaller than a word.
>
> – the *pulled* of *Arthur pulled a fast one* is not a lexical unit because, although it is a word, it is not a semantic constituent.

Let us now examine the notion of semantic constituent.

2.2   Semantic constituents

The meaning of a typical sentence in a natural language is complex in that it results from the combination of meanings which are in some sense simpler. (The fact that the meanings of sentences are more accessible to intuition than the meanings of words does not alter this.) These simpler meanings (which does not necessarily mean 'simple') are carried by identifiable parts of the sentence; and the way they must be combined to yield the global meaning of the sentence is indicated by the syntactic structure of the sentence.[2] Thus, the meaning of *The cat sat on the mat* is "the" + "cat" + "sat" + "on" + "the" + "mat", combined in the ways signalled by the syntactic structure, which tells us, for instance, that "on" goes with "the mat", rather than with "the cat", and so on. The syntactic structure also defines intermediate complexes, such as "the cat" and "on the mat", which, when appropriately combined, yield the global meaning of the sentence, but which themselves can be decomposed into more elementary parts. Any constituent part of a sentence that bears a meaning which combines with the meanings of the other constituents to give the overall meaning of the sentence will be termed a †**semantic constituent**. A semantic constituent which cannot be segmented into more elementary semantic constituents will be termed a †**minimal semantic constituent**. Thus *on the mat* is a semantic constituent of *the cat sat on the mat*, but not a minimal one, as it ultimately divides further into *the*, *on* and *mat*; the latter, on the other hand, are incapable of further subdivision, and are therefore minimal semantic constituents. Notice that the term semantic constituent is not used to refer to a meaning only, but to a form-plus-meaning complex; that is to say, a semantic constituent is a meaningful form (the precise sense of *meaningful* intended here will be clarified below) with a determinate grammatical function.

In most cases it is immediately clear what the semantic constituents of a sentence (or part thereof) are. But to be able to handle borderline or other problematic cases with any degree of confidence we need a firmer characterisation, grounded in more basic intuitive judgements of the kind introduced in the previous chapter. However, before going on to propose a test for semantic constituency, it might be useful to clarify the notion further in an informal way. An important indication (although, as we shall see, not a sufficient one) that a portion of a sentence is a semantic constituent is that its semantic contribution to the sentence is the same as that which it makes to other, different sentences; in other words, it carries what is in some sense a constant meaning from context to context. Consider *sacks* in the following sentences:

1. The sacks had been hung out to dry.
2. A woman was repairing sacks.
3. Everywhere there were sacks full of potatoes.

Sentences 1, 2 and 3 all contain the meaning "sacks"; the only formal element they have in common is the graphic sequence *sacks*. We can therefore be reasonably confident in identifying *sacks* as the bearer of the meaning "sacks". However, this is not sufficient to guarantee semantic constituency. Take *black* in 4 and 5:

4. A blackbird sang softly in the willow-tree.
5. A black bird sang softly in the willow-tree.

Intuitively, it would be difficult to deny that there was a connection between the semantic contributions of *black* in the two sentences: blackness is not irrelevant to blackbirds (even if it is true that not all blackbirds are black) – this is proved by the normality of *blackbirds, crows and other black birds*. Yet equally clearly there is a difference. Put simply, the meanings of *black* and *bird* do not add up to the meaning of *blackbird*, but do yield that of *black bird*. In other words, *black* in 4, although not devoid of meaning, is not a semantic constituent: it does not carry one of the set of simpler meanings which on combination yield the global meaning of the sentence. To arrive at the overall meaning of 4, *blackbird* must be taken as a minimal semantic constituent. On the other hand, *black* is, of course, a semantic constituent of 5.

An important diagnostic test for semantic constituency, and one which utilises one of the basic intuitive judgements introduced in the previous chapter, is the test of †**recurrent semantic contrast**.[3] Suppose we take our previous sentence *The cat sat on the mat* and substitute for one of its constituent parts, *cat*, a different, but syntactically identical, element such as *dog*. The result of this substitution is of course change in the meaning of the sentence. Now it so happens that we can make the same substitution of forms in an otherwise completely different sentence, producing an exactly parallel change of meaning:

6. $\dfrac{\text{cat}}{\text{dog}}$ (The — sat on the mat) = $\dfrac{\text{cat}}{\text{dog}}$ (We bought a —)

This test precisely locates the form responsible for a given meaning, and at the same time ensures that its role is that of a semantic constituent; from 6 we can therefore conclude that *cat* is a semantic constituent of *The cat sat on the mat*. Observe now what happens when we attempt to set up an equation like 6 using a portion of a sentence which is clearly not a semantic constituent. Suppose we replace the *-at* of *mat* by *-oss*. The result is certainly a change of meaning: *The cat sat on the moss*; but in this case it is impossible to find a different sentence in which the same substitution of forms produces a parallel change of meaning. In other words, we cannot show a recurrent semantic contrast, although it is, of course, possible to find sentences where the substitution of forms can be made without a recurrence of the semantic contrast:

7. $\dfrac{\text{-at}}{\text{-oss}}$ (He doesn't like his new b—)

It may be thought that in 8 we have an equation which indicates (wrongly) that *-at* is a semantic constituent:

8. $\underline{\text{-at}}$ (The cat sat on the m—) = $\underline{\text{-at}}$ (The m— is wet)
    -oss   -oss

It is true that 8 exemplifies a recurrent semantic contrast, but this is possible only because of the presence of *m—* in both sentences. It is essential, in carrying out the test, to use sentential frames which ideally do not share any elements (although in practice it is usually sufficient if the immediate pre- and post- environments of the substituted items are distinct). It is also important that the substituted items should belong to the same syntactic class; that is, there should be no change in the syntactic structure of the frame as a result of the substitution. The reason for this is that we want to be able to attribute all changes of meaning on substitution to differences in the semantic properties of the items being substituted.

We are now in a position to spell out precisely the basic form of the recurrent contrast test for semantic constituency:

A part X of a grammatically well-formed and semantically normal sentence S^1 is a semantic constituent of S^1 if

(i)   X is either omissible or replaceable by some other element Y, yielding a grammatically well-formed and semantically normal sentence S^2 which is syntactically identical to S^1 but distinct in meaning from S^1

and (ii)   there exists at least one other grammatically well-formed and semantically normal sentence S^3, containing X, but otherwise having no other elements in parallel syntactic positions in common with S^1, in which X is similarly omissible or replaceable by Y, yielding a syntactically identical but semantically distinct sentence S^4

and (iii)   the semantic contrast between S^1 and S^2 is identical to that between S^3 and S^4.

Strictly speaking, only two sentential contexts are required to prove semantic constituency, but of course a constituent limited to only two specific contexts would necessarily play only a minor role in a language. For a typical semantic constituent, there is an unlimited number of possible sentential frames.

Before going on to consider more problematic aspects of semantic constituency, let us look at a few more examples of the recurrent semantic contrast test in action. Take the prefix *in-* in *inhale*, *inconspicuous* and *impertinent*. For *inhale* and *inconspicuous*, the semantic constituency of *in-* is easily established, although the semantic identity of *in-* is different in the two cases:

9. $\underline{\text{in-}}_{\text{ex-}}$ (John —haled) = $\underline{\text{im-}}_{\text{ex-}}$ (They —port textiles)

(Here, *in-* and *im-* represent the same grammatical element: the prefix merely adapts itself phonetically to the initial consonant of the root.[4])

10. $\underline{\text{in-}}_{\phi}$ (The bulge in his pocket was —conspicuous) =

$\underline{\text{in-}}_{\phi}$ (This disease is —curable)

Turning now to *impertinent*, we can readily see that although the *im-* is replaceable by zero, it does not qualify as a semantic constituent:

11. $\underline{\text{im-}}_{\phi}$ (His remarks were —pertinent) ≠

$\underline{\text{im-}}_{\phi}$ (What you suggest is —possible)

It is not possible to discover even one other sentential context in which the *im-*/zero alternation can reproduce the contrast we find with *impertinent*. This means that unless the *im-* of *impertinent* can be 'rescued' by any of the procedures detailed in the next section (and, in fact, we shall find that it cannot), it fails to satisfy the criteria for semantic constituency. Those who detect a 'negative emotive force' in the (apparent) negative prefix not only of *impertinent*, but also of *impudent*, *indignant*, *indifferent* and possibly *inane* (in none of which is it a true semantic constituent), may be reluctant to accept this result. However, as we shall see, it is necessary to recognise several 'lesser' semantic roles besides the central one of being a semantic constituent, so that to deny semantic constituency to an element is not necessarily to deny it any semantic role whatsoever: the 'negative emotive force' can, in fact, be accommodated.[5]

It was claimed earlier that *black-* in *blackbird* was not a semantic constituent; we can now verify the claim by subjecting it to the recurrent contrast test:

12. $\underline{\text{black-}}_{\text{blue-}}$ (The teacher read a story about a —bird)

≠ $\underline{\text{black}}_{\text{blue}}$ (Cynthia wore — stockings)

This example is useful for understanding how the test works. If, in replacing *black-* in *blackbird* by *blue-*, one merely replaced "black" by "blue", then the contrast would be found to recur. But at least some of the meaning of *blackbird* belongs to the whole complex, and is not attributable to either *black-* or *bird* separately; so, when *black* is replaced, this additional meaning is lost, along with "black". Since the additional meaning is unique to *blackbird*, no recurrence of the resulting contrast is possible.

2.3 Semantic constituents which fail the test

The vast majority of items for which there is a strong intuition either of meaningfulness or meaninglessness respond in the appropriate way to the test of recurrent semantic contrast. We may confidently say that the typical semantic constituent passes the test. However, there are certain peripheral types of semantic constituent which cannot be directly subjected to the test. This may be because they occur only in association with a particular element, like the *cran-* of *cranberry*, or because they occur with a particular semantic value only in the context of one other element, like the *-en* of *oxen*, the *ab-* of *abnormal*, or *foot* in *foot the bill*; in a case of **collocational uniqueness** of either of these types, no contrast in which the unique element participates can be tested in a distinct linguistic environment. Or a semantic constituent may be untestable because it is completely determined syntactically, like *-ness* in *His kindness was overwhelming*, and thus does not participate in any contrasts at all. For some of these items – for instance, *foot* in *foot the bill* – there is a strong intuition of meaningfulness; for others, like *cran-*, intuition is less certain. Clearly, some way of deciding is needed.

There are two principal strategies for proving that a collocationally unique item is a semantic constituent. The first consists in demonstrating that the element in question participates in the same semantic contrast with a third element as a proven semantic constituent. For the purpose of this test a contrast with zero is valid. Take the *-en* of *oxen*: this contrasts with its own absence just like the *-s* of *cows*, and with a precisely parallel semantic effect:

13. $\dfrac{\text{-en}}{\phi}$ (The ox— trudged past) = $\dfrac{\text{-s}}{\phi}$ (The cow— grazed here)

The *-s* of *cows* can be shown to be a semantic constituent by the normal test:

14. $\dfrac{\text{-s}}{\phi}$ (The cow— grazed here) = $\dfrac{\text{-s}}{\phi}$ (Our dog— barked)

29

From this it seems eminently reasonable to conclude that *-en*, too, is a semantic constituent. Similarly, 15 and 16 show *ab-* in *abnormal* to be a semantic constituent:

15. $\dfrac{\text{ab-}}{\phi}$ (That's —normal) = $\dfrac{\text{un-}}{\phi}$ (He was —popular)

16. $\dfrac{\text{un-}}{\phi}$ (He was —popular) = $\dfrac{\text{un-}}{\phi}$ (They looked —happy)

The same technique can be used for *foot* in *foot the bill* and *red* in *red hair*, although perhaps marginally less convincingly. The case for *foot* rests on the presumed equivalence of contrast between *foot* and *query*, and *pay* and *query*, in 17:

17. $\dfrac{\text{foot}}{\text{query}}$ (John agreed to — the bill) =

$\dfrac{\text{pay}}{\text{query}}$ (We shall certainly — the fees)

However, some may feel that there is more to footing a bill than merely paying it: there is a hint of reluctance, of the imposition of an unwelcome demand for money on the payer, which renders the equivalence of the contrasts in 17 slightly suspect.[6] Another way of approaching *foot the bill* will be suggested below. The reason why *red* in *red hair* is unique is that the colour it refers to would not be labelled *red* if anything other than hair were being described. (Current fashions make a 'true' red for hair not impossible, so that *red hair* is now ambiguous. We are here discussing the more traditional usage.) It is not an easy colour to describe, but let us assume that, say, a carpet the colour of red hair would be described as *light reddish-brown*. We can then establish *red* as a semantic constituent via an equivalent contrast with *black*:

18. $\dfrac{\text{red}}{\text{black}}$ (She has — hair) =

$\dfrac{\text{light reddish-brown}}{\text{black}}$ (The new carpet is —)

A slightly more oblique approach to the problem of determining whether a contextually unique item is a semantic constituent is to see whether it is normal in the language to treat it in parallel with unquestionable semantic constituents. The most obvious type of 'treating in parallel' is coordination: in general, a non-constituent cannot be coordinated with a constituent without oddness:

> 19.   ? Arthur kicked the detonator of the bomb, and, consequently, the bucket.

The normality of the following sentences is therefore evidence that the collocationally unique elements *gnash* and *purse* are semantic constituents of the expressions *gnash the teeth* and *purse the lips*, respectively:

> 20.   He kept baring and gnashing his teeth.
> 21.   Samantha was pursing, licking and biting her lips.

The parallelism may be less transparent: in 22 *foot* and *scrutinise* have a parallel relation to *bill*, and in 23 *foot* and *add up* have a parallel relation to *bill*. *Scrutinise* and *add up* are clear semantic constituents, so the parallelism is sufficient to establish *foot* as a semantic constituent too:[7]

> 22.   Arthur agreed to foot the bill only after scrutinising it carefully first.
> 23.   I'm expected not only to foot the bills, but to add them up as well.

Certain uniquely determined grammatical elements present special problems. Some clearly fail the recurrent contrast test, and rightly so. For instance, the -*s* of *books* in *those books* does not contrast with anything, so there is no question of recurrence. This is a correct result: semantically speaking, the element "plural" occurs only once in the phrase *those books*. Thus the -*s* here does not independently signal plurality, but only in conjunction with the exponent of plurality in *those*. We may perhaps speak here of a **discontinuous semantic constituent**.[8] More difficult are elements like -*ness* in 24:

> 24.   His kindness amazed us all.

In spite of the fact that nothing can be substituted for -*ness*, and it therefore participates in no contrasts, recurrent or otherwise, it is different from -*s* in *those books*, and arguments can be put forward that it should be regarded as a semantic constituent. One such argument runs as follows: *kind*- in 24 has normal recurrent contrasts (e.g. with *cool*-), and is thus a semantic constituent; so also is *kindness* – it contrasts, for instance, with *hat*; since *kind*- is not synonymous with *kindness*, -*ness* must signal the semantic difference between them. The meaning(s) of -*ness* can, moreover, be glossed: "the degree to which (he was kind)" or "the fact that (he was kind)"; also, these meanings are recurrent – they appear also in *coolness* and *foolishness* (notice that if the two meanings had been signalled by two different affixes, there would be no problem about their status as constituents). It would seem reasonable, in general, that if a sequence of elements AB can be shown to be a semantic constituent, and one of the parts of the sequence satisfies the recurrent contrast criterion, then the status of semantic constituent should be accorded to the remaining part of the sequence, even if it does not satisfy the recurrent contrast criterion. This is the view we shall adopt.[9]

2.4 Indicators, tallies and categorisers

There are several types of element which fail the straightforward version of the recurrent contrast test, and cannot be rescued by any of the strategies suggested in the previous section, but which cannot, unlike the *-oss* of *moss*, be dismissed as having no semantic relevance. One type is exemplified by the *cran-*, *bil-*, *rasp-*, *goose-* of *cranberry*, *bilberry*, *raspberry* and *gooseberry*; the *bull-* of *bullfinch*, the *missel* of *missel thrush*, the *dor-* of *dormouse*; also the *pad-* of *padlock* and *gang-* of *gangway* – and many more. In none of these cases does either the first or the second element qualify as a semantic constituent:

25.   rasp- (We ate some —berries) ≠ rasp- (Don't forget the —)
      goose-   goose-

Such semantic contrasts are impossible to duplicate; for the second elements of these words, it is usually impossible even to find a recurrence of the form contrast. Where the elements are two separate words, the first can often be coordinated with other elements:

> blue and hump-backed whales
> missel and song thrushes

However, this does not prove semantic constituency, because coordination is normal only with other elements of the same sort – i.e. elements which similarly fail the recurrent contrast test. They do not coordinate with normal semantic constituents:

> ? blue and carnivorous whales

The expression *herring and common gulls* illustrates this point well, because it is normal if *common* is taken to identify a particular species of gull (in which case it is not a semantic constituent), but odd if it is taken to mean "not rare". It might be argued that the test procedure is thus shown to be at fault, since in all the above cases the first element can be shown to have a clear semantic function relative to the second element: in fact, it signals a sub-variety of the general category denoted by the second element. Thus, a raspberry is a type of berry, a bullfinch a type of finch, a dormouse a type of mouse, a padlock a type of lock, etc. As proof, it is sufficient to point to the following entailment relations:

> *It's a bilberry* unilaterally entails *It's a berry*
> *It's a dormouse* unilaterally entails *It's a mouse*

However, let us consider, for instance, *cranberry* more carefully. Granted that a cranberry is a variety of berry, what exactly does *cran-* mean? It is a curious fact that native speakers are unwilling to attempt even an approximate gloss of the meaning of *cran-*, yet there is no such hesitation with *foot* in *foot the bill*. Nor does *cran-* seem to carry any meaning into newly coined forms: we can make sense, for instance, of *billy-giraffe* and *nanny-giraffe* by analogy with *billy-goat* and *nanny-goat*, and also of *foot the fees*; but creations like *cranbeads* and *bilbeads* convey nothing, although one might have expected some interpretation such as "small round red beads" and "small round purple beads". The fact is that elements like *cran-* and *bil-* do not carry any meaning at all, in the normal sense – they merely distinguish; they are equivalent to numbered or lettered labels: "(berry) type A/type B/type C . . .". We shall call such elements †**semantic tallies** and their partner elements which indicate a general category will be termed †**semantic categorisers**. A semantic tally in combination with a semantic categoriser constitutes a minimal semantic constituent.

All the semantic tallies we have considered so far have been what might be termed †**pure tallies**, in that they have no perceptible semantic connection with any other elements in the language. However, there exist many examples of semantic tallies which do have a clear semantic connection with normal meaningful elements, without themselves being semantic constituents. Examples of this category are *black-* in *blackbird*, *blue* in *blue-tit*, and *red* in *red wine* (it must not be thought that *red* here is merely a colour term: a red wine is a type of wine, whereas a red dress is not a type of dress). This type of tally will be described as †**impure**.

It would be useful to have a general term for elements which fall short of being constituents, but which nonetheless have a semantic function relatable to the meanings the same forms carry when they are semantic constituents. We shall call these †**semantic indicators**. A distinction may be made between †**full indicators**, which retain the whole of their normal

33

constituent meaning, like *black-* and *-bird* in *blackbird* (it is true that female blackbirds are brown, but *black-* here still relates to "black", which is a salient characteristic of the species), and †**partial indicators**, like *-house* in *greenhouse* (a greenhouse is not a house; but, like a house, it is a building). As we have defined it, the category of semantic indicator overlaps with that of semantic tally, impure tallies being those which are at the same time indicators (full or partial); it includes that of semantic categoriser – a categoriser is necessarily a full indicator. We can perhaps include in the category of semantic indicator such cases as the *dis-* of *disappoint, disgust, dismay,* etc., and the *im-* of *impertinent, impudent,* etc., if the former is felt to be related to the *dis-* of *dislike* and *disapprove,* and the latter to the *im-* of *impolite*; the segments *-appoint, -gust, -may, -pertinent* and *-pudent* have no discernible semantic function, and do not need a label.[10]

2.5 Phonetic elicitors of semantic traits

The vast majority of meaningful elements in a language, whether they are full constituents or have some lesser status, are at the same time grammatical elements. Since the principal function of grammar is to indicate how units of meaning are to be combined, this is scarcely surprising. But there are some phonetic sequences which seem to have semantic value of a sort, yet they do not correspond to grammatical elements: there seems to be a direct pathway from sound to meaning, bypassing grammar. Such elements are of two kinds. Firstly there are what are usually termed **onomatopoeic** phonetic sequences: with these it is often difficult to define their exact limits. The following are examples of words which contain (and in some cases, perhaps consist of) onomatopoeic sequences: *hum, buzz, hiss, gong, splash, crack, whip, bump, clank, tinkle, hoot, coo, miaow.* Onomatopoeic words are held to 'resemble' their referents auditorially, but the degree of objective similarity may be very low (perhaps no lower, however, than the perceived visual resemblance between a cartoonist's representation of a political figure and its subject).

The second type of 'meaningful' phonetic sequence is exemplified by the initial consonant clusters in

(i) *slimy, sleazy, slut, slouch, slovenly, slob, slattern, slither, slink,* etc.

(ii) *glow, glimmer, gleam, glisten, glitter, glare,* etc.

and possibly the vowel in

(iii) *coon, goofy, goon, loony, fool, drool, moon* (around), *noodle* (fig.), etc.

This phenomenon is distinct from onomatopoeia – it is sometimes called **sound symbolism**: there is no question of auditory resemblance.[11] Although not all words containing these sounds manifest the (usually somewhat indeterminate) meaning, it is capable of transferring to new coinages. For instance, a new breakfast food marketed under the brand name of SLUB would stand little chance of success; on the other hand, a flashing beacon called a GLEEPER (on the analogy of *bleeper*) might have some chance of succeeding. Sound symbolism is not just a matter of a certain number of words containing certain sounds happening also to fall into the same semantic area. No meaning attaches, for instance, to the $/\overline{\text{ei}}/$ vowel in *plate, plane, plain, pane, blade, table*, etc., which all contain the semantic trait "flat".[12]

The phonetic sequences involved in either onomatopoeia or sound symbolism are clearly not to be considered semantic constituents. It is generally difficult to find recurrent contrasts of form in which they participate, let alone recurrent semantic contrasts – and they do not respond to any of the rescue strategies. We shall call them †**phonetic elicitors** of semantic traits.

2.6 Words

Our discussion of semantic constituency has taken no account of whether the elements under consideration are parts of words, words, or sequences of words. However, the second criterion for a lexical unit was that it should be 'at least one word'. We must now therefore examine what this entails. A great deal of scholarly discussion has centred on the linguistic status of the word. It would not be appropriate to review this in detail here. For our purposes it will be sufficient to draw attention to two fairly general and constant characteristics of words across a wide range of languages. The first is that a word is typically the smallest element of a sentence which has positional mobility – that is, the smallest that can be moved around without destroying the grammaticality of the sentence (ignoring any semantic effects):

> John saw Bill.
> Bill saw John.
> Bill, John saw.

By no means all words are equally mobile in this sense, but with very few exceptions, the smallest mobile units are words. The morphemes constituting a single word have a rigidly fixed sequential order: we find *unwillingly*, but not *lywillingun* or *unlywilling*, etc.

The second major characteristic of words is that they are typically the largest units which resist 'interruption' by the insertion of new material between their constituent parts. Consider the following sentence, and observe where extra material can be inserted:

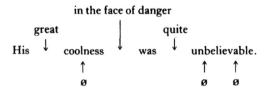

The possible insertion points clearly represent word-boundaries. In a language such as Turkish, in which words composed of a relatively large number of basic grammatical units (morphemes) are common, this characteristic of words may seem less salient. (Turkish, incidentally, also shows a very small degree of optionality in the order of morphemes within a word.) Take, for instance, the word *öl-dü* (the morphemes of the word are separated for illustration). This means "he/she/it died", the final *-dü* indicating third person singular, past tense. Quite a lot can be inserted between the root *öl-* and the past tense element, as the following word shows:

öl-dür-ül-e-mi-yecek-ti

(This can be translated as "He would be unable to be killed": the final *-ti* represents the same morpheme as *-dü*). However, there is a marked difference in the degree of interruptibility between words and phrases. In the Turkish example, although several grammatical elements can be inserted within the word, they are strictly determinate in number and identity; whereas between words, if one takes into account coordinations and parenthetical insertions, the possibilities are infinite. This can be illustrated from English; Turkish is no different in principle:

HIS great courage and imperturbable COOLNESS in the face of what must at times have seemed to him to be insuperable odds WAS, I must confess – although I do not really like him – quite UNBELIEVABLE.

We shall not pursue the matter any further here. It will be henceforth assumed that the typical unit of lexicology is the word[13] (this statement is so obvious as to have an air of tautology). However, there do exist, and not so uncommonly that they can be safely ignored, minimal semantic constituents which consist of more than one word. To these we now turn.

2.7 Idioms

It has long been recognised that expressions such as *to pull someone's leg, to have a bee in one's bonnet, to kick the bucket, to cook someone's goose, to be off one's rocker, round the bend, up the creek*, etc. are semantically peculiar. They are usually described as **idioms**. A traditional definition of idiom runs roughly as follows: an idiom is an expression whose meaning cannot be inferred from the meanings of its parts. Although at first sight straightforward, there is a curious element of circularity in this definition. Does it indicate that the meaning of an idiom cannot be inferred from (or, more precisely, cannot be accounted for as a compositional function of) the meanings the parts carry IN THAT EXPRESSION? Clearly not – so it must be a matter of their meanings in other expressions. But equally clearly, these 'other expressions' must be chosen with care: in considering *to pull someone's leg*, for instance, there is little point in referring to *pull* in *to pull a fast one*, or *leg* in *He hasn't a leg to stand on*. The definition must be understood as stating that an idiom is an expression whose meaning cannot be accounted for as a compositional function of the meanings its parts have when they are not parts of idioms. The circularity is now plain: to apply the definition, we must already be in a position to distinguish idiomatic from non-idiomatic expressions.

Fortunately it is possible to define an idiom precisely and non-circularly using the notion of a semantic constituent. We shall require two things of an idiom: first, that it be lexically complex – i.e. it should consist of more than one lexical constituent; second, that it should be a single minimal semantic constituent. Consider 26:

26.   This will cook Arthur's goose.

The test of recurrent semantic contrast reveals that *this, will* and *Arthur* are regular semantic constituents; the rest, however, i.e. *cook —'s goose*, constitutes a minimal semantic constituent, which as a whole contrasts recurrently with, say, *help* or *destroy*.[14] *Cook —'s goose* is therefore an idiom. An idiom may be briefly characterised as a lexical complex which is semantically simplex.[15] We shall regard as non-idiomatic (or †**semantically transparent**) any expression which is divisible into semantic constituents, even if one or more of these should turn out on further analysis to be idioms. Most idioms are homophonous with grammatically well-formed transparent expressions. A few are not in this sense well-formed, although some grammatical structure is normally discernible. Such cases, of which *by and large* and *far and away* are examples, are often called **asyntactic idioms**.

From our point of view, all idioms are elementary lexical units. It is interesting that although idioms consist of more than one word, they display to some extent the sort of internal cohesion that we expect of single words. For instance, they typically resist interruption and re-ordering of parts. Some of the restriction of syntactic potential of idioms is clearly semantically motivated. For instance, the reason that *to pull someone's left leg* and *to kick the large bucket* have no normal idiomatic interpretation is that *leg* and *bucket* carry no meaning in the idiom, so there is nothing for *left* and *large* to carry out their normal modifying functions on (in general, a modifier needs a semantic constituent to modify).[16] However, idioms also tend to resist interruption by material which, as long as it remains 'outside' the idiom, is semantically compatible:

27a. Arthur apparently has a chip on his shoulder.
  b. ? Arthur has a chip, apparently, on his shoulder.
28a. After a shaky start, we took them to the cleaners.
  b. ? We took them, after a shaky start, to the cleaners.

The same is true of re-ordering. Many grammatical processes involving re-ordering of constituents are ruled out for semantic reasons, particularly those whose semantic function is to highlight a specific semantic constituent: thus, *What John pulled was his sister's leg* has no idiomatic reading, whereas *What John did was pull his sister's leg,* which leaves the idiom 'physically' intact, has.[17] But semantically innocuous re-orderings are also to some extent resisted:

29a. John has a bee in his bonnet about it.
  b. ? John has a bee about it in his bonnet.

At the same time, idioms show their status as phrases in various ways, too. For example, if an idiom may be inflected, the inflectional affixes are carried by the grammatically appropriate elements within the idiom, whether or not they are semantic constituents; that is to say, the elements of an idiom retain at least some of their grammatical identity:

30a. John has bees in his bonnet about many things.
  b. *John has bee-in-his bonnets about many things.

Likewise, in certain regular grammatical re-formulations the parts of an idiom may behave as they would in a transparent expression: thus we have a *leg-pull*, formed on the same pattern as *hand-shake*. For these reasons, it would not be appropriate to assimilate idioms to the category of words.

The question of precisely which syntactic processes a particular idiom will undergo is an extremely complex one, and is not strictly relevant here. In some respects it seems to be idiosyncratically determined, and in other respects predictable.[18] As a first approximation, we may say that an idiom's syntactic behaviour is broadly determined by two factors: the syntactic structure of the literal counterpart of the idiom (if it has one), and the fact that distinguishable syntactic constituents are not semantic constituents, and therefore are not open, for instance, to adjectival and adverbial modification, nor can they be isolated for emphasis, etc.

2.8 Degrees of opacity

A semantically non-transparent expression may be described as **semantically opaque**. It is important to emphasise that, as we have defined it, transparency is the end-point of a continuum of degrees of opacity, much as "cleanness" is the end-point of a continuum of "degrees of dirtiness" (see chapter 9). We have located the decisive break in semantic character between "fully transparent" and "to some degree opaque", rather than between "completely opaque" and "not completely opaque", as this groups together more satisfactorily elements with significantly similar properties. The idea of semi-opaque expressions is already implicit in the notion introduced earlier of 'semantic indicator': a semi-opaque expression must contain at least one semantic indicator. We must now be somewhat more precise concerning the concept of "degree of opacity". There would seem to be two components to this notion. The first is the extent to which constituents of opaque expressions are 'full' semantic indicators: clearly *blackbird*, with two full indicators, is less opaque than *ladybird*, with one partial indicator only (*-bird*), which in turn is less opaque than *red herring* or *in a brown study*, neither of which contains any indicators at all. The other factor affecting degree of opacity is the discrepancy between the combined contribution of the indicators, whether full or partial, and the overall meaning of the idiom. It is of course difficult to measure such a discrepancy objectively, but it does seem that, for instance, some of the so-called **'irreversible binomials'**[19] such as *fish and chips*[20] are less opaque than, say, *blackbird*, even though both contain only full semantic indicators. It may even come as a surprise to some to learn that *fish and chips* is opaque at all; but one needs only to consider that not any kind of fish, nor any method of cooking and presentation, will qualify for the description, and that this is not true of, say, *chips and fish* or even *fish with chips*, both of which are transparent. (It is probable that *fish and chips* is ambiguous, with one opaque and one transparent reading, the two being optionally distinguishable in pronunciation; *chips and fish*, on the other hand, is not ambiguous, and does nòt have the two pronunciation options.)

As degree of opacity diminishes, we approach the somewhat indeterminate transitional zone between opacity and transparency: indeed, some of the irreversible binominals are hard to categorise as one or the other: *salt and vinegar* (in chip-shop parlance), *soap and water*, etc. In principle, all opaque sequences are minimal lexical units and therefore should be listed separately in an ideal dictionary. A practical lexicographer, however, would probably draw his line in a different place from ours: he might well argue that phrases such as *fish and chips*, *bread and butter*, etc., while undoubtedly slightly opaque in the technical sense, present few problems of interpretation to speakers familiar with the normal constituent meanings of the parts, and are thus not worth listing.

2.9 Idioms and collocations

The term **collocation** will be used to refer to sequences of lexical items which habitually co-occur, but which are nonetheless fully transparent in the sense that each lexical constituent is also a semantic constituent. Such expressions as (to pick a semantic area at random) *fine weather*, *torrential rain*, *light drizzle*, *high winds* are examples of collocations. These are of course easy to distinguish from idioms; nonetheless, they do have a kind of semantic cohesion – the constituent elements are, to varying degrees, mutually selective. The semantic integrity or cohesion of a collocation is the more marked if the meaning carried by one (or more) of its constituent elements is highly restricted contextually, and different from its meaning in more neutral contexts. Consider the case of *heavy* in *heavy drinker*. This sense of *heavy* requires fairly narrowly defined contextual conditions: one may speak of *a heavy smoker*, or *a heavy drug-user*, a car may be *heavy on petrol*, etc. For this sense of *heavy* to be selected, the notion of "consumption" in the immediate environment seems to be a prerequisite. In a neutral context like *It's —*, *heavy* has a different meaning. We are still, however, in the realms of transparent sequences, because each constituent produces a recurrent semantic contrast:

31. $\dfrac{\text{heavy}}{\text{light}}$ (He's a — smoker) = $\dfrac{\text{heavy}}{\text{light}}$ (They were — drinkers)

32. $\underline{\text{drinker}}$ (He's a heavy —) = $\underline{\text{drinker}}$ (They're light —s)
      smoker   smoker

Semantic cohesiveness is even tighter if the meaning of one of the elements of a collocation requires a particular lexical item in its immediate context (cases where all the elements are uniquely selective in this way seem not to occur). Such is the case with, for example, *foot the bill* and *curry favour*. With expressions such as these, we are obviously approaching another transitional area bordering on idiom. It has already been argued in some detail that *foot the bill* is semantically transparent. It is also un-idiom-like in the fact that *bill* is fairly freely modifiable:

> I'm expected to foot the bill.
> > the electricity bill.
> > all the bloody bills!

Yet it has some distinctly idiom-like characteristics, too. One of these is that *foot* (in the relevant sense) demands the presence of a specific lexical partner; pronominal anaphoric reference to a previously occurring *bill* apparently will not do:

Son: I've just got the bill for the car repairs.
Father: ? I hope you don't expect me to foot it.

Furthermore, it resists interruption:

> ? I'm expected not only to foot, but also to add up, all the bills.

Collocations like *foot the bill* and *curry favour*, whose constituents do not like to be separated, may be termed †**bound collocations**.[21] Although they display some of the characteristic properties of idioms, bound collocations are nevertheless, as far as we are concerned, lexically complex.

2.10 Idiom and 'dead' metaphor

There is a type of expression which is frequently included in the category of idiom, but which, it will be argued, ought to be kept distinct, and that is what is sometimes called 'frozen' or 'dead' metaphor. The topic of metaphor is too broad to receive a detailed treatment here; let us simply say that a metaphor induces the hearer (or reader) to view a thing, state of affairs, or whatever, as being like something else, by applying to the former linguistic expressions which are more normally employed in references to the latter. In, for instance, *The huge locomotive snorted and belched its way across the plain* we are invited to look at the locomotive as if it were a gigantic animal. This, of course, changes our perception of it, and it seems to take on characteristics such as "temperamental", "dangerous when roused", "difficult to control", and so on. The metaphorical strategy of interpretation is most likely to be triggered off by a perception of incongruity or inappropriateness in the sentence when interpreted literally. If, however, a metaphor is used sufficiently frequently with a particular meaning, it loses its characteristic flavour, or piquancy, its capacity to surprise, and hearers encode the metaphorical meaning as one of the standard senses of the expression. Interpreting it then no longer requires the activation of the metaphorical strategy, working through the literal meaning, but merely requires the looking up, as it were, of a dictionary entry, in much the same way, presumably, that idioms are interpreted. However, very often the link with the original 'live' metaphor, and hence with the literal meanings of the parts, is not wholly lost. Dead metaphors for which this is true can be 'revived' by substituting for one or more of their constituent parts elements which (in their literal uses) are near-synonyms, or paraphrases. Consider the following pairs of sentences:

33a.　They tried to sweeten the pill.
　b.　They tried to sugar the medicine.
34a.　You must have taken leave of your senses!
　b.　You must have left your senses behind!
35a.　We shall leave no stone unturned in our search for the culprit.
　b.　We shall look under every stone in our search for the culprit.

The first sentence in each pair contains a dead metaphor; in the second sentence, the metaphor is revitalised by the substitution of a near-synonym or paraphrase. The same process carried out on true idioms dramatically demonstrates the difference between the two types of expression:

36a.　John pulled his sister's leg.
　b.　John tugged at his sister's leg.
37a.　Tonight we're going to paint the town red.
　b.　Tonight we're going to colour the city scarlet.
38a.　They took us to the cleaners.
　b.　They took us to the laundry.

Something similar happens on translation. A literal rendering of an idiom is very rarely capable of serving as even an approximate translation; it is most likely to be either uninterpretable, or quite unrelated in meaning to the original expression. Consider the French idioms *faire des gorges chaudes de quelque chose* and *donner sa langue au chat*. A literal translation of the first is scarcely interpretable: *to make warm throats of something*; the second translates into something a little easier to construe: *to give one's tongue to the cat*. But neither of these translations gives the slightest clue to the idiomatic meaning of the original French expression; the first means "to laugh loudly and maliciously at something" and the second "to give up" (e.g. when asked a riddle). (It is by no means uncommon for an idiom in one language to be at least roughly equivalent to a lexically unrelated idiom in another language: the French *monter un bateau à quelqu'un* is quite close to *to pull someone's leg*, or *to have someone on*. Whether lexically unrelated idioms can ever be considered exact translation equivalents, however, is debatable.) Literal translation fares rather better with dead metaphors; the results are usually a little odd, but are nonetheless interpretable in the manner of live metaphors. In the following, the (a) sentences are dead metaphors, and the (b) sentences are literal translations:

39a. Why keep a dog and bark yourself?
 b. Pourquoi avoir un chien et aboyer soi-même?
40a. You're barking up the wrong tree.
 b. Ce n'est pas à cet arbre là que vous devez aboyer.
41a. Il a changé son cheval borgne pour un aveugle.
 b. He has changed his one-eyed horse for a blind one.
42a. Il était prêt à aller décrocher la lune pour elle.
 b. He was ready to go and unhook the moon for her.

Interestingly, a high proportion of dead metaphors have similar (although not often identical) dead metaphor equivalents:

43a. to put the cat among the pigeons.
 b. mettre le loup dans la bergerie.
44a. A cat may look at a queen.
 b. Un chien peut bien regarder un évêque.
45a. Let sleeping dogs lie.
 b. Ne pas réveiller le chat qui dort.
46a. to call a spade a spade.
 b. appeler un chat un chat.
47a. It's enough to make a cat laugh.
 b. Cela ferait rire les pierres.

These close equivalents among dead metaphors can present the translator with a dilemma (one of many!). If he translates word-for-word, he will achieve greater fidelity in one respect (*mettre le chat parmi les pigeons*, for instance, evokes the same picture as *put the cat among the pigeons*), but to the detriment of fidelity in another respect (*Faire cela, c'est mettre le chat parmi les pigeons* is a live metaphor, while *Faire cela, c'est mettre le loup dans la bergerie* is not); if, however, he puts a greater value on the latter type of fidelity, then he must sacrifice the former.

Not surprisingly, dead metaphors as a rule present fewer problems to foreign learners of a language than idioms do. Their interpretability, however, must not be exaggerated; their meanings are not necessarily wholly predictable on first acquaintance. Indeed, some can only be appreciated as metaphors with hindsight, as it were; it is only when the figurative meaning is pointed out that the path from the literal to metaphorical meaning becomes traceable.

While idioms and dead metaphors must be distinguished, it should also be recognised that they have certain characteristics in common. (It is probable that the majority of idioms began their lives as metaphors; and synchronically, transitional cases, which are idioms for some and metaphors for others, are not uncommon.)[22] Dead metaphors have in common with idioms that their constituent elements do not, in the straightforward sense, yield recurrent semantic contrasts: consider, for instance, the contrast *stone/knob* in *We shall leave no — unturned*. They are not, therefore, semantically transparent. On the other hand, the effect of synonymous substitution and the continuing relevance of their literal meanings make it unsatisfactory simply to call them 'opaque'. We shall therefore describe them as 'translucent'. (It should be noted that translucency is not the same as the semi-opacity of, for example, *fish and chips*.) Dead metaphors also have a certain syntactic rigidity; the quality of being 'dead' is closely tied to a particular syntactic form, and with any modification the metaphor springs to life: compare *He has one foot in the grave* and *One of his feet is in the grave*.

Even if translucency and opacity can be satisfactorily distinguished, it is not necessarily the case that a particular expression can be unambiguously characterised as one or the other. This is because the two properties may coexist in one and the same expression. Take the case of *She gave him a piece of her mind*. A good part of the meaning of this expression is accessible via normal metaphorical interpretation – it may be inferred that some opinion has been communicated. But a crucial element of meaning cannot be construed in this way, namely, the negative, scolding aspect; because of this, the expression *to give someone a piece of one's mind* must be considered semi-opaque – and, by the same token, only semi-translucent.

44

Because of their non-transparency and syntactic frozenness we shall consider dead metaphors to be minimal lexical units.

Notes

The most explicit account of the basic theoretical notion of this chapter – the semantic constituent – can be found in Haas (1985). (Haas does not use the expression *semantic constituent*, but refers, instead, to elements with 'reproductive distinctiveness'.)

2.1

1. There are, of course, honourable exceptions. See, for instance, Cowie's introduction to *Applied Linguistics*, vol. 2, no. 3 (devoted to 'lexicography and its pedagogical applications'), and his article 'The treatment of collocations and idioms in learners' dictionaries' in the same volume.

2.2 The principal reference for this section is Haas (1985).

2. What is known in formal semantics as the 'principle of compositionality' states: the meaning of a composite expression is a function of the meanings of its component expressions. Lyons (1981: 144)
3. See Haas (1985: 13).
4. The *im-* of *import* and the *in-* of *inhale* are, within one theory of morphological structure, described as **allomorphs** (i.e. variant forms) of the same **morpheme** (i.e. basic grammatical unit). For a fuller discussion, see Allerton (1979: ch. 10). For an exposition of different approaches to the description of morphological structure see Matthews (1974).
5. Notice that *-pertinent* and *-pudent* fail the test of semantic constituency, too. Many apparently complex words in English turn out to be single semantic constituents: *receive, deceive, conceive, invert, convert, pervert, revert, distract, contract, attract, disappoint, disgust, dismay*, etc. This fact, however, does not necessarily oblige us to regard these words as *morphologically* simple.

2.3

6. The 'additional' meaning is expressive, not propositional in nature (this distinction is discussed in 12.2). This is why a sentence like *? John didn't foot the bill, he paid it* is odd: for a sentence of the form *A didn't X, he/she Y-ed* to be normal, the propositional meanings of X and Y must be different (and neither included in the other).
7. See Cowie in the introduction to the *Oxford Dictionary of Current Idiomatic English*, vol. 2 (Cowie, Mackin and McCaig (1983)).
8. For discussion of discontinuous elements see Harris (1951: 182–4) and Allerton (1979: 123–5).
9. Haas (private communication) does not agree that elements such as *-ness* are semantic constituents. I can see some advantage in distinguishing them as a special sort of semantic constituent.

2.4

10. It does not follow, just because a semantic trait of negativity is associated with *im-* of *impertinent* (or *dis-* of *disappoint*), that *-pertinent* (or *-appoint*) must therefore be the bearer of the rest of the meaning of the whole word. This would only be true if *im-* was functioning as a normal negative prefix,

in which case it would be a semantic constituent. The point is that although *im-* in some sense carries a semantic trait which is part of the overall meaning, the rest of the meaning does not cohere into a unitary concept – it does not form, as it were, a semantic gestalt. The same is true of *cran-* in *cranberry*. Just because *-berry* can be associated with the meaning "berry", it does not follow that *cran-* carries the meaning "cranberry" minus the meaning "berry". (There is further discussion of this point in 6.2.)

2.5 See Ullmann (1962: 82–92) for discussion of onomatopoeia and sound symbolism (also called **phonaesthesia**).

11. Bolinger (1980: 17–24) does not make a distinction between onomatopoeia and sound symbolism, only between **arbitrary** units of communication (in which there is no resemblance between the physical form of a unit and its referent) and **iconic** units ('their physical form resembles, and by that resemblance suggests, something in nature' (p. 19)). Lyons (1977: 102–5) classifies onomatopoeia as 'primary iconicity' and sound symbolism as 'secondary iconicity'.

12. At least according to my intuitions, and those of many classes of students that I have consulted informally.

2.6 For a fuller discussion of the word as a linguistic unit see Lyons (1968: 194–206). It should be borne in mind that in this chapter we are considering the word only from the point of view of its syntagmatic extent.

13. In this book, the word, rather than the **root** (open class morpheme), is taken as the basic unit of lexical semantics. It is true that most of what we call lexical meaning is carried by roots. However, the word is intuitively a more satisfactory unit; and it would be inconvenient to be restricted to talking only of roots in discussing a semantic relation such as reversivity (see 10.5), which may hold between two morphologically simple words (e.g. *fall*: *rise*), and one simple and one complex word (e.g. *mount*: *dismount*) or two complex words (e.g. *increase*: *decrease*).

2.7 For general discussion of idiomaticity and related matters from various points of view see Bar-Hillel (1955), Healey (1968), Weinreich (1969), Fraser (1970), Mitchell (1971), Makkai (1972) and Cowie (1981b). The characterisation of idioms adopted here is not identical to that in any of the works cited: I owe it to Haas.

14. The sort of contrast envisaged here is as follows:

$$\frac{\textit{That cooked Arthur's goose}}{\textit{That pleased Arthur}} = \frac{\textit{This will cook Mary's goose}}{\textit{This will please Mary}}$$

It is clear that the condition of substitution within a constant syntactic frame cannot be strictly observed here (although it can for most idioms). However, what is required, fundamentally, in the recurrent contrast test is a species of semantic constancy in the frame. The easiest way of controlling this is to insist on syntactic constancy – but the latter is not strictly necessary. Consider the contrast between *That cooked Arthur's goose* and *That pleased Arthur* in the above equation. Both sentences have a semantic structure which can be represented as follows:

Nominal notion	+	Verbal notion	+	Nominal notion
("cause of action process")				("entity affected by action or process")

In other words, the contrast is between two verbal notions within a constant semantic frame. The same is true of the contrast on the other side of the equation. Furthermore, the two verbal notions are associated with the same contrast of form on both sides of the equation.

15. I owe this succinct formulation to Haas.

16. *He kicked the proverbial bucket* is not really an exception to this, as *proverbial* does not have the normal semantic role of a modifier: it seems to act here as a kind of metalinguistic comment on the whole expression. More problematic, at first sight, are cases like *His goose was well and truly cooked* and *He has a large chip on his shoulder*. The possibility of these modifications does not, however, prove either that *cooked* and *chip* carry an identifiable part of the (idiomatic) meaning of their respective idioms, or that their literal meanings contribute in any direct way to the idiomatic meanings. Modifications such as these seem to be interpreted in two stages. First, they are applied to the literal meanings of what they modify (their **heads**); then, secondarily, this process is taken as a semantic model, and is applied analogically to the idiomatic meaning of the whole expression. The result is that the meaning of the whole idiom is intensified. It is not clear what general regularities govern such cases, although most examples seem to involve semantic intensification. (It must be borne in mind that idioms, like any other aspect of language, can be bent to creative and innovative use. An editorial in the *Times Higher Educational Supplement* (21 Sept. 1984) described a certain issue as a 'reds-under-the-bed herring'. Our account of idioms does not aspire to encompass such cases.)

17. Notice that *It's my/John's goose that was cooked , not yours* and *It's my/Arthur's leg he's pulling, not yours*, both of which, at least for me, have a normal idiomatic interpretation, do not constitute evidence of semantic 'life' in the elements of the idioms. What is being topicalised in these sentences is *John, Arthur*, etc., which are semantic constituents, and not part of the idioms; the possessive affix (which is part of the idiom) simply has to accompany the noun to which it is attached. (*My* and *your* in these sentences must be analysed as "I"/"you" + "possessive": only the possessive forms part of the idiom.)

18. Newmeyer (1974) proposes that modifications to idioms have to be compatible with both their literal and their idiomatic interpretations. This could explain why, for instance, *Arthur kicked the bucket slowly and painfully* is less normal than *Arthur died slowly and painfully*. It is not clear, however, how generally applicable this principle is.

2.8

19. This is the name given by Malkiel (1959) to expressions usually of the form *X and Y* (where X and Y are noun phrases), whose semantic properties change when the order of the noun phrases is reversed. Examples are: *apple pie and custard, soap and water, bread and butter, cloak and dagger, pots and pans*, etc. Usually one ordering is more common than the other; in our terms, the most common ordering is usually semantically opaque. Sometimes both are opaque, but with different meanings: *salt and pepper* (condiments); *pepper and salt* (colour).

20. Readers not familiar with British culture should perhaps be informed that *fish and chips* is a traditional British popular food, having something of the position of hamburgers or hot dogs in the U.S.A., consisting of fish (usually cod), dipped in batter and deep-fried, and eaten with chips (French fries).

(True devotees claim that, to be enjoyed at their best, they ought to be wrapped in newspaper and eaten with the fingers.)

2.9 For general discussion of collocations see Mitchell (1971), Mackin (1978), Cowie (1981b). For collocational restrictions, see Allerton (1984) and 12.2 below.

    21.   This term was suggested to me by David Wolstenholme.

2.10 For metaphor see Brooke-Rose (1958), Black (1962), Ullmann (1962), Richards (1965), Mooij (1976), Levin (1977).

    22.   A glance through Long and Summers (1979) reveals that true idioms are much less numerous than dead metaphors.

3
The paradigmatic and syntactic delimitation of lexical units

3.1 Introductory

In the previous chapter a number of important decisions were taken which enable us to establish the location of lexical elements within sentences, that is to say, to delimit them syntagmatically. We must now confront the rather more daunting problems of differentiating lexical units paradigmatically.

It will be necessary to introduce a distinction, which has up to now not been needed, between two kinds of element relevant to lexical semantics. The two types will be called †**lexical units** and **lexemes**.[1] In this book our main, although by no means exclusive, concern is with the former. Lexical units are those form–meaning complexes with (relatively) stable and discrete semantic properties which stand in meaning relations such as antonymy (e.g. *long* : *short*) and hyponymy (e.g. *dog* : *animal*), and which interact syntagmatically with contexts in various ways to produce, for instance, the different sorts of anomaly discussed in chapter 1. A particular lexical unit, of course, expresses its semantic identity through such relations, but its essence cannot be exhaustively characterised in terms of any determinate set of such relations. The meaning aspect of a lexical unit will be termed a †**sense**. Lexemes, on the other hand, are the items listed in the lexicon, or 'ideal dictionary', of a language; these will be discussed in 3.10.

It may be wondered why it is necessary, or even advantageous, to have two sorts of unit for lexical semantics. The reason is that they have different functions, which impose different constraints on their nature. Senses need to represent unitary 'quanta' of meaning, but they do not need to be finite in number. There is nothing in the notion of oppositeness, for instance, which dictates that there should necessarily be only a finite number of opposite pairs in a language. A lexeme, on the other hand, may well be associated with indefinitely many senses, but the set of lexemes must be finitely enumerable. Consider, by way of illustration, the example of *topless*. We may speak of (a) *a topless dress* or (b) *a topless dancer*.

Each of these is lexically distinct, in that it has, for instance, different typical contrasts (e.g. *long-sleeved* for (a) and *nude* for (b)), and the two readings are called forth by different types of context. They are also relatively stable across contexts: for instance, *a topless swim-suit* would seem to exemplify the same sense of *topless* as (a), and *a topless barmaid* the same as (b). Why then can we not simply say that *topless (a)* and *topless (b)* are different (although perhaps related) lexemes? One important reason is that the number of possible distinct uses of *topless* seems to be, in principle, open; so any attempt to draw up a determinate closed list would be of questionable validity. In addition to the examples mentioned above, one might also encounter *a topless bar, I hear Torquay has gone topless.* And can we entirely rule out *topless by-laws*, or *the topless watchdog committee* (with the function of monitoring the behavioural effects of toplessness)? Another example of such openness is provided by what we shall call the †**unit-type** ambiguity. For instance, *jacket* in *I like this jacket* may be understood to refer to a particular individual jacket (the unit), or to a type of jacket. However, there seems, in principle, to be no limit to the number of possible type readings in such cases. Suppose someone in a greengrocery picks up an apple and says: *Is this the fruit you mean?* Besides the unit reading, the speaker may be intending to refer, among other possibilities, to: that variety of apple (e.g. Cox's Orange Pippin); apples in general; fruit from a particular supplier; home-grown apples; etc., etc. While in particular contexts some readings may well be much more likely than others (if this were not the case, many utterances would be harder to understand than they are), the number of possible readings is clearly limited only by imagination. (Except, of course, that the type cannot be more general than the lexical item used to refer to it: *this apple* cannot refer to fruit in general.) It seems that there is a high degree of creativity in the lexicon which we must take account of. The creativity inherent in the grammar of a language has often been pointed out: an unlimited number of sentences may be produced from a finite set of elements together with rules for their combination.[2] Lexical creativity is probably of a similar order and, like syntactic creativity, must have a finite aspect. It will be assumed in this book that a (relatively) closed set of lexical units is stored in the mental lexicon, together with rules or principles of some kind[3] which permit the production of a possibly unlimited number of new (i.e. not specifically stored) units.

3.2 Selection and modulation of senses

One of the basic problems of lexical semantics is the apparent multiplicity of semantic uses of a single word form (without grammatical difference). There seems little doubt that such variation is the rule rather than the exception: the meaning of any word form is in some sense different in every distinct context in which it occurs.

However, that does not mean that the 'word-form-in-context' is the appropriate unit for lexicological purposes. There are two distinct types of variation in the semantic contribution that a word form makes to different sentences – or, to look at it from a different point of view, two ways in which the sentential context of a word form may affect its semantic contribution to the sentence. It will be argued that one of these types of variation involves the selection, by the context, of different units of sense, while the other type is a matter of contextual modification of a single sense.

The difference between the two contextual effects can perhaps be approached initially by considering two corresponding ways in which a word form, in a single context, may be open to more than one interpretation. *Cousin* and *bank* in 1 and 2, respectively, illustrate the difference:

1. Sue is visiting her cousin.
2. We finally reached the bank.

Cousin in 1 can, of course, refer to either a male or a female cousin. But the sentence can function as a satisfactory communication without either the hearer perceiving, or the speaker intending to convey, anything concerning the sex of the person referred to. This is because *cousin* has a general meaning which covers all the more specific possibilities (not only with regard to sex, but also with regard to an indefinitely large number of other matters, such as height, age, eye-colour, etc.). *Bank* in 2 can also be interpreted in more than one way (e.g. "margin of river" or "establishment for the custody of money"); but it has no general meaning covering these possibilities. Furthermore, the interpretation cannot be left undecided: both speaker and hearer must select a reading (the same reading) if the sentence is to play its part in a normal conversational exchange. We shall say that the word form *cousin* is **general** with respect to the distinction "male cousin"/"female cousin";[4] *bank*, on the other hand, will be said to be **ambiguous** with respect to the sense distinction "financial institution"/"side of river". In other words, the two meanings "male cousin" and "female cousin" are both associated with the same lexical unit *cousin*, whose meaning is more general than either; they therefore do not represent distinct senses of *cousin*. The meanings "financial institution" and "side of river", on the other hand, do represent two distinct

51

senses, so there are two lexical units *bank* corresponding to these senses. (Every word form is general with respect to some semantic distinctions, and (at least potentially) ambiguous with respect to others.) Let us now examine in greater detail the different ways in which contexts exert a restrictive influence on the meanings associated with word forms which occur within them.

There are two fundamental ways[5] in which the effective semantic contribution of a word form may vary under the influence of different contexts. First, a single sense can be modified in an unlimited number of ways by different contexts, each context emphasising certain semantic traits, and obscuring or suppressing others; just as a dirty window-pane will allow some parts of the scene beyond it to be seen clearly, and will partially or completely obscure other parts – and a different pane will affect the same scene differently. This effect of a context on an included lexical unit will be termed †**modulation**; the variation within a sense caused by modulation is largely continuous and fluid in nature. The second manner of semantic variation concerns the activation by different contexts of different senses associated with ambiguous word forms. This will be termed †**contextual selection** (of senses); in the nature of things, this sort of variation proceeds in discrete jumps rather than continuously. The two types of variability are normally operative together; that is, a selected sense is also subject to modulation by the context which forced its selection. Let us first look a little more closely at modulation.

We shall discuss sense modulation under two main headings: first, changes in the status of semantic traits along the dimension of necessity – which will be termed †**promotion** and †**demotion**; and second, the highlighting and background of traits. As an example of promotion and demotion, consider the semantic traits associated with *nurse* in 3 and 4:

3. A nurse attended us.
4. A pregnant nurse attended us.

In 3, the trait "female" is expected, and the trait "male" unexpected; but in 4, although *nurse* represents the same lexical unit as in 3, "female" is at the very least canonical (if not criterial), while "male" is demoted to anomalous or impossible status.[6] As a further example, consider 5:

5. Arthur poured the butter into a dish.

Out of context, or in a neutral context, "liquid" is either a possible or unexpected trait of *butter*. But in 5 it is at least canonical. Sentence 5 also illustrates another aspect of modulation, which we shall call †**linkage** of traits. It is clear that the butter referred to in 5, if it is normal, is not only liquid, but also hot; "hot" is therefore a canonical trait. Now, "hot" is merely a possible trait of *butter* in, for instance, *Arthur put the butter into a dish*; and it is certainly not the case that any lexical unit functioning as the direct object of *pour* has "hot" as a canonical trait – in *Arthur poured the milk into a dish*, for instance, "hot" is, again, merely possible. It is the combination of *pour* with *butter* (in direct object position) – or, more directly, the interaction of the traits "butter" and "liquid" – which promotes "hot" from possible to canonical status. This is a very simple example; it is easy to conceive of extremely varied and complex patterns of linkage appearing in various contexts. This will not, however, be elaborated on here; we shall merely note that it is an important aspect of modulation.[7]

Another effect of contextual modulation on the sense of a lexical unit involves the relative [†]**highlighting** or [†]**backgrounding** of semantic traits. Different sorts of trait can be affected in this way. Two examples will suffice. First, some part of an object (or process, etc.) may be thrown into relief relative to other parts. For instance, *The car needs servicing* and *The car needs washing* highlight different parts of the car. (This is not to say that *car* refers to something different in each of these sentences – in both cases it is the whole car which is referred to.[8]) Second, it is commonly the case that what is highlighted or backgrounded is an attribute, or range of attributes, of the entity referred to. For instance, *We can't afford that car* highlights the price of the car, *Our car couldn't keep up with his* highlights its performance, and *The car crushed Arthur's foot* its weight. It is in respect of 'contextually modulated sense' that a lexical unit may be justifiably said to have a different meaning in every distinct context in which it occurs.

We have been speaking, so far, of the effects of context on the meaning of a single lexical unit. But a context normally also acts in such a way as to cause a single sense, from among those associated with any ambiguous word form, to become operative. When a sentence is uttered, it is rarely the utterer's intention that it should be interpreted in two (or more) different ways simultaneously. It is probable that deliberate equivocation in respect of the intended sense of word forms is always to some extent odd. This means that, for the vast majority of utterances, hearers are expected to identify specific intended senses for every ambiguous word form that they contain. The process of sense selection is, of course, extremely complex, with many interacting factors. However, in general, one can say that a hearer selects that combination of lexical readings which leads to the most normal possible utterance-in-context. In other words, a hearer will generally assume that the producer of an utterance wants to communicate something, and has chosen the linguistic context of his utterance with a view to furthering this aim.[9] Broadly speaking, we can identify two types of normality – sentence-internal normality and contextual normality (it is probably the case that the latter is the stronger determinant of sense selection). Very often a sentence contains more than one ambiguous word form; in such cases, there will occur a kind of mutual negotiation between the various options so as to achieve the most normal combination. This process is illustrated in 6:

> 6.   Several rare ferns grow on the steep banks of the burn where
>   it runs into the lake.

It is highly unlikely that any reader of this sentence will interpret *rare* in the sense of "undercooked" (as in *a rare steak*), or *steep* in the sense of "unjustifiably high" (as in *steep charges*), or *bank* in the sense of "financial institution", or *burn* in the sense of "injury caused by fire", or *run* in the sense of "progress by advancing each foot alternately never having both feet on the ground simultaneously", etc. There is only one selection of senses here which yields a normal sentence (i.e. the sentence form is not ambiguous). Contextual normality involves such matters as relevance, informativeness and consistency. Consider 7:

> 7.   A: It's dark in here, isn't it?
>   B: Yes. Aren't there any lights?

B's utterance (in the context of A's) is normal if *lights* is interpreted to mean "sources of illumination", but would be of, at best, obscure relevance if interpreted to mean "lungs of sheep". (Notice, however, that B's utterance does not display internal abnormality on either interpretation.)

So far we have taken it for granted that the distinction between ambiguity and generality is intuitively obvious. In some cases it is, but in others it is not; this judgement certainly does not figure amongst the basic set of intuitive judgements on which we base our analyses. We must now, therefore, consider in some detail the question of explicit diagnostic tests for ambiguity and generality.

3.3 'Indirect' tests for ambiguity

One approach to the diagnosis of ambiguity relies on finding, for two occurrences of a word form, different relations of meaning with other items. These relations may be of the paradigmatic variety (e.g.

oppositeness, synonymy, etc.) or they may be of the so-called †**paronymic** sort (that is to say, involving identity of root, but difference of syntactic category, as, for instance, with *act* : *actor*, *race* : *racy*.[10] We shall describe evidence of this type as 'indirect'; arguments will be put forward that indirect evidence has severe drawbacks as a method of diagnosing ambiguity. The following three 'tests' for ambiguity will serve to illustrate the approach.

     I.   If there exists a synonym of one occurrence of a word form which is not a synonym of a second, syntactically identical occurrence of the same word form in a different context, then that word form is ambiguous, and the two occurrences exemplify different senses.

Thus, for example, one might suggest *lucifer* as a synonym for *match* in 8 (but not in 9), and *contest* as a synonym in 9 (but not in 8):

    8.   Guy struck the match.
    9.   The match was a draw.

From this, the principle expressed in 1 would allow us to conclude (correctly, in this instance), that *match* was ambiguous, and in 8 and 9 represented different senses.

    II.   If there exists a word or expression standing in a relation of oppositeness to one occurrence of a word form, which does not stand in the same relation to a second, syntactically identical occurrence of the same word form in a different context, then that word form is ambiguous, and the two occurrences exemplify different senses.

In 10, for instance, *dark* (but not *heavy*) stands in a relation of oppositeness to *light*, whereas in 11 *heavy* is a satisfactory opposite, but *dark* is not:

    10.   The room was painted in light colours.
    11.   Arthur has rather a light teaching load.

Light is therefore, according to the test, an ambiguous lexical form, and 10 and 11 manifest different senses.

    III.   If there exists a word which stands in a paronymic relation to one occurrence of a word form, but does not stand in the same relation to a second, syntactically identical occurrence of the same word form in a different context, then that word form is ambiguous, and the two occurrences exemplify different senses.

55

Consider *race* in 12 and 13:

> 12.   The race was won by Arkle.
> 13.   They are a war-like race.

The verb *to race* and the noun *racing* are paronymically related to the occurrence of *race* in 12, but not to that in 13; on the other hand, *racial* and *racist* are related to *race* in 13, but not in 12. Hence *race*, according to the test, is an ambiguous lexical form, and 12 and 13 manifest different senses. Once again, the diagnosis seems intuitively correct.

Other tests of the same general type may be proposed, but none bring anything radically new to the picture. They all suffer from a major weakness, which is that for every instance in which a word form possesses different synonyms, opposites, morphological derivatives, or whatever, in different contexts, there are several possible explanations, only one of which involves ambiguity of the word form; hence, further evidence of a different sort is required to determine which explanation is correct in any given instance. Suppose there exists a word form W, which in context $C(1)$ stands in a particular meaning relation to another element $A(1)$, but in context $C(2)$ stands in the same meaning relation not to $A(1)$, but to $A(2)$:

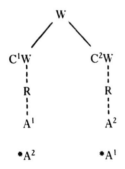

There are at least three possible reasons why W should have different relational partners in $C(1)$ and $C(2)$. One is, of course, that W is ambiguous, and $C(1)$ and $C(2)$ select different senses. This is presumably what happens in the cases of *light*, *match* and *race* discussed above. Another possibility is that $C(1)$ and $C(2)$ modulate a single sense of W in mutually exclusive ways. Thus *monarch* in 14 has *queen* but not *king* as a synonym, whereas in 15 it has *king* but not *queen*:

> 14.   The Ruritanian monarch is expecting her second baby.
> 15.   The child's father is the reigning monarch.

In such a case there would be no evidence of ambiguity. A third possibility is that A(1) and A(2) are sensitive to differences between C(1) and C(2) to which W is indifferent. Consider the following case of *thin* and its opposites:

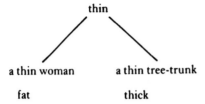

It does not seem illuminating to say either that *thin* is ambiguous, or that these contexts restrict its meaning in mutually exclusive ways.[11]

It is clear that nothing can be reliably inferred from the mere fact that a word form has different meaning relations in different contexts, and independent evidence concerning ambiguity or generality is required. But if such evidence is available, then it is superfluous to appeal to differential relations.

Indirect tests can be used in another way, which in some cases can seem more reliable. Instead of looking for different relations in different contexts to prove ambiguity, one may adduce sameness of relations as evidence of generality. Thus, the fact that *thin* in both of the contexts illustrated above has *slender* as a synonym could be cited as evidence that it is not ambiguous after all. However, using indirect criteria in this way is no more reliable: one simply falls into a different trap, because the item which stands in the 'same' meaning relation in different contexts to the lexical form being tested may itself be ambiguous. There is an intuitively clear example of this involving *thin*:

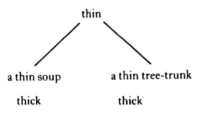

It is of course true that one of the main purposes of distinguishing discrete senses is to have available a unit which can stand in relations such as synonymy and oppositeness. However, it seems clear that these units must be established in some other way. Fortunately there are more successful and reliable ways of distinguishing ambiguity from generality, and to these we now turn.

3.4 **Direct criteria for ambiguity**

Three different types of criteria for ambiguity will be proposed. It may ultimately be possible to show that they all reduce to a single basic criterion, but here they will be presented separately. Generally speaking, unless there are specific reasons why one or other of the criteria should be inapplicable (some of these reasons will be discussed below), we shall expect an ambiguous item to satisfy all the criteria.

The first criterion is frequently difficult to apply in practice, but it is conceptually important. It is that the senses of an ambiguous word form should not in every case be totally conditioned by their contexts, unlike the interpretations which arise as a result of contextual modulation. This means that an ambiguous word form set in a disambiguating context may well carry more information than can be accounted for in terms of interaction between the context-independent meaning of the word form, and the semantic properties of the context. In cases of contextual modulation, on the other hand, ALL information is derived from these sources. Consider sentences 16 and 17:

16. Arthur washed and polished the car.

17. John lubricated the car.

The most likely interpretation of 16 is that not every part of the car underwent washing and polishing, but the exterior surface only. What is the basis for this conclusion? It is derived entirely from the general meaning of *car*, together with the semantic properties of the context (remember that general knowledge concerning cars and operations carried out on them is, on the view of meaning adopted in this book, embedded in the meanings of *car*, *wash*, *polish*, etc.). A similar account can be given of the most likely interpretation of *car* in 17. Or take the case of *monarch* in 14 (repeated here for convenience):

14. The Ruritanian monarch is expecting her second baby.

We can be virtually certain that the monarch in question is a queen, because of the restricting effect of the context on the general meaning of *monarch*. Notice that a similar interpretation would arise, and no loss of information would result, if *monarch* were replaced by a synonym or paraphrase such as *sovereign*, or *crowned head* (and *automobile* would interact in the same way with the context if it were substituted for *car* in 16 and 17). Contrast these, however, with *bank* in 18 and 19:

18. Her husband is the manager of a local bank.

19. At this point, the bank was covered with brambles.

Let us try to account for the (most probable) different interpretations of *bank* in the way that we did for *car*. It is first necessary to decide on a synonym or paraphrase of the context-invariant meaning of *bank*. This already poses problems, but let us say, for the sake of argument, that it is equivalent to *place*. We can then observe the effect of substituting *place* for *bank* in 18 and 19:

20.   Her husband is the manager of a local place.
21.   At this point, the place was covered with brambles.

There is quite clearly a loss of information, so we have failed to show that the interpretations of *bank* are the result of contextual modulation of a general meaning. It may be concluded, therefore, that the different contexts are selecting discrete senses of *bank*. Another instance of incomplete contextual determination is to be observed with *dog*. Let us for the moment take it as established that *dog* has a general sense, denoting the whole species, irrespective of sex. In sentences such as 22, however, *dog* has a more specific meaning, and refers only to males:

22.   John prefers bitches to dogs.

Now it might be argued that the resultant sense of *dog* here is caused by contextual modulation of the general sense: *dog* cannot in this context refer to females if logical consistency is to be preserved, which leaves only males as possible referents. Consider now, however, 23:

23.   Incredibly, John prefers an aged, half-blind bitch to a dog, as his canine companion.

If the interpretation of *dog* in this sentence were the result of contextual modulation of the general sense, it ought to include reference to, for instance, young females with good eyesight. But once again, it refers to male dogs only. This reading cannot be explained by contextual modulation, so it must be the result of selection from a set of discrete possibilities. In fact, the same is true of 22. That contextual modulation of the general sense of *dog* cannot explain the specific interpretation in 22 is shown by the lack of a parallel specific interpretation of *canine* (in its jocular use as a noun) when it is substituted for *dog*:

24.   ? John prefers bitches to canines.

(We shall consider below why 24 should be anomalous.)

Some understanding of the way the semantic effects of selection may be independent of, and indeed may transcend, those properties of the context which are responsible for the selection can be gleaned from the following analogy. Suppose that it is known that a certain event is to occur on a certain day, but may take place at only one of two possible times, namely, 12.00 noon or 12.00 midnight. If one were subsequently to receive a report that when the event occurred, the sun had set, one would be able to infer that it had taken place at exactly 12.00 midnight. The precision of this inference goes well beyond what is explicitly present in the report, which acts rather like a trigger setting off one of two pre-existing possibilities. In a similar manner, the context of *dog* in 22 and 23 acts like a trigger which activates one of a set of pre-existing bundles of semantic properties, each having a precision and richness not directly sanctioned by the context. In principle all ambiguous items should be capable of manifesting these characteristics.

Our second criterion for ambiguity is that separate senses should be †**independently maximisable.** Under certain conditions, the application of certain terms must be maximised within the current universe of discourse, even at the expense of oddness. Consider 25 (which resembles 24):

25. ? Mary likes mares better than horses.

One might have thought that the context makes it clear that *horses* is to be interpreted as "stallions"; however, such an interpretation is not available for this type of sentence. The reason is that since mares have been mentioned, they fall within the current universe of discourse, and by the rule of maximisation (the details of which are not entirely clear) must be included in the reference of *horses*. This, of course, leads to logical inconsistency, and hence oddness. (Notice, however, that there is no anomaly if the reference of *horses* is EXPLICITLY restricted: *Mary prefers mares to horses which can sire foals* or *Mary prefers mares to these horses* uttered in a situation where only stallions are present.) On the other hand, 26, unlike 25, is perfectly normal:

26. John prefers bitches to dogs.

The general sense of *dog* would of course give rise to anomaly in 26, because of the rule of maximisation. The reason 26 is not odd is that *dog* has another sense, which even when maximised excludes bitches, and this is automatically selected by the context. By contrast, 27 selects the general reading of *dog* (the specific reading would be odd here, but not for reasons connected with maximisation):

27. Arthur breeds dogs.

Thus 26 and 27 taken together constitute strong evidence that *dog* is ambiguous.

The existence of two independent senses of *dog*, each independently maximisable, is responsible for the fact that A's question in 28, if the dog in question is female, can be truthfully answered either 'Yes' or 'No' (depending on which sense the respondent believes the questioner to be intending):

28. A: Is that a dog?
    B: (i) Yes, it's a spaniel.
       (ii) No, it's a bitch.

There is no parallel set of circumstances in which the question in 29 can be truthfully answered 'Yes' or 'No':

29. A: Is the subject of this poem a monarch?
    B: (i) Yes, it is a queen.
       (ii) ? No, it is a king.

Because there is only one sense of monarch, namely, the general one, and because its reference must be maximised, if the subject of the poem was a king or a queen, then 'Yes' is the only truthful answer. As with 28, situations can be imagined in which the questions in 30 and 31 can be truthfully answered either negatively or positively:

30. A: Has Charles changed his position?
    B: (i) Yes, he's now sitting next to the chairman.
       (ii) No, he still supports corporal punishment.
31. A: Did Arthur make it to the bank?
    B: (i) Yes, he's a strong swimmer.
       (ii) No, he was arrested as soon as he came out of the water.

The same should be true, in principle, of any truly ambiguous expression.[12]

Ambiguity tests of the third kind utilise the fact that independent senses of a lexical form are antagonistic to one another; that is to say, they cannot be brought into play simultaneously without oddness. Contexts which do activate more than one sense at a time give rise to the variety of oddness we have labelled zeugma:

32. ? John and his driving licence expired last Thursday.

The simultaneous bringing into play of two senses can be effected either by coordination, as in 32, where *John* and *his driving licence* select different senses of the verb *expire*, or by anaphora, as in 33:

33.   ? John's driving licence expired last Thursday; so did John.

So did is an anaphoric verb phrase; that is to say, its referential properties operate not directly, but indirectly, through a previously mentioned verb phrase, in this case *expired last Thursday*, which must be re-applied, this time with *John* as subject. But since this demands a different sense from the one appropriate to its first occurrence, the result is zeugma.

A general term cannot give rise to zeugma in this way:

34.   My cousin, who is pregnant, was born on the same day as Arthur's, who is the father.

Arthur's refers anaphorically through *cousin*. The context makes it clear that the two cousins are of different sexes; however, the sentence is not zeugmatic, so we may conclude that *cousin* does not have two senses "male cousin" and "female cousin".

Antagonism of senses also lies behind the so-called **identity test** for ambiguity.[13] In 35, each part of the sentence contains an occurrence, either direct, or indirect via anaphora, of the ambiguous adjective *light*, and can therefore in theory be interpreted in two ways:

35.   Mary is wearing a light coat; so is Sue.

However, the whole sentence does not have four (i.e. 2×2) interpretations, but two only. This is because the same reading of *light* must be selected in each part: either both ladies are wearing "undark" coats, or both are wearing "unheavy" coats. What is termed the **crossed interpretation**, with each part of the sentence manifesting a different sense, is prohibited. This prohibition is not a mysterious property of the grammatical process of anaphora; it is simply a consequence of the fact that *light* resists, as it were, the simultaneous activation of more than one of its senses. General terms allow crossed interpretations:

36.   Mary has adopted a child; so has Sue.

There are four possible distributions of sexes compatible with this sentence, since there is no requirement that the two children should be of the same sex.

3.5   Some difficult cases
In this section the operation of ambiguity tests will be illustrated

by applying them to a selection of difficult cases. The difficulties mostly concern tests based on the antagonism of sister-senses (i.e. senses associated with a single lexical form). It is not possible simply to dispense with such tests, because there are occasions, especially when dealing with highly context-bound readings which do not appear in ambiguous sentences, when they are the only practicable way of diagnosing ambiguity.

ɪ   The first example involves the unit-type ambiguity. This is quite easy to demonstrate by means of the *Yes/No*-test:

37.   A: Is this the jacket you want?
      B: (i) Yes. (it's the type I want)
          (ii) No. (this particular one is shop-soiled)

But it is much more difficult to show antagonism: many contexts which might be expected to manifest it do not:

38.   This is our best-selling jacket: do try it on.

Jacket in the first clause clearly must have a type reading – one cannot repeatedly sell the same individual jacket. One might have thought that only a particular unit of the type could be 'tried on', but that seems not to be the case. One must beware of drawing hasty conclusions in this area. As it happens, it is possible to find contexts which isolate the two readings, and when these are yoked together, zeugma results. Sentence 39 allows only the 'unit' reading for *skirt* (this seems to be a property of *belong*):

39.   That skirt belongs to Mary.

Sentence 40 can only bear a type reading:

40.   My sister has the skirt Sue is wearing now.

Try to link these two readings together anaphorically, and the antagonism becomes plain:

41.   ? The skirt Sue is wearing belongs to Mary; my sister has it, too.

ɪɪ   It not infrequently happens that ambiguous readings are related in such a way that in certain contexts one reading entails the other. Such cases are a common cause of apparent failure of the zeugma-test (often called the 'pun-test') or the identity test. The two readings of *dog* are a case in point.[14] In 42, for example, it appears that a crossed interpretation is possible, in that Mary's dog could well be male, and Bill's female:

42.   Mary bought a dog; so did Bill.

63

Does this contradict the evidence presented above that *dog* is ambiguous? The answer is that it does not. When *dog* occurs in a sentential context in which the specific interpretation entails the general interpretation, we cannot be sure which sense is operative when reference is made to a male dog: the two senses under these circumstances are effectively inseparable. Hence the normality of 42 when the dogs referred to are of opposite sexes cannot be used as evidence against the existence of two senses of *dog*, since it can be fully accounted for by claiming that only the general sense is operative. However, the situation is much clearer when *dog* occurs in a context where neither sense entails the other, as in 43:

43. Arthur wants to know if that is a dog; so does Mike.

A moment's thought will convince the reader that the crossed reading is prohibited here: this sentence cannot be used to describe a situation where Arthur knows that the animal in question is an alsatian, but is unsure of its sex, while Mike knows that it is female, but thinks it might be a wolf. The pun-test, too, demands non-entailing contexts:

44a. Dogs can become pregnant at 12 months. (general sense only)
  b. Dogs mature later than bitches. (specific sense only)
  c. ? Dogs can become pregnant at 12 months, but mature later than bitches.

III Entailment between readings also bedevils attempts to demonstrate antagonism between the "exactly" and "at least" interpretations of numerals and other expressions of quantity.[15] The *Yes/No*-test suggests that this is a genuine ambiguity:

45. A: Have you got £10 in your wallet?
  B: (i) Yes. In fact, I've got £12.
     (ii) No, I've got £12.

However, *John has (exactly) £10* entails *John has (at least) £10*, which perhaps explains why 46 is not zeugmatic:

46. You need £100 in your account to qualify for free banking. Arthur has it, now that he has added £50 to the £50 that was already there.

The first mention of £100 clearly demands an "at least" interpretation; what Arthur has is "exactly" £100; one might therefore not expect the *it* of the second sentence to be able to refer anaphorically to £100 in the first sentence without antagonism. However, because of the entailment referred to above, the original and anaphoric occurrences of £100 can both be given the "at least" interpretation, thus avoiding antagonism. It is possible to construct isolating contexts which reveal antagonism, but they are extremely cumbersome:

47a. John, with £11, and Bill, with £12, both have the £10 necessary to open a savings account. ("at least")

b. Tom, too, now has £10, having spent £2 out of his original £12. ("exactly" reading forced by *now*)

c. ? John, with £11, has the £10 necessary to open a savings account; Tom, too, now has it, having spent £2 out of his original £12.

IV The case of *door* is interesting (a group of related words such as *window*, *hatch*, *sky-light*, etc. behave similarly). Two senses of *door* may be observed in 48, which can be truthfully answered either 'Yes' or 'No' in the following situation: the door in question has a 'cat-flap', and is standing open; the cat goes through the cat-flap, but not through the doorway:

48. Did the cat go through the door?

Once again, difficulties arise with the antagonism criteria. It might be predicted, for instance, that 49 would be zeugmatic, since what is smashed (the door-panel) is different from what is bricked up (the doorway):[16]

49. The door was smashed in so often that it had to be bricked up.

But there is no anomaly of any kind. Again, it appears that contexts of a particular kind must be avoided if the test is to succeed. In this case it is the part–whole relationship which is to blame. For certain predicates, applicability to parts entails applicability to wholes corresponding to the parts. Thus, if I touch the *table-leg*, by doing so I necessarily touch the *table*; if the *tea-pot handle* is broken, so is the *tea-pot*, and so on. It seems likely that this entailment is interfering with antagonism in 49 – both events are interpreted as happening to the 'global door', of which the door-panel is a part. The remedy, as before, is to avoid such contexts, and to use, to isolate the senses, only those contexts in which part does not entail whole (or, better still, contexts where part entails not-whole). When this is done, the antagonism of the senses is easily seen:

50. ? We took the door off its hinges and then walked through it.

65

The moral to be drawn from these examples is that apparent compatibility of readings must not be too hastily accepted as proof of generality: each case must be examined carefully to determine whether there are special factors preventing the appearance of zeugma. It may be reasonably confidently assumed that the different criteria for ambiguity which have been described in fact are sensitive to the same underlying semantic property, and that in the absence of 'special factors' will provide identical diagnoses.

3.6 Non-lexical sources of ambiguity

It is important to realise that not all sentence ambiguity originates in lexical ambiguity; furthermore, our tests for ambiguity are not, in general, capable of discriminating between lexical and non-lexical varieties. Usually this is not a serious source of practical difficulty, since most cases are intuitively clear; but it is unfortunately not easy to formulate explicit criteria for recognising lexical ambiguity. We shall adopt a 'default' definition and characterise as lexical all ambiguities for which there is no convincing non-lexical explanation. This means that something at least must be said about alternative types of ambiguity, although a detailed treatment would be well beyond the scope of this book.

We can crudely classify the sorts of ambiguity found in sentences as follows:

1. Pure syntactic ambiguity:
   old men and women
   French silk underwear
2. Quasi-syntactic ambiguity:
   The astronaut entered the atmosphere again
   a red pencil
3. Lexico-syntactic ambiguity:
   We saw her duck.
   I saw the door open.
4. Pure lexical ambiguity:
   He reached the bank
   What is his position?

Types 3 and 4 are of direct relevance to us, and are discussed in some detail in the present chapter; types 1 and 2, on the other hand, are irrelevant, and we need to know how to exclude them.

By 'pure syntactic ambiguity' is meant ambiguity in which the variant readings of a sentence involve identical lexical units; the ambiguity is thus necessarily a matter merely of the way the elements are grouped together.

For instance, the meaning of *old men and women* differs according to whether *old* goes with *men* only:

(old men) and women

or with *men and women*:

old (men and women)

Likewise, *French silk underwear* may be underwear made of French silk ((*French silk*) *underwear*) or French underwear made of silk (*French* (*silk underwear*)). Such cases are characteristically very insensitive to the semantic properties of the constituent lexical items: *melodious trills and scales*; *porcelain egg container*. The so-called 'ambiguities of scope' can be included in this category; although they are often lexically restricted, they can be fully accounted for in terms of 'what goes with what'. Take, for example, sentence 51:

51. I don't like him.

Innocuous though it may seem at first sight, this can be interpreted (at least in the written form) in two ways: either "I dislike him" (the most usual reading), or, in suitable contexts, "It's not true that I like him" (for instance, in *I don't dislike him, but I don't like him either*). There is no need to postulate different negative elements, or different meanings of *like*: it is enough to allow the negative element either to take the whole of the rest of the sentence as its scope (*Neg* (*I like him*)), in which case the meaning will be "It's not true that I like him," or the single element *like* (*I Neg-like him*), in which case the meaning will be "I dislike him."[17]

'Quasi-syntactic' ambiguities require careful consideration because there may be a temptation to diagnose them as cases of lexical ambiguity. This is because there is no straightforward syntactic explanation of the ambiguity: not only are the lexical units identical for the two interpretations, but they are identically grouped, too. And yet this type of ambiguity bears a striking resemblance to the scope ambiguities described above. Consider the case of *The astronaut entered the atmosphere again*. The two meanings are (i) "the astronaut entered the atmosphere for (at least) the second time" and (ii) "the astronaut returned to the atmosphere (after what could have been his/her first trip into space)". This ambiguity can be accounted for without the need either for two different elements *enter*, or two different elements *again*, if we regard the meaning of *enter* as being constituted out of more elementary semantic entities which are related quasi-syntactically:

"enter" = [COME TO BE] [IN]

The two readings can then be represented as follows:

    (i)   ([COME TO BE] [IN]) [AGAIN]
   (ii) [COME TO BE] ([IN] [AGAIN])

The availability of an explanation along these lines (however it might be formalised in relation to the syntax) renders a lexical solution unnecessary.[18] Another example is *a red pencil*, which has the two readings (i) "a pencil painted red" and (ii) "a pencil which writes red". It may be thought that in reading (ii), *pencil* should be taken to refer only to the core of the pencil. This is not so, however: there is little doubt that in both interpretations *pencil* refers to the whole object (or at least potentially does so). Notice that *I have a red pencil and a blue one* has no crossed interpretation, which is what we expect from a genuine ambiguity. Yet *The red pencil is the chewed one* is quite normal on both readings, which would not be expected if on one of the readings *pencil* referred only to the core. It seems that the adjective *red* can apply either to the whole of the referent of the noun that it accompanies, or to a salient, or major functional, part of it. The same potential ambiguity is present in *a stainless steel hammer*, and even (although pragmatically less likely) *a felt pen*. It is not clear at present exactly what the rules are in such cases, nor whether the choices of readings are as clear-cut as they at first seem. What is clear, however, is that we are not dealing with lexical ambiguity.

3.7 Establishment of senses

    A lexical form may well be associated with an unlimited number of possible senses, but these are not all of equal status. If we take seriously the notion of 'unlimited number', there must be, for any lexical form, potential senses which have never been realised in use: equally, every lexical form has at least one relatively well-utilised sense. We may thus envisage a gradient of what we shall term †**establishment** of senses. (Individual speakers may, of course, differ markedly in respect of the degree of establishment of different senses, but a substantial measure of consensus may be assumed.)

The difference between established senses and potential senses is not merely one of frequency of use, although this is undoubtedly an important component of the difference: established senses are presumably represented differently in the mind's lexicon. It seems appropriate to distinguish two kinds of contextual selection, according to whether the selected sense is established or not. In the former case, where selection is from among pre-established senses, the context acts merely as a kind of filter: we shall refer to this as †**passive selection**. Where, on the other hand, the selected sense is not established, the context acts rather as a stimulus for a productive process, namely, the activation of a set of rules or principles which 'generate' the sense in question. The latter type of selection will be called †**productive**. The difference between the two types of selection may be assumed to be of psycholinguistic importance.

There is a possible test for the establishment of a sense, which has consequences for the second family of tests for ambiguity described earlier. It appears that it is possible to assert one of the senses of a lexical form, using the bare form, while at the same time denying (explicitly or implicitly) another of the senses, only if the asserted sense is fully established. A few examples will make this clear. Take the case of *novel*, which can have the readings (i) "narrative text" or (ii) "physical object (embodying a narrative text)". The two readings may be observed in 52 and 53 respectively:

52.　His new novel will be published next spring.

53.　Why is your desk always piled high with novels?

Now consider 54 and 55:

54.　I'm not interested in the cover design, or the binding – I'm interested in the novel.

55.　? I'm not interested in the plot, or the characterisation, or anything of that nature – I'm interested in the novel.

Notice that 54 is more or less normal: the "physical object" reading is explicitly denied, and *novel* is consequently understood with the "text" interpretation. Sentence 55, on the other hand, is uninterpretable: since the "text" reading has been excluded, it appears that there is no other possible reading, so the sentence is anomalous. It would make sense if we were free to take *novel* to refer to the physical object; but in this sentence such an interpretation is not available. It seems reasonable to conclude that only the "text" reading is fully established. In the case of the numerals, it is the "exactly X" reading which is fully established according to this test. Thus the final £*10* in 56, if it carries the main sentence stress, can only mean "exactly £10":

56.　A: I would earn at least £10 an hour there.
　　　B: Well, here you'll earn £10.

However, the bare mention of £*10* cannot carry the "at least" interpretation in contrast to an explicitly expressed "exactly £10":

57. A: I would earn just £10 an hour there.

    B: ? Well, here you will earn £10.

If the "at least" reading had been available, the sentence would not be odd. From this we may conclude that the "at least" sense of numerals is not established. In the case of the unit–type ambiguity, it is the unit readings which pass this test (cf. 58), while the 'type' readings fail (cf. 59):

58. I don't want that type of jacket, I want that jacket.

59. ? I don't mean that individual dog, I mean that dog.

In all the above cases, the lexical form in question has only one established sense. This, however, is not a rule: more than one sense may be established, as the normal interpretability of all the following examples shows:

60a. I'm not only interested in male dogs, I'm interested in dogs.

 b. I'm not interested in all members of the canine race
     irrespective of sex – I'm interested in dogs.

61a. I didn't put my money in the side of a river, I put it in the
     bank.

 b. I didn't moor the boat to a financial institution, I moored it
     to the bank.

62a. Charles has moved to another seat in the conference hall, but
     he has not changed his position.

 b. Charles hasn't changed his mind on EEC membership, but
     he has changed his position.

These examples point to a limitation on one of the tests for ambiguity elaborated earlier. It appears that certain ways of applying the criterion of independent maximisability are valid only for established senses. Sentences of the form of 26, for example, require established senses. Negative results in such cases must therefore be checked either against other criteria, or against other ways – such as the *Yes/No*-test – of applying the same criterion. (Positive results, of course, present no problems.)

The number of fully established senses is presumably finite at any one time (though it may differ for different members of the language community, and at different times for the same speaker). It might therefore be thought advantageous to limit the class of lexical units to these. However, although our attention will naturally be more strongly drawn to established senses, to limit the discussion in principle to these would lead to a distorted picture of word-meaning. This is because less-than-fully-established senses are lexicologically almost indistinguishable from fully established ones, in that they enter largely the same range of syntagmatic and paradigmatic relations of meaning (the sentences cited above, of course, show that they are not absolutely identical). We shall therefore not limit our investigations in any principled way to established senses; whether a sense is established or not is, however, of significance for lexicography.

3.8 Sense-spectra

It has been argued up to now that although word-meaning is in a sense infinitely variable, nonetheless discrete units – 'atoms' or 'quanta' of sense – can be identified which at least in some respects are stable across contexts, and which are the appropriate basic units for lexical semantics. Certain aspects of word-meaning, however, are difficult to reconcile with this view: particularly awkward are what we shall term †**sense-spectra**.

There are cases where variant readings of a single lexical form would seem to be more appropriately visualised as points on a continuum – a seamless fabric of meaning with no clear boundaries. This would not necessarily conflict with the picture of word-meaning developed so far if a single superordinate sense could be found which covered all the variants. However, there do appear to exist examples of gradual variation which cannot be made to share a superordinate; in such cases the absence of boundaries between senses is an embarrassment. The appearance which sense-spectra present can be compared with a so-called 'dialect continuum': speakers from village A can communicate with those from village B, who are able to converse with speakers from C; these, in turn, can communicate with speakers from village D. However, speakers from A cannot hold a conversation with speakers from D, and without the evidence of the intervening stages, one would be tempted to say that they spoke different languages. But it is impossible to say at what point along the continuum the change from one form of the language to another occurs, or to determine how many distinct forms there are. Another analogy is with the evolutionary biologist's notion of a 'ring-species': a population A, of some species, interbreeds with a neighbouring population B, B with C, C with D, and so on, round the world, until population X is reached, whose territory adjoins that of the original A. But A and X do not interbreed: they give every appearance of being distinct species. Again it is impossible to say where the change-over from one species to the next occurs, and how many species there are. The fact seems to be that in such cases it is inappropriate to think in terms of discrete variation. In the semantic analogues to these continua, two readings which are close together on the continuum can be coordinated without zeugmatic incompatibility (this is the semantic parallel to mutual intelligibility and interbreeding), whereas readings which are far apart are incompatible. Examples of this· are far from rare: on the contrary, this state of affairs would seem to be the norm, for example, for senses which have undergone 'metaphorical extension'.[19]

As an example of this sort of semantic continuum, which we shall call a †**sense-spectrum**, consider the following use of *mouth*:

63. John keeps opening and shutting his mouth like a fish.
64. This parasite attaches itself to the mouths of fishes, sea-squirts, etc.
65. The mouth of the sea-squirt resembles that of a bottle.
66. The mouth of the cave resembles that of a bottle.
67. The mouth of the enormous cave was also that of the underground river.

Allowing for a degree of non-anomalous unusualness in the sentences (such sequences are, for various reasons, rather difficult to construct) it seems that we have got from *John's mouth* to *the mouth of the river* without encountering zeugmatic incompatibility. The normal conclusion from this would be that the readings of *mouth* in 63–67 were contextual modulations of a single superordinate sense. This is ruled out, however, not only by the difficulty of finding a paraphrase of the supposed superordinate sense, but also by the clearly zeugmatic nature of 68:

68. ? The poisoned chocolate entered the Contessa's mouth at the same instant that the yacht entered that of the river.

This is, of course, a simplified picture of a sense-spectrum: it should be thought of as having, at least potentially, many dimensions, and as continually growing, amoeba-like.[20]

One of the points on the sense-spectrum presented above – and this is typical of the metaphorical variety – has a special status, which manifests itself in two principal ways. First, it is the only sense which can appear in a neutral, or minimal context, as in 69:

69. At school, we are doing a project on mouths.

It seems unlikely that 69 could be taken to include river mouths. All the other possibilities are highly context-bound, in that they can only appear in relatively explicit contexts – compare the a and b sentences in the following:

70a.　? The body was found near the mouth.

　b.　..............................the mouth of the cave.

71a.　? This bird is often to be seen near mouths.

　b.　.....................................the mouths of rivers.

　　　(cf. also: ....near estuaries.)

72a.　? The candle was stuck in the mouth.

　b.　...............................the mouth of the bottle.

The independent sense is often also the 'literal' sense, in that it is the only one, or at any rate the most plausible one, from which all the others can be derived by metaphorical interpretation. (It may sometimes happen that of two senses, either one could plausibly be a metaphorical extension of the other, as with, for example, *expire* (driving licence, etc.) and *expire* (person).) In the case of *mouth*, if one knew what an animal's mouth was, and one were to hear, for the first time, a reference to *the mouth of a river*, I surmise that there would be little difficulty in construing the meaning; but suppose one were familiar only with *mouth* used to refer to the mouth of a river, and one heard a reference to *the horse's mouth*, it is by no means certain that one's attention would be directed to the appropriate end of the horse!

The proper descriptive treatment of sense-spectra, and points along them, is somewhat problematical. A full sense-spectrum is not a satisfactory lexical unit: it does not, for instance, enter into any recognised lexical relations. Individual points along a spectrum, on the other hand, seem at first sight to be insufficiently distinguished from one another. However, there are reasons for believing that these are the most appropriate lexicological units. Although when viewed as part of a spectrum their distinctness is questionable, they typically function in widely different semantic fields, and within these their discreteness and stability are not in question. Take the case of *mouth of river*: it participates in a significant number of meaning-relations:

　　　　mouth :source　　　(opposites)
　　　　mouth :river　　　　(part–whole)
　　　　mouth :bed　　　　(coordinate parts)
　　　　mouth :estuary　　　(superordinate–hyponym)

None of these relations are shared by, for instance, *mouth of bottle*. Furthermore, the sense of *mouth* (*of river*) is stable across a variety of contexts (i.e. subject only to modulation) provided that "of river" is understood.

So far, so good. But here we are faced with a dilemma. If we allow the existence of distinct sets of lexical relations to individuate senses along a sense-spectrum, we are re-instating the indirect criteria dismissed earlier as being inadequate. If, on the other hand, we adopt a complex unit such as *mouth of river* as a basic lexical unit, this would be inconsistent with our earlier decision not to regard, for instance, *foot the bill* as a single unit. We shall adopt here the first of these solutions, as being the least objectionable of the two. That is to say, we shall recognise sense-units along a sense-spectrum – to be called †**local senses** – by their participation in distinct lexical fields (here, to be understood merely as sets of lexical items interrelated by determinate meaning relations such as oppositeness, hyponymy, part–whole, etc.). This method of delimiting senses will be confined to sense-spectra.

The true extent of the phenomenon is not at present clear, but not all sense-spectra are of the metaphorical sort. It seems likely, for instance, that the senses of *handle* form a spectrum:

> handle   of door
>   of drawer
>   of suitcase
>   of umbrella
>   of sword
>   of knife
>   of spoon

There is more than a suspicion of zeugmatic tension when the end-items are yoked together:

> ? He grasped the handle of the door in one hand, and that
>   of the spoon in the other.

The different senses of *handle* can be delimited in the manner suggested above for *mouth*.

3.9 Syntactic delimitation

Lexicological units must not only be delimited paradigmatically, that is, within a constant syntactic frame: we want also to be able to say of two occurrences of a lexical form in different syntactic environments whether they are occurrences of the same lexical unit, or two different units. Consider the occurrences of *open* in the following:

> 73a. The open door.
>   b. The door is open.
>   c. The door won't open.
>   d. John will open the door.

How many different items *open* are represented here? The sort of criteria which we used for paradigmatic delimitation are of no help here.

It would seem reasonable to adopt as a general principle that any two occurrences of a lexical form which represent two different grammatical elements should be regarded, *ipso facto*, as lexically distinct. However, there does not seem to exist an accepted notion of 'grammatically different element' which is sufficiently well-defined to carry the whole burden of distinguishing lexical units. Mere occurrence in syntactically different environments is not a sufficient criterion for the grammatical distinctness of two elements. For instance, the following two occurrences of *man* can be said to be in syntactically different environments:

74a. Arthur saw the man.
  b. The man's brother was here.

However, there are various reasons for saying that *man* is the same grammatical element in 74a and b. An important one is that the possible substitutes for *man* (preserving grammaticality, but not necessarily semantic normality) are virtually identical in the two positions. We might therefore demand difference of grammatical paradigm as a minimum requirement for distinctness. However, this is not sufficient, either, although it may well be necessary. Consider the following examples:

75a. The   main   customer
         old
         *asleep
  b. The customer is   asleep
                old
                *main
76a. Michael is eating   his sandwiches.
              preparing
              *laughing
  b. Michael is laughing
              eating
              *preparing

It is extremely dubious, in spite of the differences in grammatical paradigm, whether anything would be gained by classifying the two occurrences of *old*, or those of *eat*, as grammatically, hence lexically, distinct. Other purely grammatical criteria may be suggested, but none seem capable of guaranteeing the desired results.

A more satisfactory way of delimiting lexical units is to look for grammatical differences which correlate with differences of meaning. Take, for example, the occurrences of *open* cited above (73a–d). Grammatically distinctive traits can be found for each of these. Looking, for instance, at grammatically equivalent substitutions, *main* is possible only in a, *ajar* only in b, *disappear* only in c, and *hit* only in d. Other differences may be cited: only in c and d can *open* take *-s* as an affix, and only in a and b can *open* be modified by *wide*; c and d differ in that the noun phrases which form normal subjects of *open* in c are those which form normal objects of *open* in d (and similarly with odd subjects in c), so that, for example, the normality of *The book opened* is paralleled by that of *John opened the book*, and the oddness of *? The page opened* by that of *? John opened the page*. Most, but not all, of these grammatical differences are correlated with semantic differences. Taking the meaning of *open* in 73b as basic, we can paraphrase 73c (not exactly, but quite closely) as "the door came to be open", and 73d as "John caused the door to come to be open." In any sentence, the appropriate interpretation of *open* can be determined from its grammatical nature (i.e. whether it is adjective, transitive or intransitive verb, etc.). The fact that the occurrences of *open* in 73b, c and d exemplify a regular correlation between semantic and grammatical properties provides a justification for regarding them as lexically distinct. However, there is no similar way of differentiating 73a and b semantically, so, in spite of grammatical evidence of distinctness, they are to be considered lexically identical.

3.10 Lexemes

One of the most remarkable features of language is the fact that it 'makes infinite use of finite resources'. This dictum is more familiar in its application to grammar. But it is valid also for the lexical domain. We have already had glimpses of the indeterminate multiplicity of lexical senses: a lexicographer, however, needs a finitely enumerable set of lexical elements with which to work. The appropriate unit for this purpose is the **lexeme**: a dictionary contains (among other things) an alphabetical list of the lexemes of a language. We shall characterise a lexeme as a family of lexical units.

However, before outlining the principles governing the assignation of lexical units to lexemes, it is necessary to introduce a refinement into our conception of a lexical unit. We have so far assumed that it is a word form associated with a single sense, and that a difference of word form entails a difference of lexical unit. But this is not quite satisfactory. Strictly speaking, we would be obliged, on this view, to regard, for instance, *obey*, *obeys* and *obeyed* as representing different lexical units. It would, however, be more advantageous for our purposes to be able to say that they were alternative manifestations of the same lexical unit *obey*. To characterise the form aspect of a lexical unit, therefore, we need to generalise across – or abstract from – a set of word forms. In order to characterise this more abstract notion of lexical unit more precisely, a distinction must be made between **inflectional** and **derivational** affixes. An affix is a grammatical element, belonging to a closed set, which can only function as a component of a word: *dis-, un-, -ment, -ise, -ed, -s* are all affixes. Each affix is obligatorily attached to a **stem**[21] containing or consisting of an open set item: *dis-obey, un-popular, central-ise, dismount-ed, long-er,* etc. A stem may be simple (as *obey* in *dis-obey*), or complex (as *disobey* in *dis-obeyed*). Affixes are of two sorts – derivational and inflectional. Derivational affixes produce new lexical units: *true : untrue, kind : kindness, help : helpful, lion : lioness,* etc. They play no direct role in the syntax of a sentence, and can be recognised by the fact that words containing them (**derived words**) can typically be replaced in any sentence, without syntactic change, by a word which does not contain the affix:[22]

> Her kindness (voice) was overwhelming.
> I found them extremely helpful (stupid).

Typically, derived words are listed as separate items in a dictionary. Inflectional affixes, on the other hand, do not produce new lexical units: *book : books, obey : obeyed, long : longer.* In principle for any word bearing an inflectional affix, it is possible to find contexts where all possible substitutes must contain either the same affix, or one belonging to the same closed set: consider the possible substitutes for *walked* in *Cedric walked home, longer* in *Mine is longer than yours* or *books* in *those books*.

We can now re-define a lexical unit. First, we may call the abstract unit of form which is realised in actual sentences as the appropriate member of a set of word forms differing only in respect of inflections a **lexical form**; and we can extend the notion of lexical form to cover an abstraction from the variously inflected manifestations of an idiom or dead metaphor. A lexical unit is then the union of a lexical form and a single sense. Let us now return to the question of assigning lexical units to lexemes.

For lexical units with identical grammatical properties, two alternative criteria for membership of the same lexeme will be proposed. The first is the most important. It is that two lexical units will be assigned to the same lexeme if there exists a lexical rule which permits the prediction of the existence of the sense of one of them from the existence of the sense of the other. The existence of a rule presupposes that senses associated with more than one lexical form fall within its scope (otherwise there would be no rule). Hence, we shall accept as evidence of the presence of a rule a recurrent semantic contrast between senses, that is to say, a contrast which holds between senses associated with at least two different lexical forms. On this basis, the unit and type readings of *jacket* in *I like this jacket* belong to the same lexeme, because the same contrast recurs with *skirt, dress, coat, hat*, etc. (We shall not concern ourselves here with the exact formulation of the regularity: we shall merely note the evidence of its presence.) Similarly, the two lexical units represented by *brilliant* in *John is brilliant* and *This is a brilliant book* are to be assigned to the same lexeme, the evidence being the recurrence of the relation with *confused, angry, bitter*, etc. A parallel situation exists with *sad* in *John is sad* and *This is a sad poem*; this relationship, too, is recurrent (cf. *light-hearted*), but is different from that observed in the case of *brilliant*. A brilliant book is (roughly) the expression of a brilliant person, but a sad poem is rather one which induces sadness in the reader. Consider, too, the two readings of *flatten out* which occur in 77 and 78:

77. The surface of the mixture began to flatten out.
78. After Kendal, the countryside begins to flatten out.

The same difference of sense recurs in the following:

79. The soil began to dry up.
80. Once you leave the Bekaa Valley, the countryside begins to dry up.

Examples such as these can be multiplied indefinitely.[23]

It is perhaps worth noting briefly at this point a special type of recurrent semantic relationship between lexical units sharing a lexical form, which is of particular significance in lexical semantics (it is discussed in greater detail in connection with markedness and neutralisation in chapter 11). The two senses[24] carried by the lexical form *dog* in 81a and b, and the two senses of *lion* in 82a and b, and of *heavy* in 84a and b stand in a relation of this type:

81a. Dogs, both male and female, make excellent pets.
   b. Dogs are more aggressive than bitches.
82a. Lions breed well in captivity.
   b. When fully grown, a lion is bigger than a lioness.

The two senses of *long* in 83a and b, and of *heavy* in 84a and b stand in a slightly different relation, but one of the same type:

83a. How long is it?
  b. How long it is!
84a. How heavy is it?
  b. How heavy it is!

The alternative criterion for assigning lexical units to a single lexeme is that their senses should be local senses belonging to the same sense-spectrum. Thus all the senses of *mouth* discussed earlier will represent lexical units belonging to a single lexeme. This criterion is quite strict, and does not allow the grouping together of all senses normally considered to be metaphorically related. For instance, there is no spectrum connecting the two senses of *expire*, so their lexical units would not be assigned to the same lexeme. The same is true of the readings of *position* that we have examined in connection with ambiguity. This differs from normal lexicographic practice, which is to group all metaphorically related senses together.

Among the lexical units which go to make up a lexeme it is possible to distinguish some that are more basic, or central, and others that are less so. It is clear that established units (i.e. those with established senses) are more central than unestablished ones: an ideal dictionary would be expected to define all the established senses within each lexeme. But even among established units we can distinguish grades of centrality. Most basic of all are lexical units which become operative in minimal, or neutral, contexts. These may be termed the †**primary lexical units** of a lexeme – a category that would include, for instance, *dog* ("species"), *heavy* ("weight"), *novel* ("text"), etc. Some lexical units, even though established, are selected only in specific restricted contexts, or in contexts where the primary units would lead to abnormality. This is true of *dog* ("male"), *heavy* ("copious consumption"), etc. Such units may be termed †**secondary** (the primary/secondary distinction here is not, of course, a strict dichotomy – the accessibility, or ease of activation, of lexical units may be assumed to vary continuously). There remain the unestablished units, generally indeterminate in number, and varying in the degree of contextual pressure required to activate them. Probably some degree of oddness is an inescapable penalty for calling an unestablished unit into service; this abnormality may be very slight, as in *A large novel fell on my head*, or it may be considerable, as in *I received a lot of kindness from him – would you like to try a bottle?*

The principle of recurrent relationships can also serve for the association of grammatically different lexical units. In such cases, the recurrent relationship must be simultaneously grammatical and semantic if the units are to be assigned to the same lexeme. The following are examples of such recurrence:

85a. John moved the rock / The rock moved.
   b. John turned the key / The key turned.
86a. Have some apple / Have an apple.
   b. Have some potato / Have a potato.
87a. Put them in a can / Can them.
   b. Put them in a box / Box them.

Notice, however, that although the following exhibit a syntactic parallel with the cases cited above, the semantic relationship is not maintained, so the lexical units must be assigned to different lexemes:

88. Get him into a corner / Corner him.
89. Put his name in a book / Book him.

Again, this is not in accordance with normal lexicographic practice, which is, first, to regard differences of major syntactic category (e.g. noun, verb, adjective) as justifying a separate main entry, irrespective of the presence or absence of recurrent relationships. In respect of minor syntactic differences (e.g. transitive *v.* intransitive verbs; mass *v.* count nouns, etc.) dictionary makers are generally somewhat inconsistent. To summarise: a lexeme is a family of lexical units; a lexical unit is the union of a single sense with a lexical form; a lexical form is an abstraction from a set of word forms (or alternatively – it is a family of word forms) which differ only in respect of inflections.

It is commonplace to describe a lexeme which has a number of senses as **polysemous** (or as manifesting the property of **polysemy**), and a lexical form which realises lexical units belonging to more than one lexeme as **homonymous**. These terms, especially *polysemous* and *polysemy*, although innocuous if used circumspectly, are not entirely ideal for our purposes, because they carry with them a view of lexical meaning in which there is a tendency to regard the lexeme as the primary semantic unit, and the different lexical units as 'merely variants'. Our approach, however, focusses on the individual lexical unit as the primary operational semantic unit, and consigns the lexeme to a secondary position.

Notes

Linguists who have worked in lexical semantics can be broadly divided into two categories: on the one hand, there are those who believe that a word form is associated with a number (perhaps finite, perhaps not) of discrete senses; and on the other, there are those who believe that the discreteness of lexical senses is illusory. Advocates of a formal–theoretical approach to meaning not unnaturally favour the first alternative – for an exposition of this view, see Kempson (1977: 79–83). Protagonists of the other view include Matthews (1979: 67–75) and Moore and Carling (1982: ch. 5). Lyons, too, seems inclined to this position (1977: 550–69). I find myself highly sympathetic to the arguments of both sides; in this chapter I present what is in some respects a compromise view – I try to have my cake and eat it. (The views expressed here differ in some respects from those presented in Cruse (1982).)

3.1

1. Kempson (1977: 82–3) uses *lexeme* to mean something very close to our *lexical unit*. For me, a lexeme is a family of lexical units. I agree with Kempson in giving primacy to the lexical unit; but I agree with, for instance, Palmer (1976: 65–71), Lyons (1977: 550–69) and Cowie (1982) in assigning multiple semantic roles to a lexeme.

2. For the notion of 'creativity' in syntax, see Chomsky (1965: 3–9). To be able to produce indefinitely many sentences from a finite set of elements and rules, at least some of the rules must be **recursive** – that is, able to apply repeatedly (see Lyons 1968: 221–2). It is not unlikely that some of the sense-creating rules are also recursive.

3. See 3.10 for some examples.

3.2

4. Kempson (1977: 128–34) uses *vagueness* to refer to what we call *generality*. We shall use *vague* in more or less its everyday sense in opposition to *well-defined*. For us, generality and vagueness can vary independently. For instance, *vertebrate* is more general than *animal* (in its everyday sense) since birds and fish are vertebrates; but it is less vague – it is easier to specify qualifying characteristics for *vertebrate* than for *animal*. (It is characteristic of scientific terms to be relatively well-defined.) For a fuller discussion of vagueness, see Alston (1964: ch. 5).

5. This preliminary account will exaggerate the sharpness of the distinction between these two. See, however, section 8 of this chapter.

6. The mechanism underlying this change of status is discussed further in 4.12 and 12.2.

7. The phenomenon of linkage is one reason for treating the principle of compositionality with the greatest circumspection (indispensable though it is to any semantics – formal or informal).

8. The reader is reminded that, strictly, *car* in the sentence *The car needs washing* 'refers' only if the sentence is uttered in an appropriate situation.

9. These assumptions form part of the 'Cooperative Principle' governing conversational exchanges suggested in Grice (1975). See also Wilson and Sperber (1981), Leech (1983: 79–103), Levinson (1983: 97–166).

3.3 Criteria for lexical ambiguity of the sort which are here labelled 'indirect' are of considerable antiquity. Ross (1981: 40–7) attributes a number of them to Aristotle. See also Cruse (1982). I am informed by N. E. Collinge (private communication) that they occur even earlier, in Plato. For a modern example of the use of such criteria see Cowie (1982).

10. For paronymy see Ross (1981: 136–41).

11. *Fat* and *thick* have different collocational restrictions and these are not shared by *thin*. (See 12.2 for discussion of collocational restrictions.)

3·4

12. This criterion may be more or less equivalently (but more precisely) expressed as follows:

> For any sentence form containing an ambiguous word form, there should exist, in principle, situations in which the sentence form can be properly used to express two distinct propositions, which are identical except for differences consequent on the choice of sense associated with the ambiguous word form, and which have opposite truth values.

Both Lyons (1977: 404) and Kempson (1977: 128–9) deny – wrongly, in my opinion – that a successful test for ambiguity can be constructed along these lines. Kempson's argument runs roughly as follows. Suppose two linguists are in dispute as to whether *John killed Bill* is ambiguous between an intentional and an unintentional interpretation (intuitively, one is free to interpret it either way), and they decide to use the criterion of different truth values to settle the matter. Imagine, now, a situation in which John kills Bill unintentionally. Linguist A, who does not believe the sentence to be ambiguous, says that it is true relative to the situation described; linguist B, who believes *John killed Bill* to be ambiguous, says that it is true on the "unintentional" reading, and false on the "intentional" reading. And they will have got no further forward – the test has resolved nothing. However, what this line of argument ignores is that we cannot properly use a particular sentence form to express whatever proposition comes into our heads. Linguist B is correct in saying that the proposition "John killed Bill intentionally" is false relative to the situation described, and the proposition "John killed Bill unintentionally" is true. He is wrong, however, in his implicit assumption that *John killed Bill* is a proper linguistic vehicle to express the proposition "John killed Bill intentionally" (or "... unintentionally"). The proper expression of this proposition would implicitly deny the proposition "John killed Bill unintentionally" – but there is no way that *John killed Bill* could be used to deny this proposition, whether implicitly or explicitly.

13. See Zwicky and Sadock (1975).

3·5

14. In Zwicky and Sadock (1975: 14) and Kempson (1977: 136) the possibility of using the identity test in such circumstances is denied. (Kempson, however, no longer subscribes to this view (private communication).)

15. See Kempson and Cormack (1981). Notice that numerals can also have an "at most" reading, as in *Can you run 100 metres in 10 seconds?* and *I'm aiming at 10 stones by Easter* (said by a slimmer). Yet another possibility is the "round number" interpretation, which is the most likely in, for instance, *I'll see you in 10 minutes* (see Wachtel (1980) and Channell (1980)).

16. The normality of this sentence is cited by Nunberg (1979: 150) as evidence that *door* is not ambiguous in this way.

3·6

17. For fuller discussion of syntactic ambiguity see Kooij (1971) and Zwicky and Sadock (1975).

18. Not all conceivable differences of interpretation attributable to variation of scope represent true ambiguities. I agree with Kempson's arguments (1977: 132–5) that *It wasn't a woman that came to the door* is not ambiguous. (If it was a girl who came to the door, it might be argued that only the trait

"adult" is being negated, but not "human" or "female", whereas if it was a man, "female" is negated, but not "human" or "adult".) This sentence does not pass the *Yes/No*-test. But I disagree with her conclusions regarding *John almost killed the hostages* (Kempson (1977: 132)) and sentences exhibiting internal and external negation – like our example 51 – (Kempson (1977: 148–154)), both of which I believe represent true ambiguity.

3.8 The existence of semi-distinct local senses on sense-spectra blurs to some extent the distinction that we have up to now sharply maintained between ambiguity and generality, selection and modulation. It now seems probable that we are, in fact, dealing with yet another continuum. This does not, however, invalidate the original distinction: there are still innumerable clear instances of both ambiguity and generality.

19. It may well be that the meaning of every lexical unit should be regarded as at least potentially a sense-spectrum.
20. See also the discussion of the meaning of *pin* in Matthews (1979: 71–2). This looks like another typical example of a spectrum.

3.10 The definition of *lexeme* adopted here differs both from that of Kempson and from that of Lyons (which represent the main current alternatives), occupying, in a sense, an intermediate position. For Kempson (1977: 79–83), every distinguished sense represents a different lexeme, and she sees no theoretical justification for groupings of senses. Lyons adopts what I take to be a more traditional approach (1977: ch. 9). If I understand him correctly, for him each of the items which stand in a relation such as antonymy is a 'lexeme-in-a-particular-sense'. He thus regards what we call the lexeme as the basic lexical item. Our approach centres on a single-sense (**univocal**) unit (in this respect, therefore, agreeing with Kempson), but at the same time recognises groupings based on relatedness of sense (in this respect agreeing with Lyons).

21. The term *stem* is sometimes used in a narrower sense, to designate what an inflectional affix is attached to, *base* being used to refer to what a derivational affix is attached to. Our usage follows Allerton (1979: ch. 10).
22. This is the case in English, at any rate. The reader should be warned that this is not a comprehensive account of the differences between inflection and derivation. For a fuller discussion, see Matthews (1974: ch. 3). (Matthews speaks of 'lexical' – rather than 'derivational' – morphology.)
23. Cf. Leech's 'rules of semantic transfer' (1974: 216–17).
24. Lexical units contract semantic relations with other units by virtue of their senses. There is therefore no difference between saying that a certain semantic relation holds between two lexical units, and saying that it holds between the senses of those units.

4
Introducing lexical relations

4.1 Preliminaries

Beginning with this chapter, and running through to chapter 12, the principal topics of discussion will be various types of semantic relation which hold between lexical units of the kind established in chapter 3. There may appear to be an element of paradox in the notion of semantic relations between lexical units whose meanings, at least on the strong version of the contextual view, are partially constituted by those very relations. It is, however, no more paradoxical than speaking of *John's arm*, when the arm in question is part of the *John* who is said to possess it (or *the chassis of the car*, for instance). In such cases we have a notion of a whole which is more, at least phenomenologically, than a mere assemblage of parts. The same is true of the meanings of lexical units: each one consists of an indefinite number of contextual relations but at the same time constitutes a unified whole. Hence it is not unnatural to speak of a lexical unit standing in a particular semantic relation to other lexical units. The paradox does not present itself in quite so acute a form if a weaker version of the contextual approach is adopted, which holds merely that the meaning of a lexical unit reveals itself through its contextual relations, without commitment as to what meaning 'really is'.

Although no meaning relation can be said to be totally without significance, by no means all conceivable relations are of equal general semantic interest. To be worth singling out for special attention, a semantic relation needs to be at least systematic, in the sense that it recurs in a number of pairs or sets of related lexical units (it will be recalled that the expression *lexical unit* is used to refer to a lexical form together with a single distinguished sense). But even recurrent sense relations are of varying general significance. There are innumerable 'low level' semantic relations restricted to specific notional areas. Take, for example, the relations between the lexical items *see* ("have a visual experience"), *look at* ("pay attention to a static visual stimulus"), and *watch* ("pay attention to a changing or potentially changing visual stimulus"). If we examine the lexical units referring to other modes of perception we find the following correspondences:

see	look at	watch
hear	listen to	
taste[1]	taste[2]	
smell[1]	smell[2]	
feel[1]	feel[2]	

Notice that although *listen to* corresponds to two different lexical units in the visual mode, it is not ambiguous; the word forms *taste*, *smell* and *feel*, on the other hand, are ambiguous in parallel ways, their senses standing in a relationship parallel to that which holds between *hear* and *listen to*. Looking now at French, we find that for terms referring to the visual mode, the *look at*: *watch* contrast is absent, the notional area being covered by a single, univocal item *regarder*. In the auditory mode, French closely parallels English, with *entendre* and *écouter*. Corresponding to *taste[1]*, *smell[1]* and *feel[1]*, French has a single item *sentir[1]*, which is non-specific with respect to the three perceptual modes; there is, however, a distinct *sentir[2]*, which corresponds to *smell[2]*. For the "pay attention" meaning in the other two sensory modes, French provides distinct lexical items: *goûter*, corresponding to *taste[2]*, and *toucher*, corresponding to *feel[2]*. Now the detailed structure of these lexical sets in English and French, although of intense concern to students of English and French, cannot be generalised to other sets; nor can the semantic contrast "have an experience in a particular perceptual mode" *v.* "pay attention to a stimulus in that mode". At this level of specificity, therefore, these facts are of limited significance for a general study of lexical semantics. However, the abstract pattern of lexical items in parallel series is of considerable general significance, and is not confined to particular notional areas. (Lexical configurations of this sort are discussed in chapter 5.) Or take the semantic relation between *dog* and *cat*. At its most specific, it has a very limited currency: it recurs between *canine* and *feline*, and between *puppy* and *kitten* – but that is about all. However, at a more abstract level, the level at which *dog*: *cat*, *church*: *cinema*, *oak*: *ash* and *tea*: *coffee* can all be said to manifest the same relation, it is of fundamental significance.

Sense relations of the more specific sort are obviously too numerous and too idiosyncratic to form the basis for a general study of lexical semantics. In this book, therefore, attention is concentrated on relations of the more abstract sort. A relatively small number of these have come to occupy focal positions in discussions of lexical semantics (such relations as antonymy, hyponymy and synonymy), and they form correspondingly prominent topics of the present and succeeding chapters.

Sense relations are of two fundamental types: paradigmatic and syntagmatic. Most of this book is devoted to paradigmatic sense relations (lexical semanticists, in general, have found them a richer vein to mine than relations of the syntagmatic variety). However, although syntagmatic relations have only one section of a chapter specifically devoted to them, it is in fact impossible adequately to discuss one type without frequent reference, either explicit or implicit, to the other type. (Abnormality, for instance, is a reflection of a syntagmatic relation.) The two types of relation each have their own distinctive significance. Paradigmatic relations, for the most part, reflect the way infinitely and continuously varied experienced reality is apprehended and controlled through being categorised, subcategorised and graded along specific dimensions of variation. They represent systems of choices a speaker faces when encoding his message. Syntagmatic aspects of lexical meaning, on the other hand, serve discourse cohesion, adding necessary informational redundancy to the message, at the same time controlling the semantic contribution of individual utterance elements through disambiguation, for instance, or by signalling alternative – e.g. figurative – strategies of interpretation.

The main purpose of the present chapter is to develop some basic concepts that will be used throughout the subsequent discussion of semantic relations. In sections 4.2–4.7 certain elementary relations between sets are used as a model to generate (i) a basic set of paradigmatic lexical relations and (ii) a set of concepts which can be applied to other relations, yielding clearly defined and systematic variants. In sections 4.8–4.12 a further set of qualifying concepts is presented which will help to identify in a systematic way a number of near relations of, and approximations to, more basic paradigmatic relations. Finally, section 4.13 introduces syntagmatic semantic relations, and briefly considers some aspects of syntagmatic–paradigmatic interconnections.

4.2 Congruence

The four basic relations between classes furnish a model not only for establishing a fundamental group of sense relations, but also for defining a set of systematic variants applicable to virtually all other paradigmatic sense relations. The basic lexical relations will be referred to collectively as †**congruence relations**, and the variants as †**congruence variants**. The relations between classes are as follows:

1. identity: class A and class B have the same members

2. inclusion: class B is wholly included in class A

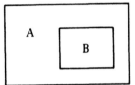

3. overlap: class A and class B have members in common
             but each has members not found in the other

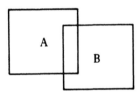

4. disjunction: class A and class B have no members in
                  common

This model can be applied to the definition of a set of lexical relations in two ways. The first possibility is to adopt a referential viewpoint. For two lexical items A and B we can ask whether the respective classes of entities they denote are identical, disjunct, overlapping, or whether one includes the other. This approach is convenient, and we shall often have recourse to it; however, it has disadvantages (even supposing that a fully adequate account can be given of such notions as "the class of dogs"). One difficulty is that the approach is not sufficiently general: many words do not in any straightforward way denote classes of potential referents (consider *air, some, usually, however*). There are also problems with words like *unicorn, roc, elf* and *dragon*. One would wish to say that there was a semantic relation between, say, *unicorn* and *animal*, yet the class of animals contains no unicorns. A better approach to the study of the semantic relations between two lexical items X and Y is to operate directly in terms of meaning, and look at semantic relations between parallel sentences in which X and Y occupy identical structural positions. The most useful primary lexical relations are established using truth-conditional relations between containing sentences. In appropriate cases (i.e. with items that denote classes of entities) this method gives results identical to those obtained with referential classes, but has the advantage of greater generality. Let us now consider the primary lexical relations (i.e. congruence relations) individually and in detail.

4.3 Propositional synonymy

The lexical relation which parallels identity in the membership of two classes is, of course, synonymy. As we shall see in chapter 12, there are different degrees of synonymity; the relation defined in terms of truth-conditional relations will be distinguished as **propositional synonymy**. Propositional synonymy may be defined as follows:

X is a propositional synonym of Y if (i) X and Y are syntactically identical, and (ii) any grammatical declarative sentence S containing X has equivalent truth-conditions to another sentence S^1, which is identical to S except that X is replaced by Y.

An example of a pair of propositional synonyms is *fiddle* and *violin*: these are incapable of yielding sentences with different truth-conditions. For instance, *He plays the violin very well* entails and is entailed by *He plays the fiddle very well*.

4.4 Hyponymy

The lexical relation corresponding to the inclusion of one class in another is **hyponymy**. Defining hyponymy is less straightforward than defining cognitive synonymy. For reasons which will become apparent in due course, it is necessary to restrict the type of sentence used in the definition. Ideally one would like to be able to give a general characterisation of suitable sentence types; unfortunately this is not at present possible. What we shall do instead is to restrict the definition to one selected sentence type which happens to work, namely, that represented by the schema *A is f(X)*, where *f(X)* is an indefinite expression, and represents the minimum syntactic elaboration of a lexical item X for it to function as a complement of the verb *to be*[1]. X will be said to be a **hyponym** of Y (and, by the same token, Y a **superordinate** of X) if *A is f(X)* entails but is not entailed by *A is f(Y)* :[2]

This is a DOG unilaterally entails	*This is an ANIMAL*
That is a STALLION	*That is a HORSE*
This is a SCARLET flower	*This is a RED flower*
He is a man who MURDERED	*He is a man who KILLED*
someone	someone

Even with sentences not of the form *A is f(X)* it is often the case that a sentence containing a hyponym unilaterally entails a parallel sentence which is identical in all respects except that it contains a superordinate in place of the hyponym:

> *John punched Bill* unilaterally entails *John hit Bill*
> *She wore scarlet shoes* unilaterally entails *She wore red shoes*

Conversely, unilateral entailment between two sentences differing only in respect of the lexical fillers of a particular syntactic slot is often an indication of a hyponymous relation between the lexical units. However, the many and varied exceptions to both these general tendencies render it impracticable to frame a more general definition of hyponymy along these lines. In the following sentences, for instance, the entailment (unilateral in each case) is in the 'wrong' direction (i.e. from superordinate to hyponym):

> *It's not red* entails *It's not scarlet*
> *All animals are forbidden* entails *All dogs are forbidden*
> *I always avoid the red ones* entails *I always avoid the scarlet ones*
> *Without the red ones there will still be too many* entails *Without the scarlet ones there will still be too many*
> *If it is red, it will be rejected* entails *If it is scarlet, it will be rejected*

It is possible to formulate rules for predicting the direction of entailment in such cases. For instance, if the hyponym and superordinate fall within the scope of a negative, or a universal quantifier (e.g. *all*, *every*, *each*), or if they form part of a conditional clause or other expression of contingency, then the direction of entailment will be reversed. However, there are complications. For instance, the three factors mentioned interact with one another, so that if any two are simultaneously applicable, the entailment is in the 'normal' direction, i.e. from hyponym to superordinate. In 1, *dogs* and *animals* are within the scope ("field of action") both of the negative *not* and the universal quantifier *all*; in 2, *scarlet* and *red* are within the scope of *not*, and form part of a conditional clause; in 3, *cars* and *vehicles* are within the scope of *all*, and are part of a conditional clause:

1. *Not all dogs are dangerous* entails *Not all animals are dangerous*
2. *If it's not scarlet, it will be rejected* entails *If it's not red it will be rejected*
3. *If all cars are forbidden, I shan't go* entails *If all vehicles are forbidden, I shan't go*

When all three factors apply, entailment is once again reversed:

4. *If not all vehicles are forbidden, I shall go* entails *If not all cars are forbidden, I shall go*

(Some readers may find this last example difficult to construe. Think of it this way: if it is the case that an incomplete embargo on vehicles will result in my going, then anything that entails an incomplete embargo on vehicles will result in my going; an incomplete embargo on cars entails an incomplete embargo on vehicles, so an incomplete embargo on cars will result in my going.) These regularities follow from elementary logical principles. However, while the logical principles are straightforward, the application to natural language is not quite so straightforward, because the crucial factors – negatives, conditionality, etc. – may not be overtly expressed. Consider, for instance, the different entailment relations in 5 and 6, and in 7 and 8:

5. *It is important to avoid red socks* entails *It is important to avoid scarlet socks*
6. *It is important to buy red socks* does not entail *It is important to buy scarlet socks*
7. *Flowers are prohibited* entails *Dandelions are prohibited*
8. *Flowers make an acceptable present* does not entail *Dandelions make an acceptable present*

There are no overt elements in these sentences to explain the differences; presumably, however, 5 and 7 contain implicit universal quantification.

These are not the only problems. In another class of instances, hyponym and superordinate in parallel positions yield no entailment at all. For example, *It turned scarlet* does not entail *It turned red*, since the referent of *it* may have been some other shade of red to begin with; nor, obviously, does the reverse entailment hold. For somewhat different reasons in each case, there is not entailment between *I chose the first rose on the list* and *I chose the first flower on the list*, nor between *Mary was disappointed to receive a rose* and *Mary was disappointed to receive a flower* (perhaps she was expecting an orchid?).

Entailment can occur between sentences differing only in respect of the lexical fillers of a particular syntactic slot even when the lexical items in question are not related by hyponymy. This introduces further complications into the task of providing a principled account of the relations between hyponymy and entailment; 9 provides an example:

9. *The boil is on John's elbow* entails *The boil is on John's arm*

It should be clear by now that the relations between hyponymy and entailment are quite complex; however, the definition of hyponymy adopted earlier bypasses these problems, so we shall pursue them no further.

There are other diagnostic tests for hyponymy which are either discriminatory but insufficiently general, or general but insufficiently discriminatory. For instance, a hyponym is often propositionally equivalent to a paraphrase in which a superordinate is syntagmatically modified.[3] The equivalence between *queen* and *female monarch*, and *kitten* and *young cat*, for instance, establishes *queen* as a hyponym of *monarch*, and *kitten* as a hyponym of *cat*. Where such equivalences can be found, they constitute satisfactory proof of hyponymy. However, by no means all hyponyms stand in a relation of propositional equivalence with an expression containing a superordinate. There is, for example, no possible syntagmatic modification of *animal* which would render it propositionally equivalent to *dog* (or *elephant, mouse, crocodile, . . .*).[4]

Hyponymously related lexical items occur normally, in the appropriate order, in expressions such as the following:[5]

> dogs and other animals
> There's no flower more beautiful than a rose.
> He likes all fruit except bananas.
> She reads books all day – mostly novels.

Any attempt to frame a definition along these lines, however, would run aground because, although such a definition could be made fairly general, it would not discriminate sharply enough to provide a guarantee of hyponymy:

> dogs and other pets
> snakes and other poisonous creatures
> There's no weapon as versatile as a knife.

None of the above expressions contain lexical items related by hyponymy according to our definitions: *? A dog is necessarily a pet*, *? A snake is necessarily a poisonous creature*, *? A knife is necessarily a weapon.*

It might be thought that it should be possible to characterise hyponymy in terms of contextual normality. A hyponym, being more specific in sense than its superordinates, might be expected as a result to be more fastidious in respect of its lexical companions; and thus the normal contexts of a hyponym might reasonably be expected to constitute a sub-set of the normal contexts of a superordinate. By and large, this is true; for example, the lexical clash in *? The cat barked* is removed when *cat* is replaced by the superordinate *animal*. But it is not invariably the case, which makes it impracticable to define hyponymy in this way, unless the exceptions to the general tendency can be characterised precisely. Unfortunately, it is not clear how to characterise those contexts, like the following, in which a hyponym can be more normal than one of its superordinates:

> Prime ministers who are women are rare.
> ? Prime ministers who are human beings are rare.

4.5 Compatibility

The lexical relation which corresponds to overlap between classes will be given the name †**compatibility**. The defining characteristics of compatibles (lexical items related by compatibility) are two. The first is that there are no systematic entailments between sentences differing only in respect of compatibles in parallel syntactic positions. So, for instance, if X and Y are compatibles, then *A is f(X)* and *A is not f(X)* are logically independent of *A is f(Y)* and *A is not f(Y)*. This criterion on its own does not guarantee any but the most tenuous relation of sense, since, for instance, *harmless* is compatible with *heavy*, and *rare* with *round*. The second defining characteristic of compatibility guarantees a genuine relationship of sense: it is that a pair of compatibles must have a common superordinate. Compatibles, therefore, have some semantic traits in common, but differ in respect of traits that do not clash. The relationship is exemplified by *dog* and *pet*. They both fall under the superordinate *animal* (in the sense of "creature"); and *It's a dog* and *It's not a dog* have no necessary links with *It's a pet* and *It's not a pet*. Another pair of compatibles is *husband* and *policeman*; both belong to the category of human males, and *Arthur is / is not a husband* and *Arthur is / is not a policeman* are logically independent.

Two varieties of compatibility can be distinguished: †**strict compatibility** and †**contingent compatibility**. X and Y are strict compatibles if they have at least one shared hyponym or hyponymous expression which is independently characterisable. Take the case of *snake* and *poisonous creature*.[6] *It's a snake* entails neither *It's a poisonous creature* nor *It's not a poisonous creature*; likewise, *It's a poisonous creature* is logically independent of *It's a snake*. *Snake* and *poisonous creature* are strict compatibles because *adder* and *cobra*, for instance, are hyponymous to both; furthermore, these species are independently characterisable – that is, they are not established solely on the basis of venomousness. (Adders and cobras are not, of course, necessarily venomous, only canonically so, since any individual snake may have had its venom extracted.) Contingent compatibility is more common. It is exemplified by *dog* and *pet*: every dog is, in principle, a potential pet. There is no independently characterisable subclass of dogs for which being a pet is a necessary or canonical trait (lap-dogs do not count, because they cannot be distinguished without invoking the characteristic of pet-hood); nor are there distinguishable sub-types of pet which are canonically or necessarily dogs (except, of course, lap-dogs, which do not count here, either, and for parallel reasons).

4.6 Incompatibility

The sense relation which is analogous to the relation between classes with no members in common is **incompatibility**.[7] Two lexical items X and Y are incompatibles if a sentence of the form *A is f(X)* can be found which entails a parallel sentence of the form *A is not f(Y)*:[8]

> *It's a cat* entails *It's not a dog*
> *It's a carnation* entails *It's not a rose*
> *John is the one who is walking* entails *John is not the one who is running*
> *John is near the building* entails *John is not in the building*

There are certain parallels between incompatibility and compatibility. Like 'mere' compatibility, 'mere' incompatibility is of relatively little interest: the fact that *affix* and *volcano* are incompatibles is not specially informative. However, a special significance attaches to sets of incompatibles (as well as to compatibles) which fall under a single superordinate:

> *animal*: *cat, dog, lion, elephant, aardvark,* etc.

Declarative sentences identical except for different incompatible terms in parallel syntactic positions (besides those used in the test) are frequently in a contrary relationship: if *I cycled to work* is true, then *I walked to work* is false, but if *I cycled to work* is false, then *I walked to work* may be either true or false. However, the relationship between incompatibility and contrariety in natural sentences, like the relationship between hyponymy and entailment, is by no means straightforward, and the expected contrariety does not always appear. For instance, the truth of *I met Mary today* does not entail the falsity of *I met Mary yesterday*, although *yesterday* and *today* are incompatibles. However, if both are true, they obviously refer to different occasions of meeting Mary – a single occasion of meeting cannot be both yesterday and today. The contrary relation will therefore show up in a sentential context that specifies, or at least implies, that a single event is being referred to, such as *I only met Mary once, and that was today/yesterday* or (somewhat less convincingly) *It was today/yesterday that I met Mary*. Another example is *I bought some apples*, which does not stand in a contrary relationship with *I bought some pears*. In this case, both sentences can be true without their necessarily referring to separate events: one may purchase apples and pears simultaneously. Contrariety will only appear here if it is specified that apples (or pears) constituted the whole of the purchase: *All I bought were some apples/pears*. Colour terms present a particular problem. Most speakers would agree, I think, that *Mary wore a red dress* and *Mary wore a blue dress* were contraries (assuming, of course, that they refer to the same occasion, and that Mary, as would be normal, wore only one dress at a time); the colour terms refer to the predominant colour of the dress, and there can be only one predominant colour. But colour terms frequently qualify only part of the object their head noun denotes; furthermore, different colour terms may typically apply to different parts, so that, for instance, *Mary's eyes are blue* and *Mary's eyes are red* are not contraries (N.B. there is no lexical ambiguity in these sentences). Clearly, to yield contrary sentences, a pair of colour terms must refer to the same area of uniform colour; but it is far from obvious how to devise linguistic contexts which will guarantee this.

Like hyponymy, incompatibility features as a typical syntagmatic relation between constituent lexical items of certain common locutions. To give one example, items in a coordinated list are typically incompatibles, and gross deviations from this lead to abnormality:

> I like mangoes and bananas.
> ? I like fruit and bananas.

However, and this is another parallel with hyponymy, strict incompatibility is not necessary, so there is no basis for a definition of incompatibility along these lines. It is perfectly normal, for instance, to say

> You meet all kinds of people here – students, bank
> managers, . . .

even though *Arthur is a student* does not entail *Arthur is not a bank manager.*

4.7 Congruence variants

We have seen how the primary relations of congruence are defined. The concepts of congruence can also be applied, secondarily, to other lexical relations. This works as follows. Suppose some lexical unit X stands in a lexical relation R to another lexical unit Y. (R must be some relation other than one of the primary congruence relations.) If every occurrence of X stands in the relation R to Y, and every occurrence of Y stands in the relation R (or its converse, if R is asymmetric) to X, then we shall say that X is a †**congruent** R of Y:

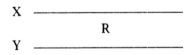

If every occurrence of X stands in the relation R to Y, but there are occurrences of Y which do not stand in the relation R to X, then we shall say that X is a †**hypo-R** of Y, and Y a †**super-R** of X:

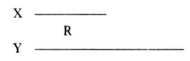

If some, but not all, occurrences of X stand in the relation R to Y, and some, but not all, occurrences of Y stand in the relation R to X, then we shall say that X and Y are †**semi-Rs**:

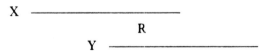

Obviously, if no occurrences of X stand in the relation R to Y, then X is not any kind of R of Y, so disjunction has no counterpart among congruence variants. The following are examples of the three congruence variants: *finger* is a congruent meronym of *hand*; *doctor* is a hypo-converse of *patient*, and *patient* a super-converse of *doctor*, because, for instance, dentists also have patients; *index* is a semi-meronym of *book*, because there are books without indexes, and indexes which are not part of a book.[9]

4.8 Partial relations

In this and the three following sections a number of general concepts will be introduced which are applicable to all, or at least most, paradigmatic lexical relations. They represent modifications of various sorts of the straightforward relations, which generally render them in some way imperfect, limited, or attenuated. We shall begin with **partial relations**.[10] These are relations which hold between lexical items whose syntactic distributions only partially coincide. (The patterns of co-incidence could, of course, be described in terms of the congruence relations introduced earlier; but no labels will be offered here except that, when congruence is perfect, the relation will be described as 'full'.) As an example of a pair of partial synonyms, consider *finish* and *complete* (in the usual sense, not the specific legal sense of "fulfil all legal requirements", as in house-buying, etc.). There are two principal syntactic differences between these two verbs: first, *finish* can occur without an overt direct object, as in *Have you finished?*, whereas *complete* in the relevant sense requires an overt direct object; second, *finish* can take a gerund complement, as in *I've finished eating*, but *complete* cannot (**I've completed reading*). There is no evidence that *I've finished*, *I've finished eating* and *I've finished my meal* involve different senses of *finish*, so we must say that *complete* is a cognitive synonym of *finish* in only a sub-set of the grammatical occurrences of the latter. It is important for the diagnosis of partial relations that the occurrences in unshared syntactic environments should not be distinct senses. (This is not always easy to determine.) Consider the case of *hide* and *conceal*. In the presence of an overt direct object, *hide* and *conceal* are cognitive synonyms – *John hid the money* is equivalent to *John concealed the money* – but *hide* is not replaceable by *conceal* in, for instance, *Go and hide!* In this case there is a clear and recurrent difference of meaning between transitive and intransitive occurrences of *hide*, and it is therefore more satisfactory to speak of *hide*[1], which is a full cognitive synonym of *conceal*, and a separate item *hide*[2].

A subtle, but fortunately uncommon, problem arises with certain lexical items; it is exemplified by *almost* and *practically*. These two are cognitively synonymous over a wide range of contexts:

10a.   I've almost finished.
  b.   I've practically finished.

11a. We're almost there.
   b. We're practically there.

In some contexts, however, the equivalence does not hold in full:

12a. I almost killed him.
   b. I practically killed him.

Sentence 12a has two possible readings, which can be roughly glossed (i) "I did something which caused him almost to die", and (ii) "I almost did something which caused him to die." Sentence 12b, on the other hand, has only one reading, which corresponds to reading (i) of 12a. These contexts cannot be characterised syntactically, although they can be characterised semantically: they require the verb to be of the 'reversible' type (see chapter 10). The different interpretations are due to differences in the scope of *almost* with respect to certain of the semantic traits of *kill*: notice how the paraphrases match the interpretations simply by moving *almost* in the sentence so as to alter its scope. We shall describe differences of this sort as †**quasi-syntactic**. The question is, though, are *almost* and *practically* partial synonyms? I am inclined to think that they should be included in this category.

4.9 **Quasi-relations**

   It not infrequently happens that an exactly appropriate lexical partner that would complete a paradigmatic relationship is missing, but a lexical item exists, with virtually the required meaning, but of the wrong syntactic category. In such cases we say that there is a **quasi-relationship**.[11] For instance, there is no superordinate for the nouns *knife, fork* and *spoon*: that is to say, there is no X such that *It's a knife, It's a fork* and *It's a spoon* all entail *It's an X*. However, we do have the mass noun *cutlery*, which has the right sort of meaning, as knives, forks and spoons are all cutlery. We shall therefore say that *knife, fork* and *spoon* are quasi-hyponyms of *cutlery*, and *cutlery* is a quasi-superordinate. Another example concerns the colour adjectives *red, orange, yellow*, etc. There is no X such that *It's red/yellow/green* entails *It's X. Coloured* will not do, since in most contexts it excludes one or more of the colours in the incompatible set. Thus *a coloured photograph* cannot be simply black, white and grey; *a coloured pencil* excludes black; *a coloured sheet of notepaper* cannot be white, and so on. In this case, *colour* serves as a quasi-superordinate.

4.10 **Pseudo-relations**

†**Pseudo-relations** occur when lexical items which do not, in fact, stand in a particular relation mimic, as it were, one or more of the contextual characteristics of that relation under special circumstances. This phenomenon will be illustrated using pseudo-synonymy, although pseudo-relations are not in principle limited to synonymy. We have already seen that two sentences differing only in respect of cognitive synonyms occupying parallel syntactic positions are in general logically equivalent. However, logical equivalence between two sentences differing only in respect of lexical items occupying a particular syntactic position does not guarantee that the lexical items in question are cognitive synonyms – they may well be pseudo-synonyms. The following examples illustrate a range of possibilities:

13a. Arthur picked a green disc from this box in which all and only the green discs are smooth.
  b. Arthur picked a smooth disc from this box in which all and only the green discs are smooth.
14a. This triangle has three equal angles.
  b. This triangle has three equal sides.
15a. We are working for a greater understanding between the parties.
  b. We are working for a better understanding between the parties.
16a. This horse has just given birth to a foal.
  b. This mare has just given birth to a foal.

The relations represented here vary in their semantic significance. Obviously the equivalence in 13 is the least interesting: the logical relationship between *smooth* and *green* is restricted to the very specific and ad hoc conditions spelt out within the sentence itself. It tells us nothing concerning the meanings of *smooth* and *green* except, perhaps, that they are (merely) compatible. The relationship in 14 is more substantial, and arises out of eternal and ineluctable properties of triangles. Nevertheless, in spite of the logical equivalence between the sentences, they state different things, and *angle* and *side* retain their distinct semantic identity: *This triangle has three equal acute angles*; ? *This triangle has three equal acute sides*. In 16, however (and perhaps in 15, too), it is possible to argue not only that the two sentences can be used to make identical statements, but more specifically that *horse* and *mare* make effectively the same semantic contribution to their respective sentences. This is because the additional semantic traits normally carried by *mare* are already inferable from the rest of the sentence, and are to that degree superfluous. It could thus be claimed that *mare* and *horse* were effectively synonymous in this context. In one sense, this is true, but it is misleading. *Horse* and *mare* in 16a and b do not represent a genuine but contextually restricted form of synonymy: their semantic distinctness remains, and can easily be made manifest. Consider, for example, 17a and b:

17a.   The second largest horse has just given birth to a foal.
   b.   The second largest mare has just given birth to a foal.

The contextual mechanism that allegedly converts *horse* in 16a into a temporary synonym of *mare* is equally operative in 17a; but in spite of this, 17a and b are not logically equivalent, and their lack of equivalence is entirely due to residual semantic differences between *horse* and *mare*. For reasons of this nature, the sentences in 13–16 will be considered to exemplify only pseudo-synonymy.

4.11   Para-relations

Many common locutions are semantically well-formed only if an appropriate semantic relation holds between certain of their lexical constituents. The required semantic relations typically resemble the sort of relations that semanticists usually deal with, but are often less stringently defined. Whereas linguists normally frame definitions of lexical relations in terms of criterial or canonical traits, natural language is very often satisfied with expected traits. A lexical relation defined in terms of expectation rather than necessity will be called a †**para-relation**.

Two typical para-relations are para-hyponymy and para-incompatibility. Strictly speaking, these are both varieties of compatibility. Para-hyponymy is exemplified by *dog* and *pet*. The *but*-test reveals that the relationship between these two is 'expected':

It's a dog, but it's a pet.   (expressive paradox)
It's a dog, but it's not a pet. (normal)

This does not, however, discriminate between para-hyponymy and para-synonymy. The former can be diagnosed by the above *but*-test pattern together with a unique order of occurrence of the related lexical items in *Xs and other Ys*:

dogs and other pets
? pets and other dogs

Para-incompatibility is exemplified by *student* and *bank-manager*; it

involves a negative expectation, so the *but*-test pattern is complementary
to that of para-hyponymy:

> He's a student, but he's also a bank manager. (normal)
> He's a student, but he's not a bank manager. (redundant)

Para-incompatibles are not normal in *Xs and other Ys*:

> ? Students and other bank managers

Unlike para-hyponyms, however, they are normal in coordinated lists:

> The people I hate most are: students, bank managers, . . .
> ? I like dogs, pets, . . .

4.12 Syntagmatic relations of meaning between lexical units

In one sense, every word in a sentence interacts semantically
with every other word, and also with words in neighbouring sentences.
But we must distinguish between a type of interaction which is precisely
regulated by the syntactic structure of the sentence, and a more diffuse
type of interaction, not dependent on syntax, but merely on discourse
propinquity. Consider sentences 18 and 19:

18. ? The Ruritanian ambassador delivered a jolly strong protest
    concerning the recent violation of his country's sovereignty.
19. ? Johnny, darling, wouldn't you like some additional butter
    on your toast?

Both of these sentences exemplify lexical dissonance (i.e. a semantic clash,
involving two or more lexical items in the same sentence (or discourse)).
In both sentences, one lexical item clashes in respect of register[12] with
the prevailing character established by the majority of lexical items in
the sentence. In 18, *jolly*, being informal, clashes with the formality established by such items as *ambassador, deliver, concerning, violation* and
sovereignty; in 19 the technical-sounding *additional* is dissonant with the
prevailing informality established by such items as *Johnny* and *darling*.
Notice that none of the items with which the dissonant word clashes most
sharply have any direct grammatical relation to it. Furthermore, in neither
case is there any clash between the dissonant word and its closest syntactic
companion; thus, *jolly* and *strong* go perfectly happily together:

20. Gosh! This coffee's jolly strong, Samantha!

as do *additional* and *butter*:

21. Additional butter in the diet would probably prove beneficial.

Semantic interactions which involve this sort of meaning[13] are not usually channelled through the syntactic structure, hence there is no syntactic dimension to any lexical dissonance which may arise. The effect of what may be loosely described as 'contextual relevance' is likewise largely independent of grammatical control. For instance, in 22, A's mention of *cheque*, by signalling a financial setting, clearly influences our most likely choice of reading for *bank* in B's utterance:

22. A: I need to cash a cheque.
    B: You'd better make straight for the bank, otherwise you'll be too late.

(It must not be forgotten, of course, that contextual relevance goes beyond the purely linguistic context and embraces the whole context of situation. The most likely interpretation of *bank* could well be different if A and B were on a boat in the middle of a river.)

Now contrast the infelicities of 18 and 19 with those of 23 and 24:

23. ? The Ruritanian ambassador delivered a highly strong protest concerning the recent violation of his country's sovereignty.
24. ? Don't use that rancid fish-paste in your sandwiches.

In each of these, the lexical clash occurs between elements locked in an intimate grammatical relationship; in both sentences the clash can be removed by appropriately replacing either of the elements involved:

25a. The Ruritanian ambassador delivered a highly emotional protest . . .
   b. The Ruritanian ambassador delivered an extremely strong protest . . .
26a. Don't use that mouldy fish-paste in your sandwiches.
   b. Don't use that rancid butter in your sandwiches.

The significance of the lexical clash thus does not extend beyond the confines of the grammatical construction in which the lexical units occur.

Grammatically controlled interactions follow strict rules. Consider the following sentence:

27. Extremely fast cars crash violently.

The grammatical relations between the elements of this sentence can be displayed by means of a labelled tree-diagram:

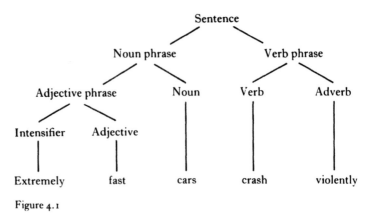

Figure 4.1

This shows, for instance, that the element most closely related to *extremely* is *fast*: these two are co-constituents of the adjective phrase construction. *Extremely* has no direct grammatical relations with any other word in the sentence. However, the whole adjective phrase *extremely fast* is a co-constituent with *cars* of the noun phrase *extremely fast cars*; and the latter joins the verb phrase *crash violently* to form the highest construction, the sentence. The grammatical structure of the sentence is thus a series of nested constructions forming a hierarchy. The structure shown in fig. 4.1 can be established on the basis of general syntactic criteria. For instance, one of the signs that *extremely* and *fast* are united in a grammatical construction is the fact that the sequence *extremely fast* can be replaced by a single element, say, *old*, which has the same relationship to *cars* as does *extremely fast*; furthermore, this substitution causes no grammatical change in the rest of the sentence.[14] (The process of substituting a single element for a sequence within a constant grammatical frame is known as **reduction**.) Similarly, *old cars* can be reduced to *they*, and *crash violently* to *disappeared* (the sentence as a whole is not reducible). It is this pattern of syntactic relationships which governs one type of semantic interaction.

Suppose we start with *extremely*. This engages directly with *fast*, its sister constituent, but only indirectly with *cars*, *crash*, or *violently*. We can produce a semantic clash by substituting *highly* for *extremely*, and restore normality by replacing *fast* with *dangerous*. The normality of *Highly dangerous cars crash violently* in comparison with *? Highly fast cars crash violently* shows that the mis-match in the latter is between *highly* and *fast*, not *highly* and *cars*, or *highly* and *crash*, etc. Moving now to the next stage of interaction, between *extremely fast* and *cars*, we find that *extremely* and *fast* do not have the same status. *Extremely* enters into no further direct interaction – it exerts its semantic influence henceforth only 'through' *fast*; it is *fast* that directly interacts with *cars*. This is shown by the fact that while it is possible to produce a semantic clash within the noun phrase which can only be resolved by replacing the adjective or the noun (? *extremely fast wines*, *extremely fast runners*, *extremely potent wines*), it is impossible to produce a clash which can only be resolved by replacing either the intensifier or the noun. The element in a construction which interacts directly with an element or elements outside the construction may be called the †**semantic head** of the construction.[15] *Fast* is thus the semantic head of *extremely fast*. Arguing along these lines it is not difficult to show that *cars* is the semantic head of *extremely fast cars*; to resolve the clash in ? *Extremely fast cars evaporate* it is no use changing *extremely* or *fast* – we must replace *cars* or *evaporate*: *Extremely fast cars disintegrate* or *Extremely fast solvents evaporate*. For similar reasons, *crash* is the semantic head of *crash violently*. The verb is equally the semantic head in a verb–object construction. For instance, the mis-match in ? *The waves repaired the lorry* is between *waves* and *repaired*: it cannot be resolved by changing *lorry*, but can be resolved by replacing either *waves* or *repaired*:

The waves overturned the lorry.
John repaired the lorry.

There is thus no direct semantic interaction between the subject and direct object of a sentence – or, to put it another way, there is no combination of subject and object which is inherently dissonant. It is not possible, using this technique, to discover which is the semantic head in the highest construction in a simple sentence, that is to say, the subject–predicate construction. This is because grammatical control of semantic interaction does not, in general, extend beyond the sentence. In syntactic theory, the verb is often taken to be the head of the sentence,[16] but for our purposes, as we shall see, there are reasons for casting the subject in this role.

Semantic co-occurrence restrictions are in principle bi-directional: that is, two constituents of a construction will each exert semantic selective pressure on the set of potential (i.e. grammatically appropriate) fillers of the syntactic slot occupied by the other. (For instance, in a *steep bank* there is mutual selection of senses.) However, grammatically controlled co-occurrence restrictions also have directional properties. To describe these, it is necessary first to make a distinction between **head-modifier** constructions and **head-complement** constructions.[17] A head-modifier construction is typically **endocentric**; that is to say, the head alone can play a grammatical role in the sentence identical to that of the whole construction:

We drank RED WINE	We drank WINE
Arthur SLEPT SOUNDLY	Arthur SLEPT
She is VERY TALL	She is TALL

There are no head-modifier constructions whose modifiers are obligatory in the sense that the construction would be ungrammatical without them; nor are there any head-modifier constructions whose modifiers, if omitted, become **latent**.[18] A head-complement construction, on the other hand, is typically not reducible syntactically to the head alone: the complement may be obligatory, like *the cat* in *Arthur stroked the cat*; or, if it is omissible, it may be latent, like the direct object in *John is watching*.

Grammatically controlled semantic co-occurrence restrictions manifest two different sorts of directional property, and these interact differently in head-modifier and head-complement constructions. First of all, it is generally possible to specify a †**selector** and a †**selectee**[19] in a construction in which co-occurrence restrictions are operating. In a head-modifier construction, the modifier is the selector, but in a head-complement construction it is the head which is the selector. Selectors may generally be identified by the fact that they presuppose one or more semantic traits of their selectees.[20] So, for instance, *pregnant* in *a pregnant X* presupposes that its selectee (in this case, the head of the construction) bears the semantic trait "female". Likewise, the verb *drink* in a verb–object construction is the selector since it presupposes that its direct object bears the trait "liquid". Thus, on their most probable readings, *His cousin is pregnant*, *His cousin isn't pregnant* and *Is his cousin pregnant?* will all be taken to contain a reference to a female cousin; and an addressee, on hearing *Drink it!*, *Did you drink it?* or *Arthur drank it* will look for the referent of *it* among liquids. Selectees, in general, do not presuppose traits of their selectors; in *Arthur's (adj.) sister*, or *Arthur (verb) rum*, nothing positive can be stated about the semantic nature of normal fillers of the semantic slots:

> Arthur's pregnant/tall/pretty/diabetic sister
> Arthur drinks/sells/abhors/wastes rum.

The most that can be said is that they must have selectional restrictions which are satisfied by the selectee.

The second directional property involves the relationship between the head of a construction and any dependent item or items. Generally speaking, a dependent item is expected to bring to a construction semantic traits not already prefigured in the head; if the dependent item contributes nothing new, the resulting combination is pleonastic.[21] Under such circumstances we say that the head **encapsulates** the meaning of the dependent item.[22] Consider the noun phrase *? a male uncle*: the trait "male" is encapsulated in *uncle*; *male* contributes nothing new, so the combination is pleonastic. The pleonasm can be cured by making the dependent item more specific so that it makes a net semantic contribution to the phrase: *my patriarchal uncle* (notice that adding specificity to the head has no effect: *? my male maternal uncle*). Similarly, in the pleonastic *? Arthur drinks liquids*, the trait "liquid" is contained in the verb, and the direct object adds nothing new. Again, it is the dependent item which must acquire additional traits if pleonasm is to be avoided: *Arthur drinks beer* (but *? Arthur quaffs liquids*).

The two sorts of directional property described above work in opposite directions in head-modifier constructions, but in parallel in head-complement constructions. Consider, first, constructions of the head-modifier type. In these, the modifier is the selector, and hence presupposes certain traits of the head. But a head is not required to carry traits not presupposed by its dependants, so when the head of a construction exactly duplicates the presupposed traits of a dependent selector (i.e. when the meaning of the head is fully predictable from the dependant), the result is perfectly normal: *a pregnant female* (animal). Furthermore, as we have seen, if the head is non-specific with respect to the presupposed traits of the selecting modifier, these traits are, as it were, transferred to the head: *my pregnant neighbour / cousin / friend*.[23] In head-complement constructions, on the other hand, the situation is different. There it is the head which is the selector, and, besides presupposing certain traits, also behaves as if those traits were encapsulated. The effect is that if the selectee possesses only those traits which are predictable from the selector, then the combination is pleonastic: *? Arthur drinks liquids*. The same is true if the selectee (i.e. the complement) is non-specific with regard to the presupposed traits of the selector: *? Arthur drinks substances*. (If, however, the complement is a definite expression, pleonasm does not arise, and traits presupposed by the head are transferred to it: *Arthur drank the substance / it*.)

The subject–predicate construction is not precisely equivalent either to a head-modifier construction or to a head-complement construction. In syntactic theory it is usual to regard the verb as the head, and the subject as dependent; but the purely semantic evidence suggests that the subject has certain of the characteristics of a head. The meaning of a (simple) sentence is qualitatively different from that of any of its constituents – it is capable of saying something that can stand on its own as a message. The sentence does not appear to have a semantic controller; that is to say, there is no evidence of privileged status for either subject or predicate in respect of semantic relations between sentences. However, the predicate displays at least one of the characteristics of a semantic dependant, and that is that it is expected to bring to the construction semantic traits not encapsulated in the subject; furthermore, in cases of pleonasm, it is the predicate whose specificity must be increased to achieve normality:

> ? The speaker is speaking.[24]
> The speaker is speaking French.
> ? The tall speaker is speaking.

Also, the predicate is the selector; it further resembles a modifier in that when its presuppositions are just matched, the result is not pleonastic:

> A dog barked.

A set of syntagmatic relations can be based on the results of putting grammatically appropriate lexical units together in a construction (all the lexical units standing in a particular syntagmatic relation to another lexical unit are, of course, specific to particular constructions, or sets of constructions). If the combination is normal, we shall say that the lexical units involved are **†philonyms**; if the combination is pleonastic, we shall speak of head and **†tautonym**; if dissonance results, the lexical units will be labelled **†xenonyms**.[25] The relations philonymy, tautonymy and xenonymy are connected in a systematic way with paradigmatic relations, and with presuppositions and encapsulations.

The sorts of correlation which exist can be illustrated by considering presuppositions. Take, first, the presuppositions of the head of a head-complement construction with respect to its complement. The meaning of a complement exactly matches the presuppositions of its head if the following conditions are satisfied:

   (i)   It is a tautonym of the head.[26]
   (ii) All its superordinates are tautonymous.
   (iii) All its compatibles and incompatibles are xenonyms.
   (iv) All its hyponyms are philonyms.

Thus, in the case of *drink*, *liquid* satisfies these conditions: superordinates, such as *substance*, or *fluid* (in the scientific sense which includes gases) are tautonyms; incompatibles, such as *solids*, are xenonyms; and all hyponyms – *beer, water*, etc. – are philonyms.[27] The presuppositions of a modifier cannot be pinpointed in this way, because a head which exactly duplicates them does not yield pleonasm. In such cases what we need to discover is the most specific head all of whose incompatibles are xenonyms – that is, a head such that, for any hyponym, at least one incompatible can be found which is also a philonym of the modifier. Consider *a pregnant —*. Clearly *woman* is a philonym, but its meaning does not precisely match the presuppositions of *pregnant* because it has incompatibles (e.g. *ewe, mare*) which are also philonyms. *Animal* is a philonym all of whose incompatibles are xenonyms (e.g. *plant, affix*). But this does not precisely match the presuppositions of *pregnant*, either, because it has at least one hyponymous expression – *female animal* – all of whose incompatibles are xenonyms. *Female animal*, on the other hand, comes close to satisfying the criteria.[28]

Syntagmatic and paradigmatic relations of sense can be used to define degrees of dissonance. Three such grades will be suggested (although it must be borne in mind that the reality is a continuum): these are †**inappropriateness**, †**paradox** and †**incongruity**. Inappropriateness is diagnosed by the fact that it is cured by substituting a propositional synonym for one of the items involved in the clash. Thus, *The aspidistra kicked the bucket* exemplifies inappropriateness because replacing *kick the bucket* with its cognitive synonym *die* removes the dissonance. Those presuppositions of a selector, which, if not satisfied by the selectee, give rise to inappropriateness, will be termed the **collocational restrictions** of the selector.[29] We shall speak of paradox when (a) there is no possibility of resolving dissonance by synonymous substitution, but (b) there exists a (not too remote) superordinate of either xenonym which is a philonym of the other. So, for instance, a *male aunt* is dissonant, but a superordinate of *aunt*, namely, *relation*, is a philonym of *male*; in *We fell upwards*, *fell* may be replaced by its superordinate *moved*, which is not xenonymous; in *A cat barked*, replacing *cat* with *animal* resolves the dissonance. It is characteristic of incongruity that there is no superordinate of either xenonym which can restore normality (except, perhaps, at the highest level of generality, such as *thing*, or *entity*, for nouns, or *do something* for verbs). This is the case with, for instance, *a lustful affix* (*a lustful thing?*). Those presuppositions of a selector whose non-satisfaction leads to paradox or incongruity will be called its **selectional restrictions**.[30]

On occasions, the results of combining two lexical units in a construction are not what would be predicted on the basis of the principles described above. The most noteworthy cases are those which one would expect to be pleonastic, but are not. Consider the following examples:

> Arthur murmured softly in Bertha's ear.
> Arthur rushed quickly to the door.
> Arthur ambled slowly across the lawn.
> Arthur was shouting loudly.

In each of the above, one would intuitively say that the meaning of the adverb was encapsulated in the meaning of the verb. This judgement is supported by the paradoxical result of replacing the adverb by its antonym:

> ? Arthur murmured loudly in Bertha's ear.
> ? Arthur rushed slowly to the door.
> ? Arthur ambled quickly across the lawn.
> ? Arthur was shouting softly.

It seems that in these cases, instead of pleonasm, there is an intensification of the adverbial notion (cf. *very very good*). Something similar occurs in *a bad headache* and *a terrible catastrophe*; notice, however, that *? a bad catastrophe* is pleonastic, which suggests that the dependent item must not be weaker than the notion encapsulated in the head. It appears that this phenomenon requires the encapsulation by a head of a gradable modifying notion.

In another type of instance, we find apparent duplication of traits with no discernible semantic effects. Consider the case of *gnash the teeth* and *purse the lips*. The predictability of the direct objects of *gnash* and *purse* is revealed by the pleonastic nature of

> ? What Mary pursed were her lips.
> ? What Arthur gnashed were his teeth.

Why, then, are *purse the lips* and *gnash the teeth* not pleonastic? The answer may quite simply be that semantically redundant dependent elements may occur without the penalty of abnormality provided they are syntactically obligatory, as are the direct objects of *gnash* and *purse*. Cases like these should be distinguished from a superficially parallel set of cases such as *shrug the shoulders* and *pout the lips*. In a sense, the meaning of the objects is encapsulated in the verb here, too, and so we would expect the expressions to be pleonastic. But there is a difference: the object in these expressions is omissible. However, the omission of the object has a subtle semantic consequence. *Shrug* and *pout* in *Arthur pouted* and

Celia shrugged refer to a gesture used as a conventional signal; *Arthur pouted his lips* and *Celia shrugged her shoulders*, however, are non-committal about whether a signal was intended, and indicate merely that a certain movement was performed. In other words, the precise sense of *pout*, *shrug* (and probably also *nod*, *stamp*, *wave*) depends on whether or not the direct object is present. That being so, the direct object cannot be said to be totally redundant.

Notes

4.4

1. See Miller and Johnson-Laird (1976: 241–2).
2. *Hyponym* and *superordinate* were first used to denote the terms in this relationship by Lyons (1963: 69–71). See also Lyons (1968: 453–5 and 1977: 291–5). It is also possible to define hyponymy in terms of the normality of sentences of the form *f(X) is necessarily f(Y)*, with the same conditions as before on the nature of f(X) and f(Y): X is a hyponym of Y if *f(X) is necessarily f(Y)* is normal, but *f(Y) is necessarily f(X)* is not (the latter condition is to exclude synonyms). Thus, *A dog is necessarily an animal* is normal, but *An animal is necessarily a dog* is not. Items not related hyponymously do not satisfy this definition:
   A cat is necessarily a dog. (abnormal)
   A dog is necessarily a cat. (abnormal)
3. See Lyons (1977: 293).
4. This point is further elaborated in 6.2.
5. See Hoenigswald (1965: 191–6).

4.5

6. This is not strictly a lexical item, but it will serve to illustrate the point (the semantic relationship is not restricted to single lexical units).

4.6

7. This term, too, originated with Lyons (1963: 59–61).
8. Defined in this way, incompatibility includes all varieties of oppositeness. However, in this book opposites will be treated independently (chapters 9–11) and, unless otherwise indicated, *incompatibility* will normally be used to refer to contrasts which are not inherently binary (see 11.6 for inherent and contingent binarity).

4.7

9. For meronyms, see chapter 7; for converses, see 10.6.

4.8

10. Not related to Lyons's *partial synonymy* (1981: 50–5).

4.9

11. See Lyons (1977: 299).

4.12 Syntagmatic lexical relations have been discussed by Continental (especially German) structural semanticists under the heading of 'lexical solidarities' (see especially Coseriu (1967, 1968, 1976)). Anglophone linguists typically speak of 'selection(al) restrictions' (see, for instance, Leech (1974: 141–6) and Lehrer (1974: 54)). Selectional restrictions, first introduced by Chomsky (1965) for purely syntactic purposes, have given rise to much theoretical discussion: for a comprehensive overview see Kastovsky (1980b).

12. For the semantic significance of register see 12.2.

13. It is specifically 'expressive' and 'evoked' meaning whose syntagmatic influence is not controlled by grammar. These notions are discussed in 12.2.

14. See also Allerton (1979: ch. 6). For syntactic control of semantic interaction see also Katz and Fodor (1963).

15. Cf. the discussion of dependency relations in Matthews (1981: 78–84). (Matthews speaks of the 'controller' of a construction.)

16. For syntactic arguments concerning the dependent nature of the subject see Matthews (1981: 100–5).

17. See Matthews on 'Complementation and modification' (1981: 147–59).

18. For latent elements, see Matthews (1981: 125). These are identical to what Allerton calls 'contextually deleted' elements (1975). Latent elements are those which are not overtly present in an utterance, but which necessarily enter into its interpretation. Consider, first, *John is reading*. It is obvious that John is reading SOMETHING, but it is not necessary for the hearer to be able to construe the missing information from contextual clues – it can be left unspecified. Indeed, the speaker might not even know what it is that John is reading. The direct object of *read* in *John is reading* is described by Allerton as having undergone 'indefinite deletion'. Now consider *John is watching*.

  Again, John must be watching SOMETHING, but in this case the hearer is expected to identify the specific target of John's observational activity. For Matthews, the direct object of *watch* is latent; for Allerton, it has undergone contextual deletion. Contextually and indefinitely deleted elements can easily be distinguished using a version of the identity test: in *John is reading, and so is Bill*, there is no implication that they are reading the same thing – this is characteristic of indefinite deletion; *John is watching, and so is Bill*, however, is normal only if John and Bill are watching the same thing – this is characteristic of contextual deletion. (By our criteria, *watch* in *John is watching* – in common with all definite expressions – behaves as if it were infinitely ambiguous. We shall not pursue the implications of this here, except to point out that ambiguity of this sort is not to be taken as evidence of the existence of an infinite number of distinct senses.)

19. These are called 'determining' and 'determined' elements in Kastovsky (1980b).

20. There is now an extensive technical literature on presupposition. The interested reader might consult, in the first place, Kempson (1973) and Levinson (1983: ch. 4). For examples of the use of presuppositions to account for lexical co-occurrence restrictions, see Bierwisch (1970b), Lakoff (1971), Fillmore (1972). The expression *presupposed meaning* is used here in a pre-theoretical sense (cf. Lyons (1977: 599)) to refer to semantic traits (i.e. presuppositions) which are, as it were, taken for granted in the use of an expression or word, but not actually asserted, denied, questioned, or whatever, in the utterance in which they appear. Particular presuppositions can be regularly and characteristically associated with specific lexical items – hence their interest to us. For instance, the verb *die* presupposes that the referent of its grammatical subject is (or was) living. Thus *It died*, *Did it die?* and *It didn't die* all presuppose that *it* refers to an organism of some sort; that is to say, someone eavesdropping

on a conversation in which any of these sentences occurred would be able to conclude with some confidence that *it* (barring metaphorical usage) referred to an organism. It is this constancy of inferability, irrespective of whether the sentence containing *die* functions as a statement or question, etc., that qualifies the trait "animate" to count as a presupposition of *die*.

21. Cf. Kastovsky (1980b: 89).

22. For this use of *encapsulate* see Lyons (1977: 262). Gruber (1976) speaks of 'lexical incorporation'.

23. Cf. Weinreich's 'transfer features' (1966: 459).

24. *Speaker* must be interpreted here as "person who is speaking".

25. I imagine these coinages will be transparent enough: *philonym* is based on the Greek *philos* ("friend, lover"); *xenonym* is from *xenos* ("stranger, foreigner"); *tautonym* is intended to evoke *tautology*. Strictly speaking, these relationships do not hold between lexical items as such, but between lexical roots (in a particular sense) standing in a particular structural–semantic relationship. So, we not only have *The dogs barked*, but also *the barking dogs* and *the barking of the dogs*, etc. In these, the underlying structural–semantic relationship between *dog* and *bark* is the same. (This sort of relationship is sometimes referred to as a 'deep case' relationship (see Fillmore 1968, 1971, 1977) or a 'semantic role' relationship (cf. Allerton 1982: 41–2).) Halliday (1966) refers to a set of related words manifesting a constant set of selectional restrictions (such as *strong, strength, strongly, strengthen* and *argue, argument*, in *a strong argument, the strength of the argument, He argued strongly* and *His argument was strengthened*) as a 'formal scatter'.

26. There may, of course, be no single lexical unit functioning in this way; but there is always at least a tautonymous expression.

27. Some of these, e.g. *petrol*, will give rise to the variety of abnormality to which we gave the name *improbability*, but none will give rise to dissonance.

28. It is perhaps arguable that "maturity" should be brought into the specification.

29. Inappropriateness (and hence collocational restrictions) can be generalised to any case in which dissonance can be cured by replacing an element by a cognitive synonym. This topic is discussed further in 12.2.

30. The distinction made here between selectional restrictions and collocational restrictions is referred to in Bierwisch (1970b: 10f) as one between general and idiosyncratic restrictions. Kastovsky (1980b: 77) speaks of inherent and contextual semantic features.

5
Lexical configurations

5.1 Introductory

This chapter deals with the two most formally complex types of lexical configuration, namely, hierarchies and proportional series. In the case of hierarchies only general formal characteristics are discussed: specific types of hierarchy are treated in some detail in chapter 6 (taxonomic hierarchies), chapter 7 (part–whole hierarchies) and chapter 8 (non-branching hierarchies). Proportional series are dealt with in more specific detail as they do not appear anywhere else in the book. Other possible configurations, which will not, however, be discussed here at any length, are doublets (exemplified by pairs of opposites – see chapters 9, 10 and 11), and clusters, which are groupings of lexical items characterised by a lack of structure (some groups of synonyms appear to be of this nature – see chapter 12).

5.2 Hierarchies

A hierarchy, which need not consist of lexical items, is a set of elements related to one another in a characteristic way. Two structural types of hierarchy may be distinguished: those which branch, and those which, because of the nature of their constitutive relations, are not capable of branching. The two possibilities are illustrated diagrammatically in figs. 5.1(a) and 1(b):

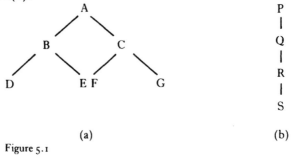

(a)   (b)

Figure 5.1

We must distinguish between hierarchies of the branching type which in particular manifestations happen not to have branches, and hierarchies which cannot branch. Only the latter may be termed non-branching. Suppose a botanist working on the taxonomy of the (hypothetical) Peruvian bladder-grass family (Vesicaliaceae) discovered that it contained only one genus, *Vesicalia*, and that the genus had but one species, *V. peruviensis*. The taxonomy of this family would then not have any branches. But it would not count as a non-branching hierarchy; branching can be regarded as a canonical feature of a taxonomic hierarchy.

Hierarchies are further sub-classified by the relations which structure them; there is thus more than one kind of branching hierarchy, and more than one kind of non-branching hierarchy. (Within each type, hierarchies may be distinguished by the elements they contain.) The most fundamental structural relation of any hierarchy – without it there would be no hierarchy at all – is what we shall call the **relation of dominance**.[1] This is the 'vertical' relation – the one which connects A to B and C, B to D and E, and C to F and G in 1(a), and P to Q, Q to R and R to S in 1(b). In a well-formed hierarchy, the relation of dominance is constant throughout the structure. A branching hierarchy requires, in addition, a †**relation of difference**; this is the 'horizontal' relation, which holds, for instance, between B and C, D and E, and F and G in 1(a). The relation of difference, too, must be constant throughout a well-formed hierarchy.[2]

The minimum requirement for a hierarchy is a set of interrelated elements structured by a suitable relation acting as a relation of dominance. Two properties are essential for the relation of dominance of a hierarchy. First, it must be **asymmetric**; that is to say, it must have a directional character. Suppose it is known that a certain element A stands in a relation R to a second element B. If R is an asymmetric relation, then it necessarily follows that B does not stand in the relation R to A (the relation of B to A in that case is the converse of R). For instance, if A is longer than B, then it follows that B cannot be longer than A; hence, "– is longer than –" is an asymmetric relation. A **symmetric** relation, on the other hand, holds simultaneously in both directions; "– is similar to –" is a symmetric relation, so if A is similar to B, then it necessarily follows that B is similar to A. The second indispensable property for the relation of dominance of a hierarchy is the capacity, in principle at least, to form indefinitely long chains of elements. We shall describe a relation which has this property as †**catenary**. An example of a non-catenary relation is "– husband of –" (it is also asymmetric): if A is the husband of B, then B cannot, in turn, be the husband of a third person C. Compare this with the catenary relation "– father of –", which generates chains of indefinite length: A is the father of B, who is the father of C, who is the father of D, etc. The relation of dominance of a hierarchy can equally well be **transitive** or **intransitive**.[3] A relation is said to be transitive if the fact that it holds between two elements A and B, and also between B and some third element C, guarantees that it holds between A and C. The relation "– is longer than –" is thus transitive, because if A is longer than B, and B is longer than C, we can be sure that A is longer than C. In the case of an intransitive relation, on the other hand, the fact that it held between A and B, and between B and C, would entail that it did not hold between A and C. For instance, if A were the father of B, and B the father of C, then A could not be the father of C; the relation "– father of –" is thus intransitive.[4]

A set of elements interrelated by an asymmetric, catenary relation R is a hierarchy if, and only if, it possesses the following properties:[5]

> (i) There is one and only one element which stands in the relation R to all the other members of the set (if R is transitive), or which stands either in the relation R or some higher power of R to all the other members of the set (if R is intransitive).

(The 'higher powers' of an intransitive relation arise when there are chains of elements each related to the next by the relation in question; thus, if A is the father of B, B of C, and C of D, then A stands in the 'third power' of the relation "– father of –" to D.) It can easily be seen that A in 1(a) and P in 1(b) fulfil this requirement (assuming, of course, that the lines in the diagrams symbolise the relation of dominance). We can avoid reference to transitivity by saying that there must be one and only one element which stands in some power of R to all the other members of the set. In this case, 'some power of R' must be taken to include the first power of R, i.e. R itself. The unique initial element in a hierarchy will be called the 'origin'.

> (ii) If A and B are two elements of the set which both stand in some power of R to a third element of the set C, then either A stands in some power of R to B, or B stands in some power of R to A.

In other words, any three such elements in a hierarchy must be capable of being arranged to form a continuous chain:

$$A\text{–}R^m\text{–}B\text{–}R^n\text{–}C \quad \text{or} \quad B\text{–}R^m\text{–}A\text{–}R^n\text{–}C$$

This condition is automatically satisfied by any non-branching hierarchy; its particular significance, however, is in respect of branching hierarchies, as it ensures that the branches do not converge. Consider the structure illustrated in fig. 5.2:

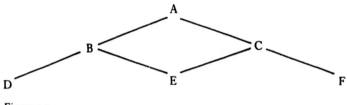

Figure 5.2

It can be seen that B and C both stand in the relation of dominance to E, but neither stands in that relation to the other; hence, the structure is not a hierarchy, according to our definition.[6]

A branching hierarchy requires a relation of dominance with a very particular property, namely, that of being, as we shall say, †**differentiable**. To be differentiable, a relation must be capable of being directed along mutually exclusive pathways in an indefinite number of successive stages. By no means all possible relations of dominance are differentiable. Consider the relation "– larger than –". This can serve as the relation of dominance of a non-branching hierarchy: *mountain :hillock :mound*. It cannot, however, act as the relation of dominance of a branching hierarchy, as it is not of the sort which can be successively differentiated. Suppose we have a set of elements A, B and C, such that A is larger than B and C, the latter pair being of equal sizes. We can picture their relationships in a way that looks like the beginning of a branching hierarchy:

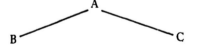

But suppose we now attempt to extend the hierarchy and add a fourth element D under B. It immediately becomes clear that the apparent branching hierarchical structure is illusory, since not only B, but also C, stand in the relation "– larger than –" to D:

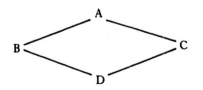

115

The relation "– larger than –" can thus generate only a non-branching hierarchy; in such a hierarchy we would have to say that B and C above jointly occupied the same position. Consider now the relation "– initiated (into the Eleusinian mysteries) –". Imagine an individual A, who initiated two other persons B and C:

In this case it is possible to add a fourth element D to the hierarchy, such that B, but not C, initiated D:

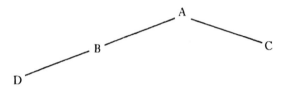

The relation "– initiated –" is thus differentiable, and can, provided it is appropriately directed, form the relation of dominance of a branching hierarchy.

An example of a differentiable relation with lexical significance is the relation of dominance of a taxonomic (i.e. classificatory) hierarchy. The lexical items in a taxonomy may be thought of as corresponding to classes of things in the extra-linguistic world. Suppose we start off with the class of animals. This can be divided into a number of sub-classes which have no members in common, such as dogs, horses, elephants, and so on. Each of these sub-classes can then be further subdivided into sub-sub-classes which likewise have no members in common; for example, the class of dogs into spaniels, alsatians, poodles, and so on. This process can be repeated, at least in principle, indefinitely, without convergence (i.e. without producing classes that have members in common). Another differentiable relation with lexical relevance is the relation between an entity and its parts. For example, the human body divides into the trunk, the head, the arms and the legs; these parts are disjunct in the sense that they do not overlap. Each part is in principle divisible into smaller disjunct parts, and successive repetition of this process produces a branching hierarchy. It is perhaps no accident that these two branching hierarchies, which are the only types of any general lexical significance, have relations of dominance which are not merely differentiable, but which in some sense are inherently differentiated. There cannot be a taxonomy without differentia-

tion into more than one sub-species: the creation of one sub-division presupposes the existence of at least one other. The same is true of parts:
it is not possible to divide an entity into only one part (although it is
possible to divide an entity into parts which are not lexically discriminated
– see chapter 7). Occasional non-branching nodes may be tolerated in
a branching hierarchy provided it is one with clearly established levels.
For instance, in the hypothetical case of the Peruvian bladder-grass, there
is in reality only one class of plants. That class qualifies as a species because
all the members will breed with other members of the class, but not with
plants from outside the class; but there would be no justification for saying
that the class also represented a genus and a family, if the larger taxonomy
of which it forms part did not exhibit branching at these levels.

Each element of a hierarchy occurs at a particular level. The notion
of level in a hierarchy can be construed in two different ways. There
is first of all what may be termed the technical conception of a hierarchical
level.[7] To determine to which technical level an element belongs, one needs
only to count the number of nodes downwards from the origin (each element constitutes a node): the unique first element constitutes level 1,
all elements one node removed from the origin constitute level 2, all elements two nodes removed constitute level 3, and so on (in a non-branching
hierarchy, there is only one element at each level):

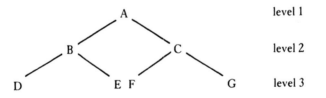

level 1

level 2

level 3

This method of determining levels precludes structures like that shown
in fig. 5.3(a):

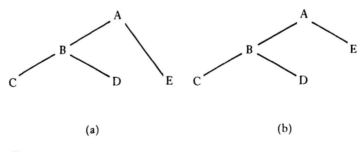

(a)   (b)

Figure 5.3

117

The element E, since there are no nodes intervening between it and A, should technically form part of level 2, as in 5.3(b). In this sense of level, all hierarchies have determinate levels.

It may well happen, however, that the users of a hierarchy (in the case of a lexical hierarchy the speakers of the language) have positive intuitions concerning which items belong together at a given level; and these intuitions may conflict with the level assignments according to technical criteria. In other words, structures like that shown in 5.3(a) may on occasions be felt by speakers to be 'correct'. For instance, many speakers of English feel that the sub-classification of garden birds into sparrows, robins, thrushes, blackbirds, etc. is comparable not with the division of animals into dogs, cats, sheep, and so on, but with the sub-classification of dogs into spaniels, poodles, alsatians, and the like. This makes no biological sense, of course, but it has a certain psychological validity, in that the significance to most members of our society of the difference between, say, a thrush and a blackbird is roughly comparable to that between a collie and a spaniel. If the classification of living creatures is structured in this way, there will inevitably be a conflict with technically determined levels. Where there are definite intuitions about which elements belong at a given level, we may speak of †**substantive** levels. In an ideal hierarchy, technical and substantive levels would be congruent; however, in cases of conflict between the two (which is, of course, possible only in the case of a branching hierarchy), primacy should be given to substantive levels.

In this section we have been considering the properties of hierarchies in general. All the characteristics outlined apply in principle to the hierarchies which fall within the scope of lexical semantics, that is to say, those which are composed of lexical items, and those structuring relations are relations of sense holding between those lexical items. The various types of lexical hierarchy also, however, have many specific properties, and these form the subject matter of chapters 6, 7 and 8.

5.3 Proportional series

The simplest proportional series consists of a single 'cell' which has four elements:

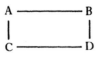

The relations between the elements must be such that from any three of the elements the fourth can be uniquely determined. The configuration is thus structured by the following relations of proportionality:

A is to B as C is to D
B is to A as D is to C
A is to C as B is to D
C is to A as D is to B

The quintessential proportionalities are, of course, numerical:

$$
\begin{array}{ccc}
2 & \!\!\!\!\!\!\!\!-\!\!\!\!-\!\!\!\!- & 3 \\
| & & | \\
4 & \!\!\!\!\!\!\!\!-\!\!\!\!-\!\!\!\!- & 6
\end{array}
$$

but lexical analogues of these are common. One example is

mare	stallion
ewe	ram

Placing the lexical items in a proportional series in this way is justified by the following recurrences of semantic contrast:

$$\frac{\text{mare (It's a —)}}{\text{ewe}} = \frac{\text{stallion (It's a —)}}{\text{ram}}$$

$$\frac{\text{mare} \ \ (\text{It's a —})}{\text{stallion}} = \frac{\text{ewe (It's a —)}}{\text{ram}}$$

These two equations are equivalent to the following four proportionality statements:

Mare is to *stallion* as *ewe* is to *ram*.
Stallion is to *mare* as *ram* is to *ewe*.
Mare is to *ewe* as *stallion* is to *ram*.
Ewe is to *mare* as *ram* is to *stallion*.

Notice that the following configuration does not constitute a proportional series according to the above definition:

$$
\begin{array}{ccc}
\text{apple} & \!\!\!\!-\!\!\!\!-\!\!\!\!- & \text{fruit} \\
| & & | \\
\text{dog} & \!\!\!\!-\!\!\!\!-\!\!\!\!- & \text{animal}
\end{array}
$$

Firstly, none of the contrasts are recurrent:

$$\frac{\text{apple (It's a(n) —)}}{\text{dog}} \neq \frac{\text{fruit} \ \ (\text{It's a(n) —})}{\text{animal}}$$

$$\frac{\text{apple (It's a(n) —)}}{\text{fruit}} \neq \frac{\text{dog} \ \ (\text{It's a(n) —})}{\text{animal}}$$

Second, it is not the case that from any three elements the fourth can be uniquely predicted. The identity of X can be uniquely determined in 1a and b, but not in c or d:

> 1a *Apple* is to *fruit* as *dog* is to *X*.
> b *Apple* is to *dog* as *fruit* is to *X*.
> c *Fruit* is to *apple* as *animal* is to *X*.
> d *Fruit* is to *animal* as *apple* is to *X*.

In the sense that *apple* has the same relationship to *fruit* as *dog* has to *animal* (i.e. '— is an immediate taxonym of —' – see chapter 6 for the meaning of *taxonym*), that relation is of the sort known as 'many-to-one'. A relation is many-to-one if several elements can stand in that relation to some other element, but for each of these there is only one element to which they can stand in that relation. Such relations occur in hierarchies, but for a proportional series all the structuring relations must be 'one-to-one', that is to say, each relation must be such that for any element there is just one other element to which it can stand in that relation, and only the first element can stand in that relation to the second. There is a more specific one-to-one relation between *apple* and *fruit*, but it is not recurrent; that is to say, there is no animal that has a unique position among other animals analogous to the position of apples among different sorts of fruit. To constitute even a minimum cell of a proportional series, two recurrent one-to-one relations are necessary.

Any basic cell is in principle extendible along one or both of its axes. A proportional series which can be extended along both axes simultaneously will be called †**open**. The cell illustrated in fig. 5.4(a), for instance, can be extended as in 5.4(b):

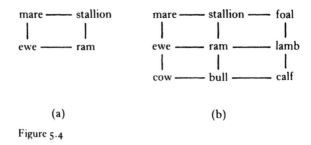

(a)   (b)

Figure 5.4

Some proportional series, however, can only be extended along one axis at a time; if an attempt is made to extend them along both axes simultaneously, unfillable structure points are created. Proportional series of this sort will be termed †**closed**. Consider the following example:

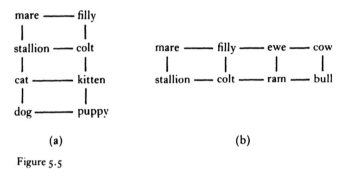

mare ——— filly

stallion ——— colt

This can be extended either as in fig. 5.5(a) or as in 5.5(b):

(a)

(b)

Figure 5.5

but not both together:

mare ——— filly ——— ewe

stallion ——— colt ——— ram

cat ——— kitten ——— ?

We shall assume in the discussion which follows that an ideal, well-formed proportional series is open.

A given lexical form may appear at more than one structure point in a proportional series, but only if it is ambiguous:

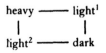

horse ——— mare ——— stallion

dog[1] ——— bitch ——— dog[2]

As a diagnostic test for ambiguity, the ability to occupy more than one point in a proportional series is more reliable than, for instance, the mere possession of two different opposites. Both *light* (*dark* and *heavy*) and *patient* (*doctor* and *dentist*) can be said to have more than one opposite, but only with the former can we construct a cell:

heavy ——— light[1]

light[2] ——— dark

121

In the case of *patient*, *doctor* and *dentist*, the necessary relations of proportionality cannot be found: *DOCTOR is to PATIENT as DENTIST is to PATIENT* is perhaps a satisfactory proportion, but *DOCTOR is to DENTIST as PATIENT is to PATIENT* most certainly is not. The evidence for ambiguity is stronger if the separate occurrence of a lexical form in a proportional series is established in different proportional sets, as in the case of

$$mare : bitch :: horse : dog^1,$$
$$mare : stallion :: bitch : dog^2.$$

The intuitive judgement of the validity of the proportionality is much harder to make when two senses associated with a single word form are directly contrasted, as in *horse : stallion :: dog^1 : dog^2*.

A particular axis of a proportional series may be †**consistent** or †**inconsistent**. Consider the two examples illustrated in fig. 5.6.

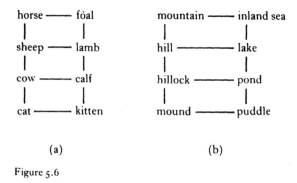

(a)   (b)

Figure 5.6

Series (b) is consistent in a way in which (a) is not. This is because the relation between *mountain* and *hill* is the same as that between *hill* and *hillock*, and *hillock* and *mound*, with the result that the following proportionality holds: *mountain* is to *hill* as *lake* is to *pond*. In fig. 5.6(a), however, the *horse* : *sheep* relation is not identical to the *sheep* : *cow* relation; therefore, given the following three elements of a proportion: *horse* : *sheep* :: *lamb* :? the fourth element is not uniquely determined. Consistency of this type in proportional series is somewhat uncommon.

All extended proportional series can be broken down into a number of linear series of cells, as in figs. 5.6 and 5.7, and this is the form in which we shall study them. The vast majority of series involve two kinds of contrast: one type is found in only a limited number of lexical pairs; the other type recurs much more freely. For instance, only a handful of lexical pairs manifest the *horse* : *sheep* contrast:

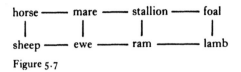

Figure 5.7

The *mare* : *stallion* contrast, on the other hand, recurs in dozens of pairs. The relatively restricted contrasts are invariably carried by open set elements; the freely recurring contrasts may be carried by open set items (as in *mare* : *stallion*), but the members of a pair of lexical items manifesting such a contrast frequently share the same open set element (i.e. the root), the contrast being signalled by one or more closed set elements) i.e. affixes):

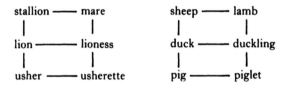

We shall adopt the convention of representing the relatively recurrent contrasts between horizontally adjacent lexical items in a series (e.g. *sheep* :*lamb* above), and the relatively restricted contrasts between vertically adjacent items (e.g. *sheep* : *duck* above).[8]

There are two lexical relations specifically associated with proportional series. But before these can be discussed, another lexical relation must be introduced, which, although it figures prominently in lexical proportional series, is not in principle restricted thereto. This relation will be called †**endonymy**. It is based on the notion of semantic encapsulation, and involves the incorporation of the meaning of one lexical item in the meaning of another. The term whose meaning is included in this way will be called the †**endonym**, and the containing term will be called the †**exonym**. Some examples of endonymous pairs are as follows (the endonym is given first): *animal* : *horse, horse* : *mare, horse* : *stable, hand* : *finger, hand* : *glove, foot* : *kick*. Notice that the relationship between superordinate and hyponym, and in certain instances between holonym and meronym, are special cases of endonymy. The essential defining characteristic of this relation is its capacity to give rise to pleonasm. The *but*-test provides a convenient way of illustrating this; all the sentences in 2 are pleonastic;

2a. It's a horse, but it's an animal.
  b. It's a finger, but it's part of a hand.
  c. It's a glove, but it's for covering the hand.
  d. It's a stable, but it's for horses.
  e. He kicked me, but with his foot.

There may sometimes be problems in deciding which member of a pair is the endonym and which the exonym, although in most cases we can trust our intuitions. If the terms are hyponymously related, then the superordinate is the automatic choice for endonym; being less specific in sense, it is therefore less complex semantically. The same is probably true of the holonym in a pair related meronymously. Take the case of *hand* and *finger*. Although the relationship is canonical in both directions – a canonical finger is a part of a hand, and a canonical hand has fingers – *hand* is in one sense the less specific and hence less complex term, the term which carries less semantic information. Very often the question can be decided by the relative adequacy of definitions. For instance, "a building for lodging horses" is an adequate definition of *stable* (or at least is on the right lines); but while "a stable-dwelling animal" might serve to identify *horse*, it is not an adequate definition. (There is, in fact, no adequate definition of 'natural kind' terms like *horse* – see chapter 6 – so if one term of an endonymous pair is a natural kind term, and the other is a nominal kind term, then the natural kind term is automatically the endonym.) A similar argument applies to *glove* and *hand*: "an item of clothing designed to cover the hand" is a satisfactory definition of *glove*, but "the glove-wearing part of the body" is decidedly odd as a definition of *hand*.

The most interesting cases of endonymy are those where the relation between endonym and exonym is recurrent, giving rise to a proportional series:

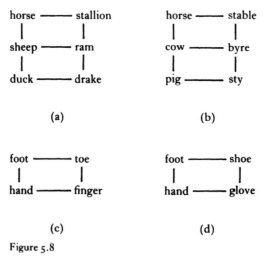

Figure 5.8

The structures shown in fig. 5.8 illustrate one of the fundamental lexical relations associated with a proportional series. This is the relation between *stallion*, *ram* and *drake*, between *stable*, *byre* and *sty*, between *toe* and *finger* and between *shoe* and *glove*. Lexical items related in this way will be termed †**analogues**. Analogues may be defined as exonyms related in parallel ways to different endonyms (the parallelism in this case must pass the appropriate tests of proportionality).

The second lexical relation associated with a proportional series is intuitively of some significance, but it is harder to pin down satisfactorily. Consider first the relation between co-exonyms. This is easy to define, but is not, intuitively, of great significance: *sow*, *bacon*, *ham* and *sty* are co-exonyms of *pig*. Somehow, they are too diverse. Even when we add the requirement of recurrence in a proportional series, we are still left with a somewhat heterogeneous set:

```
sow ———— boar ———— sty ——— pork
 |          |          |         |
cow ———— bull ———— byre — beef
```

However, co-exonyms become more interesting if they are more highly constrained – if, for instance, they are required to fall under a single superordinate concept involving the endonym (the vagueness of this formulation is acknowledged). Consider the following two proportional series (the endonyms are given in brackets):

```
(foot) ———— toe ———— sole      (university) — lecturer — student
  |           |          |           |             |          |
(hand) ———— finger— palm       (prison) ———— warder — convict
```

According to our definitions, *toe* : *finger*, *sole* : *palm*, *lecturer* : *warder* and *student* : *convict* are all pairs of analogous exonyms. However, the relation between, for instance, *finger* and *palm*, and between *lecturer* and *student* is also significant. These are not simply co-exonyms: the former pair also fall under the superordinate concept "part of hand", and the second pair share the superordinate concept "persons canonically relevant to the functioning of a university". In other words, they are related, in a sense, in parallel ways to their common endonym. Items related in this way will be called †**lexical siblings**: co-partonyms like *finger* and *palm* and co-hyponyms like *sow* and *boar* are sub-types of siblings. There is very often no superordinate lexical item for a set of siblings, so the groupings they represent tend to be passed over when taxonomic structures are studied.

A proportional series, then, may consist of parallel strings of endonyms

125

and analogous exonyms, as in fig. 5.9(a), or parallel strings of analogues, as in fig. 5.9(b):

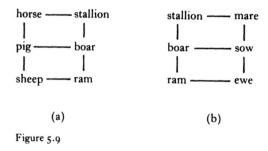

(a)   (b)

Figure 5.9

Notice that in fig 5.9(b) the columns consist of analogues, and the rows consist of siblings; that is to say, the sibling relationship is associated with the recurrent contrast, and the analogue relationship with the restricted contrast. This is a frequent, but not a necessary, correlation: in the following series, the analogue relationship is associated with the restricted contrast:

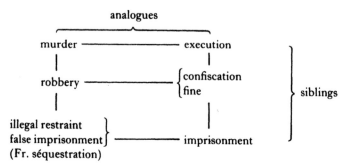

It may be wondered why *murder* and *execution* are classified as analogues rather than siblings – if the latter diagnosis were adopted, a regular correlation between siblinghood and recurrent contrast would be maintained. After all, they are both exonyms of *kill*. However, *murder* and *execution* are also exonyms of two distinct endonyms, namely, *crime* and *punishment*, and since their relation with these (i.e. taxonymy – see chapter 6) is stronger than their common relation with *kill* (i.e. mere hyponymy), it takes precedence.

The range of imperfect relations outlined in chapter 4 applies to proportional series and their associated lexical relations. For instance, the following series illustrates congruence mis-match:

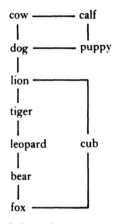

In terms of the primary congruence relations, nothing more can be said about the relationship between, say, *lion* and *cub* other than that they are compatibles (not all cubs are lions, and not all lions are cubs). This is not very informative. It is more illuminating to say that *cub* is a super-exonym of *lion*, *fox*, etc., a super-analogue of *calf* and *puppy*, and a super-sibling of *lioness*, *vixen*, etc. It would not be correct to repeat the item *cub* at each relevant structure point of the above series, because it is not ambiguous, at least not in the way that requires us to recognise more than one lexical item *cub*. The univocality (i.e. non-ambiguity) of *cub* is shown by the normality of:

> The vixen and the lioness are playing with their respective cubs.

> The lioness is playing with her cubs; the vixen, on the other hand, is washing hers.

However, *cub* is one of those items, like *watch*, which displays the property of latency. It was pointed out earlier (chapter 4, note 18) that *watch* behaves, when no explicit direct object is present, as though it meant "watch X", where X must be recovered from the context by the hearer. *Cub* is similar: it behaves, when no animal species is explicitly mentioned, as though it meant "X-cub", with X being contextually recoverable. This is why it is somewhat odd to say, without preamble:

> ? I saw three cubs this morning.

(It is even odder to say this when what one has seen are a fox cub, a lion cub and a bear cub.)

Of some significance are proportional series based on a 'to some extent' proportionality. (A distinction may be drawn between †**strict** and †**lax** proportional series.) Some of the series already illustrated may more

127

properly be said to belong to this category. Generally speaking, for a lax proportional series, we shall insist on the requirement that in every cell any item must be uniquely predictable from the remaining three items, even though the exact recurrence of the semantic contrasts is suspect, as in

university : student : : prison : convict : : hospital : patient

The parallelism here, although not perfect, nonetheless gives important information concerning the semantic relations between the lexical items. More subtle non-equivalence can be found. Informants unhesitatingly assent to the validity of the proportion *man : woman : : boy : girl*. It must be recognised, however, that the equivalence of contrast is not perfect: it is perfectly normal to refer to first year female undergraduates as 'girls'; it is not normal to refer to first year male undergraduates as 'boys'.[9]

The sex-contrast in proportional series gives rise to a rather tricky problem. Consider the following set:

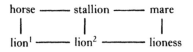

The problem concerns the identity of the stem in *lioness* (and similar forms): is it *lion¹+ess*, or *lion²+ess* (or even *lion³+ess*)? The answer we give to this question will affect our description of the semantics of the affix. If the affix simply means "female", and its meaning is compounded with that of the stem in the way that "red" and "hat" are combined to give the meaning of *red hat*, then the stem of *lioness* must be *lion¹*, otherwise the combination would be odd. However, this is not the only possible meaning for the affix: it could mean something like "female counterpart of", in which case *lion²* would be a more appropriate stem. Words referring to humans at first seem to provide an answer to the puzzle. Consider, for example, *prince : princess, duke : duchess*, and *waiter : waitress*. In these cases there is no general term for the 'species', corresponding to *horse* and *sheep*, only morphologically simple terms denoting males, and affixed terms denoting females. The most parsimonious analysis would therefore seem to be that *-ess* means "female counterpart of", and that *lioness* is *lion²+ess*. However, we have not tapped all available sources of evidence. Suppose we were given the task of devising affixed words to replace simple terms referring to female animals, such as *ewe* and *mare*. Which would be the most acceptable (or least unacceptable) replacements, *ram-ess* and *stallion-ess*, or *sheep-ess* and *hors-ess*? My intuitions are strongly in favour of the latter. If this evidence is accepted, then it follows that *-ess* means "female", and prefers to attach itself to a 'species' term. In that case, the correct analysis of *lioness* would appear to be *lion[1]+ess*. But we would then have to recognise two senses of *prince*: *prince[1]*, which refers to the 'species', and appears only in the context of a following *-ess*, and *prince[2]*, which refers to the male of the species. However, there is still more evidence, and a third possible analysis. The names of some female animals are formed by pre-fixing *she-* to the name of the species: *she-bear*, *she-wolf*. The preference of *she-* for the name of the species is shown by the greater acceptability of *she-pig* and *she-horse*, compared with *she-boar* and *she-stallion*, which are slightly paradoxical. This preference also applies in the case of terms referring to humans: *she-child*[10] would be a better replacement for *girl* than *she-boy*, and *she-monarch* a better replacement for *queen* than *she-king*. What happens, then, if we try to produce a pre-fixed term to replace *princess* and *duchess*? My intuitions are that *she-prince* and *she-duke* are mildly paradoxical, like *she-boy* and *she-boar*. Now if *princess* were really composed of *prince[1]+ess*, as our last analysis suggested, it would be reasonable to expect this general sense of *prince* to be available for prefixation by *she-*. Since it is apparently not available, we are led to the conclusion that there is no general sense of *prince*, distinct from that of the free form. All these facts can be accommodated, however, if we postulate two senses of *-ess*: *-ess[1]*, which means "female", and appears in *lioness*, *tigress* and *leopardess*, and *-ess[2]*, which means "female counterpart of", and appears in *princess* and *duchess*.[11]

Proportional series in which the recurrent contrast involves lexical items belonging to different syntactic categories (quasi-series) are numerous, and of some importance.[12] The most interesting of these from our point of view are those in which the relations of quasi-endonymy and paronymy play a part. As we shall see, quasi-series of this type throw up some quite tricky problems; but we shall begin with the most straightforward cases, namely, those in which there is a recurrent, overt morphological relationship which parallels the semantic relation of endonymy:

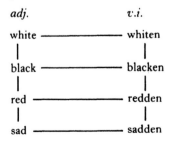

In these instances, the meaning of the verb encapsulates the meaning of the adjective; this is demonstrated by the fact that defining *blacken* in terms of *black* is noticeably simpler and more direct than the reverse:

> *blacken* = "turn black"
> *black*   = "colour of something which has blackened"

The relationship between one word and another belonging to a different syntactic category and produced from the first by some process of derivation will be called **paronymy**; the derivationally primitive item will be called the **base**, and the derived form the **paronym**. Generally speaking, unless there is good evidence to the contrary, it will be assumed that semantic complexity parallels derivational complexity, and that in a normal case of base and paronym, the base is an endonym of the paronym. This is particularly clear when the derivational process is affixation, since there is then usually little doubt as to the direction of derivation. Since both paronymy and endonymy, for us, are relations not between lexemes as such, but between what we call 'lexical units' (i.e. single senses associated with lexical forms), it is important to identify the relevant senses in any given relationship. Consider the following:

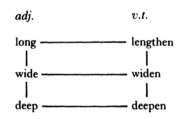

In these it is not the most usual sense of the adjective which is encapsulated in the verb: to widen something is not to make it wide (necessarily), but to make it wider than it was, which could still be relatively narrow. The sense of *wide* which is encapsulated in *widen* is thus not the one which appears in *It's wide*, but the one which appears in *How wide is it?* and in the comparative form *wider* (for a detailed discussion on this and related points see chapter 11).

It is possible to describe the relationship between base and paronym, or more strictly, between free base and base-in-paronym, in terms of congruence variants. Consider the items in fig. 5.10. They illustrate a congruent relationship: an *inflator*, for instance, is designed for inflating, neither more nor less; the recurrent semantic modification brought about by the derivational process represents a plausible semantic load for an affix. These items, which represent the commonest pattern of relations,

130

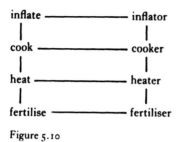

Figure 5.10

establish a reference point. Consider now *chopper* (in the sense of "small axe") and *walker* (in the sense of "rambler"). In both of these it can be argued that what is encapsulated is something more specific than the sense of the verb base. A chopper is certainly designed for chopping, but not, for instance, onions or parsley; not everyone who can walk is a walker (in the relevant sense). In a pair like *write* and *writer* ("one who writes books"), the noun encapsulates a sense of *write* more specific than the most frequent one, but that more specific sense can also be carried by the free base, as in *John writes for a living*, so there is no need to postulate non-congruence. The case of *walker* is perhaps debatable, but it could be argued that although a more specific sense of *walk* appears also in *walking* (as in *to go walking*, or *to be out walking*) and in *walk*(n.), as in *to go for a walk*, there is no comparable specific interpretation of the simple verb *walk*, as in *John walks now* or *Mary is walking*. If this is true, then *walker* is a hypo-paronym of *walk*. The case of *chopper* is surely clearer: there is no evidence of two senses of *chop* in *chop wood* and *chop onions*, and since *chopper* is restricted to the former, it must be a hypo-paronym of *chop*. A similar example (although not belonging to the above series) is *miller*, which is related to only one type of mill (not, for instance, a cotton mill). Possible examples of super-paronymy, where the meaning associated with the base in its encapsulated form is superordinate to the meaning of the free base, are *joiner* (who does more than mere joining), and *potter* (not all of whose products can be appropriately described as pots). It is even possible to include in this scheme cases like *conduct* and *conductor* (of a bus) where there is no obvious semantic relation between base and paronym. The relation between free base and base-in-paronym could be viewed as incompatibility, and included as a congruence variant ('hetero-paronymy'). (This variant is not applicable to most lexical relations.)

However, there is another (not necessarily incompatible) way of dealing with paronymous relations – one which establishes an analogy with the

131

literal/idiomatic distinction. The existence of a proportional quasi-series like that illustrated in fig. 5.10 may be taken as evidence of the existence of a derivational semantic rule – a recurrent association of a morphological process and a particular semantic change. All cases which fall under such a rule may be thought of as regular: interpreting a derived form of this type is analogous to the semantic construal of a transparent sequence like *The cat sat on the mat*. All cases where the semantic nature of the derived form is not what would be predicted from the rule (unless, of course, they fall under a different rule) are analogous to idioms. We shall reserve the term *paronym* for the semantically regular formations; semantically idiosyncratic derived forms will be called †**false paronyms**.[13] The category of false paronyms includes super-paronyms, hypo-paronyms and hetero-paronyms;[14] it also includes instances where semantic complexity does not follow morphological complexity (as is arguably the case with, for instance, *beauty* : *beautiful*).

In principle, the foregoing account of paronymous relations applies also to **zero-derived** paronyms, i.e. those with no affix or other overt sign of category change (stress pattern, for instance), like *comb* (n.) : *comb* (v.), *hammer* (n.) : *hammer* (v.), and *saw* (n.) : *saw* (v.).[15] However, at least some cases of zero-derivation present special problems in that semantic complexity does not always seem to follow derivational complexity. It is convenient to bring into the discussion at this point pairs of lexical items which display the same semantic relationship as, for instance, *inflate* and *inflator*, but which have no formal relationship; examples of such pairs are: *dig* : *spade*, *sweep* : *broom*, *shoot* : *gun*, *write* : *pen*, *steer* : *rudder*. It can be argued with a degree of plausibility that the verb in these cases is the endonym and the instrumental noun the exonym. The basis for this view is the relative independence of the sense of the verb, and the relative dependence of the sense of the noun on that of the verb. Take the case of *dig* and *spade*. One can characterise the action of digging without invoking the notion of a spade, but one cannot satisfactorily characterise a spade without invoking the notion of digging. This pattern of dependence reflects itself also in the relations between mutual definitions: *A spade is an implement for digging* is both more direct and more accurate than *To dig is to use a spade in the function for which it was designed*. The relationship between *dig* and *spade* may be contrasted with the to some extent similar, but nonetheless distinct, relationship between *drive* and *vehicle* (also *ride* and *bicycle*, and *sail* and *boat*). Here the dependency relation is clearly reversed. What counts as driving cannot be described without mentioning vehicles; vehicles are not designed to serve an independent and pre-existing function of driving – rather, driving is whatever is necessary to get a vehicle to go, and as vehicles change, so does the nature of driving. Compare *To drive is to operate a vehicle*, which captures the essence of *drive*, and *A vehicle is something one drives*, which misses the essence of *vehicle*.

Let us return now to the zero-derived examples introduced in the previous paragraph. It appears that the relationship between verb and noun in the case of *comb, hammer* and *saw* (and many others) is virtually identical to that between *dig* and *spade*, witness the intuitively satisfactory nature of the proportions *dig*:*spade*::*comb* (v.):*comb* (n.) and *dig*:*comb* (v.)::*spade*:*comb* (n.). If the argument concerning *dig* and *spade* is correct, this means that *comb* (v.) is an endonym of *comb* (n.), and the result is generalisable, in principle, to the other examples. This is not at all problematic in cases like *rattle* (v.) and *rattle* (n.), *stamp* (v.) and *stamp* (n.), and *hoist* (v.) and *hoist* (n.), where lexicographers, lexicologists and intuition all agree that the noun is derived from the verb. But there is a potential embarrassment: the aforementioned authorities also agree that in the case of *comb, hammer, saw, iron* and *brush* the noun is primary, at least historically, and the verb secondary. An isolated instance would not be embarrassing – we should simply say that it was a case of false paronymy. But what we seem to have is a quasi-series, consisting of related verbs and nouns, in which the nouns are most satisfactorily defined in terms of the verbs (i.e. the verbs are semantically more basic), while the historical evidence indicates that the verbs are derived from the nouns. Now it is possible that our semantic principle – that semantic primitivity should go hand in hand with morphological simplicity – is wrong; or it may be no more than a general tendency. But it is an intuitively plausible principle, and there are other possible explanations of our apparent anomaly. One is that zero-derivations are not under the same semantic constraints as overt morphological derivations: it is perhaps significant that the only overt derivations in the proportional series we are considering (*inflate*:*inflator*, etc.) are semantically 'regular'. Another possibility is that historical evidence is not an infallible guide to current relationships: perhaps *comb* (n.) should be considered to be synchronically (i.e. in the present state of the language) derived from *comb* (v.).[16] If it is accepted that derivation has a semantic dimension, then it must also be accepted that in some cases – especially those where the stabilising influence of overt morphological form is absent – a semantic shift may change the effective direction of derivation.

Lexical semantics

Notes

5.1 What are here called lexical configurations are often referred to as lexical fields, or word fields. Field theorists tend to view whole configurations as linguistic entities; for us, however, lexical configurations are merely by-products, as it were, of particular sense relations. For details of lexical field theory see Trier (1934), Geckeler (1971), Lehrer (1974: ch. 2), Miller and Johnson-Laird (1967: 237–67), Coseriu (1975), Lutzeier (1981 and 1983).

5.2

1.   See Bunge (1969).
2.   Cf. Stebbing (1952: 109) on the necessity for a constant *fundamentum divisionis* in classification.
3.   Miller and Johnson-Laird (1976: 240) state that the relation of dominance in a hierarchy must be asymmetric and transitive. They are correct as far as asymmetry is concerned, but transitivity is not necessary.
4.   For an elementary treatment of the logic of relations see Tarski (1965: ch. 4).
5.   This definition is a conflation of two separate definitions – Bunge's definition of an intransitive hierarchy (1969: 5), and van Valen's definition of a transitive hierarchy (1964: 408).
6.   Cf. Bever and Rosenbaum (1971: 593–5) on 'non-convergence'.
7.   See, for instance, Kay (1971: 877).

5.3 The existence of proportional series such as *man : woman : : stallion : mare* is sometimes cited as evidence for the autonomy and discreteness of traits like "horse", "human", "male" and "female", within a componential theory of meaning (see, for instance, Hjelmslev (1961) and Lamb (1964)). It is undeniable that some traits, especially those which recurrently differentiate pairs of lexical items, seem to have a higher degree of autonomy within the meaning of a word than others. It must be borne in mind, however, that the areas of the vocabulary which can be illuminatingly treated in this way (i.e. those where the items fall into convincing proportional series) are somewhat restricted. Few componentialists would limit themselves to components which can be established through proportional series.

8.   The two types of contrast discussed here correspond to two types of semantic component distinguished by certain componentialists. Coseriu (1967) and Pottier (1974) make a distinction between **semes** and **classemes**: the latter function in a range of lexical fields, and have a tendency to be grammaticalised; the former are usually distinctive in a single lexical field, and are lexicalised, but only rarely grammaticalised. (Coseriu and Pottier perhaps overstate the difference between semes and classemes: the distinction is not at all clear-cut, and there is no reason to suppose that a radically different type of meaning is involved.)
9.   Cf. Lyons (1977: 334).
10. *Child* is not quite right here: *young person* would be better semantically, but there is no suitable lexical item. With a little good will, however, I think the argument can still go through.
11. There is no need to postulate two meanings of *-ess* in, for instance, *princess* ("consort of prince") and *princess* ("daughter of king", etc.). Such words do not seem to be ambiguous: *Three princesses attended the reception* would

134

be perfectly normal if the three happened to be Princess Anne, the Princess of Wales and Princess Michael of Kent.

12. This is not intended to be a comprehensive account of the semantics of derivation. A great deal of information concerning English word-formation can be found in Bauer (1983).

13. *Paronymy* is a traditional term: our use of it is more restricted than the traditional use.

14. We have not distinguished hypo-, super- and hetero-idioms, but there is no obvious reason why we should not do so.

15. Zero-derivation is sometimes called **conversion**.

16. There are some cases of instrumental nouns and related verbs of identical form where historical indications and current semantic relations are not in conflict – historically the derivation is from noun to verb, and semantically the verb clearly incorporates the meaning of the noun:

(a) gun   (to) gun
(a) knife   (to) knife
(a) broom   (to) broom
etc.

These would not, therefore, belong to the same proportional series as *dig* : *spade* : : *comb* (v.) : *comb* (n.).

6
Taxonomies

6.1 Hyponymy and incompatibility

Consider the following fragment of a taxonomic hierarchy:

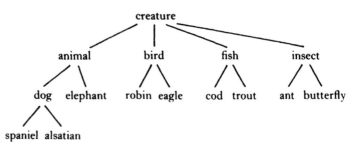

It seems fairly clear intuitively that two sense relations are essential to this configuration: daughter-nodes must be hyponyms of their respective mother-nodes (*dog*:*animal*, *insect*:*creature*, *cod*:*fish*); and sister-nodes must be incompatibles (*cat*:*dog*, *robin*:*eagle*, *bird*:*fish*). Let us accept that this is at least ideally so. We may now ask whether these two properties are not only necessary, but also sufficient, to characterise a taxonomic hierarchy – do they guarantee that any hierarchy which possesses them will be a well-formed taxonomy? The answer is that they do not. Consider the following fragment of a hierarchy:

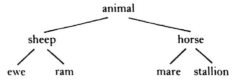

In this, sister-nodes are strict incompatibles, and daughters are strict hyponyms of mothers. Yet it is not a well-formed taxonomy. Intuitively, one would say that the principle of differentiation has not been held constant:

the division of *animals* into *sheep* and *horses* is a different sort of division from that of *sheep* into *ewes* and *rams*. We must therefore inquire into the nature of the division which gives rise to well-formed taxonomies.

It is worth noting, too, that there is no inherent connection between hyponymy and incompatibility: two hyponyms of the same superordinate need not be incompatibles:

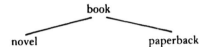

It would be more satisfying if we were able to characterise a taxonomy in terms of a relation of dominance and a principle of differentiation which were more intimately related. This will be attempted in the next section.

6.2 Taxonymy

It will be argued in this section that the key to a taxonomic lexical hierarchy is a sense relation which will be called †**taxonymy**. This may be regarded as a sub-species of hyponymy: the taxonyms of a lexical item are a sub-set of its hyponyms. Taxonymy (or more precisely, its converse) is the relation of dominance of a taxonomy: the corresponding horizontal relation – the relation between sister-nodes – will simply be labelled †**co-taxonymy**, to underline the intimate connection between the two.

A useful diagnostic frame for taxonymy is:

An X is a kind/type of Y

If X is a taxonym of Y, the result is normal:

1a. A spaniel is a kind of dog.
  b. A rose is a type of flower.
  c. A mango is a kind of fruit.

In each of the examples in 1, X is a hyponym of Y. However, not all hyponyms give a normal result in this frame:

2a. ? A kitten is a type of cat.
  b. ? A queen is a type of monarch.
  c. ? A spinster is a kind of woman.
  d. ? A waiter is a kind of man.

Unfortunately, the expression *kind of* is not univocal, and it is necessary to be able to recognise those senses which are irrelevant for the diagnosis of taxonymy. There are three of these. The first is illustrated in 3:

3. He was wearing a kind of flattened, three-sided turban – I don't know exactly what it was.

This is a signal that the speaker is referring to something unfamiliar, for which he has no ready label, and is offering an approximate description. It is reducible phonologically to /kənəv/ (/ə/ is the unstressed vowel of the first syllable of *about*). Taxonyms do not yield normal sentences in the frame when this reading is operative:

4. ? A dog is a ... /kənəv/ ... animal.

The second irrelevant sense of *kind of* typically carries a falling–rising intonation pattern; it indicates doubt as to the appropriateness of the predication which follows:

5. I suppose a parish priest is a kind of social worker.

This sense, too, gives an odd result with taxonyms:

6. ? A dog is a kind of animal.

The third irrelevant sense of *kind of* occurs in, for instance, *What kind of person is she?* and *That kind of person never pays his bills*. Questions of the form *What kind of...?* are ambiguous. Someone asking *What kind of tree is that?* is most probably requesting a taxonym: *It's a hornbeam* (rather than, say, *It's one that likes acid soil*). On the other hand, someone who asks *What kind of tree are you thinking of putting in the corner of the garden?* might well be satisfied with an answer like *One that gives a good show of spring blossom*. Likewise, *What kind of person is she?* is unlikely to be a request for a taxonym (if, indeed, there are any taxonyms of *person*); something like *Reliable and efficient* is more probably the sort of answer expected. Notice, however, that *What kinds of...?* is a request for taxonyms:

7. A: What kinds of animals did you see at the zoo?
   B: (i) ? Big ones, little ones, ...
      (ii) Lions, tigers, monkeys, zebras, ...

The diagnostic frames for co-taxonymy which show most clearly the close relationship with taxonymy are:

An X is a kind of Y, and a Z is another kind of Y

and

An X is a kind/type of Y, and so is a Z

8.   An armadillo is a type of animal, and so is an aardvark.

All the examples given so far have been living things. While these may turn out to be the paradigm instances of taxonyms, the relation is readily recognisable among artefacts:

9.   An ocarina is a kind of musical instrument.
10.   A car is a type of vehicle.

Verbs generally seem to show hierarchical structuring to a more limited extent than nouns; however, just as hyponymy is quite common among verbs, a relation paralleling nominal taxonymy occurs, too. It is recognised by means of the test frame *X-ing is a way of Y-ing*. This discriminates among verb hyponyms in a way closely parallel to the way *X is a kind of Y* does with nouns. Thus, although *murder* and *strangle* are both hyponyms of *kill*:

> To murder someone is necessarily to kill him.
> To strangle someone is necessarily to kill him.

only *strangle* is normal in the test frame:

> ? Murdering is a way of killing
> Strangling is a way of killing.

Likewise, *travel* and *walk* are both hyponyms of *move*, but only *walk* is a taxonym. By this test, then, the taxonyms of *kill* would be such verbs as *strangle, garotte, hang, drown*, etc.; and the taxonyms of *move* (in the sense of "locomote"), would be *walk, run, crawl, fly, hop, swim*, etc. Notice that although *murder* is not a taxonym of *kill*, it is a taxonym of *commit a crime*, along with *rob, rape, assault, defraud*, etc. It is also worthy of note that the nouns corresponding to these verbs satisfy the test frame for noun taxonyms, which provides confirmation that the diagnostic frame for verbs does indeed select taxonyms:

> Murder/rape/fraud is a type of crime.

Recognising taxonymy is one thing; describing its essential nature is another and more difficult task. It is not easy to discover invariable semantic properties which differentiate all taxonyms from other hyponyms. However, there are two or three lines of approach which seem to throw some light on the matter. First of all, we can observe a strong correlation between taxonyms and what are called **natural kind** terms, and between non-taxonymic hyponyms and **nominal kind** terms.[1]

One of the ways in which natural kind terms differ from nominal kind terms is that the latter correspond in a fairly precise way to analytic definitions containing a superordinate with a modifier. Thus, in general, the replacement of, say, *stallion* by *male horse* yields a logically equivalent sentence:[2] *I saw a stallion* entails and is entailed by *I saw a male horse*. The same relation exists between *kitten* and *young cat*, *spinster* and *unmarried woman*, etc. In the case of a nominal kind hyponym, therefore, the nature of its greater specificity is clear: we can picture the hyponym as encapsulating a syntagmatic modification of its superordinate. Natural kind terms, however, are different, and the nature of the greater specificity of a natural kind term relative to its superordinate remains somewhat obscure. Consider the relation between *horse* and *animal*. We know that *horse* is a hyponym of *animal*, but there is no modification of *animal* which will yield an expression equivalent to *horse* in the way that *male horse* is equivalent to *stallion*. (It is no good saying that *equine animal* is equivalent to *horse*: *equine* is totally parasitic on *horse* – it means "resembling or pertaining to horses" – so *equine animal* is not a genuine analysis of the meaning of *horse*). Similarly, while one can say that a mare and a stallion differ in respect of sex, there is no comparable way of expressing the difference between, say, a horse and a cow. Intuitively one would be inclined to say that horses and cows differed in an indeterminately large number of ways; in the same way, in order to give an account, which matched the average person's knowledge, of what sort of an animal a horse was, would require an encyclopaedic description of indeterminate size and complexity. (Dictionaries often do not attempt definitions of such terms, but merely give a few distinguishing features, like the hump of a camel. It is important to realise that a set of features adequate to identify an object does not amount to a full description of that object.) Incidentally, this aspect of the meaning of natural kind terms throws some light on the problem of the semantic status of *cran-* in *cranberry*, etc. We know that a cranberry is a kind of berry, so the form of .the word sets up an expectation that the prefix should carry the traits of meaning which distinguish the species from the genus (using these terms loosely). But since *cranberry*, *raspberry*, etc. are natural kind terms, their relations with their superordinates can only be described encyclopaedically, and there is no conceptually autonomous portion of meaning parallel to "male" or "young" for the prefixes to carry.

Another way in which natural kind terms differ from nominal kind terms is that the former show certain resemblances to proper names in the way that they refer. In particular, they share with proper names the property of being **rigid designators**.[3] This means that referents would not lose their entitlement to their current labels whatever changes in our perception of their nature were to come about. An illustration will make this clear. Suppose that all cats were discovered one day to be not animals at all, but highly sophisticated self-replicating robots, introduced to earth millions of years ago by visitors from outside our galaxy. Would this discovery lead us to exclaim 'Aha! Cats do not exist!'? Or would we not continue to call the referents 'cats', and say that cats were not what we took them to be? Surely the latter is the case; this is part of what is meant by a rigid designator. By way of contrast, consider another eventuality. Suppose it were discovered that there were no genuine male horses, only parthenogenetic females, and that what we previously took to be stallions, actually, despite strongly suggestive activities with mares, had nothing whatsoever to do with the conception of foals, but were really animals of another species (discoveries of this nature are by no means unknown in biology). Confronted with these facts, would we exclaim 'Aha! Stallions are not what we took them to be!'? Or would we not say 'So stallions don't exist, after all'? It seems clear in this case, that if there were no male horses, then there could not be any stallions either, because that is what *stallion* means. In other words, *stallion* (and this is true of nominal kinds in general) is not a rigid designator.[4]

A third property which distinguishes natural kind terms from nominal kind terms is their capacity for use with a 'type' reading. One may say, for instance, pointing to a dog, perhaps a collie, 'that dog makes an excellent sheep-dog', meaning "that breed of dog"; similarly, 'that horse makes a first-rate hunter' may be said indicating a particular horse, but with the breed of horse as the intended interpretation. However, this usage, for most speakers, is not possible with nominal kind terms. Thus *this bitch makes an excellent sheep-dog* can only refer to one particular animal, and cannot be interpreted to mean "bitches of this breed".

The characteristics of natural kind terms are not only to be found in the names of natural species and naturally occurring substances, but also (despite the term *natural*), amongst names of artefacts, such as *violin*, *cathedral*, *lorry*,[5] etc. The meaning of *violin*, for example, cannot be established by dictionary definition: it is not equivalent to any expression of the form *an X musical instrument*. One can make as good an argument as that for *cat* that *violin* is a rigid designator.

It is more difficult to verify the relation between taxonymy and natural kinds in respect of verbs. One reason is that it is not clear that the concept of natural kind can be applied to verbs. Verbs such as *walk, crawl, swim,* and *see, hear, taste,* etc., can probably be argued with some plausibility to be rigid designators: radical changes in our perception of the fundamental nature of the processes and actions they refer to would not lead us to abandon them as labels. Perhaps this is sufficient justification for regarding them as natural kind terms. If so, then many verb taxonyms are natural kind terms. But a number of these verbs seem to be analytically definable: *swim* = "move through water using bodily appendages"; *see* = "perceive through the eyes". It is possible that these glosses merely provide identificatory features, rather than true equivalents; however, this distinction seems more difficult to establish in the case of verbs.

It seems, then, that the notion of a natural kind term, is, at the very least, intimately associated with the notion of a taxonym. Suppose we make a stronger claim, and say that a taxonym must be a natural kind term. What evidence can be ranged against such a claim? (Let us assume, for present purposes, that verbs like those discussed in the previous paragraph are, in fact, natural kind terms.) Consider first the following taxonymy:

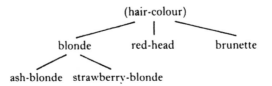

(hair-colour)

blonde   red-head   brunette

ash-blonde   strawberry-blonde

(There is no superordinate for this set; *woman* will not serve:

? A blonde is a kind of woman.)

What is needed is a term which focusses on hair-colour in the way that all the other terms do. It is, of course, unlikely that such a term would exist, since at that level of specificity no particular colour is designated. (The lack of a most inclusive term here is presumably not unrelated to the lack of an origin in the colour-adjective and shape-adjective hierarchies.) The point about this hierarchy is that all the constituent terms are nominal kind terms, yet they are satisfactory taxonyms and co-taxonyms. At first sight this seems to call into question the close association between taxonymy and natural kinds. However, the association can be maintained: all the terms are cognitively synonymous with paraphrases of the form *woman–girl with X-coloured hair.*[6] This means that the terms

contrast solely in respect of their X-traits. That this is so is confirmed
by the fact that a proportional series can be constructed:

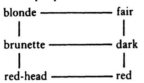

When we examine these X-traits – "fair", "red", "dark" – they turn
out to be of the natural kind variety. In other words, the hierarchy depends
on contrasts of the natural kind sort, in spite of being made up of nominal
kind terms.

There is, however, more serious counter-evidence to the claim that taxonyms must be natural kind terms. Consider the taxonymy of *crime*: *bur-
glary*, *murder*, *theft*, *fraud*, etc. Each of these is established by precise
definition, and is thus a nominal kind term par excellence. None of them
is a rigid designator. If we discovered a loophole in the law (or received
a new revelation) which meant that killing other people was sanctioned
under all circumstances, we would be obliged to say not that murder was
different to what we thought, but that murder did not exist as a crime.
In this case, the connection between taxonyms and natural kinds cannot
be saved by the strategy used for terms referring to ladies' hair-colours.
Perhaps the true essence of taxonymy lies elsewhere?

Another possible approach to the characterisation of taxonymy is in
terms of the good category principle.[7] Perhaps what we are doing when
we sub-divide a superordinate category in a taxonomic fashion is to create
the 'best' categories that we possibly can; that is, we create categories
with the highest possible degree of resemblance between co-members,
combined with the maximum possible distinctiveness from members of
other categories (especially sister categories). The taxonyms of X, on this
view, would then be those lexical items which denote the best categories
that the category denoted by X could be divided into. Certainly, if we
are going to sub-divide the class of animals, we could hardly do better
than horses, giraffes, elephants, mice, etc. We can go further and suggest
that the reason the division of sheep into rams and ewes, and of horses
into mares and stallions, is taxonomically anomalous is that it is not the
one which produces the best categories: it may be surmised that the rams
and ewes of a given breed of sheep will resemble one another more strongly
than, say, rams of two different breeds. But this argument has a drawback.
Suppose there existed a species of birds with very marked sex-differentia-
tion in a large number of salient aspects: appearance, behaviour, culinary

value, etc. Now suppose this species came in several varieties (like domestic fowl). It is far from inconceivable that in such a species males of different varieties should resemble one another more, over a wide range of characteristics, than the male and the female of the same variety. In such circumstances, the good category principle would lead to the avian equivalent of *stallion* and *mare* for that species of bird. (It is not unknown for biologists to mistakenly classify as two different species males and females of what later turn out to be a single species.) Yet such a division of our hypothetical category would be taxonomically incorrect. It is clear, therefore, that a taxonomist must, on occasions at least, ignore the good category principle; in that case, what principle does he follow?

It is possible that we have been looking in the wrong direction for an answer – or rather, looking for the wrong kind of answer. The everyday names of natural species provide the central examples of natural kind terms; they are also paradigm instances of the good category principle at work. Perhaps when we taxonomise some other field, there are no invariable principles to be applied which inevitably lead to unique taxonomies; perhaps we merely seek to create the closest analogues we can to natural species. Exactly how close we get will of course depend on the nature of the category being sub-divided.[8] In sub-dividing a biological category (e.g. a species into varieties) one would expect biological criteria to predominate. That could be why a taxonomic sub-division of a species cannot consist of a single sex. To be maximally like a species, a sub-species or variety would at least have to be capable of reproducing itself. In other semantic areas, we simply do the best we can, mimicking natural species by, for instance, creating where possible sub-classes that require encyclopaedic characterisation, in preference to classes that can be characterised by means of a couple of clear-cut semantic traits. This would be a pessimistic conclusion for semantic theory – but it is one that should not be dismissed too hastily.

We have up to now assumed that a taxonym must necessarily be a hyponym. It would certainly be a pity to have to relinquish the close association between taxonymy and hyponymy. However, if we are to maintain this particular connection, there are a few awkward facts to explain. Consider the taxonyms of *kill*. *Strangle*, *drown*, *hang*, etc. are undoubtedly hyponyms; but *shoot*, for instance, is not (? *To shoot someone is necessarily to kill him*) yet it belongs naturally with the rest:

> Strangling, drowning, hanging, shooting and stabbing are
> ways of killing.

One hesitates to draw a line after *hanging* merely to save the relationship with hyponymy. However, it will be remembered that expression-schemata generally diagnostic of hyponymy, such as *Xs and other Ys*, also admitted para-hyponymy. It seems that our diagnostic frames for taxonymy 'leak' in the same way, and we therefore need to recognise para-taxonymy as a lexical relation. In this way the close relationship with hyponymy is preserved: strict taxonyms must be strict hyponyms; para-taxonyms must be para-hyponyms.

In this discussion, no attempt has been made to treat taxonymy and co-taxonymy independently. This would, in fact, be impossible: unlike hyponymy and incompatibility, taxonymy and co-taxonymy are conceptually inseparable. This is another way of saying that taxonymy is an inherently differentiated relation.

6.3 Characteristics of natural taxonomies

Taxonomic lexical hierarchies (taxonomies) have been extensively studied in a wide range of languages by anthropological linguists and others. Certain general characteristics of natural taxonomies emerge from these studies. One is that they typically have no more than five levels, and frequently have fewer. These levels are commonly labelled as follows:

unique beginner	(plant)
|	
life-form	(bush)
|	
generic	(rose)
|	
specific	(hybrid tea)
|	
varietal	(Peace)

It will be noticed that the labels have a strong biological orientation. This is because ethnolinguists have been mainly interested in the way human communities classify living things. There is no doubt, however, that lexical taxonomies occur throughout the lexicon. Of the level labels in common use, only *life-form* is totally unsuited for use with non-biological taxonomies; the simple term *kind* has been suggested as an alternative.[9] The limitation to a maximum of five levels is a characteristic of 'natural' or **folk taxonomies** – those with widespread use throughout a speech community – which may be expected to exhibit general linguistic and cognitive constraints. There also exist various specialist (e.g. technical or scientific) taxonomies, which are, in general, more closely attuned to current scientific

145

orthodoxy, and to the needs of the discipline or craft which they serve; some of the features of natural taxonomies (e.g. a limited number of levels) do not appear to apply to them.

The most significant level of a taxonomy from the point of view of the speakers of a language is undoubtedly the **generic level**. This is the level of the ordinary everyday names for things and creatures: *cat*, *oak*, *carnation*, *apple*, *car*, *church*, *cup*, etc.[10] Items at this level are particularly likely to be morphologically simple, and to be 'original' in the sense that they are not borrowed by metaphorical extension from other semantic areas.[11] This is also the level at which the greatest number of items is likely to occur, although it is obvious that if every generic item in a taxonomy had several specifics, then the number of items would be greater at the specific level. The point is, however, that most branches of taxonomic hierarchies terminate at the generic level. Items which occur at specific and varietal levels are particularly likely to be morphologically complex, and compound words are frequent.

It was suggested in chapter 5 that in an ideal hierarchy all branches have nodes at each level; in this respect natural taxonomies often fall short of the ideal. Consider the taxonomic systems of those speakers of English for whom the names of birds like *blackbird*, *robin* and *starling* are at the same taxonomic level as *collie*, *spaniel* and *alsation*; their taxonomies must either be structured as in fig. 6.1, or as in fig. 6.2. In either case

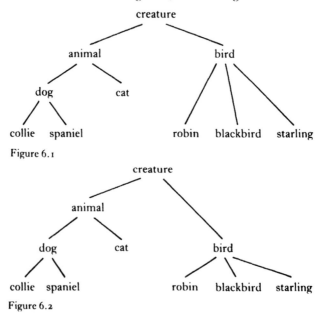

Figure 6.1

Figure 6.2

there are gaps: in fig. 6.1 at the generic level, and in fig. 6.2 at the level of kind (life-form). Given the psychological importance of the generic level, the more likely structure is that shown in fig. 6.2. Similar gaps can be found among taxonomies of artefacts. Musical instruments provide one example:

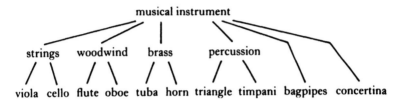

Most instruments belong to a kind, but there is no obvious candidate kind for *bagpipes* (although they belong to a fairly clear-cut family of instruments), or *concertina*. Or, thinking about the things (other than food) which go on the table at mealtime (*tableware?*), there appears to be no label denoting the kind that *breadboard* belongs to (if, indeed, it can be said to belong to a kind):

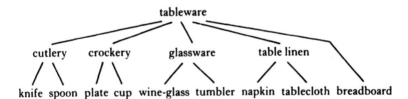

The lexical items in a taxonomic hierarchy may be considered to be labels for nodes of a parallel hierarchy of conceptual categories. Now while the existence of a label without a corresponding conceptual category must be regarded as highly unlikely, it is not impossible for what is intuitively recognised as a conceptual category to be without a label. Sometimes there may be clear linguistic evidence for the existence of the unlabelled category. For instance, the items which yield a normal sentence in the frame *He/she was wearing X/an X* constitute a natural class which includes *spectacles*, *underpants*, *necklace*, etc. There is no label for this category. Another example is the set of devices for telling the time, associated together perhaps by normal occurrence in the frame *John looked at the X to see what time it was.* Again there is no superordinate (other than the rather rare or archaic *timepiece*) for the class, although it is conceptually pretty clear.[12] In some cases the linguistic motivation for grouping a set of lexical items together as taxonyms of a non-existent superordinate may not be so immediately apparent. Consider the class of movable items one buys when moving into a new house: *furniture* (*chairs, tables, beds,* etc.), *appliances* (*refrigerator, television, washing-machine,* etc.), *carpets, curtains,* etc. Once again there is no label for this overall category. Nor is there a simple diagnostic frame. But the use of *everything* in *Of course, we had to buy everything when we bought our first house ... beds, carpets, cooker ...* is suggestive (it means "everything in a category we both know about, but I can't name"). These categories with no names, but for whose existence there is definite evidence, are called **covert categories**: they most frequently occur at the higher levels of a hierarchy.

We have so far treated all taxonyms of a superordinate as if they were of equal status. But in some respects they are not: speakers regard certain items as being 'better' examples of a category than others. For instance, 11a, 12a and 13a are generally judged to be more normal than 11b, 12b and 13b:

11a.   An apple is a better example of a fruit than an olive.
   b.   ? An olive is a better example of a fruit than an apple.
12a.   A car makes a better vehicle than a tractor.
   b.   ? A tractor makes a better vehicle than a car.
13a.   A pigeon is a better example of a bird than an ostrich.
   b.   ? An ostrich is a better example of a bird than a pigeon.

Those examples which emerge from such tests as the best examples of their categories are called the **prototypical** members of the category.[13] Many categories have a somewhat problematical peripheral region. There is no real problem about, for instance, *ostrich*, which, although rather different from the prototypical bird, is nonetheless indubitably a bird. But consider, for example, the status of *shoes* with respect to the superordinate *clothes*. We can, with a clear conscience, tell a customs official that we are carrying 'nothing but clothes' if our suitcase contains trousers, jackets, shirts, underwear, socks and several pairs of shoes. But surely it would not be normal – in fact it would be downright misleading – to say of a shoe-box with only a pair of shoes in it that it contained clothes, or to say that a shoe-shop sold clothes.[14] The same would be true, for me, of the relation between *sandals* and *shoes*: I would expect to find sandals in a shoe-shop, and I would not feel I had been misled if I found a pair of sandals in what had been described to me as a bag of shoes. On the other hand, I would feel that the full truth had not been told if the bag turned out to contain nothing but sandals. A similar relation holds between *ruler* and *tool*: I would hesitate to describe a ruler as a tool (an *instrument*, perhaps?), but I would expect a set of carpentry tools to include one. Even covert categories can have **peripheral** categories. It is normal to speak of 'wearing' a perfume, and a complete answer to the question 'What was she wearing?' could well include a mention of perfume. On the other hand, in answer to a policeman's inquiry 'Was Miss X wearing anything when you entered the room, sir?' one would feel obliged, in the interests of honesty, to answer in the negative if the lady in question had been naked but fragrant at the time. (One might be less sure what to answer if she had been wearing only a watch, or a pair of spectacles; the distinction peripheral/non-peripheral is not a sharp one.)

It is not uncommon for a lexeme to include lexical units functioning at more than one level of taxonomic specificity. Consider the following examples:[15]

14a. A hand has five fingers.
 b. The thumb and two fingers were missing from the hand.
15a. The meal consisted of meat, potatoes and two vegetables.
 b. You must eat plenty of potatoes and other vegetables.
16a. An ape is a tailless monkey.
 b. Apes are mostly larger than monkeys.

Sister lexical units of a lexeme with different levels of specificity often differ in their freedom of occurrence; usually only one of the items is likely to occur in a neutral context, the other(s) requiring a greater or lesser degree of contextual pressure.[16] For instance, *I've hurt my finger* would normally be taken to exclude the thumb, even though there is no bias in the (linguistic) context of *finger*.

We are now in a position to distinguish two distinct kinds of 'gap' in a hierarchy. First, there are those which represent covert categories supported by intuition and by linguistic evidence, and which therefore ought to be represented in the tree-diagram of the hierarchy (perhaps by the symbol ⌀). Secondly, there are gaps where there is no evidence for the existence of a node at all (the gaps in figs. 6.1 and 6.2. are of this nature).

Quasi-relations are relatively common in taxonomic hierarchies. We have already encountered (in chapter 4) the use of *colour* as quasi-superordinate of the set of colour adjectives (*red*, *green*, etc.), and *shape* as quasi-super-ordinate of the set of adjectives denoting geometrical shapes (*round*, *triangular*, etc.). In taxonomies consisting, at the lower levels, of ordinary count nouns, items at higher levels are quite often mass nouns (contracting singular concord with a verb: *The cutlery/crockery is all here*):

or less frequently collective nouns (contracting plural concord with a verb: *The woodwind/brass are all here*):

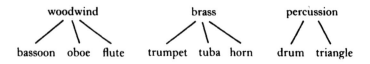

It is perhaps worth while at this point introducing a minor terminological refinement. We have so far regarded quasi-relations as possessing a type of symmetry: if X is a quasi-R of Y, then Y is a quasi-R of X. This is when there are no grounds for distinguishing the statuses of X and Y. But in a taxonomic hierarchy there is what might be considered a 'normal' syntactic class for the members. This can be ascertained by examining the items at the generic level. Suppose we have a hierarchy in which all the generic, specific and varietal items are count nouns, but the kind terms are mass nouns. In such a case it would seem justifiable to discriminate between the count noun and the mass noun items in a quasi-relationship. In the case, for instance, of *cutlery* and *knife* it would be better to call *cutlery* a quasi-superordinate of *knife*, but not to call *knife* a quasi-taxonym, since it is a perfectly regular taxonym – it is the superordinate which is out of line. If we adopt this convention, then it appears that quasi-superordinates are far more frequent than quasi-taxonyms. There is thus a parallel with covert categories, which are also more frequent as superordinates; covert categories are different, however, in that they can only be established by superordination – that is to say, it is only the behaviour of a set of taxonyms which can point to the existence of a covert category.

Co-taxonyms are expected to be incompatibles; that is to say, sister taxonomic categories are not expected to overlap. With nouns this is invariably the case, but it is possible to find apparent counter-examples among verbs. Take, for instance, the verbs denoting methods of cooking. In answer to the question *What ways of cooking are there?*, one is likely to receive among the answers *frying, broiling, roasting, baking, boiling, steaming*. Most of these are mutually incompatible, as one would expect.

But it has been pointed out that a *broiled chicken* is also a *roast chicken*. This might, of course, indicate that *broil* and *roast* are synonyms; in the present instance, however, this is not the case, since not every roast chicken is a broiled chicken (for instance, if it is roasted in an oven). Another possibility is that *broil* is a hyponym of *roast*, in which case they should not appear as co-taxonyms in the hierarchy. This would be supported by the normality of *To broil a chicken is necessarily to roast it*. However, the apparent normality of *Broiling is one way of cooking and roasting is another* is unexpected if *broil* is a hyponym of *roast* (cf. *? A dog is one kind of animal and a spaniel is another*). The simultaneous evidence of co-taxonymy and hyponymy strongly suggests that *roast* has two senses, *roast*[1] being superordinate to *roast*[2] and *broil*. If this were the case, the taxonomy of cooking terms should appear as follows (only a fragment is illustrated):[17]

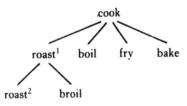

In this way the principle of incompatible co-taxonyms would be preserved. Unfortunately, this picture does not represent the facts, either: a *broiled steak*, for instance, cannot be described as a *roast steak* – it is only when whole carcasses are *broiled* that they also count as *roasted*. So, although *roast*[2] and *broil* are incompatibles, *broil* is not a hyponym, but a compatible, of *roast*[1]. Another example of overlapping co-taxonyms is to be found among the verbs of locomotion for living creatures:

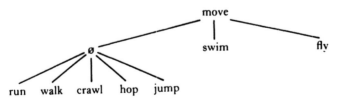

According to my intuitions, there is a covert category in this hierarchy: there is no superordinate term for the verbs denoting locomotion on land (but the argument is not affected if *run*, *walk*, and so on are considered to be at the same taxonomic level as *swim* and *fly*). Once again, co-taxonyms are, by and large, incompatibles, but, for instance, *crawl* and *walk* would not be distinct for a mouse, a fly, or a lizard (although, of course, they

151

would be distinct for a human being); and possibly *jump* and *hop* would not be distinct for a frog or a kangaroo.

What does this mean for our account of taxonymy? It appears to be a property of predicative terms such as verbs and adjectives that their meanings are context-dependent to a much greater extent than those of nouns; their meanings are, in fact, dependent in various ways on those of closely associated nouns. There is therefore an extra measure of indeterminacy about the meaning of a verb or adjective out of context. It is perhaps not surprising, therefore, that hierarchies composed of unattached verbs should fail to display the rigid semantic structuring shown by hierarchies composed of nouns. However, as soon as the predicative term is tied down to a particular subject noun phrase, its meaning becomes more determinate, and the expected strict hierarchical properties re-appear. Thus, in answer to the question *In what ways can a fly move?* it would not be normal to reply *It can fly, crawl or walk*: one must give a set of properly incompatible co-taxonyms. It follows that the only way to get the cooking verbs to behave in a strict hierarchical fashion is to tie them to a particular noun phrase (or set of noun phrases referring, potentially, to a linguistically relevant category or its members): *What ways are there of cooking a chicken?*

In 6.2 taxonymy is presented as an inherently differentiated relation, that is, one which guarantees divergent branching. It might appear to follow from this that we should never encounter structures like

where C is a taxonym of both A and B, which are not synonyms, nor is one a taxonym of the other. Actually, such cases do occur, although they are not very frequent. They are, however, compatible with taxonymy being inherently differentiated, provided that A and B can be shown to belong to different taxonomies. That is to say, taxonomies may be allowed to intersect without compromising the principle of non-covergent branching. The following is an example of intersecting taxonomies:

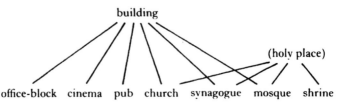

What should not occur with an inherently differentiated relation of dominance is convergent branching in the same taxonomy. That is to say, if we begin with the most inclusive term of the taxonomy, and construct the hierarchy from the top downwards, using a frame such as *The types of X are A, B, C . . . etc.* then no convergence should occur.

6.4 Over-specification, under-specification and the generic level

One of the linguistic variables under our control as speakers of a language is the semantic specificity of expressions. We can invest an expression with a very light semantic load:

> We found a THING in the attic.

or we can pack in a lot of meaning:

> We found a SEVENTEENTH CENTURY SILVER SNUFF-BOX in the attic.

However, if we wish to communicate effectively, we must submit to certain constraints on the choice of level of specificity in particular situations. For instance, a referring expression must contain enough information for the addressee to be able to identify the intended referent.[18] The amount of information (and hence, in general, the degree of specificity) that is required will vary from situation to situation. One can easily imagine a situation where, in order to obtain a particular book, one merely has to say *Please give me that book*. In, say, a library, or a bookshop, however, that could well be inadequate, and something more specific like *Please give me the French–Somali dictionary at the end of the second shelf from the top* might be required. The need to refer successfully thus sets a lower limit to the level of specificity of a referring expression. Other considerations govern the level of specificity of non-referring expressions. For instance, in attributing membership of a category to some referent already identified, as in:

> A: What's that?
> B: It's an X.

the principal aim of B's answer would normally be to tell A something that he did not already know. So, for instance, if A and B were walking round the monkey-house at a zoo, then neither *It's an animal* nor *It's a monkey* would be likely to constitute a satisfactory answer to A's question. (Of course, matters are complicated considerably if, for instance, the

153

speaker is deliberately attempting to be droll; for the sake of simplicity, we shall confine our attention to situations of optimum banality.) Here, too, the situation sets a clear lower limit to level of specificity.

For the two types of expression discussed above, there is a functionally determined lower limit to specificity. There is, however, no comparable functionally determined upper bound to specificity, and the speaker has a certain amount of freedom in this respect. Generally speaking, except in special circumstances which will be detailed in a moment, overspecification throws into relief any semantic traits over and above the basic functionally prescribed minimum:

17. I was attacked by that huge black alsation he keeps in his garden.
18. I want that gold-plated quartz analogue watch you are wearing.

It is not being suggested that there are no constraints on overspecification: a person who consistently overspecifies runs a grave risk of being judged a pedant and bore. But the constraints are of a vaguer sort, and the penalties for infringement more peripheral.

There are two ways of increasing the specificity of an expression. The first is to add syntagmatic modifiers: *the book, the red book, the tattered red book, the tattered red book on the table in the hall*, etc. The second way of increasing specificity, and the one which more directly concerns us, is to replace one or more lexical items in an expression by hyponyms (including, of course, taxonyms): *It's an animal, It's a monkey, It's a colobus*. The second method is usually preferred if suitable lexical items exist (indeed, if the required extra specificity is of the taxonymic sort, then there is no choice).

We have seen that overspecification may be deliberately used for its semantic effects. According to what has been said so far, however, there appears to be no comparable role for underspecification, at least not within the framework of functional adequacy. As it happens, underspecification for special communicative effect is possible, due to certain characteristics of lexical items belonging to the generic level of a taxonomic hierarchy. We have already described these as being the 'normal, everyday names for things'. What this means can be made more precise: provided the basic functional requirements are met, a generic term produces an unmarked utterance (the rest of the sentence permitting) even when, from the strict functional point of view, it represents an overspecification. For instance, *I'm going to take the dog for a walk* would constitute a neutral statement of intention even in circumstances where *animal* would carry enough information for successful reference, as when spoken, say, by a person known to have only one domestic animal. An overspecifying generic term does not produce the characteristic effects of overspecification observable in 17 and 18.

There are two noteworthy consequences of this peculiar property of generic terms. The first is that a generic term can never be used as a marked overspecification: either it is neutral, or it is functionally an underspecification. The second consequence is that in a context where a generic term carries more information than is strictly necessary for successful reference, there exists a possibility of producing a marked, but functionally adequate, underspecification by using a superordinate of the generic term. So, for instance, the person with one pet can say, without fear of referential breakdown, *I'm going to take the animal for a walk*. But this is no longer neutral – to produce a neutral utterance, the speaker must use *dog*. The effect of avoiding the generic term in this way is often to add negative emotive overtones to the utterance.

It seems, then, that to account fully for the semantic contribution of certain lexical items to certain utterances in certain situations we need to know their location in a taxonomic hierarchy relative to the generic level. This is an inherent property of lexical items, and is not predictable from other aspects of meaning.

Notes

6.2 Taxonomic classification has been widely studied (see the references for 6.3), but to the best of my knowledge the conceptual distinction between hyponymy and taxonymy was first explicitly made in Cruse (1975).

1. A detailed discussion of nominal and natural kinds can be found in Pulman (1983: ch. 6). The expression *nominal kind* is from Schwartz (1979, 1980).
2. This is perhaps too strong: some may feel that a gelding is a male horse, but is not a stallion. (I am not sure about a 'regular' gelding, but I feel that a stallion that had lost his male attributes in an accident would still be a stallion – although a non-canonical one.) For the distinction being made here it is probably sufficient to think of equivalence in terms of canonical traits, rather than insisting on criterial equivalence.
3. For rigid designators see Kripke (1972).
4. I give here my own intuitions on the matter. However, I find that in an average class of students, about a third will have intuitions corresponding to mine, a third will feel strongly that there is no difference between *horse* and *stallion* – i.e. they are both rigid designators – while the remaining third will be unable to make up their minds.
5. Cf. Lyons (1981: 72–3).
6. Perhaps one should say *person with X-coloured hair*; these terms are used predominantly of female persons, but probably not necessarily.

7. For principles and theories of categorisation see Rosch (1973), Rosch and Mervis (1975), Rosch *et al.* (1976), Rosch (1978). For critical discussion of Rosch's ideas see Pulman (1983: ch. 4).

8. By *we* here I mean "we human beings". These statements must be interpreted metaphorically: I am not suggesting that individual persons consciously devise taxonomies in this way.

6.3 For discussion of folk taxonomies by anthropological linguists see Berlin, Breedlove and Raven (1973), Brown *et al.* (1976), Berlin (1978), Hunn (1983), Rhodes (1985). See also Pulman (1983: ch. 4). I have taken a number of examples from Rhodes.

9. Rhodes (1985).

10. Cf. Brown (1958).

11. See the characterisation of basic vocabulary items in Berlin and Kay (1969: 5–7).

12. I am assuming that *timepiece* (which in any event is somewhat archaic) does not cover, for instance, sundials.

13. See the references in note 7 above.

14. Rohdenburg (1985) describes this situation by saying that, say, *clothes* is capable of 'inclusive' reference to shoes, but not 'exclusive' reference.

15. From Rohdenburg (1985).

16. Although markedness is usually discussed only in connection with binary contrasts, it is arguable that these examples exemplify the same, or at least a closely similar, phenomenon. Many of the points made in chapter 11 concerning marked and unmarked terms are applicable here, too.

17. See Lehrer (1974) for a detailed study of cooking terms.

6.4 The topics of this section are discussed in greater detail in Cruse (1977).

18. Cf. Grice's 'Maxim of Quantity' (1975: 45–6).

7
Meronomies

7.1 Introductory: parts and pieces

The second major type of branching lexical hierarchy is the part–whole type, which we shall call meronomies.[1] It was suggested in chapter 6 that perhaps the classification of living things serves as a model for all natural language classifications. In a similar way, it is possible that originally the division of the human body into parts served as a prototype for all part–whole hierarchies:

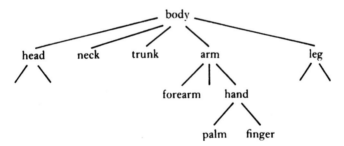

But it may well be that nowadays the structural make-up of a complex artefact such as a car forms a more significant prototype. Be that as it may, there is no doubt of the central importance of fully integrated and cohesive physical objects, with well-differentiated parts, in the concepts of "part" and "whole". We shall accordingly, at least to begin with, confine our attention to these. In this section we shall take an informal look at some of the characteristics of parts and wholes. Let us first consider some of the differences between the notion of "piece" and the notion of "part".

Suppose someone were to take a hacksaw and cut, say, a typewriter into a number of arbitrary portions. While these portions could properly be referred to as *pieces* of the typewriter, they would not normally be said to be *parts* of the typewriter; reducing a complex artefact to its parts (confusingly called 'taking it to pieces') normally requires the undoing

157

of screws and other means of attachment. The contrast between parts and pieces is potentially operative even with highly integrated wholes such as animal bodies: there is a clear difference between such a body hacked to pieces, and one carefully dissected into its parts.

Any potential piece is spatially included within its whole (of course, once the potentiality is actualised, and the potential piece becomes a piece, it is no longer included within its whole). But this is not sufficient to qualify a particular quantity of previously included substance for the label *piece*. First, the notion of a piece presupposes the notion of topological stability – one cannot have a piece of steam, for instance. Second, a piece must be spatially continuous; that is to say, it must be possible, at least in principle, to move from any point within a piece to any other point within the same piece, without being forced at any time to traverse material not belonging to the piece, or to cross empty space.

The relation "– piece of –" is transitive, asymmetric and catenary; furthermore, it is inherently differentiated. The sawing operation could be carried out on the resulting pieces of the typewriter, and the process repeated, in principle, indefinitely; and at no point could any piece be said to be a piece of two different pre-existing pieces, except when one of those two pieces resulted from the cutting up of the other. The relation is thus capable of generating a well-formed, branching hierarchy, whose nodes are separated in time (the claimed pieces of the True Cross, if genuine, would constitute such a hierarchy). It is not, however, capable of giving rise to a lexical hierarchy, because there is no reason, unless one be imposed in an ad hoc fashion, why an arbitrary division of one whole should yield pieces in any way analogous to the pieces resulting from a similarly arbitrary division of another whole of the same type. Such constraints as there are on what constitutes a piece allow every individual whole to be partitioned in a different way. Pieces, therefore, do not fall into sub-classes with sufficient constancy of attributes to qualify for lexical labels.

We have seen that sawn-off bits of a typewriter do not constitute, except accidentally, parts of the typewriter. What, then, are the characteristics of parts, and how do they differ from pieces? Still thinking about central instances of the part–whole relation, we can say, first of all, that parts share with pieces the characteristics of topological stability and spatial continuity; both also have a determinate topological relationship with their wholes, and with their sister parts.

Turning now to differences, it seems that a typical part is distinguished from a piece by three main characteristics: autonomy, non-arbitrary boundaries and determinate function with respect to the whole. Take first the feature of autonomy. Something described as 'a piece of an X' must once have formed an integral constituent of a properly constituted X; a piece of a typewriter must once have been incorporated in an actual typewriter – an exact replica of such a piece would not itself count as a piece of the typewriter. This is not true, in principle, of a part, except contingently, as with, for instance, the parts of the human body (and even that may change one day!). Thus, the items in a display cabinet labelled 'The parts of a typewriter' need never have belonged to the same, or, indeed, any, actual typewriter; furthermore, exact copies of them would count equally well as parts. (Notice that this means that *part* is not a hyponym of *piece*.)

The second characteristic feature of parts is that their boundaries are motivated. A part is normally delimited from its sister parts by a (relative) discontinuity of some sort. It is therefore often possible to point to the parts of an assembled whole (the notion of pointing to the pieces of an integral whole is somewhat nonsensical). The extreme case is when a part is completely detachable, like the wheel of a car. Less extreme, but still clear cases might involve the mobility of a comparatively rigid portion relative to another more-or-less rigid portion. For instance, several parts of the human body are delimited by joints: the *thigh* by *hip* and *knee*, and the *forearm* by *elbow* and *wrist*. Or a relatively extended region may be connected to another relatively extended region by a narrow 'bridge', the latter forming a boundary between parts: such is the case with *leaf* and *branch* or *twig*. In this case, the bridge region is considered to form part of the leaf, perhaps because in deciduous plants it falls with the leaf-blade in autumn. (An interesting question is why the elements of a jigsaw should be called pieces, rather than parts. It is perhaps because the divisions are totally unmotivated with respect to the picture that they go to make up.)

The third characteristic feature of parts is the possession of a definite function relative to their wholes; obvious examples are: *eye* for seeing, *brake* for stopping, *handle* for carrying, *spout* for pouring. Function can sometimes delimit a part when there is no obvious discontinuity, as with the *tip* of the *tongue*.

So far we have been discussing the nature and characteristics of parts, their relations with wholes, and their distinction from pieces. We must now turn to a consideration of the lexical items used to designate parts and wholes, and the semantic relations between them. The semantic relation between a lexical item denoting a part and that denoting the corresponding whole will be termed **meronymy**; we shall give the name

159

†**co-meronymy** to the relation between lexical items designating sister parts. Although there is an intimate connection between an extra-linguistic part–whole hierarchy and the corresponding lexical hierarchy, the two are nonetheless distinct, and must not be confused. In many cases, the two hierarchies are not isomorphous. The human body meronomy, for instance, has only one node for *arm* and one for *leg*; but the corresponding extra-linguistic part–whole hierarchy has two nodes for each. It is necessary to distinguish, therefore, between two different sorts of lexical hierarchy consisting of lexical items referring to parts. There is first of all a true meronomy, whose structure is determined by purely linguistic criteria; and there is what might be called a †**labelled part–whole hierarchy** which is formally identical to the corresponding extra-linguistic hierarchy. Our concern will for the most part be with true meronomies.

7.2 Defining meronymy

Meronymy is subject to a greater number of complicating factors than taxonomic relations are; instead of there being a single clearly distinguished relation, there is in reality a numerous family of more-or-less similar relations. In this section we shall deal with what may be regarded as the central, or ideal, meronymic relationship, and the complications which arise from the factors of optionality and necessity, lack of congruence, and from the existence of sense spectra. This will enable us to define a fairly cohesive core group of relations. A number of more distant relatives of meronymy will be discussed in 7.5.

We shall begin by considering a definition of meronymy which is undoubtedly too restrictive, in that it excludes some intuitively clear examples of the part–whole relation, but which characterises what we shall take to be the central variety of the lexical relation:

X is a meronym of Y if and only if sentences of the form *A Y has Xs/an X* and *An X is a part of a Y* are normal when the noun phrases *an X, a Y* are interpreted generically.

Virtually all word pairs which one would wish to recognise as having a meronymic relation will yield normal sentences in the test-frame *A Y has Xs/an X*:

> A hand has fingers.
> A piano has a keyboard.
> A car has wheels.
> A saw has teeth.
> A book has pages.

On its own, however, the frame is too generous, as it accepts any characteristic attributes, and not only parts:

> A wife has a husband.
> A sound has a pitch and a volume.

(It is possible that *have* is ambiguous, but this is extremely difficult to demonstrate convincingly.) The second frame, *An X is a part of a Y*, also leaks:

> A huge bank balance is a part of his attractiveness to women.
> Changing nappies/diapers is part of being a mother.

Only meronyms, however, will satisfy both frames:

> ? A husband is a part of a wife.
> ? A volume is a part of a sound.
> ? His attractiveness to women has a bank balance.
> ? Being a mother has changing nappies.
> A hand has fingers.
> A finger is a part of a hand.

Although the two-part test gives a fair guarantee of a meronymic relationship in word pairs which satisfy it, it excludes intuitively clear cases of parts and wholes:

1a. ? A handle is a part of a bag.
 b. ? A bag has a handle.
2a. A sepal is a part of a flower.
 b. ? A flower has sepals.
3a. ? A root is a part of a word.
 b. ? A word has a root.

A test-frame which does not leak, and which accepts all the above cases, is:

> *The parts of a Y include the X/Xs, the Z/Zs, etc.*
> The parts of a flower include the sepals, the petals, . . .
> The parts of a word include the root, . . .
> The parts of a door include the handle, the lock, . . .

(These examples are also normal in *the X and other parts of a Y*.) We shall take it that this test establishes a significant family of relations, and we shall examine three factors which govern the different results obtained with it and with the stricter two-part test.

The first of these factors is the optionality or necessity of the relation. The reason 1b is odd while *A hand has fingers* is normal is that a *handle* is an option for a door, whereas *fingers* are necessary to a *hand*. The notion of necessity appropriate here is not the logical necessity which manifests itself in entailment. It is not logically necessary for a human body, for instance, to have two ears; after Van Gogh had cut off one of his ears, he still had a body, and the detached ear was still an ear. But his body was thenceforward defective (and so, in a sense, was the ear). We shall speak in such cases of canonical necessity, and describe *ear* as a canonical meronym of *body*, and *body* as a canonical **holonym** of *ear*. A truly optional relationship, like that between *door* and *handle*, will be termed **facultative**: *handle* is thus a facultative meronym of *door*. Both facultativity and canonicity may be either unilateral or bilateral; this gives rise to the following variant relations between a meronym X and a holonym Y:

I.   X is a canonical meronym of Y; Y is a canonical holonym of X

II.   X is a canonical meronym of Y; Y is a facultative holonym of X

III.   X is a facultative meronym of Y; Y is a canonical holonym of X

IV.   X is a facultative meronym of Y; Y is a facultative holonym of X

It is variant I which is selected by the stricter of the two tests for meronymy given earlier. It is exemplified by *finger* and *hand*; *finger* may thus be described as a bilaterally canonical meronym of *hand*. Variant II is the rarest of the four. Convincing examples are hard to find, but the sort of relationship envisaged here is something like that between a lichen and either its algal or fungal component. A lichen is a symbiotic association between a fungus and an alga, and requires both; but the two components are each capable of living as free organisms in their own right, and their association to form a lichen is thus optional. We may therefore say that *fungus* is a unilaterally canonical meronym of *lichen*, and *lichen* is a unilaterally facultative holonym of *fungus* (I have made the simplifying assumption that any fungus can associate with any alga: this is not, in fact, the case). Variant III is also fairly rare in its strictest form, although it is more common between items which are not congruent (see below). It is exemplified by *leader* and *newspaper*: it is open to any *newspaper* to have, or not to have, a *leader*, but *leader* (in the relevant sense) only occurs as part of a *newspaper*. *Newspaper* is therefore a unilaterally canonical holonym of *leader*. Variant IV, a bilaterally facultative relation, is the weakest of the set, and perhaps only marginally deserves to be considered a lexical relation at all. Take the relationship between *university* and *museum*: any university is free in principle to have a museum, and any museum could in principle stand as an autonomous whole in its own right. Neither a university without a museum, nor a museum that is not part of a university, can be considered defective. The only motivation for recognising a sense relation between *university* and *museum* would be to account for the normality of sentences such as *The museum is a part of the university* and *The university has a museum* in their non-generic interpretation (but not, it must be emphasised, *? A museum is a part of a university*). The case for recognising a lexical relation would be stronger if we insisted on an expected relationship, at least in one direction. Such is not the case with *university* and *museum*, but it is arguably the case with *university* and *medical school*:

It's a university, but it doesn't have a medical school.
It's a medical school, but it isn't part of a university.

It would perhaps be more appropriate to describe *medical school* as a para-meronym of *university* (it will be recalled that para-relations are defined on expectation rather than necessity).

The second factor which prevents pairs of lexical items passing the stricter test for meronymy is mis-match in respect of congruence. Of the four congruence relations, disjunction is not applicable to meronymy, but the other three are. Our discussion so far has presumed full congruence. We are therefore concerned here with inclusion and overlap. Inclusion can manifest itself in one of two ways. First, the meronym may be more general than the holonym, in that without ambiguity it stands in the same relation to at least one other holonym. An example of this is *nail* and *toe*. *A toe has a nail* is normal, but *A nail is a part of a toe* is not, because a nail might equally be a finger-nail: *nail* is thus more general than *toe*. Following the convention established in chapter 4, therefore, we may say that *nail* is a super-meronym of *toe*, which entails that *toe* is a hypo-holonym of *nail*. (Taking account of the matters discussed in the previous paragraph, a fuller specification of the relation between *toe* and *nail* would be that *nail* is a bilaterally canonical super-meronym of *toe*.) Super-meronyms are quite common; other examples are *page*:*book* and *wick*:*candle*. The second possibility is for the holonym to be the more inclusive term in a mis-matched pair. This relationship can manifest itself in one of two ways which we shall not distinguish terminologically. Take the case of *sepal* and *flower*. At first sight this may appear to be a case of optionality: a flower may or may not have sepals. However, this is not an option for particular flowers, in the way that any man may choose to have, or not to have, a beard: for a given species of flower, sepals are either canonically present, or canonically absent. Thus, *flower* is more inclusive than *sepal*, and covers cases which have sepals, and those which do not. Since, as we have already seen, a sepal is necessarily a part of a flower, we must therefore describe *flower* as a bilaterally canonical super-holonym of *sepal*. In the other variety of super-holonym, some members of the class of wholes have one sort of part, while others have a different part in a structurally analogous position; this is exemplified by *body* in relation to *penis* and *vagina*. A possible example of a non-congruent pair involving a facultative relation is *beard* and *face*: a beard is an option only for some faces (i.e. men's), but a face is necessary to a beard, so *beard* is a unilaterally facultative hypo-meronym of *face*, and *face* a unilaterally canonically super-holonym of *beard*. (It is possible, however, that *beard* is more accurately described as an attachment of *face* – see next section.) Strictly speaking, *lichen* is a unilaterally facultative hypo-holonym of *fungus*, since not all fungi enter into a symbiotic relation with an alga. The other type of non-congruent relationship applicable to meronymy is the overlapping sort. Consider the relation between *stalk* and *leaf*; not all leaves have stalks, and flowers, as well as leaves, may have stalks. *Stalk* must therefore be described as a semi-meronym of *leaf* (of the bilaterally canonical variety).

A third factor which interferes with the stricter test for meronymy is the existence of sense-spectra with local senses. Take the example of *handle*. To some extent, *handle* behaves like a super-meronym of, say, *door*, since *the handles of doors and drawers* is normal. But this is normal only because the local senses are close to one another. If the argument in chapter 3 is correct, there is no superordinate meaning for all uses of *handle*. It would therefore be more accurate to describe *handle* as a local meronym of *door* (*door* and the local sense of *handle* are congruent). We shall recognise super-relations only when there is a true superordinate meaning. Relations involving local senses may, of course, vary along the dimension of necessity; so, for instance, *handle* is a canonical local meronym of *spoon*, but a facultative local meronym of *door*, since there is no spoon without a handle, but handle-less doors are quite common. (To indicate that a homeless door-handle is non-canonical, and that *door* serves to locate the local sense of *handle*, *door* can be described as a canonical locating holonym of *handle*.)

One more type of part–whole relation remains to be considered under the present heading. It is exemplified by the relation between *blade* and *leaf*. What is peculiar about this relation is that a blade may constitute either part of a leaf (if the leaf has a stalk) or the entire leaf (if the leaf is without a stalk). We shall call this relationship †**holo-meronymy**: *blade* may therefore be described as **holo-meronym** of the holonym *leaf*. Holo-meronymy must not be confused with the relation between a fungus and a lichen, where a fungus may either exist independently, or as part of a lichen; or with the relation between a museum, which may constitute an autonomous whole, and, say, a university of which it may form part. The point is that a fungus cannot, on its own, constitute a lichen, nor can a museum, on its own, constitute a university; whereas a blade can, on its own, constitute the whole of a leaf.[2]

7.3 Aspects of transitivity: integral parts and attachments

Hyponymy is an unproblematically transitive relation: it follows from the fact that a spaniel is necessarily a dog, and a dog necessarily an animal, that a spaniel is necessarily an animal. Taxonymy is less clear, but it seems better to treat it as intransitive: it seems misleading to describe a spaniel as a type of animal. Meronymy is more complicated, as in most other respects. Notice, first, that the relation "– piece of –" is, like hyponymy, straightforwardly transitive: a piece of a piece of the True Cross is still a piece of the True Cross, and will be confidently expected by the faithful to have the same miraculous properties. The complications, in other words, are strictly a property of parts.

There are two causes of 'failure' of the transitivity of the part–whole relation, which may in some instances be simultaneously operative. The first involves the notion of †**functional domain**. Consider the sentences in 4 and 5:

4a. The jacket has sleeves.
 b. The sleeves have cuffs.
 c. The jacket has cuffs.
5a. The house has a door.
 b. The door has a handle.
 c. ? The house has a handle.

Why is 4(c) a valid conclusion from 4(a) and 4(b), while 5(c) is not a valid conclusion from 5(a) and 5(b)?[3] (Sentence 5(c) is also odd, but this is not the problem: normality and logical validity are two different things. The reason 5(c) is odd is that ordinary houses do not usually have handles.

165

The doll's house has a handle, for instance, is relatively normal, but is still not a valid conclusion from *The doll's house has a door* and *The door has a handle*.) The answer involves two facts about *handle*.

As we have already noted, a part typically has a more or less determinate function with respect to some whole. The more inclusive element within which the part functions may be termed its functional domain. For instance, a typical function of a handle is to enable something to be moved by hand; the functional domain of such a handle is whatever moves when appropriate manual force is applied to it. A functional domain may be restricted or generalised. The functional domain of a handle, for instance, is typically restricted. A door-handle, say, serves to open and close a door; but although the door may be part of something larger, like a house, the door-handle does not have any direct function with respect to this. The functional meaning of *handle*, in other words, does not transfer to nodes higher up the hierarchy than the one immediately dominating it. *Handle* may be contrasted in this respect with *cuff*, which has a generalised functional domain. The difference is that the function of a cuff is mainly a decorative one, which it fulfils equally with respect to *sleeve* and *jacket*. In other words, the functional aspects of the meaning of *cuff* are effectively transitive.

The second significant fact about *handle* is that its functional domain is established only with reference to specific contexts. Many parts have their functional domains encapsulated within their meanings. We know that *stamens* function with respect to *flowers*, and *fingers* with respect to *hands*; specifying the domain in such cases gives rise to redundancy: *? flower-stamen*, *? hand-finger*, etc. *Handle*, however, since it forms part of a sense-spectrum, has a multitude of different possible functional domains. In any actual occurrence, the domain is fixed by the context, as part of the local sense. In particular, in an expression of the form *The X has a handle*, X will be taken as the functional domain of *handle* (at least in the absence of a more powerful indication). Hence, *handle* in *The house has a handle* can only with great difficulty (if at all) be taken to refer to the door-handle, but must be interpreted as referring to a house-handle. It will be appreciated that this in itself would not cause a breakdown in transitivity were it not for the fact that the functional domain of *handle* is restricted. If the door of a house incorporated, say, a bronze relief by Ghiberti, like the doors of the Baptistery in Florence, it would be much less odd to say *This house has a bronze relief by Ghiberti*. Notice, too, that the functional domain can also be indicated by Y in an expression of the form *the Y-handle*; in an expression of the form *The X has a Y-*

handle, the more intimate connection between Y and *handle* will result in Y being taken as the functional domain of *handle*. This has the effect, as it were, of liberating X from the functional aspects of *handle*, so that *The house has door-handles* (or better still, *The house has porcelain door-handles*) is relatively normal.

Transitivity failures are also caused by a special type of part which we shall term an †**attachment**.[4] Attachments have two defining characteristics. First, it must be normal to describe them as being attached to some larger entity (which we shall call the †**stock**):

> A hand is attached to an arm.
> The handle is attached to the door.
> The ears are attached to the head.

It is odd to refer to **integral parts** (i.e. those which are not attachments) in this way:

> ? The palm is attached to the hand.
> ? The handle is attached to the spoon.

(Whether *handle* is an attachment or not depends on its local sense in particular contexts.) Secondly, attachments must satisfy our criteria for parts:

> A hand is a part of an arm.
> An arm has a hand.
> The parts of the arm are: the upper arm, the elbow, the
>   forearm, the wrist and the hand.

The wholeness of an entity is destroyed if an integral part is missing, but this is not necessarily true if the missing part is an attachment:

> A: Did you find the whole arm?
> B: (i) Yes, but the hand was missing.
>   (ii) ? Yes, but the forearm was missing.

An attachment is, however, typically an integral part of the overall whole, so that, for instance, a human body cannot be described as complete if the hands are missing, nor can the hands be described as being attached to the body.

There is a difference between integral parts and attachments with regard to certain aspects of transitivity. Certain predicates, if applied to an integral part of something, necessarily apply also to the whole:

> *I touched her elbow* entails *I touched her arm*
> *The table-leg was damaged* entails *The table was damaged*
> *There were burns on his fingers* entails *There were burns on his hands*

When such predicates are applied to an attachment, however, they do not necessarily apply to the whole, although with one exception they are not excluded:

> His arm was unhurt, but there were burns on his hand.
> The door was clean, but the handle was contaminated.

The exception is that a part of an attachment does not count as a part of the stock; hence *finger*, for instance, does not count as part of *arm*:

> ? An arm has fingers.
> ? A finger is a part of an arm.

The part relation is transitive, however, where integral parts are concerned; in other words, if X is an integral part of Y, then a part of X will also count as a part of Y. This can be illustrated with *knee-cap*, *knee* and *leg*. Since *knee* is an integral part of *leg* (? *The knee is attached to the leg*), *knee-cap*, which is a part of *knee*, counts also as a part of *leg*:

> A knee-cap is a part of a leg.
> A leg has a knee-cap.

7.4 Characteristics of meronomies

A well-formed part–whole hierarchy should consist of elements of the same general type. It is not immediately clear how to articulate this notion precisely, but it is easy to see that some such concept is necessary. If one element in a meronomy denotes a cohesive physical object, for instance, then all the other items in the set must too (for instance, the *weight* of a *body* does not figure among its parts); if one item refers to a geographical area, so must all the others (hence Westminster Abbey is not a part of London); if one item is an abstract noun, all the others must be as well – and so on. This principle helps to explain why there are numerous limited meronomies, instead of just one, with *universe* as its most inclusive element, and some sort of sub-atomic particle or particles at the lower bound. Consider the most familiar sort of meronymy – the one with *body* as its origin. Why does the hierarchy go no higher? To perhaps *family*, then *population*, *terrestrial biomass*, ...? What qualifies *body* to be considered a WHOLE? Part of the answer is that *body* is the most inclusive entity encompassing *finger, leg, head*, etc. that is of the appropriate type. Going from *body* to *family*, for instance, would mean a change from a cohesive physical object to an entity with no physical cohesiveness whatsoever, constituted by a set of invisible relationships. Families do have parts, of course, but these are persons, not bodies.

We have seen that a well-formed taxonomic hierarchy must preserve a constant principle of differentiation throughout. This feature has a meronymic parallel. Consider the ways of dividing the human body. We can either divide it into parts such as *trunk, head, limbs*, etc., or we can equally validly divide it in quite another way, into *skeleton, muscles, nerves, blood vessels*, etc. Parts of the first type have a greater degree of spatial cohesiveness, and presumably, also, perceptual salience (when viewed from the outside, at any rate). They will be called †**segmental parts**; as we traverse a whole along its major spatial axes, we typically encounter the segmental parts sequentially. Parts of the second type have a greater functional unity, a greater consistency of internal constitution, but they are spatially inter-penetrating, running along the major axes of the body. These will be termed †**systemic parts**. Each of these principles of division is as valid as the other, but it seems that ordinary language has a preference for segmental parts. Many wholes can be partitioned in ways parallel to the human body. A *house*, for instance, may be divided into *living-room, dining-room, kitchen, hall, bedrooms, cellar, loft*, etc. (segmental parts); or *brickwork, joinery, plasterwork, plumbing, wiring*, etc. (systemic parts – notice that these are quasi-meronyms of *house*, because they are mass nouns, whereas *house* is a count noun). The case of *house* (and other buildings) is further complicated by the fact that the segmental parts can be seen either in terms of spaces (e.g. rooms), or in terms of the structural elements which define those spaces (for instance, the *walls, floors* and *ceilings* are also parts of a *house*). Whatever type of division is adopted for a particular hierarchy, it must remain constant throughout the structure. One must not, for instance, if one is partitioning the *body*, on reaching *finger* go on to *bone, muscle* and *nerve* – even though fingers can be so divided – as this would not preserve constancy. (There are other reasons, of course, for not going beyond *finger*: the lexical items available (*bone*, etc.) refer to parts which are not confined to the finger. But presumably there do exist scientific names for these particular bones, muscles, etc.; these, however, would not do, either.)

The relation of meronymy is not an ideal guarantor of a well-formed hierarchy, unlike taxonymy. It is, of course, differentiable, but unlike the extra-linguistic part–whole relation, is not inherently differentiated.

169

That is to say, convergence cannot be ruled out unless certain restrictions are placed on the participants in a hierarchy. The trouble arises out of the existence of super- and hypo-relations, in particular super-meronyms like *nail*:

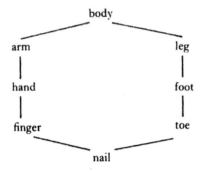

In the corresponding extra-linguistic hierarchy there is, of course, no convergence, because the finger-nails and the toe-nails are different parts; but the same lexical item is used to refer to them, so the lexical hierarchy does converge. (Convergence due to sense-spectra can be avoided by insisting that the elements in the hierarchy be local senses; this escape-route is not available, however, for genuine super-meronyms.) To secure a well-formed hierarchy we would have to confine the elements to congruent pairs – every meronym should be congruent with its holonym. Doing this, however, would exclude many normal part names; it would seem better to accept that meronomies may not be perfect hierarchies. The phenomenon of non-congruent relations also allows meronomies to intersect. A striking case of this is provided by the male and female human body meronomies. Strictly speaking, there are two separate meronomies for males and females, which intersect heavily – they even share the most inclusive element *body*. It is noteworthy that intersection between part–whole hierarchies is by and large a purely lexical phenomenon: actual sharing of parts between extra-linguistic wholes seems rare, except as an abnormality, as in Siamese twins.

Meronomies typically have rather weakly developed substantive levels. The properties which give rise to equi-level intuitions seem usually to be analogous (or homologous) structure or function, and perhaps also size-range. In the human body-meronomy, for instance, where levels are relatively well-developed, the homologies between *arm* and *leg* give rise to the feeling that not only *arm* and *leg*, but also *hand* and *foot*, and *finger* and *toe* are equi-level. (In English this is reinforced by the existence of the term *limb*, which covers *arm* and *leg*; many languages designate the toes by an expression which is the equivalent of *foot-fingers* – apparently none, though, refer to the fingers as 'hand-toes', presumably because of the psychological primacy of the hand.)[5] There are, however, no homologies between the head and the arm, for instance, so that intuitions as to whether, say, the ear-lobes and the fingers are at the same hierarchical level are, to say the least, uncertain.

The existence of gaps (i.e. covert categories) was noted for taxonomic hierarchies: it was most frequently either the origin or one or more kind terms which were found to be missing. In the case of meronomies, the most inclusive term is never covert: there are no meronomies of unnamed wholes. One type of covert part does however occur relatively frequently: there often is no separate name for the major, essential functional part, especially of artefacts. Take the example of *spoon*. A spoon has a *handle*, but what do we call the other part, which corresponds to the *blade* of a *knife*? Informants when questioned about this usually search for a while, then either say, 'But that is the spoon,' or suggest something like *bowl*. But this, while fairly apt, is obviously an ad hoc creation – there simply is no everyday name. Another example is *fork*. This also has a handle, but again there is no name for the rest. It might be suggested that the *prongs* constitute the rest; but this is not quite right – the part of a fork excluding the handle bears some resemblance to a hand, and the prongs are analogous to fingers, but there is no name for the fork analogue of *hand*. Or take a *teapot*, whose parts are *handle*, *spout* and *lid* – but what about the bit in the middle which holds the tea? Again, informants tend to say, 'But that is the teapot.' Sometimes *body* is suggested. This is interesting; presumably the analogy is with *body* in the sense of "trunk", with *handle*, *spout*, etc. being seen as analogues of limbs. In a not dissimilar situation, *body* has developed two distinct senses, as in *The body of a man was found in the shed* and *There were burns on his arms and legs, but none on his body*. (That this is true ambiguity is shown by the interpretability of *The body found in the woods had tatoos all over the body*, and the zeugmatic nature of *? The body found in the woods had tattoos all over it, but had none on the arms or legs*; compare these with the relative uninterpretability of *? The human arm found in the woods had tattoos all over the arm*, and the non-zeugmatic nature of *The arm found in the woods had tattoos all over it, but had none of the hand*.) One wonders why a similar development has not occurred with *teapot, fork, spoon* and, indeed, *arm*.

7.5 Close relatives of the part–whole relation

Up to now we have been more or less concentrating on the central instances of part and whole, which we have taken to be well-differentiated parts of clearly individuated and cohesive physical objects (and even with these restrictions a considerable number of variations have been observed). In reality, however, these central instances of the relation are only imperfectly distinguishable from other members of a cluster of roughly similar relations; the central instances, in other words, shade off imperceptibly into less central and ultimately peripheral instances. The whole area is extremely diffuse and complex. An attempt will be made in this section to isolate the main dimensions of variation, and to identify the most salient near-relatives of the core part–whole relation.

A number of dimensions of variation can be identified which correlate with centrality and peripherality in part-like relations. One such dimension is concreteness: *bodies*, *trees*, *cars* and *teapots* are concrete, but one may also speak of parts of non-concrete entities such as events, actions, processes, states, and abstract nominal notions like *adolescence* and *courage*. A second dimension of variation is the degree of differentiation amongst parts: the parts of a *body*, or *car*, are highly differentiated; the parts (i.e. members) of a *team* may or may not be clearly differentiated, but in general will be less so than the parts of a body; the parts of a unit of measure such as *hour*, *metre*, or *pound* are not differentiated at all. A third dimension of variation is structural integration: the *members* of a *team* are more integrated than the *stones* in a *heap*, or the *books* in a *library*, but are less so than the parts of a body. Degree of integration, we may take it, correlates with centrality. The fourth factor we shall consider is whether the items in a relationship are count nouns or mass nouns; this presumably reflects degree of individuation. In almost all the part–whole pairs we have discussed up to now, both meronym and holonym have been count nouns. But there are part-like relations where one or both terms are mass nouns: *The car is part steel* (whole = count, part = mass); *Sand consists of grains* (whole = mass, part = count); *Milk is an ingredient of custard* (whole = mass, part = mass).

We shall begin our survey of meronym-like relations by looking at relations between non-concrete entities. Quite close to concrete parts are places situated within the boundaries of other places, such as *France : Europe*. These are often well-differentiated, and can give rise to well-formed branching hierarchies:

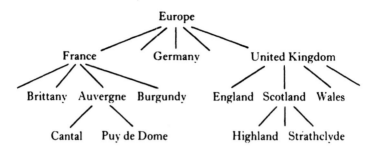

They display some of the typical contextual properties of parts:

> France is a part of Europe.
> The parts of Europe are: France, Belgium, Holland, etc.

but not all:

> ? Europe has France, Belgium, etc.

From the point of view of lexical semantics, parts such as these are of less significance, because they are really pieces, in our terminology, rather than parts with properties which can be generalised to delimit parts of other wholes of the same type. They are accordingly designated by proper nouns rather than common nouns. There are, however, cases which more closely approach the concrete part–whole pattern – perhaps they should be included in this category. The relation between *capital* and *country* is an example:

> A capital is a part of a country.
> A country has a capital.

Likewise, a *city* or *town* has a *centre*, and possibly also a *red-light district*, and so forth. (*Capital* can be more precisely characterised as a super-meronym of *country*, as *empires*, *provinces* and *states* (of the U.S.A.) also have capitals; *centre* on the other hand, is a local meronym.)

Entities with a temporal structure may also have parts. Most of these fall into the category of event nouns, which may be recognised by the fact that they occur normally in the frame *The X* + (*be*) = (*time expression*):

> The concert was yesterday.
> The next performance is at 7.30.

They also typically *occur, take place, coincide*, can be *cancelled, postponed, delayed* and *brought forward*. Many event nouns are clearly derived

173

from verbs: *performance, arrival, killing, initiation*; others are not: *birthday, Christmas, concert, match, ceremony*. Verbs which give rise to event nouns refer typically to either **activities** (broadly, things that one 'does') or **processes** (roughly, changes of state that 'happen to' people or things). Activities may be further sub-divided into **accomplishments** (verbs which, like *cough, kick, hop,* typically receive an iterative interpretation in the frame *He started X-ing*); **actions** (verbs which are not interpreted iteratively in *He started X-ing,* but are not normal in *He almost X-ed*: *He started playing the violin,* ? *He almost played the violin*); and **achievements** (verbs which resemble actions but which are normal in *He almost X-ed*: *He has almost learnt to play the violin*).[6] Any entity which has a differentiated temporal structure (i.e. at least a beginning, a middle, and an end) may have segmental or systemic (parallel) parts, the former being the more usual. In the case of nouns derived from process, achievement, or accomplishment verbs, it may be more normal to refer to the parts (if they are segmental) as stages or phases. Actions, which have no temporal structure, can only have systemic parts. The following exemplify some of the possibilities; first, segmental parts:

> The most popular part of the show is the strip-tease.
> The parts of the show are: the strip-tease, . . .
> The show has a strip-tease.
> The run-up, the delivery, and the follow-through are parts/ phases/stages of the action of bowling.
> The phases of the action of bowling are: the run-up, . . .
> ? The action of bowling has a run-up, . . .

second, systemic parts:

> The most extraordinary part of the show was the decor.
> ? The parts of the show are: the decor, . . .
> Learning to control oneself is a part of growing up.
> ? The parts of growing up are: learning to control oneself, . . .
> Bowing is the most difficult part of playing the violin.
> ? The parts of playing the violin are: bowing, fingering, . . .

Abstract objects which are realised as a temporal sequence, such as *opera, symphony, play,* or *ballet,* often have clear (usually segmental) parts. A *symphony,* for instance, usually has *movements,* some of which have differentiated labels: *slow movement, scherzo, finale* (these are strictly supermeronyms, since they also potentially have *concerto* and *sonata* as their holonyms); *movements* themselves may have distinguished parts: *introduc-*

174

tion, exposition, development, recapitulation, coda. Plays and *operas* are typically divided into *acts* and *scenes*, and *poems* are often divided into *stanzas*. Different acts, scenes and stanzas are normally distinguished by numbers, rather than names. The fact that major musical forms often have named parts presumably testifies to the tighter formal constraints under which composers typically work.

Non-temporal states and qualities may be described as having parts:

> Being slim is part of being fit.
> Self-control is part of maturity.

But these are very peripheral and do not display other typical contextual characteristics of parts:

> ? Maturity has self-control.
> ? The parts of maturity are: self-control, . . .

Even more peripheral are what might be called features of events, states, etc. These can be referred to as parts, but they are characterised by a type discrepancy, and are more normally called **features**:

> Christmas pudding is a part (feature) of Christmas.
> Changing nappies/diapers is a part (feature) of being a
>   mother.
> Rebelliousness is a part (feature) of adolescence.

Units of measure and their sub-units constitute a special class of abstract part-wholes, one of whose characteristics is a total lack of differentiation. They do not strictly belong in this chapter as they give rise only to non-branching hierarchies; they are more fully discussed in the next chapter, and are mentioned here purely for the sake of completeness.

Entities such as groups, classes and collections stand in relations which resemble meronymy with their constituent elements. These entities are essentially collectivities, in that their ultimate parts are elements which themselves, under another aspect, are independent wholes of the more basic sort. They are less structurally integrated than typical physical objects, and their parts are often less differentiated, too. We shall begin with what will be termed the †**group-member** relation. Groups seem to be largely restricted to associations of human beings; examples are: *tribe, team, cabinet, committee, family, orchestra, jury, squad, audience,* etc. Most groups have no specific lexical items to designate their members; a few, however, do: *tribe : tribesman, jury : juror/juryman, senate : senator.* The distinguishing characteristics of group nouns in English are, first, that in the singular they can contract singular or plural concord with a verb:

The tribe/jury/team/family is/are under investigation.

and, second, they occur normally in the plural:

Of all the tribes/juries/families I have known, this one is the oddest.

They designate groupings which have a purpose or function: the members are not associated merely because they share certain attributes. Members of groups display some of the properties of parts:

A juror is a part of the jury.
A jury has jurors.

but not all:

? The parts of a jury are the jurors.

More distantly related to partonymy is a relation which we shall call the †**class-member relation**. It is exemplified by such pairs as *proletariat*: *worker*, *clergy*: *bishop*, *aristocracy*: *duke*, etc. What we shall call a †**class** is an assemblage of humans justified more by the possession of common attributes than a common purpose; a class is thus less organically cohesive than a group, and its members less like true parts:

A bishop is a part of the clergy.
? The clergy has bishops.
? The parts of the clergy are: the bishops, the archbishops, . . .

Class nouns are generally uncomfortable with the plural inflection: *proletariats*, *clergies*, *aristocracies*, and prefer plural concord with a verb: *The clergy were (was?) unhappy with the decision*.

Yet another relation involving a collectivity is the †**collection-member** relation. Collections are typically inanimate: *heap*, *forest*, *wardrobe* (in the sense of "collection of clothes"), *library* (in the sense of "collection of books"). The members of collections are not normally lexically distinguished (I know of no example in English): the relation from member to collection (*tree*:*forest*, *book*:*library*, *stone*:*heap*) is therefore facultative. The converse relation is sometimes necessary, as in *forest*:*tree* and *library*:*book*; but the relation between *stone* and *heap*, for instance, is bilaterally facultative. Collection nouns occur readily in the plural, but when singular cannot contract plural concord with the verb:

*His library are in excellent condition.
*The forest have been felled.

Terms referring to groups of animals seem to be poised between group and collection. My intuitions are that *The herd are grazing* is slightly odd, but that *The (wolf) pack have succeeded in cornering the stag* is not, perhaps because of the hint of human-like cooperation.

There is a family of relations involved with what things are made of, the part-like component being a mass noun denoting a substance or material. In cases where the whole is also a mass noun, we may speak of **constituents** or **ingredients**. The distinction between these two is basically that the ingredients of X are the substances that one starts out with when one prepares X, whereas the constituents of X are the substances which enter into the final composition of X. The ingredients and constituents of X may, or may not, be the same. If they are the same, *ingredient* is more likely to be used if X is something to eat or drink; otherwise *constituent* is more likely. It is just as likely, however, that they are not the same – the constituents may arise by natural processes in the course of manufacture, and ingredients may lose their identity through chemical reactions and the like. Thus, although alcohol is a constituent of wine, it is not an ingredient, because it is not used in the preparation, but arises naturally as a result of fermentation. Ingredient-hood is sometimes lexically marked, although rather rarely; for example, *shortening* has a necessary ingredient relation to *pastry*. In cases where the whole is a count noun, we have the †**object–material** relation, as in *tumbler:glass*. Notice that it is not normal to describe glass either as an ingredient or a constituent of the tumbler. It appears that in general, for *A, B and C are ingredients of X* to be normal, X must be a mass noun. However, this restriction does not apply to *A, B and C are ingredients for/for making X*.

Finally, some mention should be made of substances which on close examination turn out to consist of discrete 'particles'. There may well be names for the particles, in which case we have the †**substance–particle** relation, which holds between a mass noun 'whole' and a count noun 'part': *sand/salt:grain, snow:flake, rain:drop*, etc. Generally speaking, one may say of a grain of sand, or salt, 'This is sand/salt,' and of a snow-flake, 'This is snow,' and so on. This is typical of the substance–particle relation. An apparent exception is *cloth:thread* – one cannot say of a single thread 'This is cloth.'

7.6 Meronomies and taxonomies

In this section, the principal resemblances and differences between meronomies and taxonomies will be briefly surveyed.

There is a fundamental difference between the two in the way that they relate to extra-linguistic facts. The terms of both types of hierarchy denote classes of entities. The classes denoted by the terms in a taxonomy form a hierarchy which is more or less isomorphous with the corresponding lexical hierarchy. However, the classes denoted by the elements of a meronomy – toes, fingers, legs, heads, etc. – are not hierarchically related; that is to say, the hierarchical structuring of a meronomy does not originate in a hierarchy of classes. It is rather the way the individual parts of each individual whole (e.g. Arthur's body) are related which generates the hierarchical structuring that forms the basis of a meronomy. A meronomy thus has closer links with concrete reality than a taxonomy. The classes denoted by the terms of a meronomy are formed by associating together analogous parts (e.g. Arthur's nose, Tom's nose, Mary's nose, etc.) of isomorphous wholes (e.g. Arthur's body, Tom's body, etc.). The difference between the two types of hierarchy can be expressed by saying that corresponding to a taxonomic hierarchy there is a hierarchy of classes, whereas corresponding to a part–whole hierarchy there is a class of hierarchies.

There are other, less fundamental, differences between meronomies and taxonomies, which perhaps find their explanation in the more basic difference. For instance, there seems to be a greater profusion of variants and near-relatives in the case of the part–whole relation: meronymy must be considered a less well-defined relation than taxonymy. A meronomy is also less well-structured in that it does not often display clear levels; and it is typically less cohesive due to the frequency of super- and hypo-relations. On the other hand, the identity of the most inclusive item is typically more clearly established for a meronomy, and is never covert. These features are presumably causally related in some way to the fact that a meronomy is more intimately tied to concrete physical reality than a taxonomy is.

It would be wrong, however, to underplay the conceptual element in part–whole relations and in the relation between meronym and holonym:[7] these are not MERELY patent properties of physical objects. Take, for instance, the question of whether a part is facultative or not. We cannot decide this simply by examining examples of a particular type of whole to see whether they all possess the part in question. It is just as much a lexical question as to whether, for instance, A + B is designated by the same lexical item as A alone. If it is, then B can be described as a facultative part of A; but if A + B is lexically distinguished from A, either as a hyponym or as an incompatible, then B is no longer facultative. For example, suppose we observe that certain chairs are virtually identical to other chairs except for the possession of arms. If the lexical item *armchair* did not exist, we should say that *arm* was a facultative meronym of *chair*; however, since the term *armchair* does exist, there is a designated sub-class of *chair* for which *arm* is a necessary meronym, so *arm* must be described not as a facultative meronym, but as a hypo-meronym of *chair*.[8] Or take the case of *hamburger* and *cheeseburger*: a cheeseburger is just a hamburger with cheese in it, but there is no optionality, because the addition of cheese changes the hamburger into something else, and for that something else cheese is a necessity. Likewise, the question of whether a finger can be said to be part of an arm cannot be settled by examining human bodies – it is a linguistic question. Super-meronymy and hypo-meronymy are obviously matters of lexical semantics rather than properties of objects. Even the question of which bits of a whole to differentiate lexically is no less a conceptual matter than the question of which bundles of attributes to dignify with a class label.

Although there are differences between meronomies and taxonomies, it is perhaps the similarities between them which are the more striking. Both involve a kind of sub-division, a species of inclusion between the entity undergoing division and the results of the division, and a type of exclusion between the results of the division. Any taxonomy can be thought of in part–whole terms (although the converse is not true): a class can be looked on as a whole whose parts are its sub-classes. Corresponding to each of the common nouns constituting a typical taxonomy, there exists a proper noun labelling the class as an individual. Thus alongside *dog* and *cat* we have *the species Dog* and *the species Cat*. Now although a *greenfinch*, for instance, is a *finch*, we cannot say *? The species Greenfinch is the genus Finch*. On the other hand, we can say *The genus Finch consists of the species Greenfinch, ...etc.*, but not *? A finch consists of a green-finch, ...*, or even *? Finches consist of greenfinches, ...* A taxonomy can in this way be transformed into a meronomy, demonstrating, surely, that there is an intimate connection between the two. Could it be that they are alternative manifestations of a single underlying principle? Up to a point, this is plausible: in both cases, sub-division is carried out in such a way as to create elements in which two parameters are maximised, namely, internal cohesiveness and external distinctiveness. In the case of classes, cohesiveness consists in degree of resemblance between members; in parts, cohesiveness is to be interpreted as physical integrity. Distinctness in classes means unshared attributes; in parts it means unconnectedness. This dual principle works quite well for both meronymy and taxonymy, and expresses in a satisfying way the close connection between the two.

179

Notes

7.1

1. In the anthropological literature these lexical structures are usually called par-
    tonomies (see, for instance, Brown (1976) and Anderson (1978)). Note that
    a meronomy is a lexical hierarchy whose relation of dominance is the lexical
    relation of meronymy (cf. taxonomy and taxonymy).

7.2

2. I am assuming, for the sake of simplicity, that *blade* (of leaf), *blade* (of oar,
    paddle, etc.) and *blade* (of knife, etc.) are distinct lexical units. It is possible,
    however, that these three senses are merely local senses on a single sense-
    spectrum.

7.3

3. This question is posed in Lyons (1977: 313). The answer given in Cruse
    (1979a: 30–2) is not quite correct.
4. Attachments are discussed in Brown (1976: 407) – though not under that
    name – and Cruse (1979a: 33–5): both come to the same conclusion concerning
    the involvement of attachments in the apparent lack of transitivity in the "part
    of" relation. A different view is presented in Chaffin and Winston (1984).

7.4

5. See Brown (1976: 408–9).

7.5 For a number of the varieties of part–whole relation discussed in this section I have
drawn on Chaffin and Hermann (1984) and Chaffin and Winston (1984).

6. These distinctions were introduced by Vendler (1967). See also Dowty (1979).

7.6

7. The part–whole relation does not figure at all in the work of Continental struc-
    tural semanticists such as Coseriu and Geckeler. Lutzeier (private communica-
    tion) does not consider it to have any relevance to lexical semantics. This
    would also appear to be the opinion of Dahl (1979).
8. J. Lyons (personal communication) informs me that armchairs do not necessar-
    ily have arms, but that *fauteuils* do. However, the *Concise Oxford Dictionary*
    defines *armchair* as being "with side supports"; this corresponds to my
    intuitions.

8
Non-branching hierarchies

8.1 Introductory

Up to now the discussion of lexical hierarchies has centred on the branching variety. The present chapter will be devoted to the non-branching variety. These fall into two major sub-types. First, there are those which are closely bound up with branching hierarchies – they can, in fact, be regarded as secondary derivations from them. Second, there is quite a large family of independent non-branching hierarchies, not derived from or connected in any way with branching hierarchies, which arise from non-differentiable relations of dominance. We shall begin with non-branching hierarchies derived from branching ones.

8.2 From branching to non-branching

A branching hierarchy can only serve as the basis for a non-branching hierarchy if it has well-defined levels. As an illustration we shall take a hierarchy from the system of grammatical description known as tagmemics.[1] It is not necessary to understand (or agree with) all the theoretical assumptions behind the hierarchy – it is chosen because it is

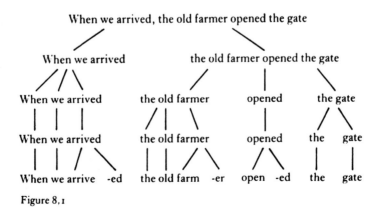

Figure 8.1

one of the few hierarchies of the part–whole type which has clear levels throughout. As with all part–whole hierarchies, we begin with an entity – in this case a sentence – which can undergo successive division into parts.[2] It will be noticed, that, for instance, *we* occurs at three different levels. Actually, within this system, it is not the same theoretical entity which recurs – only the phonetic/graphic realisation is the same. The first occurrence (from the top) is a noun phrase, the second a word, and the last a morpheme. The possibility of such 'anomalies' is a consequence of the relation of holo-meronymy, which occurs frequently in linguistic structures: a morpheme is capable of constituting a whole word, and a word is capable of constituting the whole of a phrase.

Sentences are not like human bodies: when well-formed they do not all have to contain the same inventory of parts. Some are more complex than others, and consist of a larger number of parts. However, the multiplication of parts is not haphazard, but is subject to certain constraints, in the absence of which it would not be possible to label the parts. Certain structural points in a sentence may be filled either by a single grammatical element, or by a more complex sequence which has identical syntactic relations with the rest of the sentence. For example, *John*, which occupies the subject position in *John saw Bill*, may be replaced by *the old man*; similarly, *old* in *the old man* can be replaced by *very tall*, and so on. This possibility of orderly expansion is part of what is meant when the structure of a sentence is described as hierarchical. It also allows us to find homologies between the structures of very different sentences, and to recognise structural parts with stable functions that can be labelled with common nouns. Some of the labels for the parts of the sentence analysed in fig. 8.1 are, according to the tagmemic system of grammatical description, as shown in fig. 8.2.

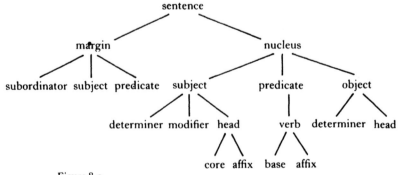

Figure 8.2

In the hierarchy illustrated in fig. 8.2, it will be noticed that, for instance, *subject* and *predicate* fall under both *margin* and *nucleus*, and *modifier* and *head* are dominated by both *subject* and *object*. What we have, therefore, is not a meronomy, but something more like a labelled part–whole hierarchy. It is not possible to construct a true meronomy from the set of terms referring to parts of sentences, partly because there is so much super-meronomy. The hierarchy in fig. 8.2 has another peculiarity. The system of grammatical description from which the terms were taken operates in terms of 'structural slots' and 'fillers' of those slots: a sentence, for example, has a *margin* slot and a *nucleus* slot, each of which must be filled by a clause; a clause, in turn, has a *subject* slot, an *object* slot and a *predicate* slot (among others), the first two of which are filled by noun phrases, and the last by a verb phrase. Strictly speaking (within this system), it is the fillers which have parts; fig. 8.2, however, consists of slot labels. So, for instance, *subject*, *predicate* and *object* are not 'parts of' the *nucleus*; more correctly, the clause which fills the *nucleus* slot has parts which fill the clause slots *subject*, *predicate* and *object*. Be that as it may, we still have a branching lexical hierarchy with well-defined levels, isomorphous with the part–whole hierarchy represented in fig. 8.1, which allows the derivation of a non-branching hierarchy. The simplest way of deriving a non-branching hierarchy from a branching one is to provide labels for the levels. Corresponding to the hierarchies in figs. 8.1 and 8.2, then, is the following non-branching hierarchy:

sentence level
|
clause level
|
phrase level
|
word level
|
morpheme level

Notice that these labels have some resemblance to proper nouns in so far as they denote unique (abstract) entities, rather than classes of entities; they differ from typical proper nouns, however, in that there is a statable – and recurrent – semantic relation between adjacent items (albeit a fairly complex one).[3] This method of producing a non-branching hierarchy is available for all branching hierarchies with levels. A botanical taxonomy, for instance, yields the following:

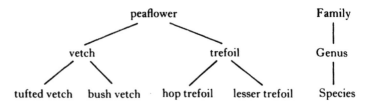

For garden flowers, this would extend downwards to *Variety* and *Strain*; higher up the hierarchy we find *Order*, *Phylum* and *Kingdom*. These are names for the levels available within a particular system of classification.

Another way of deriving a non-branching hierarchy from a branching one is to suppress differentiation and provide a single superordinate at each level for all the items at that level. (The best we can do along these lines in a body meronomy is to describe fingers and toes as *digits*, and arms and legs as *limbs*.) Corresponding to the levels in figs. 8.1 and 8.2, then, we also have the following series of common nouns:

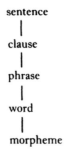

All the items at phrase level are *phrases*; those at word level are *words*, and so on. (Actually, this is not quite true, even in the example given: *when* is not a phrase, although within this system it occurs at phrase level. But we shall ignore the complications introduced by 'atypical mapping' between levels.) In this latest version of a non-branching grammatical hierarchy, there is a simple sense relation between the terms, namely, meronymy without differentiation of meronyms: a *sentence* consists of one or more *clauses*, a *clause* of one or more *phrases*, a *phrase* of one or more *words* and a *word* of one or more *morphemes*. (With *morpheme*, we reach the end of the line: we do not say that a morpheme consists of sound segments (phonemes), because that would introduce a type-inconsistency, as phonemes are not grammatical units.)

There is one type of hierarchy for which this method of deriving a non-branching string does not work, and that is a taxonomy. The reason for this is not difficult to grasp. For each level of a hierarchy, a term is needed of which all items at that level are hyponyms, but of which no items at any other level are hyponyms. For example, for the following hierarchy, a term X is needed such that *It's a vetch* and *It's a trefoil* entail *It's an X*, but *It's a bush vetch* and *It's a hop trefoil* do not entail *It's an X*:

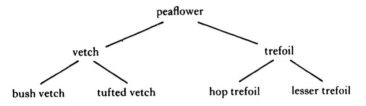

Obviously there can be no term having the properties of X, because of the transitive nature of the relation of hyponymy: since *hop trefoil* is a hyponym of *trefoil*, anything which is superordinate to the latter is also necessarily superordinate to the former. How, in that case, do we obtain the series of common nouns *family*, *genus*, *species*, etc. (as in *Five species of tulips grow in our garden*)? The answer is that they are not directly derived from a taxonomy – the derivation requires an extra step. First, the taxonomy must be transformed into a kind of meronomy, by re-interpreting classes as individuals. So, instead, for instance, of having the common noun *peaflower*, which can refer to individual members of a class, we replace it with *the Peaflower Family*, which designates the whole class viewed as a single entity; in the same way, vetch is replaced by *the Genus Vetch*, and so on. Once this transformation is carried out, it is possible to assign a superordinate to the items at a given level which is unique to those items: there is thus a level of *families* (including the Peaflower Family, the Buttercup Family, the Daisy Family,[4] etc.), a level of *genera*, a level of *species*, etc. The sense relation between adjacent members of the resulting lexical string is again meronymy without differentiation: a *family* consists of *genera*, a *genus* consists of *species*, and so on.

It is possible to derive a non-branching lexical hierarchy from a branching extra-linguistic hierarchy, even when no branching lexical hierarchy corresponds to it. There are two main reasons why there may be no lexical items corresponding to the nodes of the branching extra-linguistic hierarchy. The first is that there may be no motivation for differentiation: an entity may be divided into identical parts, each of which is further divided into a number of identical parts. This is generally the case, although there are exceptions, with units of measure. A *metre*, for example, is divided into a hundred *centimetres*, each of which is further divided into

185

ten *millimetres*; there would seem to be little motivation for giving separate names to each of the hundred centimetres of a metre. It is an intriguing question why separate names should be given to the days of the week, and the months of the year (in some languages years are also named), but not to the metres in a kilometre, or the pence in a pound.[5] In fact there are two systems for designating days: one uses a movable reference point which is constantly updated as we move through time (*yesterday*, *today*, *tomorrow*);[6] the other indicates fixed points like milestones (with a repeating pattern of numbers) along a road (*Sunday*, *Monday*, etc.).

The second reason why there should be no lexical items corresponding to the nodes of a branching extra-linguistic hierarchy is that the elements which occupy them do not qualify for lexification. If the elements are individuals, for instance, and not classes, then they only qualify for proper name labels. This is the case with a military hierarchy. The relation of dominance in the extra-linguistic hierarchy is "– directly commands –": any individual in the armed forces who is neither at the highest nor at the lowest rank both directly commands a number of other individuals and is himself, together with others, under the direct command of someone at the next higher rank. The individuals who constitute the hierarchy do not each have distinctive common noun labels; they are separately designated only as, for instance, *Corporal* X, *Sergeant* Y, *Major* Z. However, the levels of the hierarchy – i.e. the military ranks – ARE named, and the names form a non-branching hierarchy: ..., *colonel, lieutenant-colonel, major, captain*,... There are, in fact, two parallel sets of terms (not phonetically distinct), similar to those observed in the case of the grammatical hierarchy. Members of the rank-naming set have some proper-noun-like characteristics (*He was promoted to the rank of major/Major*); the other set consists of common nouns (cf. *There were three generals and four colonels on the committee*), each of which designates a class to which all the individuals at a particular level in the hierarchy belong. (It would not be strictly correct to describe the common noun *major* as a superordinate of all the elements of the hierarchy at that level, because the elements are individuals, not classes. The relation between *Major X* and *major* is not the same as that between *alsatian* and *dog*, but is parallel to that between *Fido* and *dog*. That is to say, *Major X* designates a member of the class of majors, not a sub-class; only in the latter case would it be proper to speak of hyponym and superordinate.)

It is interesting to speculate on how a set of terms could be devised for military personnel which formed a branching hierarchy. It seems that there are only two possibilities. Either we impose a taxonomic structure, and give different labels to different K I N D S of soldier, so that, for instance, an infantry captain and an artillery captain would be designated differently. Or we could label the individuals concerned according to the P A R T S of the army over which they had command. This apparent limitation of possibility highlights the fundamental importance of meronymic and taxonymic relations. A further point of interest is that there would appear to be a close correspondence between the two hierarchies thus created; that is to say, there is a close relation between the most natural K I N D S of soldier and the most natural P A R T S of the army:

> ? A colonel is a kind of soldier.
> An infantryman is a kind of soldier.
> ? The main parts of the army are the officers and the men.
> The main parts of the army are: the infantry, the artillery, etc.

This can be taken as reinforcement of the idea mooted at the end of chapter 7, that a single principle might underlie both meronomies and taxonomies.

8.3 Chains, helices and cycles

There are many sets of lexical items which form non-branching hierarchies according to our criteria, but which bear no relation whatsoever to hierarchies of the branching sort. All that is needed for a non-branching hierarchy is a principle of ordering which will enable the terms of the set to be arranged in a unique sequential order with a first item and a last item (i.e. not in a circle). Since the ordering principle must be consistent throughout the hierarchy, this means that we need a relation that is asymmetric and catenary.[7] However, to be lexically significant, such ordering must be in some sense inherent in the meanings of the items in the ordered set, or, at least, inherent in the meanings of some of the members of the set; sets belonging to types to be discussed in this section often display only partially inherent ordering. The difference between inherent and non-inherent ordering of lexical items may be illustrated by means of the following two sets:

(i) *mound, hillock, hill, mountain*
(ii) *mouse, dog, horse, elephant*

Both of these sets can be unambiguously ordered in terms of size:

(i) A mountain is bigger than a hill.
  A hill is bigger than a hillock.
  A hillock is bigger than a mound.

187

(ii) An elephant is bigger than a horse.

A horse is bigger than a dog.

A dog is bigger than a mouse.

However, only set (i) is inherently ordered. The difference between the two types of ordering shows up if we attribute different ordering with respect to size:

1a. We saw a dwarf elephant which was smaller than a horse.

b. There was a pigmy horse barely the size of a dog.

c. The story concerned a race of giant mice bigger than dogs.

These sentences suffer from little more than a mild dose of improbability. Contrast this with the paradoxical nature of 2a and b:

2a. ? Behind the house is a dwarf mountain, smaller than a hill.

b. ? Behind the house is a giant hillock, the size of a mountain.

There are two important semantic differences between the items in set (i) and the items in set (ii). The first is that the semantic trait of "relative size" is criterial in set (i), but only expected in set (ii). This can be established as follows:

It's a mountain entails *It's bigger than a hill*

It's an elephant does not entail *It's bigger than a horse*

It's an elephant, but it's bigger than a horse.

(expressive paradox with pleonastic colour)

It's an elephant, but it's no bigger than a horse.

(normal sentence, but odd elephant, if fully grown)

The second difference between the two sets lies in the semantic relations among the respective members. The members of set (ii) contract the type of multi-dimensional contrasts with one another (and with other generic level animal names) which are characteristic of natural kind terms. There is no special foregrounding of size traits, so that in 3, for instance, it is not obvious or necessary that reference is being made to the relative sizes of John and Bill:

3. John is like an elephant; Bill is like a horse.

The members of set (i) also contract multi-dimensional contrasts, but only with items outside the set, such as *plain, lake, river*, etc. With each other, however, they display another mode of contrast: they contract a uni-dimensional contrast in respect of size. The size traits of the members of set (i) are thus foregrounded. This is why the most likely interpretation of 4 is that John is bigger than Bill:

4. John is like a mountain; Bill is like a hill.

The items in set (i) do not merely form an ordered sequence; they also represent (or, more precisely, encapsulate) degrees of a graded property, namely, size. However, in many cases of ordered sequences of lexical items, there is no salient property X such that, of two adjacent elements in a sequence, one must be 'more X' than the other; in such cases one can merely say that one occurs further along in the sequence than the other (since the ordering relation needs to be asymmetric, it is always possible to specify a direction). Thus, for instance, in the sequence *Sunday, Monday, Tuesday, Wednesday, . . .* there is no property X such that *Tuesday* is 'more X' than *Monday*: the most that one can say is that *Tuesday* comes later in the sequence than *Monday*. In the rest of this section, we shall be looking at sequences of this sort: the majority are sets of coordinate parts. Sequences based on degrees of a scaled property, like those in set (i) above, will be discussed in 8.4.

In a sense, all distinguished parts of a normal object are ordered – they all have a unique place within the whole. But the only orderings which are relevant to non-branching hierarchies are those in which parts are strung out in linear sequence on either a spatial or a temporal axis. There are two principal modes of organisation of such sequences: they may exhibit pure linear ordering, in which case they will be termed †**chains**; or they may have a hybrid linear/cyclical ordering which we shall call †**helical**. The following are examples of lexical chains:

> shoulder, upper arm, elbow, forearm, wrist, hand
> source, upper reaches, lower reaches, mouth/estuary
> introduction, exposition, development, recapitulation, coda
> birth, childhood, adolescence, adulthood, old age, death

Notice that the spatial examples do not have to form a straight line – a unique sequential ordering is all that is required. None of the sets considered so far are pure chains, since the constituent lexical items also encode information as to the nature of the whole whose parts are denoted. An example of a pure chain would be *beginning, middle, end*.

The sets of lexical items which will be termed †**helices** are a sub-type of chain. They show the typical characteristics of chains, with a first item, a last item, and a unique ordering in between:

>Sunday is the first day of the week.
>
>Monday comes immediately after Sunday.
>
>. . .
>
>Friday comes immediately after Thursday.
>
>Saturday is the last day of the week.

However, the relation "— stands immediately between — and —" organises these terms into an apparently cyclical structure:

>Monday stands immediately between Sunday and Tuesday.
>
>Tuesday stands immediately between Monday and Wednesday.
>
>. . .
>
>Sunday stands immediately between Saturday and Monday.
>
>Monday stands immediately between Sunday and Tuesday.

The same relation organises the colours of the spectrum into a circle, too. But there is a difference. The colour-terms *red, orange, yellow, green, blue, purple* form what is perhaps the only truly cyclically organised set in the language:

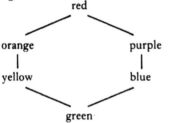

This set does not constitute a hierarchy: the structuring relation does not have the necessary directional properties. There is no top, and no bottom; there is no unique item related in the relevant way to all the other items in the set. However, the names of the days of the week do not really form a circle. In the sequence *Sunday, Monday, . . . Saturday, Sunday*, the first and last items do not refer to the same day: in the course of each circuit, time moves forward one week. The combination of linearity and cyclicity may be taken as the defining characteristic of a helix.

The links of a helical chain typically refer to periods of time:

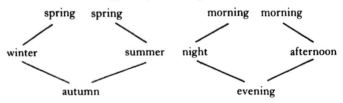

The incidence of helical ordering in time expressions is perhaps a reflection of the human propensity for imposing a rhythmical structure on the flow of time, and arises from the same deep impulse as music and dance. (There are, of course, natural models for recurrent patterns of temporal change in, for example, the diurnal, lunar and seasonal rhythms.) The constituent items of helical chains may have precise boundaries (*Monday : Tuesday, June : July*) or vague boundaries (*afternoon : evening, autumn : winter*). None of the segmentation found in helical chains seems to be wholly un-motivated, although the repeat period may be: the day, the lunar month and the year are 'natural' periods, but the week and the twelve-year cycle of Chinese year names are arbitrary. Many cases show a combination of naturalness and arbitrariness: the day is a natural period related to the rotation of the earth about its axis, but the location of the point where one day passes into the next is arbitrarily imposed.

Each of the sets of lexical items we have so far discussed in this section, whether they are linear or helical chains, has an overall expected ordering; but not all the constituent lexical items of the sets have ordering information encoded as critical parts of their meaning. Consider the parts of the arm: the hand is canonically at the end of the arm furthest away from the point of attachment to the body. But if, because of some developmental anomaly, a hand were to appear attached, say, to the middle of the upper arm, it would still be referred to as a hand; this is presumably because the central traits of *hand* are concerned with form and function rather than with relative position. If, on the other hand, we were to attempt to describe a malformation of the arm by saying that the elbow was where the wrist should be, and vice versa, this would be judged anomalous, because *elbow* and *wrist* have, as critical traits of their meaning, information concerning position relative to upper arm and forearm, and forearm and hand, respect-ively. We would be more likely to say that the elbow resembled a wrist and the wrist an elbow. Inherent ordering seems to be typical of names of joints. In the case of the parts of a musical movement in classical sonata form, we have again a mixture of inherent and contingent ordering. Although it might be unexpected, and even artistically incongruous, the development could precede the exposition. Both of these are characterised by the nature of the musical material they contain. But the recapitulation could neither precede nor immediately follow the exposition, since in the former case it would not be a repetition, and in the latter case it would be MERELY a repetition; the coda cannot come anywhere but the end, nor the introduction anywhere but the beginning. The majority of terms in helical chains are inherently ordered. Inherent ordering is definitely the rule in sets with a significant conventional component. For instance, *The government has decided to interchange Monday and Friday* can only be understood to refer to a decision to change the meanings of the words *Monday* and *Friday* – otherwise the sentence is paradoxical. With 'natural' sets, the facts are less clear. In some cases there is no doubt. For example, the oddness of *The effect of the close approach of the comet was that afternoons immediately followed nights and preceded mornings* is not due simply to physical implausibility: a major reason for the sense of anomaly is that whatever changes were brought about by the approach of the comet, we would still apply the term *morning* to the period of light immediately following *night*, because that is what it means. I am less certain about the names of the seasons in English. It seems to me that although *In that country, autumn passes straight into summer* may jolt our expectations, it is nonetheless interpretable as indicating that a temperate season in which leaf-fall occurs is followed by a hot season. If this were true, it would imply that *autumn* was characterised more by what happened in it than by relative position. On the other hand, it is normal in English to use *autumn* to refer to the mild season following summer in the Eastern Mediterranean, even though it closely resembles our spring, and indeed is called in Turkish *sonbahar* – literally "last (or second) spring". This would indicate that position was more important than climate or characteristic events.

8.4 Ranks, grades and degrees

In a number of ordered sets the constituent lexical units relate to different values of some variable underlying property. There are two distinct types of underlying scale: those which vary continuously, and those which vary in discrete jumps. Lexical units which operate on a discontinuous scale will be called ✝**rank-terms**. Such terms, not surprisingly, do not lend themselves to grading. Terms which operate over a continuous scale may be gradable or non-gradable; the non-gradable ones will be called ✝**degree-terms** and the gradable ones ✝**grade-terms**.[8]

The level terms associated with a military hierarchy (coincidentally called ranks in everyday language) are good examples of ranks. The variable property underlying these is also normally called rank: in respect of rank, a colonel is higher than a major. This property does not vary continuously: no major outranks any other major, nor is it normal to say:

? John is only just a major – Bill is nearly a lieutenant-colonel.

(This sentence might be interpretable in a situation where a steady progression through the ranks was expected. It would mean that John had only just become a major, and that Bill was about to become a lieutenant-colonel. The continuously varying property, therefore, would be time, not rank.) Probably the most important set of ranks is the set of natural integers. The property of numerosity, like military rank, increases by discrete jumps: no sets of X items outnumbers any other set of X items. Witness also the oddness of *? There are only just twelve students in our group; in yours there are nearly thirteen.* Sets of number names combine features of sets of measure terms (which are discussed below) and of helical chains. In English we have two sets of terms resembling helical chains, which are continuously re-cycled, one inside the other, so to speak, as higher and higher numbers are named. These are the 'units' – *one, two, three, four, . . . nine*, and the 'tens' – *twenty, thirty, forty, . . . ninety*. In addition to these helix-like sets, there is a set resembling measure terms: *hundred, thousand, million, billion*, etc. (which form in principle, but not in practice, an endless series).[9] There are many sets of lexical items which encapsulate numbers, especially units: they are all ranks, too:

> first, second, third, fourth, fifth, sixth, . . .
> — half, third, quarter, fifth, sixth, . . .
> — twins, triplets, quadruplets, quintuplets, sextuplets, . . .
> monadic, diadic, triadic, tetradic, pentadic, . . .
> —   —   triangle, square, pentagon, hexagon, . . .
> single, double, triple, quadruple, quintuple, sextuple, . . .

Turning now to lexical units operating over a continuously varying scale, we find, as we have already noted, two types, namely, degree-terms (non-gradable) and grade-terms (gradable). Let us first see how degree-terms can be distinguished from rank-terms. An example of a set of degree-terms is provided by the terms used in examination assessments: *fail, pass, credit, distinction.* (There are different variants, but they are structurally alike. *Pass* is used here in the sense in which it is incompatible with *credit* and *distinction.*) The difference between this set and a typical set of rank-terms is that whereas one major, for instance, cannot outrank another, one *pass* can be of higher academic merit than another. Hence it is perfectly normal to say: *John just scraped a pass, but Bill nearly got a credit.* A number of sets of degree-terms represent a temporal sequence: an example of this is *baby, child, adolescent, adult* (I am assuming that there is a sense of *child* which is incompatible with *baby*, my evidence being the normality of *babies and children*); another example is the set of words denoting stages in the life of a salmon – *parr, smolt, grilse, kelt.* The terms in sets like these will not, however, be regarded as degree-terms merely because they constitute a time sequence; there must also be some property which increases continuously with time, such as maturity (as in the sets just cited). In the absence of such a property, items in temporally sequenced sets are merely partitions of a period of time – i.e. they are rank-terms. A rather awkward and marginal case is *egg, caterpillar, chrysalis, butterfly*. It is difficult to think of a property that a chrysalis manifests to a higher degree than a caterpillar, and that a caterpillar also manifests to a higher degree than an egg. Yet it would presumably be inconsistent to regard them as anything other than degree-terms.

Although it could be argued that some types of measure unit, particularly those of distance and time, have a connection with a branching part–whole hierarchy with no differentiation of parts, we shall relate them to a unidimensional continuous scale, and categorise them as degree-terms. They differ, however, from other types of degree-term in that whereas the degrees in a set usually represent a more or less linear progression in terms of values of the underlying property, measure terms typically increase geometrically (again, more or less). So, for instance, whereas *one, two, three, four*; *Monday, Tuesday, Wednesday, Thursday*; *fail, pass, credit, distinction*; and *baby, child, adolescent, adult* all represent either equal or roughly equal intervals along their respective scales, *second, minute, hour, day*; *millimetre, centimetre, metre, kilometre*; *ounce, pound, stone, hundredweight, ton*; and *hundred, thousand, million, billion* increase geometrically (again roughly).

Grade-terms differ from degree-terms in that they are gradable (although the outermost items in a set may resist grading to a variable extent). They are therefore mostly adjectives. The following are examples of sets of grade-terms:

> freezing, (cold), cool, warm, (hot), scorching
> atrocious, (bad), indifferent, average, fair, (good), excellent
> minuscule, tiny, (small), (big), huge, gigantic

(items in parentheses are not strictly incompatibles of their neighbours, but cover regions of the scale not covered by other terms). The boundaries between grade-terms are typically somewhat vague, but the vagueness is less marked when the terms are explicitly contrasted with one another.

There exist degree-terms that might appear to encapsulate grades, but which, if they do, have some puzzling properties. Consider the set

> mound   hillock   hill   mountain

These vary along the dimensions of size, so one might expect them to have some demonstrable relation to sets of grade-terms such as *tiny*, *small*, *large*, *huge*. One might surmise, for instance, that *mountain* meant (very roughly) "huge earth-protuberance", *hill* "large earth-protuberance", *hillock* "small earth-protuberance", and *mound* "tiny earth-protuberance". The glosses for *mountain* and *hill* are not without plausibility; those for *hillock* and *mound*, however, are deficient in an important respect. The set of size adjectives is polarised, and *large* and *huge* 'face in the opposite direction from' *tiny* and *small*. This shows up when they are intensified (cf. the discussion of antonyms in chapter 9). The supposed encapsulations, however, are not polarised. If one were told that X was 'more of a mountain' than Y, one could presumably conclude that X was larger than Y; the same conclusion would be drawn from *X is more of a hill than Y*. This is in line with the suggested glosses for *hill* and *mountain*. However, it is much less clear what conclusion could be drawn from *X is more of a hillock than Y* and *X is more of a mound than Y*. It is certainly not that X is smaller than Y: my intuitions are uncertain, but I feel that I would be most likely to infer that X was larger than Y in both cases. (Notice that from *X is more of a dwarf than Y* and *A is more of a giant than B* it would be normal to conclude that X was smaller than Y, and A larger than B. Clear cases of polarised encapsulations do, therefore, occur.) Perhaps more plausible candidates for encapsulation in the earth-protuberance set are

moderately large, fairly large, very large, extremely large

Even for these, however, the evidence is not strong, and it is perhaps wrong to look for any determinate lexical items or expressions that are encapsulated.

Notes

8.2

1. For an introduction to tagmemics see Cook (1978). This example is used here purely as an illustration of a well-developed hierarchical structure, without commitment as to its truth, or value as a grammatical description.
2. The divisions made here do not correspond precisely to those that would appear in a typical IC-analysis.
3. Cook gives these level names capital letters.
4. The botanical family-names *Buttercup Family* and *Daisy Family* are named after their best-known genera. The name *Peaflower Family* is slightly different, because there is no Genus Peaflower. While the semantic motivation of the name *Buttercup Family* can be explained as "the family which includes the

Genus Buttercup", the parallel explanation of Peaflower would be "the family whose members have flowers resembling those of the Genus Pea". Botanists, at least when writing for laymen, often refer to genera and species as follows: Plants such as Early Purple Orchid ... and Bluebell ... are characteristic. Fitter, Fitter, and Blamey (1974: 310) The names of common flowers, such as *buttercup, daisy, dandelion, bluebell,* etc. occur much more frequently as common nouns than as proper nouns, and can probably be considered to be primarily common nouns. The relation between *Bluebell* and *bluebell* parallels that between the two occurrences of *Middleton* in *That is Arthur Middleton* and *She married one of the Middletons of Hartlepool.* The difference is that *Middleton* is primarily a proper noun, and secondarily a common noun. (Notice that surnames lend themselves more readily to transformation into common nouns than do forenames.)

5. Of course, in the cultures in which the names arise, days, months, etc. may be functionally distinct, in that characteristic activities, observances and so on may be prescribed for them. But there is no logical reason why, for instance, the fifth mile of a journey should not be consecrated to Jupiter, and the sixth to Venus, or whatever.

6. Elements such as *today, tomorrow, here, there, this, that, now, then, I, you, he, she,* etc., which serve to locate what is being referred to in space or time relative to the time and place of utterance, are known as **deictic** elements, and the phenomenon in general is known as **deixis**. For an elementary treatment of deixis, see Lyons (1981: 228–35). For more detailed discussion, see Lyons (1977: ch. 15) and Levinson (1983: ch. 2).

8.3

7. See definition of *catenary* on p. 113.

8.4

8. Lyons (1977: 289), following Lehrer (1974: 29), distinguishes, among ordered sets of incompatibles, between 'ranks', whose members are non-gradable, and 'scales', whose members are gradable. The members of Lyons's ranks, therefore, may for us be either rank-terms or degree-terms, according to the nature of their underlying scale.

9. The highest number with a single-word name to date is a googolplex. The second highest is a googol (the mathematician who coined these terms is alleged to have asked his nine-month-old baby for a suitable name). A googol is written as follows:

10,000,000,000,000,000,000,000,000,000,000,000,000,000,
000,000,000,000,000,000,000,000,000,000,000,000,000,000,
000,000,000,000

A googolplex is written as 1 followed by a googol zeroes. This is an extremely large number.

9
Opposites 1: complementaries and antonyms

9.1 Oppositeness

Of all the relations of sense that semanticists propose, that of oppositeness is probably the most readily apprehended by ordinary speakers. Indeed, if my children are typical, the basic notion is well within the grasp of three-year-olds. It is also perhaps the only sense relation to receive terminological recognition in ordinary language; most languages seem to have a non-learned term for it: Arabic: *'aksi*; Chinese: *tao-fan*; French: *contraire*; German: *gegensatz*; Hungarian: *ellentét*; Turkish: *karşı*, etc.

Opposites possess a unique fascination, and exhibit properties which may appear paradoxical. Take, for instance, the simultaneous closeness, and distance from one another, of opposites. The meanings of a pair of opposites are felt intuitively to be maximally separated. Indeed, there is a widespread idea that the power of uniting or reconciling opposites is a magical one, an attribute of the Deity, or a property of states of mind brought about by profound meditation, and so on. The closeness of opposites, on the other hand, manifests itself, for instance, in the fact that the members of a pair have almost identical distributions, that is to say, very similar possibilities of normal and abnormal occurrence. It is also reflected in the frequency of speech errors in which the intended word is substituted by its opposite. Philosophers and others from Heraclitus to Jung have noted the tendency of things to slip into their opposite states; and many have remarked on the thin dividing line between love and hate, genius and madness, etc. The paradox of simultaneous difference and similarity is partly resolved by the fact that opposites typically differ along only one dimension of meaning: in respect of all other features they are identical, hence their semantic closeness; along the dimension of difference, they occupy opposing poles, hence the feeling of difference.

In spite of the robustness of the ordinary speaker's intuitions concerning opposites, the overall class is not a well-defined one, and its adequate characterisation is far from easy. One can distinguish, however, central, or prototypical, instances, judged by informants to be good examples of the category: *good*:*bad*, *large*:*small*, *true*:*false*, *top*:*bottom*, etc.; and more or less peripheral examples, judged as less good, or about whose status as opposites there is not a perfect consensus, such as *command*:*obey*, *mother*:*father*, *town*:*country*, *clergy*:*laity*, etc. (Even *tea*:*coffee* and *gas*:*electricity* are felt by some speakers to have a degree of oppositeness, but only in situations where they represent a two-way choice.) I shall make some attempt in a later chapter to specify the characteristics which distinguish the good from the less good examples of the category.

Within the somewhat indeterminate general class of opposites there is a small number of relatively well-defined sub-types (concerning which the intuitions of ordinary speakers are paradoxically uncertain) with interesting and systematic properties. It is these which will occupy most of our attention in this and the two following chapters. There will remain, however, a large number of opposites about which little will be said, because they apparently do not lend themselves to significant generalisations, nor do they display interesting recurrent patterning. For instance, most of our distinguished sub-types serve as bases for morphologically derived forms. Generally speaking, the lexical derivatives of a pair of opposites are themselves opposites, sometimes with interesting properties in their own right (e.g. *lengthen* and *shorten* from *long* and *short*), but most often they display no interesting properties that are not related in an obvious way to those of the base forms. Another class of opposites about which little systematic can be said are impure opposites, that is to say, those which encapsulate, or include within their meaning, a more elementary opposition. For instance, *giant*:*dwarf* can be said to encapsulate the opposition between *large* and *small* (but this opposition does not exhaust their meaning); likewise, *shout* and *whisper* encapsulate *loud* and *soft*, *criticise* and *praise* encapsulate *good* and *bad*, and *stalactite* and *stalagmite*, *up* and *down*. As far as can be ascertained at present, these are idiosyncratic and unpredictable in both their occurrence and their properties.

We shall now turn to the description of the basic types of lexical opposite, beginning with **complementaries**.[1]

9.2 Complementaries

Of all the varieties of opposites, complementarity is perhaps the simplest conceptually. The essence of a pair of complementaries is that between them they exhaustively divide some conceptual domain into two mutually exclusive compartments, so that what does not fall into one of the compartments must necessarily fall into the other. There is no 'no-man's-land', no neutral ground, no possibility of a third term lying between them. Examples of complementaries are: *true* : *false, dead* : *alive, open* : *shut, hit* : *miss* (a target), *pass* : *fail* (an examination).

We can recognise complementaries by the fact that if we deny that one term applies to some situation, we effectively commit ourselves to the applicability of the other term; and if we assert one term, we implicitly deny the other. Thus *John is not dead* entails and is entailed by *John is alive*; and *The door isn't open* entails and is entailed by *The door is shut*.[2] Complementarity can also be diagnosed by the anomalous nature of a sentence denying both terms:

? The door is neither open nor shut.
? The hamster was neither dead nor alive.
? The statement that John has blue eyes is neither true nor false.

Opposites which are not complementaries do not yield anomaly under these circumstances:

Her exam results were neither good nor bad.
The temperature was neither rising nor falling.

The relation of sense holding between the members of a pair of complementaries is not weakened, or called into question, by the existence of situations where it is difficult to decide which term is appropriate: the relation between *dead* and *alive*, for instance, is not at all affected by medico-legal uncertainty as to what constitutes the point of death. Such referential indeterminacy afflicts all words, without exception. The point about complementaries is that, once a decision has been reached regarding one term, in all relevant circumstances, a decision has effectively been made regarding the other term, too.

Since a pair of complementaries bisects a particular conceptual domain, their peculiar properties manifest themselves only within that domain. In some cases, it is possible to define a domain within which two words have a complementary relationship independently, as it were, of the words themselves. For instance, we could say, given that we are talking about members of the species *Lion*, that a particular animal must in normal circumstances be either a *lion* or a *lioness*; therefore, within this domain, *lion* and *lioness* are complementaries. However, we shall not define complementaries in this way. For us, the limits of the relevant domain will be set by the normal presuppositions of use of the words themselves. If someone says: 'What's in this box is not alive', we have a right to conclude that the box contains something that was once alive. Likewise, if someone says: 'John did not succeed in entering the building,' it would be normal to infer that John had been trying to enter the building. Hence, *dead* and *alive* are complementaries, because, within the domain they themselves define, i.e. organisms, denial of one term entails the assertion of the other. Similarly, within the domain defined by *succeed*:*fail*, namely, that of attempting to do something, *not succeeding* is equivalent to *failing*. This is not the case, however, with *lion* and *lioness*. It is not a normal inference from *It says on this cage that the animal is a lioness, but that is obviously wrong* that the cage contains a lion. That is to say, *lion*:*lioness* are complementaries only within a domain which is imposed, as it were, extrinsically. We shall say merely that *lion*:*lioness* encapsulate the complementary opposition between *male* and *female*. The latter are true complementaries by our definition, because in ordinary circumstances a hearer would take it for granted that *No, it's not a female* referred to a living thing, and given this restriction of domain, would confidently conclude that the referent of *it* was male.

It must be remembered that language is designed neither by nor for logicians, and while definitions of sense relations in terms of logical properties such as entailment are convenient, they are also partially misleading as a picture of the way natural language functions. This is because complementarity (for instance) is to some extent a matter of degree. There are cases that would satisfy the most fastidious of logicians: for instance, if someone is doing something, he can either *continue* doing it, or *cease* doing it, and this would seem to exhaust the possibilities that are conceivable in any circumstances. But with many terms, a proviso 'in all normal circumstances' seems necessary before the inferences which establish complementarity can be accepted as valid. This is perhaps true, for example, of *dead* and *alive*; could one not say of ghosts, or better still, vampires, that they existed in a state which was neither death nor life? Similarly, the existence of hermaphrodites and animals of totally indeterminate sex weakens the relationship between *male* and *female*. An even weaker relationship would hold between terms which required the proviso 'generally speaking': it is probably the case that if someone is not *left-handed*, then, generally speaking, we can conclude that he is *right-handed*. There is, in other words, a continuum between contradiction (e.g. *This proposition is true*:*This proposition is false*) and contrariety (e.g. *John is tall*:*John is short*). The intermediate points along this continuum are occupied by cases for which intermediate values are to a greater or lesser degree unexpected, or difficult to conceive of. There is no clear cut-off point along the continuum. Our tests give clear-cut results only for pairs near one end of this continuum.

Complementaries are, generally speaking, either verbs or adjectives. It is convenient to consider the two types separately. An interesting feature of verbal complementaries, which distinguishes them from the adjectival sorts, is that the domain within which the complementarity operates is often expressible by a single lexical item, which itself contracts distinctive relations of oppositeness with one of the members of the complementary pair. Consider the pair *obey*: *disobey*. The relation of complementarity between these manifests itself only in the context of a successfully transmitted command: if there is no command, or if the command is directed elsewhere, or if it has not been heard or understood, or if the issuer of the command has no right to demand obedience, then it is not proper to speak of obeying and disobeying.[3] The verb *command* therefore sets the scene for the complementarity of *obey* and *disobey* to appear. Most speakers feel that there is a relation of oppositeness (not, of course, complementarity) between *command* and *obey*. Interestingly, when asked for the opposite of *command*, most will reply with *obey*, but when asked for the opposite of *obey*, the invariable response is *disobey*, presumably because *obey*: *disobey* are 'better' opposites than *command*: *obey*. There are four types of opposite whose characteristic relations can hold between the lexical item which expresses the necessary presupposition for a pair of complementaries, and one of the members of the complementary pair. These four are: reversives, interactives, satisfactives and counteractives.

Let us first consider how reversivity and complementarity interlock in generating lexical triplets. Take the set *be born*: *live*: *die*. The outer pair, *be born* and *die* are reversives (these are discussed in detail in the next chapter; for the time being they may be characterised as denoting "change in opposite directions" – in the present instance, "entering life" and "leaving life"); *live* and *die* are complementaries: *He shall not live!* is equivalent to *He shall die!*, and *He shall not die!* to *He shall live!* For all complementaries of this group, the basic opposition is between "continuance of a state" and "change to an alternative state". Other triplets with more or less analogous relationships (although there are differences of detail which we shall not go into) are: *start*: *keep on*: *stop*, *learn*: *remember*: *forget*, *arrive*: *stay*: *leave*, *earn*: *save*: *spend*.

The opposites that are here termed †**interactives** have a 'stimulus–response' type of relationship: the verb expressing the precondition for complementarity denotes an action which has as its goal the elicitation of the response denoted by its interactive opposite, which, in turn, is one of the terms of the complementary pair. An example of a set of lexical items related in this way is *command* : *obey* : *disobey*. In the context of a command, *obey* and *disobey* are complementaries, while *command* and *obey*, representing 'stimulus' and 'response', are interactives. The following are further examples of such triplets: *request* : *grant* : *refuse*, *invite* : *accept* : *turn down*, *greet* : *acknowledge* : *snub*, *tempt* : *yield* : *resist*.

The term †**satisfactive** is given to what is probably a rather weak form of oppositeness in which one term denotes an attempt to do something, and the other denotes successful performance. Satisfactives are included, with some hesitation, largely on the grounds that they participate, along with complementaries, in triplets which are very similar to those which contain interactives. Examples of satisfactives are: *try* : *succeed*, *seek* : *find*, *compete* : *win*, and *aim* : *hit*. Not everyone feels these to be opposites; but some do, and there is undoubtedly a binary relation of some sort between the members of a pair. With the exception of *seek* : *find*, all the instances quoted form triplets: *try* : *succeed* : *fail*, *compete* : *win* : *lose*, *aim* : *hit* : *miss*.

As a final example of lexical triplets involving complementaries, consider the following cases: *attack* : *defend* : *submit*, *charge* : *refute* : *admit*, *shoot* (in football) : *save* : *let in*, *punch* : *parry* : *take*. The first and second terms of each triplet represent a new type of opposite. The first term denotes an aggressive action, and the second denotes measures to neutralise it. We shall call this type of opposition †**counteractive**. Notice that the members of the complementary pair represent an active and a passive response to the original action or, perhaps more revealingly, counteraction and lack of counteraction. (It is perhaps worth noting in passing that in many cases there is a verb expressing a less direct, but more dynamic, response to an initial aggressive action: *attack* : *counter-attack*, *punch* : *counter-punch*, *charge* : *counter-charge*, etc. These dynamic counteractives seem never to be expressed by distinct lexical roots in English, but only by pre-fixation with *counter-*. It is not clear why this should be so; intuitively, it does not seem fortuitous.)

It has been claimed that complementary adjectives are not normally **gradable**;[4] that is to say, they are odd in the comparative or superlative degree, or when modified by intensifiers such as *extremely*, *moderately*, or *slightly*. This is true, to a greater or lesser degree, of many adjective complementaries in English: *? extremely true*, *? fairly dead*, *? a little shut*, *? more married than most*, *? moderately female*, etc. But it is also true that very often one member of a pair lends itself more readily to grading than the other. Thus *dead* is less gradable than *alive*:

? very dead, ? moderately dead, ? deader than before
very alive, moderately alive, more alive than before

and *shut* is less gradable than *open*:

(tight shut), *? slightly shut, ? moderately shut, ? more shut than*
before
wide open, slightly open, moderately open, more open than
before

There is also, however, a class of what at first sight appear to be more or less fully gradable complementary adjectives: *clean : dirty* and *safe : dangerous* will serve as examples:

moderately clean, very clean, fairly clean, cleaner
slightly dirty, quite dirty, fairly dirty, dirtier
moderately safe, very safe, fairly safe, safer
slightly dangerous, quite dangerous, fairly dangerous,
more dangerous

Pairs such as these have not been generally recognised as complementaries,[5] perhaps because the usual tests give slightly equivocal results. Consider the pair *clean : dirty*: many speakers reject the entailments in 1 and do not find 2 anomalous:

1. *It's not clean* entails and is entailed by *It's dirty*
2. It's neither clean nor dirty.[6]

It seems that the bald statement *It's dirty* is reserved for distinctly dirty things, and would not be appropriate for only very slightly dirty things. However, a strengthening of the test produces clear results which differentiate these apparently gradable complementaries from antonyms such as *long* and *short*: *It's not clean* entails and is entailed by *It's at least slightly dirty*, and 3 is paradoxical for everyone:

3. ? It's neither clean, nor even slightly dirty.

These results may be contrasted with those obtained for *long* and *short*: *It's not long* does not entail *It's at least slightly short*, and 4 is not paradoxical:

4. It's not long, nor is it even a little bit short.

Other complementaries of this type are: *accurate : inaccurate, pure : impure, satisfactory : unsatisfactory, smooth : rough, drunk : sober, straight* : *bent*, *honest* : *dishonest*, *fresh* : *stale*, *well* : *unwell*. These opposites have a number of puzzling properties which make them difficult to classify and describe. The position that will be taken here is that there are, in fact, two senses of (for example) *clean* : *clean*[1], which appears in contexts such as *It's clean*, and which has a complementary relation with *dirty*; and *clean*[2], which appears in *How clean is it?* and *It's cleaner now*, and which has an antonymic relation to *dirty*. (Antonyms are discussed in detail below.)

9.3 Antonyms

Examples of antonyms have already been introduced, without definition, for purposes of comparison. The term will be used in this book with the restricted sense defined by Lyons,[7] rather than with its other most frequently encountered sense as a cover term for all types of lexical opposite. Antonymy is exemplified by such pairs as *long* : *short*, *fast* : *slow*, *easy* : *difficult*, *good* : *bad*, *hot* : *cold*. Antonyms share the following characteristics:[8]

(i) they are fully gradable (most are adjectives; a few are verbs)

(ii) members of a pair denote degrees of some variable property such as length, speed, weight, accuracy, etc.

(iii) when more strongly intensified, the members of a pair move, as it were, in opposite directions along the scale representing degrees of the relevant variable property. Thus, *very heavy* and *very light*, for instance, are more widely separated on the scale of weight than *fairly heavy* and *fairly light*.

(iv) the terms of a pair do not strictly bisect a domain: there is a range of values of the variable property, lying between those covered by the opposed terms, which cannot be properly referred to by either term. As a result, a statement containing one member of an antonym pair stands in a relation of contrariety with the parallel statement containing the other term. Thus, *It's long* and *It's short* are contrary, not contradictory, statements.

Furthermore, *It's neither long nor short* is not paradoxical, since there is a region on the scale of length which exactly fits this description.

Many properties can be conceptualised in terms of "more" and "less", thus creating a scale. We can think of such a scale as having an origin, or zero (corresponding to the absence of the scaled property), and extending more or less indefinitely in the direction of "more of" the property.

Of a pair of antonyms associated with such a scale, one will, as it were, tend towards zero, while the other will tend in the contrary direction. The terms of an antonymous pair are symmetrically disposed around a neutral region of the scale, which will be called the †**pivotal region**, and which cannot be referred to by either member of the pair. In the majority of cases, the pivotal region is not designated linguistically by any lexical item (*tepid* and *lukewarm*, referring to the pivotal region between *hot* and *cold*, are exceptional).

The scale on which a pair of antonyms operate is, however, not quite so straightforward as the preceding remarks imply. In fact, to picture how a typical pair of antonyms work we need to refer to two scales – an absolute scale, which covers all possible values of the scaled property from zero to infinity, and a relative scale, which is movable relative to the absolute scale, and whose values are directly relatable to the terms of the antonymous pair. Take the example of *long:short*. These terms cannot be assigned to any constant length, or even to a range of lengths: the values (on the absolute scale) that they denote vary with every referent to which they are applied. Compare *a long/short river* and *long/short eyelashes*.

The way a pair of antonyms operates can be represented diagrammatically as shown in fig. 9.1. The vertical dimension in this diagram is not significant: it has the purpose, simply, of permitting the representation

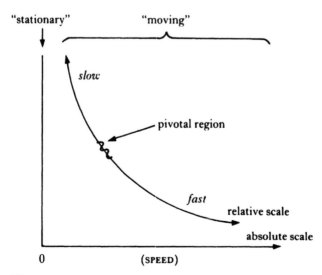

Figure 9.1

of an important property of *slow*. The value of *slow*, although it 'tends towards' zero speed, never actually reaches it, but approaches it, as mathematicians say, asymptotically. This is not a physical fact, but a linguistic one: we cannot say *completely slow* when we mean "stationary". The behaviour of *slow* is typical of that of 'zero-oriented' members of antonym pairs; thus, we cannot say *completely cheap* when we mean "free of charge", nor *completely short* when we mean "having zero length".

It has been said that antonyms, even when not explicitly comparative in form, are always to be interpreted comparatively.[9] That is to say, expressions like *It's long* or *That's a long one* are to be understood to mean "longer than X", where X is some implicit reference point on the scale of length. (It would be more accurate to say "longer to a surprising or significant degree than X", since the amount of excess length which is needed to qualify a referent as *long* is different for different referents, and depends on inherent variability.) This is a species of definiteness: just as an addressee on hearing *Give me the book* must identify the particular book being demanded, so must someone hearing *Isn't he tall?* identify the particular reference point intended by the speaker. The most frequent reference point is some sort of average value within a class. But the hearer must also, of course, identify the relevant class. *A tall man entered the room* is likely to refer to someone taller than the average adult male human; *Isn't he tall?*, however, may mean "tall for his age, family, class at school, tribe, or profession" (e.g. if he is a jockey), or "taller than the last time the speaker saw him", etc.

9.4 Sub-classes of antonyms

Antonyms can be divided into three (possibly four) sub-types. I shall delimit the types initially on the basis of the relationship between the semantic properties of those lexical units of the adjective lexemes which appear in sentences of the form *It's X*, and the semantic properties of the lexical units which appear in corresponding comparative forms (although, as we shall see, there are other correlated differences). There are basically two possible relationships, one involving what we shall call †**pseudo-comparatives**, and the other †**true comparatives**. Consider, first, the relation between the occurrences of *heavy* in 5 and 6:

5. This box is heavy.
6. This box is heavier than that one.

Notice that a preceding assertion that the box is *light* yields oddness in the case of 5, but not with 6:

7. ? This box is light, but it's heavy.
8. This box is light, but it's heavier than that one.

In other words, *heavier* does not mean "heavy to a greater degree", but "of greater weight". We shall therefore describe *heavier* as the pseudo-comparative of *heavy* (in, e.g., *It's heavy*). (Evidence will be offered below that two distinct, but related, senses of *heavy* are involved here – *heavier* is the true comparative of one, and the pseudo-comparative of the other.) Consider, now, the relation between the occurrences of *hot* in 9 and 10:

9. It's hot today.
10. It's hotter today than yesterday.

A preceding assertion that the weather is *cold* produces oddness in both cases:

11. ? It's cold today, but it's hot.
12. ? It's cold today, but it's hotter than yesterday.

It seems that *hotter* DOES mean "hot to a greater degree". We shall therefore describe *hotter* as the true comparative of *hot*, and it will be argued that 11 and 12 contain the SAME sense of *hot*.

We are now in a position to define the three groups of antonyms:

Group I: there is a pseudo-comparative corresponding to each member of a pair.

> It's short, but it's longer than the other one.
> It's long, but it's shorter than the other one.
> e.g. *heavy : light, fast : slow, high : low, deep : shallow,*
> *wide : narrow, thick : thin, difficult : easy*

Group II: there is a pseudo-comparative corresponding to one member of a pair, but the other member has a true comparative.

> John's a dull lad, but he's cleverer than Bill.
> ? Bill's a clever lad, but he's duller than John.
> e.g. *good : bad, pretty : plain, kind : cruel, polite : rude*

Group III: both members of a pair have true comparatives.

> ? It's hot, but it's colder than yesterday.
> ? It's cold, but it's hotter than yesterday.
> e.g. *nice : nasty, sweet : sour, proud of : ashamed of, happy : sad*

Group II has a sub-group consisting of those hybrid opposites like *clean* :

dirty and *safe* : *dangerous*, which in the positive degree behave like complementaries. In respect of their graded uses, however, there is no doubt that they belong to Group II:

> ? It's still clean, but it's dirtier than before.
> It's still dirty, but it's cleaner than before.

Accordingly, two sub-groups will be distinguished. It would be useful to have names for these antonym types. We shall therefore call those in Group I †**polar antonyms**, those in Group II †**overlapping antonyms**, and those in Group III †**equipollent antonyms**. Group II(b), a sub-class of overlapping antonyms, will be termed †**privative antonyms**.[10]

The three groups that have been established also display differences with respect to certain other properties. First, members of the three groups differ in respect of the sort of properties they typically refer to. Polar (Group I) antonyms (e.g. *long* : *short*) are typically evaluatively neutral, and objectively descriptive. In the majority of cases, the underlying scaled property can be measured in conventional units, such as inches, grams, or miles per hour. Overlapping (Group II) antonyms all have an evaluative polarity as part of their meaning: one term is commendatory (e.g. *good*, *pretty*, *polite*, *kind*, *clean*, *safe*, *honest*) and the other is deprecatory (e.g. *bad*, *plain*, *rude*, *cruel*, *dirty*, *dangerous*, *dishonest*). What distinguishes privative antonyms in this respect is not entirely clear: it may be that they characteristically refer to situations where the desirable state is less the presence of some valued property than the absence of an undesirable one, such as dirt or danger. All equipollent (Group III) antonyms – there are not many of them – refer to distinctly subjective sensations or emotions (e.g. *hot* : *cold*, *happy* : *sad*), or evaluations based on subjective reactions, rather than on 'objective' standards (e.g. *nice* : *nasty*, *pleasant* : *unpleasant*).

Second, the three groups differ in respect of the possibility of forming questions on the pattern of *How X̀ is it?*, with the main (nuclear) stress of the sentence on *X* (all antonyms occur normally in *how*-questions with the stress on *how* or *is*); and they differ too, with regard to the semantic nature of the questions thus formed. Consider the question *How heavy is it?* Just as *X is heavier than Y* tells us nothing about the actual weight of X or Y, the questioner here expresses no presumption or expectation concerning the weight of the questioned item. Such expressions will be described as †**impartial** (in this case, impartial with respect to the contrast between *It's heavy* and *It's light*). On the other hand, *How hot is it?* and *It's hotter than before* both carry a presupposition that *hot*, rather than *cold*, would be an appropriate description of the questioned item.[11] These expressions will be described as †**committed**. (Notice that although *How heavy is it?* is impartial, *H*ŏ*w heavy is it?* is committed.) The characterisation of the three groups in respect of *How X is it?* questions (which will henceforth simply be referred to as *how*-questions) is as follows:

Polar: Only one member of a pair yields a normal *how*-question (cf. *How long is it?* but *? How short is it?*), and this question is impartial.[12]

Overlapping: Both terms of a pair yield normal *how*-questions, but one term yields an impartial question (e.g. *How good is it?*), and the other term yields a committed question (e.g. *How bad is it?*).

Equipollent: Both terms of a pair yield normal *how*-questions, and both questions are committed (*How hot is it?*, *How cold is it?*).

It is worth noting that quantified comparatives of the form *twice as/half as X* show the same patterning as *how*-questions in respect of normality and impartiality.[13]

This is a convenient point to raise the matter of distinctions of lexical units within lexemes. Consider the occurrences of the form *long* in 13, 14 and 15:

13. It's long.
14. This one is longer than that one.
15. How long is it?

How many different lexical units *long* occur in these sentences? The following evidence is relevant. First of all, 16 is zeugmatic. This suggests that the sense of *long* which appears in 15 is different from that which appears in *It isn't long* (and presumably also in 13):

16. A: How long is it?
    B:? It isn't.

On the other hand, if B's answer in 17 can be taken as equivalent to a comparative, it is not odd in the way that would be expected if 15 and 14 contained different senses:

17. A: How long is this one?
    B: More so than the last one, but still a bit short.

(cf. also:

A: What is the length of this one?
B: Greater than that of the last one, but still short.)

On this evidence, then, it would seem that 14 and 15 contain one and the same sense of *long*, and 13 a different one. This is confirmed by the suggestion of zeugma in 18, which indicates a distinction between 13 and 14:

18. A: Is this one long?
    B: ? No – more so than the last one, though.

The *long* in *twice as long* is harder to test, but it seems reasonable to assume that it is the same as that in 14 and 15. Similar considerations lead to the conclusion that *short* in *It's short* and *It's shorter* represent distinct senses; likewise *clean* in *It's clean* is different from *clean* in *It's cleaner* and *How clean is it?* The two senses of *long* (likewise those of *heavy*, *wide*, *fast*, *clean*, etc.) are, of course, systematically related and their respective units are to be assigned to the same lexeme. Notice that in 19, 20 and 21 there is no need to postulate different lexical units *hot*:

19. It's hot.
20. It's hotter than yesterday.
21. How hot is it?

Many of the differences between the groups can be given an intuitively satisfying explanation if we assume that for overlapping and equipollent antonym pairs (but not polars) the properties denoted by each of the members of a pair are conceived as being quasi-autonomous. That is to say, whereas SHORTNESS, for example, is no more and no less than the absence of LENGTH, GOODNESS and BADNESS, CLEVERNESS and DULLNESS, and HOTNESS and COLDNESS are to some extent independent properties. At a more abstract level, of course, there is a common underlying gradable property for both members of a pair (otherwise they would not be opposites): MERIT for *good* : *bad*, TEMPERATURE for *hot* : *cold*, etc. But at a more superficial level, the properties have a certain independence. We can thus say that whereas a single scale underlies a pair of polar antonyms, there are two scales underlying a pair of overlapping or equipollent antonyms. This already offers a natural explanation for certain of the differences between polar antonyms, on the one hand, and overlapping and equipollent antonyms on the other. It is reasonable to assume that the normality of *twice/half as X* and *How X is it?* depends on the existence of a scale of X-NESS. *Short*, *slow* and *shallow*, for example, are odd in these frames because there is no scale of SHORTNESS, SLOWNESS, or SHALLOWNESS. (*A speaker is, of course, free to create an ad hoc scale: How slow is it?*, although not fully normal, is by no means uninterpretable.)

The relationship between the senses associated with a pair of polar antonyms can be portrayed diagrammatically as shown in fig. 9.2. We need
now to be able to picture overlapping and equipollent antonyms in a way

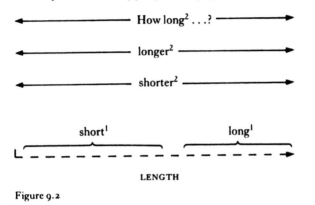

Figure 9.2

which will account naturally for their differences. Consider, first, the equipollent type, represented by *hot*: *cold*. Since nothing that is *colder* can
be *hot*, and nothing *hotter* can be *cold*, then if we assume that each term
is restricted to its own scale it appears that nothing can fall simultaneously
on the two scales; or, to put it another way, there is no overlap between
the scales of COLDNESS and HOTNESS. The relationship between the scales
can therefore be represented as shown in fig. 9.3.

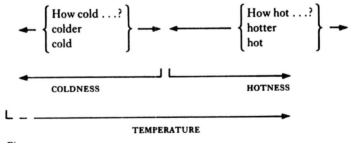

Figure 9.3

There is an important difference between the *hot*: *cold* contrast and the
long: *short* contrast: the difference between *hot* and *cold* is in a sense absolute, rather than relative. The distinction is based neither on an average
nor on a norm, but ultimately on a difference of sensation quality. However,
although the distinction between *hot* and *cold* is absolute, once we are
on one or other of the scales a principle of relativity applies. The temperature required for a day to qualify as *hot* is much lower than that required
of an oven, which in turn is lower than that required of a furnace.

211

Let us now consider how *warm* and *cool* fit into the picture. The facts are somewhat complex. First, the normality of all the following sentences suggests that each of the terms operates on its own scale:

How hot is it?	X is twice as hot as Y.
How warm is it?	X is twice as warm as Y.
How cool is it?	Z is twice as cool as Y.
How cold is it?	X is twice as cold as Y.

How cool is it? and *twice as cool* are the least normal of these expressions, but even here the oddness is not of the same order as that of *? twice as short*. (It is interesting to note that hotness, warmness and coldness – but not coolness – are physiologically distinct sensations.) If we accept the linguistic evidence for the existence of separate scales, then the picture is as shown in fig. 9.4.

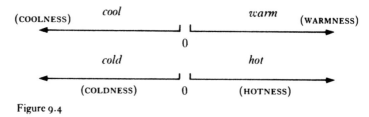

Figure 9.4

This arrangement, however, fails to account for the peculiar distribution of *cooler* and *warmer*. The problem is that *cooler* can be used of any temperature provided that it does not fall within the range of *cold*, and *warmer* can be used of any temperature that does not fall within the range of *hot*. Thus we can speak of one *hot* furnace being *cooler* than another, and of the temperature at the North Pole as being *warmer* than that of the surface of the moon. It is almost as if there were two different lexical terms *cool*: *cool*[1], which had its own scale, and denoted a moderate degree of coldness, and *cool*[2], which acted as a polar antonym of *hot*; similarly, there might be a *warm*[1] with its own scale, and a *warm*[2], which was a polar antonym of *cold*. This would yield a picture like that shown in fig. 9.5. In this way the observed range of *cooler* could be explained as the

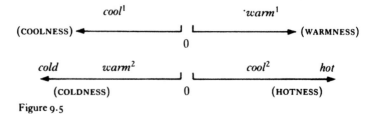

Figure 9.5

combined ranges of *cooler*[1] and *cooler*[2] and, similarly, *mutatis mutandis* with *warmer*. An obvious difficulty with this proposal is that there do not, at first sight, appear to be any normal uses of *cool*[2] and *warm*[2] to denote, respectively, 'relatively *cool* on the *hot* scale' and 'relatively *warm* on the *cold* scale'. A day on which the temperature is 'mildly hot' is a *warm* day, and by no stretch of the imagination a *cool* day. There do occur, however, in special circumstances, uses of *cool* and *warm* which correspond closely to what one would expect from *cool*[2] and *warm*[2]:

Place the mixture in a cool oven.
This substance burns with a cool flame.
Put it in the warm part of the refrigerator.

An *oven* and a *flame* can perhaps be regarded as inherently *hot*, and a *refrigerator* as inherently *cold*: under these circumstances, *warm* and *cool* behave like polar antonyms of *cold* and *hot*. If the above analysis is correct, then we have four opposite pairs: *hot*:*cold*, *warm*[1]:*cool*[1] *hot*:*cool*[2], and *cold*:*warm*[2]. This account sheds some light on the properties of, and relations between, *cold*, *cool*, *warm* and *hot*, but it cannot be denied that many problems remain, and it could be that a rather different sort of model is required from the one we have been using.

In the case of overlapping antonyms, exemplified by *good*:*bad*, things that are *bad* may nonetheless be *better*; whatever is *good*, however (for the majority of speakers), cannot be normally qualified as *worse*. Thus the scale of BADNESS must overlap the scale of MERIT (over which *good*[2] operates), but not extend into the region on the MERIT scale covered by *good*[1]. The relationships between the terms associated with the scale of MERIT can therefore be pictured as shown in fig. 9.6.

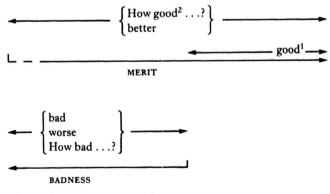

Figure 9.6

213

There is a theoretical third possibility for the relation between two sub-scales, which, if realised, would yield a fourth group of antonyms. There could be two completely overlapping scales, as shown in fig. 9.7. The predicted properties of such a group would be:

a. both terms of a pair would have pseudo-comparatives
b. both terms would yield impartial questions
c. both terms would be normal and impartial in quantified comparatives

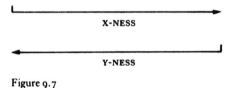

Figure 9.7

There are no fully convincing examples of this type of opposition in English, although the pair *hard*:*soft* (as applied, for instance, to cheese or butter) is difficult to classify, and might be a candidate.

9.5 Inherentness

It has been argued that the scale of MERIT on which *good* and *better* operate overlaps with that of BADNESS, a consequence of this being that something *bad* can be described as being *better* than something which is even worse. However, this general statement needs qualification and refinement, in view of cases like 22:

22a. Bill's accident was worse than John's.
  b. ? John's accident was better than Bill's.

It appears that, after all, not every *bad* thing can be normally described as *better* than something else, even when that something else is qualifiable as *worse*. The following is a selection of lexical items which do not collocate normally with better: *headache, depression, failure, debt, famine, drought, storm, earthquake, flood.* They are all nouns whose referents may be said to be 'inherently bad'. Apparently *better* will collocate normally only with nouns which can collocate normally with *good*. A related peculiarity of inherently bad nouns is that they cannot be questioned with *How good is ...?*:

23. ? How good was the drought last year?

How bad was the drought?, on the other hand, is perfectly normal. The latter restriction is the easier to motivate. In asking *How X is it?*, one is effectively saying: "Place it for me on the scale of X-NESS." In the case of floods and other inherently bad things we have a theoretical choice of questions: *How good is it?* and *How bad is it?*, i.e. "Place it for me on the scale of GOODNESS" or "Place it for me on the scale of BADNESS." Choosing the wider scale carries an implication that one is prepared for an answer anywhere along it; that is to say, one signals a readiness to accept that the item might be *good*. This is, of course, nonsense in the case of inherently bad items, so it is more normal, for these, to choose the narrower scale. The restriction of *better* to referents that are not inherently bad is less obvious in its motivation, but the rationale is presumably similar.

Peculiar collocational behaviour with inherent nouns is confined to overlapping antonyms, and is a consequence of a restricted sub-scale overlapping a wider sub-scale, thus presenting the speaker with a choice of scales when a referent falls within the region of overlap. In principle, all overlapping antonyms are capable of displaying the effects of inherentness:

24a. John's torturing of the cat was crueller than Bill's.
  b. ? Bill's torturing of the cat was kinder than John's.
  c. ? How kind was John's torturing of the cat?
25a. Cedric's insult was ruder than Crispin's.
  b. ? Crispin's insult was more polite than Cedric's.
  c. ? How polite was Cedric's insult.

For most or all of the lexical items we have so far examined it could plausibly be claimed that the 'inherent badness' was an inalienable feature of their meaning. However, this is not a necessary condition for the effects of inherentness to manifest themselves. What matters is simply that the speaker, at the time of utterance, should feel that a certain whole class of referents should be 'a bad thing', rather than a class that has good and bad members. Consider the sentence:

This year's strike was better than last year's.

This sentence would hardly occur during a conversation between managing directors, to whom all strikes are evil, but could very well occur in a conversation between shop stewards. On the other hand, *This year's strike was worse than last year's* would be more likely in a managerial discussion; it might also be uttered by a union official, but would have the opposite interpretation, i.e. that percentage support was down this year.

Polar antonyms exhibit no inherentness effects comparable to those of overlapping type. Thus, although pygmies are inherently *short*, they can be described quite normally as *taller*:

26. The pygmies on this island are taller than those on the mainland.

In the case of equipollent antonyms, while it is odd to describe an inherently *cold* referent (such as an iceberg) as *hotter* than something else, it is not necessary to invoke inherentness as an explanation, since it is odd to describe any *cold* thing as *hotter*.

Another type of interaction between an antonym operating on a restricted sub-scale and inherentness of qualified noun can be observed when 27 and 28 are compared:

27. John's headache is bad.
28. John's exam marks are bad.

In 27, *bad* does not mean "bad rather than good", as it does in 28, but rather "more than averagely bad" (cf. also *a sweet marmalade* compared with *a sweet wine*, *a hot fire* compared with *a hot day*). That is to say, with an inherently bad noun, *bad* acts like one member of an antonymous pair whose total domain is the scale of BADNESS (its partner might be something like *slight*). With respect to this scale, *How bad is your headache?* has some claim to being regarded as an impartial question. Surprisingly, it does not appear that 27 and 28 contain different senses of *bad*, since most speakers apparently do not find 29 zeugmatic:

29. When harvests are bad, so are farmers' debts.

The different interpretations of *bad* with *harvest* and *accident* must thus be attributed to contextual modulation.

9.6 Implicit superlatives

Some scales, besides having a pair of gradable lexical items that are implicitly comparative (i.e. normal antonyms), also have lexical items which are better characterised as implicit superlatives. An obvious example of this is the scale of SIZE, which is associated not only with the antonym pair *large*:*small*, but also with *huge*:*tiny* and *enormous*:*minute*, which are confined to the negative and positive extremes of the scale. Implicit superlatives can be recognised by a number of distinctive properties. First, they are, generally speaking, resistant to grading, although to varying degrees:

? very huge, ? fairly huge, ? This one is huger
? rather minute, ? very minute, ? This one is minuter
? slightly enormous, ? pretty tiny

Second, they can be modified by unstressed *absolutely*:

absolutely huge, absolutely enormous, absolutely minute

Simple antonyms sound very odd when spoken like this:

? absolutely large, ? absolutely small

Third, although they cannot be lexically or morphologically graded, they can be prosodically graded, that is to say by means of stress and intonation.[14] Thus, the 'hugeness' of something can be indicated by the pitch range of the falling tone on *huge* in *It's hùge!* According to these criteria, the following are further examples of implicit superlatives:

beautiful : ugly, brilliant : stupid, spotless : filthy, scorching : freezing

Where two terms on one part of a scale differ in intensity, but not in polarity (i.e. if they move in the same direction when intensified), there are two possibilities for their relationship: either, as in the cases just described, one term is an implicit comparative and the other is an implicit superlative; or one term may be an implicit comparative and the other an implicit attenuative. The latter possibility is exemplified by *hot : warm* and *cold : cool*. The more basic pair, *hot* and *cold*, are at the same time the 'outer' pair; *warm* and *cool* represent a weakening of this contrast. *Hot* and *cold* do not display the characteristic features of superlatives: *? absolutely hot, ? absolutely cold*.

9.7 Stative verbs

There is a group of verbal opposites which share a great many characteristics with equipollent antonyms such as *hot : cold*. Consider *like : dislike*: they represent psychological states (cf. *happy : sad*); they are fully gradable (*I quite like it, I like her enormously*); and there is a neutral area between the opposing poles (*I neither like nor dislike her – she leaves me totally indifferent*). The relation between the terms can be modelled, like that between *hot* and *cold*, as two non-overlapping scales pointing outwards in opposite directions:

dislike   like

217

As this model predicts, both terms are committed in the verbal equivalent to a comparative:

> ? I like her, but I dislike her more than Susan.
> ? I dislike her, but I like her more than Mary.

Other examples of this type are: *despise* : *admire* and *approve* : *disapprove*; similar in structural relations, but different in that the experiencer is the direct object, are *please* : *displease*.[15]

A further resemblance between verbs of this group and adjectival opposites is that they include what appear to be underlying superlatives, analogous to *huge* : *tiny* and *scorching* : *freezing*. *Love* and *hate* seem to be of this type. First, they are not so fully gradable as *like* and *dislike*:

> *I quite like him, I dislike it, a little*
> *? I quite love him, ? I hate him, a little*

Second, they are modifiable by unstressed *absolutely*:

> *I absolutely love it!, I absolutely hate it!*
> *? I absolute like it!, ? I absolutely dislike it!*

Finally, *love* and *hate*, in contrast to *like* and *dislike*, can be prosodically intensified.

The scales of HOTNESS and COLDNESS can be seen to be closely related because they both measure degrees of TEMPERATURE. That is to say, we can identify a more abstract scale which unites the two properties. Intuitively, the same ought to be true of *like* and *dislike* and the other stative verbal opposites; but it is a curious fact that there is no independent evidence for it. There is no neutral way, for instance, of asking what someone's degree of liking or disliking for something is, analogous to *What is the temperature?* We can say *How do you feel about Mary?*, but this seems too general, and could refer to any emotional colour. It is not immediately obvious whether this is a significant or a fortuitous lack.

9.8 Contrastive aspects

At present, available information concerning the existence and membership of sub-classes of antonyms in other languages than English is unfortunately too fragmentary to enable firm contrastive generalisations to be made. However, there is enough to justify a few tentative suggestions.

We have seen that oppositions between gradable adjectives can be classified into four fairly distinct types: polar antonyms (e.g. *long* : *short*), overlapping antonyms (e.g. *good* : *bad* and *clean* : *dirty*, with the latter exemplifying the sub-group of privative antonyms), and equipollent antonyms (e.g. *hot* : *cold*); we have also seen that in English, group membership tends to be correlated with certain types of meaning: polar antonyms are objectively descriptive, overlapping antonyms are evaluative, and equipollent antonyms refer to sensations, emotions and subjective reactions.

A preliminary observation is that the nearest translation equivalents in another language of a pair of English antonyms will not necessarily belong to the same structural group as the English pair. For instance, *chaud* and *froid* in French do not, like their English equivalents *hot* and *cold*, belong to the equipollent type, but to the polar type: speakers of French I have consulted find the following sentences quite normal:

> Il fait chaud, mais il fait plus froid qu'hier.
> Il fait froid, mais il fait plus chaud qu'hier.

The German pair *gut* : *schlecht* also appear to be polar antonyms, unlike their English counterparts, which are of the overlapping type.[16] (It is worth noting that for a minority of English speakers, too, *good* and *bad* are polar antonyms: for them, *John's performance was excellent, but it was worse than Bill's* is perfectly normal.[17] However, like the majority group, they judge *How good is your headache?* to be odd. For such speakers, *worse* apparently has two senses, (i) a pseudo-comparative of *bad*, which may be applied to things that are not inherently bad, and (ii) a true comparative of *bad*, restricted to inherently bad things. They find the following sentence zeugmatic, since for them the *worse* which can qualify a good set of exam marks cannot simultaneously qualify a headache, although the lexeme *worse* collocates normally with either of these singly:

That John's headache was worse than Bill's perhaps explains why his exam marks were, too, although they were, in fact, very good.

For the majority of English speakers this sentence is abnormal for different reasons, but it is not zeugmatic.) The Egyptian Arabic equivalents of *good* and *bad*, on the other hand, are privative antonyms.[18]

Looking at the three antonym groups, one might suggest that antonyms of the equipollent type (*hot* : *cold*) are, in a sense, the most 'subjective', and the polar type (*long* : *short*) the most 'objective', with the overlapping variety (*good* : *bad*) occupying an intermediate position. To put it another way, polar antonyms are the most highly conceptualised and distanced from the raw psycho-physical facts, while equipollent antonyms are the most 'primitive', being the most closely modelled on the psycho-physical facts (for instance, heat and cold are physiologically distinct sensations;

linguistically, *hot* and *cold* operate on their own distinct scales). On this basis, one might hazard a tentative suggestion. Presumably all languages will have adjectives, and very probably pairs of opposites, denoting degrees of such properties as length, temperature, beauty, merit, pleasantness, and so on. But perhaps in some languages the meanings of relative adjectives are in general more highly conceptualised than in others. In this respect, English, with some equipollent antonyms and substantial numbers of overlapping antonyms, is relatively 'subjective'. In contrast, Macedonian seems to be highly conceptualised, since all antonyms are apparently of the polar type.[19] French is perhaps intermediate between English and Macedonian: polar and overlapping antonyms (including privatives) are certainly present, but an informal questioning of informants has failed to unearth any convincing examples of equipollent antonyms. It may be that if a language has only one type of antonym, there is a strong likelihood that they will be polars; if there are two types, they will resemble our polar and overlapping antonyms; equipollents will only be represented if the other two are also present. Further research is needed before this hypothesis can be confirmed or disconfirmed.

Notes

9.1 For opposites in general see Ogden (1932), Martin (1976), Lyons (1977: 270–80), Geckeler (1980), Warczyck (1981).

   1. The term *complementary* is from Lyons (1968: 460–2). As far as possible I have adopted Lyons's terminology.

9.2

   2. It must be borne in mind that, in judging the logical relation between *John is not dead* and *John is alive*, it is necessary to assume (i) that the referential presuppositions of both statements are satisfied – i.e. there exists an appropriate person named John, (ii) the statements both refer to the same person, and (iii) that the predicate is predicable of the subject – *The table is not dead*, for instance, does not entail *The table is alive*.
   3. The conditions for the successful performance of a speech act are known as **felicity conditions**. See Austin (1962: chs. 2, 3 and 4) and Levinson (1983: 229–35 and 238–40).
   4. See Lyons (1968: 462).
   5. See, however, Cruse (1980).
   6. This must not, of course, be interpreted as a metalinguistic statement – for instance, as *It's neither 'clean' nor 'dirty'*.

9.3 Antonyms have received a good deal of attention from linguists: see, in addition to the works cited under 9.1, Sapir (1944), Ducháček (1965), Bierwisch (1967), Lyons (1968: 463–7), Pohl (1970), Ljung (1974), van Overbeke (1975), Cruse (1976), Bolinger (1977), Cruse (1980), Lehrer and Lehrer (1982), Lehrer (1985).

7. See Lyons (1968: 463–4).
8. For a more formal definition see Lehrer and Lehrer (1982).
9. See Sapir (1944).

9.4 This section is based largely on Cruse (1976) and (1980). See also Lehrer (1985).

10. For the privative nature of Group II(b) antonyms see Kastovsky (1982). The terms *privative* and *equipollent* were first introduced by Trubetskoy (1969: 74–7) to designate types of phonological opposition, along with a third term, *gradual*, which we have not made use of. The three types of opposition may be briefly characterised as follows. A privative opposition is one between two terms, one of which possesses a distinctive feature that the other one lacks. The phonemes /p/ and /b/ in English may be said to manifest a privative opposition, the feature which is respectively present and absent being that of voicing. Lyons (1977: 279) gives *animate : inanimate* as an example of a privative opposition, on the grounds that the terms denote, respectively, presence and absence of life. However, it is the referents of the terms which have, or do not have, life; it is less easy to show that the privativeness applies to the senses of the lexical items. Coseriu (1975: 40) conceives of privativeness in terms of the presence or absence of specific semantic traits. So, for instance, for him, *albus : candidus* (L.) manifest a privative opposition, since they differ in respect of the presence or absence of the trait "luminosité"; the opposition between *dominer* and *maîtriser* (Fr.) is likewise privative, the trait which is respectively absent and present being "volonté". An equipollent opposition is one between two terms each of which carries a positive differentiating feature. The phonemes /t/ and /s/ in English can be seen as manifesting an equipollent opposition, the former possessing the feature 'stop', and the latter the feature 'fricative'. Lyons's example of an equipollent opposition is *male : female*; Coseriu gives the colour terms *yellow, red*, etc. Gradual oppositions are those where the contrast between the terms of the opposition lies in their possessing different values of a single property. Distinctions of vowel height are often held to be examples of this type. Coseriu's examples of gradual oppositions are *tiède : chaud, grand : énorme, seconde : minute : heure : jour*, etc.

11. These presuppositions of *hotter, colder*, etc. would appear to be what Grice (1975: 44) calls **conventional implicatures**. (See also Levinson (1983: 127–32).)

12. Some speakers accept *How short is it?* in restricted contexts: it is invariably committed.

13. Most speakers appear to find *half as short* (etc.) more difficult to construe than *twice as short* (etc.); for a few, they would appear to be synonymous. (*Half as long* and *twice as long* are, of course, fully normal for all speakers.)

9.6

14. Cf. Bolinger (1972: 281–8).

9.7

15. Notice that *dislike* is not equivalent to a logical negation of *like*. (Confusingly, *I do not like him* has an interpretation equivalent to *I dislike him*: to obtain an unequivocal logical negation one must say *It's not true that I like him*.) Negative prefixes on gradable adjectives (such as *happy*) and stative verbs (such as *like, approve*) tend not to produce contradictory opposites (i.e. complementaries), but contrary opposites (i.e. antonyms). (This does not apply to adjectives like *clean* which denote the absence of an undesirable property.) See Zimmer (1964).

9.8

16. This was first pointed out to me by W. Haas, whose first language is German; I have since had ample confirmation from German-speaking students, who are often reluctant to accept that English is different.

17. From my questioning of many classes of students I would estimate that roughly 10 per cent use *worse* in this way. (It is possible that the fact that *worse* is not morphologically related to *bad* has something to do with this.)

18. Zikri (1979).

19. Marsh–Stefanowska (1981).

10
Opposites II: directional oppositions

10.1 Directional opposites

Underlying many lexical opposites there is a type of opposition which we shall call †**directional**. It can be seen in its purest form in the everyday notion of contrary motion (i.e. motion in opposite directions). This is relatively easy to define, in the simplest case: two bodies A and B, moving in straight lines at speeds S(1) and S(2), respectively, are moving in opposite directions if the speed of A relative to B is equal to the sum of S(1) and S(2). We shall take this as the most primitive manifestation of the directional opposition. As we shall see, no pair of lexical opposites expresses pure linear contrary motion – not even such a pair as *ascend*: *descend*. However, many opposites clearly owe their oppositeness to the fact that they encapsulate the basic directional opposition, or represent a conceptual transformation or metaphorical extension of it. These form the subject matter of the present chapter.

10.2 Directions

A direction, in the simplest case, defines a potential path for a body moving in a straight line; a pair of lexical items denoting opposite directions indicate potential paths, which, if followed by two moving bodies, would result in their moving in opposite directions, as defined above. Although there are no lexical pairs denoting pure contrary motion, there are pairs which in their most basic senses denote pure opposite directions. They are all adverbs or prepositions: *north*: *south*, *up*: *down*, *forwards*: *backwards* are examples.

Any direction from a base point must be established either with respect to some second reference point, or by reference to the orientation or motion of some entity. For instance, from any point on the earth's surface, *north* may be defined as the direction in which a body must travel in order to reach the North Pole by the shortest route; or maybe it is the direction indicated by the Pole Star; *south* can be defined in relation to the South Pole, or simply as the opposite direction to *north*. *East* and *west* can be established by reference to the points on the horizon where the sun respectively rises and sets. *Towards X* and *away from X* are opposite directions defined in relation to a variable second reference point.

Up and *down* can also be defined with respect to a second reference point (i.e. *away from* and *towards* the centre of the earth), but it is perhaps psychologically more plausible to define them in terms of the direction of motion of freely falling bodies (or, better still, the direction of the force that must be applied to prevent them falling; this would give cognitive primacy to *up*).[1] *Upstream* and *downstream*, too, can be defined using a second reference point (e.g. "towards source"/"away from source"). But this does not make any connection with the basic sense of *up* and *down*. It seems equally likely that a relationship is felt between the falling of dropped objects and the floating. downstream of objects placed in a river; in other words, the direction of the tractive force of the water is seen as analogous to the pull of gravity. There are two rotational directions: *clockwise* and *anticlockwise*, which today are presumably established by reference to the direction in which the hands of a clock move; but more primitively – perhaps under different names (e.g. *withershins* for *anti-clockwise*)[2] – these directions are defined by the apparent movement of the sun in the sky.

Forwards and *backwards*, for objects with inherent orientation (like people, or cars), can be seen either as the direction of normal motion, or the direction the object 'faces'. For objects without inherent orientation, like tables and footballs, *forwards* and *backwards* (in their spatial interpretation) are interpreted relative to the speaker, or some other person who is the current source of spatial coordinates for the discourse.[3] Paradoxically, at least for (non-orientated) objects in front of a reference person who is both stationary and not viewed as potentially moving, *forwards* denotes movement *towards* him – that is, the direction which, if followed by the reference person himself, would count as backwards. (This is perhaps because an equivalent reduction in distance could be achieved by the reference person moving forwards.)

There are many complex details of usage of direction words which it would be inappropriate to go into here; the present concern is merely to establish a category of lexical opposites.[4]

10.3 Antipodals

Building on the notion of oppositeness of direction, a category of †**antipodal** opposites can be defined, in which one term represents an extreme in one direction along some salient axis, while the other term denotes the corresponding extreme in the other direction. For instance, if we go *up* as far as we can while remaining within the confines of some spatial entity, we reach its *top*, and in the other direction the lower limit is the *bottom*; *zenith* and *nadir* represent a related contrast, not usually applied to the extremes of a coherent physical object – more often to the highest and lowest points of a range of values of some more abstract property, such as the political fortunes of a dynasty. Pairs of opposites encapsulating the notion of *upward* and *downward* extremities are common: *cellar* : *attic*, *source* : *mouth*, *peak* : *foot* (of mountain), *head* : *toe*. The same notion extended analogically yields *maximum* : *minimum*, *full* : *empty*; even Keats's *emperor* and *clown* (*Ode to a Nightingale*) owes something to this, being the *zenith* and *nadir*, respectively, of social rank at court. Not dissimilar are *always* : *never*, *all* : *none* and *black* : *white*; they certainly represent opposite extremes along notional axes, but perhaps the association with *up* and *down* is less strong. The directions *forwards* and *backwards*, within a coherent spatial entity, yield *front* and *back*, which are encapsulated in *tip* : *tail* (for animals). *Forwards* and *backwards* in the temporal dimension give *start* : *finish*, *beginning* : *end*; the latter, encapsulated, appears in *cradle* : *grave*. The directions *in* and *out* yield the antipodals *middle*/*centre* : *edge*/*periphery*/*circumference*, etc.

Once again, example and finer detail could be multiplied indefinitely; however, there seems little of a systematic nature to say.

10.4 Counterparts

Any deviation or irregularity in an otherwise uniform surface or shape has a counterpart in which essential defining directions are reversed. Thus, for instance, a *mound* projects *out* of the earth's surface; the corresponding shape projecting *into* the earth is a *depression*. Similarly, we have *bulge* : *constriction* (in a tube or pipe), *ridge* : *groove*, *hill* : *valley*, *bump* : *dent*, and the related adjectives *convex* : *concave*. Extended, the notion of counterpart can generate, for instance, *lull* : *spurt* (in activity). It may be that the *male* : *female* opposition partakes of this notion, the sexual organs being seen as counterparts. (The use of *male* and *female* in relation to electrical plugs and such-like would support this: the sexual opposition, is, however, one of those like *heaven* : *hell*, *yin* : *yang*, which do not satisfactorily reduce to any specific simpler opposition, but embody a number of different elementary notions.[5] Such oppositions frequently have profound cultural significance.)

10.5 **Reversives**

One of the most interesting classes of directional opposite consists of those pairs of verbs which denote motion or change in opposite directions. We shall call these †**reversives**. Purely spatial instances – presumably the simplest, conceptually – are not very numerous: the basic senses of *rise* :*fall*, *ascend* : *descend*, *advance* : *retreat* and *enter* : *leave* are examples. In the majority of cases, it is necessary to interpret the notion of opposite direction somewhat abstractly, or in an extended sense.

There are two main ways of characterising 'opposite direction' for reversive verb pairs. The first applies to those verbs which refer to change between two determinate states: let us symbolise these as state A and state B. The reversivity of the verb pair resides in the fact that one member denotes a change from A to B, while its reversive partner denotes a change from B to A. Consider, as examples of this type, *appear* : *disappear*, *tie* : *untie* and *enter* : *leave*. For the first pair, the relevant states are A: "being visible" and B: "being invisible". *Appear* (in the appropriate sense) means "change from being invisible to being visible", and *disappear* "change from being visible to being invisible". For *tie* and *untie*, the relevant states are "being tied" and "being untied"; for *enter* and *leave*, the relevant states are locational: "being inside something" and "being outside something". The latter two pairs illustrate an important feature of reversive opposites, namely, that the processes or actions through which the changes of state come about do not need to be precisely reversed for the two verbs of a pair. The action of *untying* a shoe-lace is not the literal reversal of the action of *tying* it (such as one might see in a film run backwards): usually one unties a shoe-lace merely by pulling the ends of the laces. What is important is that the appropriate states should come about. Likewise, *entering* and *leaving* do not necessarily involve motion in opposite directions in the simple spatial sense: a train *entering* and subsequently *leaving* a station may do so by travelling in the same direction for each. The essential thing is that the train should change from being *outside* the station to being *inside*, for *enter*, and from being *inside* to being *outside*, for *leave*. This characterisation applies to a large number of reversive pairs, of which the following is a selection: *pack* : *unpack*, *lock* : *unlock*, *screw* : *unscrew*, *dress* : *undress*, *mount* : *dismount*, *embark* : *disembark*, *cover* : *uncover*.

The second characterisation of opposite direction involves not absolute, but relative, states. Reversive verbs of this type denote changes between states defined merely as having a particular relationship to one another. Suppose we have a pair of verbs of this type, *a* and *b*, whose defining relation is R. One member of the pair, let us say *a*, will denote a change such that the initial state stands in the relation R to the final state, while its reversive partner, *b*, will denote a change such that the final state stands in the relation R to the initial state. An example of such a pair is *lengthen* : *shorten*. For something to have undergone a process of *lengthening*, it is enough that its final state should be longer than its initial state ("be longer than" represents R for this pair), whereas for *shorten* the initial state must be longer than the final state. Absolute lengths are irrelevant for both verbs. Other examples of this type are: *widen* : *narrow*, *accelerate* : *decelerate*, *heat* : *cool*, *ascend* : *descend*, *strengthen* : *weaken*, *improve* : *deteriorate*.

While it is necessary for members of a pair of reversives to be related to one another in one of the ways described above, the relationships as presented are not quite sufficient to define a pair of reversives. It is necessary to stipulate in addition that they should differ only in respect of directionality. Otherwise, *abbreviate*, for instance, would qualify as the opposite of *lengthen*, although no native speaker, I imagine, would accept this pair as opposites. *Abbreviate* fails, however, to satisfy the more stringent criteria, because its meaning differs from that of *lengthen* in more than just directionality: it is also more contextually restricted.

Syntactically, the most elementary type of reversive opposites are intransitive verbs whose grammatical subjects denote entities which undergo changes of state: *appear* : *disappear*, *enter* : *leave*, *rise* : *fall* are of this sort. A sizeable proportion of what must be considered reversive opposites, however, have a causative meaning: their grammatical subject is an agent, and it is the (referent of the) direct object which undergoes the reversible change of state: *raise* : *lower*, *lock* : *unlock*, *pack* : *unpack*, etc. belong to this category. Some lexeme pairs exemplify both types: *Mary lengthened/shortened her skirt*, *The days began to lengthen/shorten* (also *widen* : *narrow*, *lighten* : *darken*, etc.). The two grammatically distinct occurrences of *lengthen/shorten* in the above sentences are, by our criteria, different lexical units, but the recurrent nature of the relationship entitles us to assign them to the same lexeme. Some pairs appear in only one of the two grammatical functions, but there exists a parallel pair fulfilling the other function, as with *rise* : *fall* and *raise* : *lower*. There remain those verbs which have only one of the two functions and are without lexical counterparts in the other function; such is the case with *appear* : *disappear* – there is no pair meaning "cause to appear" and "cause to disappear". It is not clear whether this variation follows any systematic pattern: the impression is one of idiosyncracy.

Reversives may also be classified in another way, into two groups, which we shall call †**independent reversives** and †**restitutives**. The latter group is the smaller, and consists of pairs one of whose members necessarily denotes the restitution of a former state. Examples are: *damage*: *repair*, *remove*: *replace*, *stop*: *resume*, *kill*: *resurrect*. One can *remove* something to a place where it has never been before, but one cannot *replace* it where it has never been; bringing a statue to life does not constitute resurrection unless it was previously alive, but a person does not have to have been dead on an earlier occasion before he can be *killed*. In restitutives, therefore, there is one dependent and one independent term, and the dependence of the dependent term is of a logical, rather than a pragmatic, nature. In the case of independent reversives, there is no necessity for the final state of either verb to be a recurrence of a former state. Thus a road which *narrows* does not have to be returning to a former state of being *narrow*, after a temporary interlude of *widening*; nor when it *widens* does it necessarily regain a previous state of being *wide*.

Although independent reversives are logically independent in the manner described, there may be a greater or lesser pragmatic expectation, for one of the terms, that a previous state is being restored. Consider, for example, *fill* and *empty*. On the basis of their everyday experience with bottles, boxes, pockets, and so forth, most people probably feel that an act of *emptying* must normally be preceded by an (at least partial) act of *filling*, and that the transition to *emptiness* is a return to an original condition; they are unlikely, however, to feel the same about *fill*. This is, by and large, true: artefacts are usually manufactured *empty*, then *filled*. But, and this is especially true of natural objects, *emptying* can result in a new state. A coconut, or a skull, can be *emptied* of its contents without at any time having either undergone a process of *filling*, or been *empty* before. This is because container and contents develop simultaneously, and thus, when the container first comes into being, it is *full*. In some cases, the pragmatic expectation of the prior existence of one of the denoted states is very strong, but the dependence is still not a logical one. An example is *lock*: *unlock*. Surely a door which someone *unlocks* is returning to a former state? Normally, yes; but it is not inconceivable that a very sophisticated manufacturing procedure should produce, say, a cupboard, complete with door in the locked state, so that the first action performed on it is *unlocking*. Likewise, one can just about imagine someone being born in a howdah, on the back of an elephant, and having to *dismount* before he can *mount* for the first time. Reversives one of whose terms is morphologically marked, such as *lock*: *unlock*, *dress*: *un-*

dress and *mount* : *dismount*, belong to the independent group, as do those which, like *lengthen* and *shorten*, are derivationally related to adjectival opposites.

An interesting property of independent reversives is their behaviour with unstressed *again*. Consider the following sentences:

> The engine started, then stopped again.
> I filled it with water, then emptied it again.
> The road widened, then narrowed again.
> We mounted, then dismounted again.

Each of these sentences has an interpretation in which the action or process denoted by the second verb may be occurring for the first time, in spite of the fact that it is modified by *again* (this interpretation is impossible if *again* is stressed).[6] What apparently justifies the presence of *again* is the recurrence of a former state, even though this has no overt linguistic expression. This means that *again* is able to take as its scope only part of the meaning of the verb that it modifies. It appears that this is a peculiar characteristic of verbs which denote a transition from an initial to a final state: it is the final state which can be isolated, and can act as the scope of *again*. Such verbs may be termed †**reversible**, since, although they may not, in fact, possess a reversive partner, they potentially do. Notice that although a return to a lifeless state can be inferred from both 1 and 2, only 1 has a 'first-time' interpretation:

1. Dr Frankenstein brought the monster to life, then killed it again.
2. Dr Frankenstein brought the monster to life, then strangled it again.

For some reason, the adverbial component[7] of the meaning of *strangle* prevents *again* from taking the resultant state as its scope (as does, indeed, an overtly expressed adverbial: *Dr Frankenstein brought the monster to life, then killed it with his scalpel again* does not have a 'first-time' interpretation, either).

We can use this peculiarity of reversives to formulate a test: a pair of independent reversive opposites X and Y should be capable of occurring normally in both the following frames, with a 'first-time' interpretation for the verb modified by *again*:

> He X-ed (it), then Y-ed (it) again.
> He Y-ed (it), then X-ed (it) again.

A number of independent reversives are either morphologically derived from adjectival opposites: *lengthen*:*shorten*, *fill*:*empty*, *darken*:*lighten*, *widen*:*narrow*, *clean*:*dirty*, etc., or are semantically related to adverbial or adjectival opposites in a way identical to these, but without any morphological relationship: *accelerate*:*decelerate* (*fast*:*slow*), *increase*:*decrease* (*much*:*little*), etc. Properties of the derived reversives can frequently be correlated with properties of the underlying adjectives. For instance, if the underlying adjectives are non-gradable complementaries A and B, the meanings of the respective derived reversives are "make or become A", and "make or become B". If, on the other hand, the underlying adjectives are gradable, then the semantic properties of the derived verbs differ according to which antonym group the adjective pair belongs to. For a pair of antonyms X and Y, the derived reversives mean "make or become X-er", and "make or become Y-er". The sense which appears in the comparative form, in such cases, is the one which underlies the derived verb. So, for instance, *lengthen* and *shorten*, like *longer* and *shorter*, are not restricted in their application to *long* and *short* things, respectively; nor need the resultant states be *long* or *short*. On the other hand, just as only *bad* things can be *worse*, only *bad* things can *worsen*. *Deteriorate* seems to be related to *poor* rather than *bad*: its sense is derived from that of *poor* in *poorer*, which, unlike *worse*, is a pseudo-comparative:

> ? The weather was fine at first, then it got worse.
> The weather was fine at first, then it got poorer.
> ? The weather was fine at first, then it worsened.
> The weather was fine at first, then it deteriorated.
> ? John's toothache got poorer.
> John's toothache got worse.
> ? John's toothache deteriorated.
> John's toothache worsened.

In the case of verbs derived from privative antonyms, one of the lexemes of a pair comprises two lexical units, corresponding to two lexical units of the underlying adjective lexeme. The verb *clean*, for instance, has two senses, one derived from the sense of *clean* (adj.) which participates in a complementary opposition with *dirty*, as in *I've cleaned it* (i.e. "I've made it *clean*¹"), and the other derived from *clean*², as in *I've managed to clean it a little* ("I've managed to make it a little cleaner").

Although many reversive pairs are related to adjectival opposites, it is important to emphasise that their basic opposition does not reduce to that of the adjectival opposition. That is to say, it is perfectly possible in principle to have a pair of reversives related to a pair of adjectives that are not themselves opposites. Suppose there existed a lexical item *bleen*, meaning "to change from blue to green", and another one *grue*, meaning "to change from green to blue". These would be reversives, even though *blue* and *green* are not opposites. The pair *condense : evaporate* are of this type: they can be glossed "change from gas to liquid" and "change from liquid to gas", respectively. *Gas* and *liquid* are not opposites. The essential opposition underlying all reversives is not, in fact, derived from any other opposite type: as we have seen, it is an extension of the elementary notion of movement in contrary directions.

10.6 Relational opposites: converses

An important class of opposites consists of those pairs which express a relationship between two entities by specifying the direction of one relative to the other along some axis. Once again the paradigm cases are spatial. Clearly, for two objects A and B at different locations the direction of A relative to B is the exact opposite of the direction of B relative to A. We can therefore express the relationship between A and B in two logically equivalent ways, taking either A or B as the reference point. Thus, if A is higher than B, we can either say *A is above B* or *B is below A*. Similarly, if A is further forward than B, then we can say either *A is in front of B* or *B is behind A*. This notion is easily extended to the temporal axis: if time T(1) comes earlier than time T(2), this may be expressed either as *T(1) is before T(2)* or *T(2) is after T(1)*. Pairs like *above : below*, *in front of : behind* and *before : after* are called **converses**; these may be diagnosed, for the time being at least, by the fact that when one member of a pair is substituted for the other in a sentence the new sentence can be made logically equivalent to the original one by interchanging two of the noun phrase arguments.

Although converseness has been presented as fundamentally a spatial notion, the relation, like reversiveness (which was also claimed to be basically spatial), is not confined to the spatial domain. However, non-spatial converses can usually be interpreted as analogical or metaphorical extensions of spatial notions. Consider the pair *ancestor : descendant : A is an ancestor of B* is logically equivalent to *B is a descendant of A*. It is easy to conceive of a 'line of descent' such that an *ancestor* of A is *above* A, and a *descendant* is *below*. In this case, the spatial connection is clear enough, and is well-established in ordinary speech: *The property passed down from father to son*. A less obvious extension of the basic notion is to be seen in *husband : wife (A is a/the wife of B* entails and is entailed

231

by *B is a/the husband of A*). Even here, it is not too difficult to think of *husband* and *wife* as facing one another, as it were, along the marital axis. Other examples of this type are: *master:servant, predator:prey, guest:host, teacher:pupil*.

Lexical converses must be capable of expressing an asymmetrical relationship between two entities (at least). This of course, excludes intransitive verbs, and most adjectives in the positive degree. Transitive verbs are capable of expressing a converse relationship unaided: *A preceded B, B followed A*; noun converses, at least in English, require the verb *to be* and an expression of the possessive relationship: *A is B's master, B is A's servant*. The comparative forms of polar antonyms express a converse relationship, a fact which can be used to diagnose the category: *A is longer than B* entails and is entailed by *B is shorter than A*.[8] It occasionally happens that a pair of lexical converses can be paraphrased by means of the comparative forms of a pair of antonyms: for instance, *X is above/below Y* and *X is higher/lower than Y* are equivalent. It is also worth noting that the active and 'full' passive forms of transitive verbs (i.e. those in which the agent is expressed, as in *The chimpanzees are fed by Arthur*) stand in a converse relationship;[9] furthermore, certain pairs of lexical converses can be paraphrased using only a contrast of voice: *Monday is before Tuesday, Tuesday is after Monday*; *Monday precedes Tuesday, Tuesday is preceded by Monday*.

Nouns belonging to pairs which express a converse relationship not infrequently display a dual semantic nature. One of the terms of a pair (rarely, if ever, it appears, both) not only expresses the relationship, but also possesses descriptive meaning which is to some extent independent of it. *Doctor* and *patient* illustrate this point. One can be a doctor purely on the strength of one's qualifications, before one has entered into a relationship with any patients. It does not seem that in this case we are dealing with two distinct senses, since 3 is not zeugmatic:

3.   Arthur has just qualified as a doctor, and Miriam wants him to be hers.

The meaning of *patient* is purely relational: there is no way one can qualify as a patient in the absence of anyone dispensing treatment. Similarly, a young hawk is a *predator* even before he has hunted and captured any *prey*; moreover, *predators* often have morphological and behavioural characteristics – they are biologically adapted for their role. It is difficult to see *prey* in this light: *prey*, like *patient*, has a purely relational meaning. As in the case of *doctor*, there is no evidence that *predator* is ambiguous.

Consider now, however, the pair *parent* : *child*. Again, we have one purely relational term: *parent*. One cannot be a parent merely because one has the capacity to produce children; for parenthood, children are indispensable. *Child*, on the other hand, has a dual nature, like *doctor*, being both relational and descriptive:

4. She was a child when her parents died.
5. All their children are now grown up.

In this case, however, the evidence is that *child*, unlike *doctor*, is ambiguous. If the sense *child* has in 5 were to occur in 4, the sentence would be tautologous; and if that in 4 were manifested in 5, the result would be a paradox. The zeugmatic nature of 6 confirms the diagnosis:

6. A: Are there any children of the marriage?
   B: ? No, they are all grown up.

10.7 Indirect converses

So far we have been dealing exclusively with two-place predicates (that is, elements which express a relation between two other elements), and converseness has been diagnosed by means of the permutation test: X and Y are converses if any sentence in which X expresses a relation between two noun phrases N^1 and N^2 is logically equivalent to the sentence which results when (i) N^1 and N^2 are interchanged and (ii) X is replaced by Y, but is not equivalent to the sentences which result when operations (i) and (ii) are carried out singly. (The rider is necessary to prevent symmetrical two-place synonyms from appearing to qualify as converses, since, for instance, *A resembles B* is equivalent to *B is similar to A*.) This test also characterises as converses certain three-place, and even four-place, expressions. Sentences 7 and 8, for example, are logically equivalent, as are 9 and 10:

7. Miriam gave a snuff-box to Arthur.
8. Arthur received a snuff-box from Miriam.
9. Harry sold the sarcophagus to the Emir.
10. The Emir bought the sarcophagus from Harry.

However, there is a difference between the kind of converseness illustrated in sentences 7–10 and that which we observed with two-place expressions such as *above* : *below* and *precede* : *follow*. Consider *give* and *receive*. Although these are, in a sense, three-place expressions, it can nonetheless be argued that each expresses a central binary relation, the third element being more peripheral. This is because the syntax of these verbs provides two central valency slots, namely, those of subject and direct object, and a more peripheral slot for indirect object. The relative peripherality of the indirect object[10] is indicated, for instance, by the fact that it is never obligatory, unlike the direct object. When we examine *give* and *receive* in the light of this, we notice that, in 7 and 8, for instance, the central binary relation expressed by *give* is between *Miriam* and *the snuff-box*. In other words, *give* and *receive* are not converses of the strictest sort. The true converse of *give* would express the relation between *the snuff-box* and *Miriam*; there is no such verb, however, in English. Converse pairs in which the interchangeable noun phrases both occupy central valency slots (like *follow*:*precede*) will be called †**direct converses**; those, like *give*:*receive*, where a central and peripheral noun phrase are interchanged, will be called †**indirect converses**.[11]

The manifold interconnections among lexical items expressing a three-way relationship between nominals can be described with reference to figure 10.1. The typical tri-valent verb relates two animate nominals, one an agent (labelled 'agentive' in the figure), frequently a donor of some sort (but can also, as with *take*, be an acquisitor); one affected by the action of the agent (labelled 'dative' in the figure), who is frequently a beneficiary, or recipient (but can also, as with *take*, be a relinquisher); and a third, normally inanimate (labelled 'objective'), which is transferred from one of the animate participants to the other. R(1), R(2) and R(3) represent potential lexical items expressing each of the three possible component binary relations, with the nominals involved in these occupying

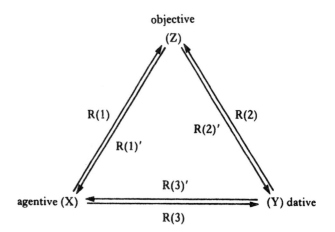

Figure 10.1

subject and direct object positions; $R(1)'$, $R(2)'$ and $R(3)'$ represent, respectively, their strict converses. For instance, one such set would be *give* ($R(1)$), *receive* ($R(2)$), and *present* ($R(3)$), the latter expressing a direct relationship between the two animate nominals: *Miriam presented Arthur with a snuff-box*.[12] None of these verbs (and this is typical) has a true converse. Other examples of such sets are (i) *take* ($R(1)$), *relinquish / give up / yield* ($R(2)$) and *dispossess* ($R(3)$):

> John took the book from Bill.
> Bill relinquished the book to John.
> John dispossessed Bill of the book.

(these verbs are not perfectly matched semantically, but they do express roughly the right relationships); (ii) *teach* ($R(1)$), *learn/study* ($R(2)$) and *instruct* ($R(3)$):

> Arthur teaches French to Miriam.
> Miriam learns French from/studies French under Arthur.
> Arthur instructs Miriam in French.

and (iii) *bequeath* ($R(1)$), *inherit* ($R(2)$) – in this case $R(3)$ is missing.

X, Y and Z in figure 10.1 represent nouns capable of participating in the expression of the same tripartite relationships as the verbs $R(1)$, $R(2)$ and $R(3)$. With nouns, it is the genitive construction which expresses the central binary relation: for instance, in *Arthur is the donor of the book-collection to the school*, *is the donor of* indicates the relation between *Arthur* and *the book-collection*, while *the school* occupies a relatively peripheral position. Many nouns of this sort, like *donor*, are angled towards one of the other participants, and cannot express the binary relation with the third: **Arthur is the donor of the school* cannot refer to Arthur's gift of books (notice the *benefactor* is differently angled: *Arthur is the school's benefactor* would be appropriate in the situation envisaged, but not **Arthur is the book-collection's benefactor*). Other nouns, like *gift*, are neutral with respect to the other two participants, and can express a binary relation with either: *John's gift to Bill, Bill's gift from John*. The angled nouns may be designated according to the participant towards which they are oriented; so *donor*, for instance, would be labelled $X(Z)$, and *recipient* $Y(Z)$ (*Miriam is the recipient of the necklace from Arthur*, but not **Miriam is the recipient of Arthur in respect of the necklace*). Another set of nouns consists of *bequest* ($Z(X)$), *inheritance* ($Z(Y)$), *heir* ($Y(X)$) and *inheritor* ($Y(Z)$). Curiously, there is no realisation of X in this set. The justification for the indicated orientations is as follows: given the truth of *John*

235

bequeathed the sculpture to Bill, it follows that the sculpture is John's *bequest*, but not Bill's *bequest*; however, the sculpture is Bill's, and not John's, *inheritance*; likewise, Bill is John's *heir*, but not the sculpture's *heir*; he is, on the other hand, the sculpture's, and not John's, *inheritor*. In the 'teaching' set of items, *teacher* is neutral with respect to Y and Z: *Mark's teacher, teacher of needlework*; *student* is likewise unoriented: *John's student, student of French*; *pupil*, however, is X-oriented: *John's pupil*, but **pupil of French*.

The conditions for direct and indirect converseness between lexical items expressing three-way relationships can now be spelled out. First, while there is no theoretical prohibition, a direct converse relationship between three-place verbs seems to be rare. Strict converseness does occasionally occur, however, between nouns such as *gift : donor* and *inheritor : inheritance*, which are angled towards one another (or, more precisely, are not oriented other than towards one another – they may be neutral):

The book was John's gift.

John was the book's donor.

The picture is Arthur's inheritance.

Arthur is the picture's inheritor.

For indirect converseness it is necessary to have either a centripetal arrangement, or a centrifugal one. This can best be explained with reference to fig. 10.1. A centripetal arrangement has two terms oriented towards the same third, such as R(1) and R(2), or X(Z) and Y(Z), all of which converge, so to speak, on Z. The verbal type is exemplified by *lend : borrow*:

John lent the book to Bill.

Bill borrowed the book from John.

Other examples are: *give : receive, bequeath : inherit, teach : learn*. The nominal type is exemplified by *donor : recipient*:

The duke was the donor of the picture of the college.

The college was the recipient of the picture from the duke.

A centrifugal arrangement of relationships occurs when two terms point 'outwards' from a common centre, like R(1) and R(3), which point outwards from X, or like Z(X) and Z(Y), which typically represent divergent orientations of terms denoting the inanimate participant. The former case is illustrated by *teach : instruct*:

John taught French to Bill.

John instructed Bill in French.

and the latter case by *bequest : inheritance*:

The house was John's bequest to Bill.

The house was Bill's inheritance from John.

(Notice that both the above pairs satisfy the permutation test.)

Similar, though more complex, principles for indirect converseness operate in what is perhaps the only four-term set in English (see fig. 10.2).

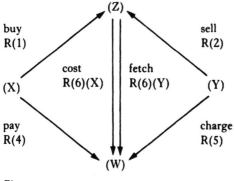

Figure 10.2

The full range of possible lexical items and their orientations is much too complex to illustrate: fig. 10.2 contains only the principal relevant verbs. Notice that the extra nominal, W, is inanimate, and is transferred in the opposite direction from Z. There is no lexical item in English to realise R(3), which relates X and Y; the reason there are two items to realise R(6) is that there are two candidates for the indirect object slot, namely, X and Y: *cost* takes X as its indirect object (*The book cost John £5*), while *fetch* takes Y (*The book fetched Bill £5*). Once again, the absence of direct converses will be noted (although, as before, they can be found among nouns belonging to the set, *purchase* and *buyer* being examples:

The book was John's purchase, John was the book's buyer). There is, however, a plethora of indirect converses. With respect to the outer terms (*buy, sell, pay, charge*), the criteria of centrifugal and centripetal orientations appear to give correct predictions:

Centripetal: *sell* : *buy:*   X sold Z to Y for W

Y bought Z from X for W

                    charge : *pay:*   X paid Y W for Z

Y charged X W for Z

Centrifugal: *sell* : *charge:*   Y sold X Z for W

Y charged X W for Z

                    buy : *pay:*   X bought Z from Y for W

X paid W to Y for Z

(*Buy* is an odd man out syntactically: it is the only one which cannot have one of the animate nominals in immediate post-verb position. This is why *pay* had to be put into a slightly unusual sentence to make the permutation of W and Z clear.) Complications arise, however, when an attempt is made to compute the indirect converse relations along the diagonals of fig. 10.2, i.e. between Z and W (and, presumably, between X and Y, too, although this cannot be tested in English). Consider *cost* and *pay*, which, according to the diagram, are centripetally related to W; yet there is no way they can be displayed as indirect converses. It appears that in four-term sets indirect converses must not only show convergent or divergent orientation of the basic binary relation, but must also be identically related to the fourth term, not involved in the centrifugal/centripetal arrangement. This condition happens to be fulfilled for *sell* : *buy* and *charge* : *pay* : *sell* and *buy*, for instance, both converging on Z, are identically related to W. For *cost* and *pay*, however, the stricter condition is not fulfilled, since although both converge on W, *cost* has X as its indirect object, and *pay* has Y. *Cost* and *charge*, on the other hand, do fulfil the more stringent conditions:

Y charged X W for Z

Z cost X W (from Y)

(*Cost* is unfortunately not an ideal candidate here, but there is nothing better in English to illustrate the point: although it undoubtedly belongs to the set, it is basically a three-place verb, and is not entirely happy when the fourth term is expressed. Allowing for three-place items in the set adds, of course, a further complication to the total picture, and multiplies yet again the theoretically possible number of lexical items in the set.)

We have so far been looking at direct and indirect converses in the context of a study of opposites. We must now re-examine the relevance of these relations to oppositeness. While there is little doubt that among converses of both types are to be found several intuitively satisfactory opposites (*above* : *below*, *husband* : *wife* and *buy* : *sell*, for instance), there are also many that either, like *gift* : *donor*, are rather feebly opposed, or they are not opposites at all, like *charge* : *cost*. The question must be raised, therefore, of whether direct converseness or indirect converseness is in itself to be considered a genuine type of oppositeness. The case for direct converseness, though not overwhelming, is better than that for indirect converseness. All two-place converses appear to be convincing opposites; as it happens, they are all direct converses, too. On the other hand, three- and four-place direct converses are felt to be relatively weakly opposed; so much so that someone asked for the opposite of *donor*, for instance, will in all probability offer something like *thief*, or possibly *recipient*, rather than the direct converse *gift*. The case for considering indirect converseness to be a type of oppositeness, however, is very weak. This is because for all those indirect converses that are also convincing opposites, an alternative explanation exists for their oppositeness. Take *lend* and *borrow*: for *lend*, there is movement of the 'thing lent' (which is one of the terms in each of the basic binary relations expressed by the two verbs) away from the subject, towards the direct object; for *borrow*, these directions are reversed. There is thus a salient element of reversivity in the opposition between this pair, which is enough to account for their oppositeness. There is no such reversivity in the relation between *buy* and *pay*, for instance, which are also indirect converses (except that *money* and *merchandise* move in opposite directions, but this aspect of meaning is not highlighted), and they are not felt to be opposites. A similar account

239

can be given of the oppositeness of *buy*: *sell*, *bequeath*: *inherit*, *give*: *receive*, etc.

10.8 Congruence variants and pseudo-opposites

In our discussion of the various types of lexical opposite we have taken for granted so far that we are dealing with canonical relations, that is to say, relations that are context-independent (unlike pseudo-relations), and that hold between participants that are congruent in respect of the relationship in question. In this section we consider relations that are non-canonical in one or both of these respects. (We do not consider here the 'quality' of the relation as such – this is discussed in 11.7.)

Of the two types of congruence variant – the 'hypo-/super-' type, and the 'semi-' type – only the former seems to be at all frequent among opposites.[13] The following are examples of two (or more) hypo-opposites standing jointly in a particular relation of opposition to a super-opposite:

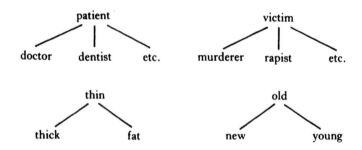

Patient and *victim* are super-converses of their respective partners,[14] and *thin* and *old* are super-antonyms of theirs. (In Japanese, there is a set of verbs meaning "to put on (an article of clothing)", each verb specific to a particular type of clothing;[15] these verbs stand jointly in a relation of reversivity with a single verb meaning "to take off (an article of clothing)".) It will be noticed that two different relationships between sister hypo-opposites are illustrated. *Doctor* and *dentist*, and *murderer* and *rapist*, are incompatibles; *thick* and *fat*, and *young* and *new*, on the other hand, differ much less radically – they differ, in fact, only in respect of collocational restrictions, and are therefore cognitive synonyms, according to our criteria (see 12.2).[16]

Given a pair of lexical opposites X and Y, we may say that any hyponym of X is a hypo-opposite of Y.[17] For many opposite pairs, there is a parallel hyponym of Y which is a hypo-opposite of X. Thus, in the case of *big*: *little*, *huge*, which is a hyponym of *big*, is a hypo-antonym of *little*; similarly, *tiny* is a hypo-antonym of *big*. In some cases there is a lack of symmetry on the two sides of the opposition. Most frequently, there is no super-ordinate of the hypo-opposites which is congruent with the super-opposite, and no hyponyms of the super-opposite to parallel the specific terms on the other side of the opposition. A comparison of sets (i) and (ii) below will make this point clear:

hyponym	X	Y	hyponym
(i) huge	big	little	tiny
(ii) doctor	—	patient	—
dentist			

Notice that in (ii) there is no conceptual difficulty concerning the meanings of lexical items to fill the gaps – the absence of these items is, to some extent at least, fortuitous.[18] Some cases of asymmetry are more strongly motivated than that of (ii). Take the case of *lengthen*:*shorten*: *shorten* has *abbreviate* as a hyponym, but there is no parallel hyponym of *lengthen*. It is difficult, but not impossible, to conceive of such a hyponym – it would have to mean something like "lengthen a word for typographical convenience". Since there is no process in our culture for such a word to designate, its non-existence is no surprise. A perhaps more radically motivated instance of asymmetry is provided by the reversive pair *kill*: *resurrect*. *Kill* has *strangle*, *drown* and *garotte* amongst its hyponyms. These are hypo-opposites of *resurrect*, but it is far from clear that they can be considered to be hypo-reversives. We have already seen (in 10.5) that *strangle*, etc. do not behave like reversible verbs. It must be doubted whether the existence of hyponyms of *resurrect* with the same differentiating traits as *strangle*, *drown*, etc. is even conceivable.

The fact that *fat* and *thick* are hypo-antonyms of *thin*, *new* and *young* of *old*, and *short* (of people) and *low* (of buildings) of *tall* has scarcely any semantic significance in context: they normally modify specific nouns (whether implicit or explicit), and in their behaviour are virtually indistinguishable from congruent antonyms. Similarly, *doctor* and *patient*, and *dentist* and *patient*, behave, in context, like congruent converses. Of course, *fat* and *thick* are cognitive synonyms, so there is no reason to expect a great difference. This is not true, however, of *dentist* and *doctor*, and it might be anticipated that *patient* would not always function as a congruent converse would. What makes, e.g., *dentist* and *patient* more like congruent converses is the fact that *patient*, like *cub* and *watch* (v.),

241

displays the property of latency. That is, even when no converse partner is explicitly mentioned, *patient* is always interpreted as "patient of X", where X is contextually definite and intended to be recovered by the hearer. In this way, any use of *patient* is functionally tied to a particular type of 'medical practitioner', so in most contexts its potentially greater generality is not apparent (the same is true of *victim*). We may say that in most contexts, *fat* and *thin*, *doctor* and *patient*, etc. are †**pseudo-congruent**.

Cases of pseudo-oppositeness occasionally occur which parallel the pseudo-synonymy of *horse* and *mare* in *That – has just given birth to a foal*. Consider the following line from Baudelaire's *Hymne à la Beauté*, a poem in which binary oppositions play an important role:

Sors-tu du gouffre noir ou descends-tu des astres?

There is presumably no way out of a *gouffre noir* except upwards, so *sortir* in this context is functionally a reversive opposite of *descendre*. Similarly, *black* and *white* are pseudo-complementaries in *In the game of chess between Arthur and Miriam, it was not a white piece that was accidentally knocked off the board*.

Notes

10.2

1. See Lyons (1977: 691).
2. *Withershins* (*widdershins*) is a Scots dialect word meaning "in a direction contrary to the apparent course of the sun" (etymology: Middle High German *wider* "against", *sin* "direction").
3. *Forwards* and *backwards* also have a temporal sense: we move forwards into the future; we cannot go backwards in time. (Apparently in some cultures it is the future, invisible and unknown, which lies 'behind'.) The use of *forwards* and *backwards* in relation to movable future events parallels the spatial use: *forwards* means "towards the speaker" (i.e. earlier in time), and *backwards* means "away from the speaker".
4. More detailed discussion can be found in Lyons (1977: 690–703).

10.3 The term *antipodal* is borrowed from Lyons (1977: 282); I have given it a slightly different definition.

10.4

5. For instance, *heaven* : *hell* could be said to embody the oppositions *up* : *down*, *good* : *bad*, *bliss* : *torment*, etc.

10.5 This section is based largely on Cruse (1979b).

6. I believe this fact was first noted by McCawley, but I have been unable to discover on what occasion.

7. The meaning of *strangle* contains the traits "kill" and "by squeezing the windpipe". The latter has a semantic function relative to the former analogous to the adverbial function of *by squeezing his windpipe* in *John killed Bill by squeezing his windpipe*.

10.6

8. The relationship between, for instance, *X is hotter than Y* and *Y is colder than X* is slightly more tricky. The position is taken in 12.2 that presuppositions do not affect truth conditions. In the interests of consistency, therefore, we should say that these two sentences are mutually entailing.
9. The converseness of, e.g., *feed* and *be fed by* is not, of course, lexical in origin, but grammatical, since both are manifestations of the same lexical unit. The converse relation between, e.g., *shorter* and *longer* is partly lexical and partly grammatical in origin.

10.7

10. '... the indirect object stands in a looser relationship' Matthews (1981:128).
11. The way in which the distinction between direct and indirect converses is made here is heavily dependent on the facts of English grammar.
12. *Present* differs from *give* and *receive* in that the peripheral noun phrase is not omissible.

10.8

13. I have a hunch that this is not fortuitous.
14. In so far as a doctor may be without patients, it could be argued that *doctor* and *patient* are semi-converses. If only criterial traits are taken into consideration, then this is undoubtedly true. However, there is something imperfect about a doctor with no patients – almost like a dog with no tail: in other words, *patient* could be held to be a canonical converse of *doctor*. In dealing with some sense relations it seems more illuminating to take account of canonical as well as criterial traits.
15. See Backhouse (1981).
16. Although Backhouse does not explicitly say so, my impression is that the "put on" verbs are cognitive synonyms.
17. Notice that this does not necessarily work in the same way for superordinates of X: for instance, *move*, a superordinate of *rise*, is no sort of an opposite of *fall*.
18. It is perhaps not entirely fortuitous that in the case of *doctor* and *patient*, etc., and *victim* and *murderer*, etc., the finer lexical differentiation is on the side of the active participants.

11
Opposites III: general questions

11.1 Impartiality

The occurrences of *thick* in 1 and 2 are of the type which was described in chapter 4 as impartial with respect to the contrast between *thick* and *thin* in *a thin branch* and *a thick branch*:

1. How thick is it?
2. Mine is thicker than yours.

To these we may add 3:

3. Its thickness is one centimetre.

The uses of *hot* in 4 and 5, on the other hand, were described as committed with respect to the contrast between *hot* and *cold*:

4. How hot is it?
5. This one is hotter than that one.

It is now necessary to distinguish two degrees, or modes, of impartiality: these will be referred to as †**strong impartiality** and †**weak impartiality**. Sentences 1, 2 and 3 illustrate strong impartiality. This involves two distinct senses: the sense of *thick* in 1, 2 and 3 is not the same as that in *It's thick* (see chapter 4 for the arguments on which this conclusion is based). Although the two lexical units *thick* are distinct, their relationship is a systematic one, and they therefore must be assigned to the same lexeme. Strong impartiality appears only in connection with gradable opposites, i.e. antonyms, and is associated with the existence of a scale which covers all possible values of the variable property denoted by the members of a pair. Corresponding to strong impartiality, we have strong committedness. A strongly committed use of a term presupposes the applicability of that term in a simple predication in the positive degree. Sentences 4 and 5, for instance, both presuppose, or take for granted, the truth of *It's hot*.

Unlike strong impartiality, which is not restricted to any particular sentence type, weak impartiality occurs only in 'yes–no' questions. It does not depend on the existence of two senses. In English, weak impartiality appears typically with non-gradable complementaries such as *dead* : *alive*, *married* : *single*, etc. Compare the two questions in 6 and 7:

     6.   Is he married? (or not?)
     7.   Is he single? (or not?)

(For some speakers, the difference is more striking if *or not?* is appended to the question.) Question 6 is distinctly the more 'open-minded'; it expresses no expectations concerning, or interest in, a particular response. It is the alternative that would be used by a totally disinterested person, such as a collector of information for official statistics. Question 7, in contrast, is 'loaded', and requires more specific contextual justification. The same open-mindedness characterises *Are your parents alive (or not)?* and *Is John in (or not)?* as against *Are your parents dead?* and *Is John out?*

In answering 1, if the object in question is *thin*, it is not necessary for the answerer to dissociate himself from the term used in the question – in fact, it is abnormal to do so:

     8.   A: How thick is it?
          B: (i)   Fairly thin.
              (ii) ? It isn't, it's thin.

This is because the lexical unit *thick* in the question is not the one which contradicts *It's thin*. In answering 6, however, since it contains the same unit *married* as in *He's married*, a reply to the effect that the person referred to is a bachelor normally requires the answerer to deny the statement implied by the question:

     9.   A: Is he married?
          B: No, he's single.

Weak impartiality, although characteristic of non-gradable adjectives in English, is not universally restricted to these. In French, for instance, there is no way of asking a strongly impartial question on the pattern of *How long is it?* One may say *Quelle est la longueur de ta jupe?* (which is strongly impartial), but in everyday French one is at least equally likely to hear *Elle est longue, ta jupe?* This is weakly impartial: it contains the same sense of *longue* as *Elle est longue*, and although it anticipates no particular response, if the skirt in question happens to be *courte*, the statement implied by the question must normally be denied:

    10.   A: Elle est longue, ta nouvelle jupe?
           B: Non, elle est courte.

Questions like *Is he single?*, *Is John out?*, *Elle est courte, ta jupe?* are weakly committed. They do not presuppose the nature of the reply, but they express a particular attitude to the corresponding implied statement, often an expectation of its truth.

A striking feature of the impartiality phenomena is that when present, they are asymmetrically disposed with respect to the basic opposite pair. Thus the lexeme *long* has a lexical unit which appears in *how*-questions, the comparative *longer*, and the nominalisation *length*; the lexeme *short* also includes among its lexical units one which has an impartial sense, but, for reasons which are at present still mysterious, this only appears in *shorter*. In the case of polar antonym pairs (e.g. *long*:*short*) it is invariably the lexical unit which denotes a relatively high degree of the underlying graded property (e.g. *long, deep, high, fast, heavy, strong*, etc.) which is co-lexemic with the most widely distributed impartial unit.[1] Overlapping antonyms (e.g. *good*:*bad*) are more complex – they will be discussed in greater detail below; there are no impartial occurrences of equipollent antonyms (e.g. *hot*:*cold*).

11.2 Polarity

Many opposite pairs are formally asymmetrical, in that one member bears a negative affix, while the other has no corresponding formal mark: *happy*:*unhappy*, *like*:*dislike*, etc. For a very few, in English, both members have a formal mark: *increase*:*decrease*, *accelerate*:*decelerate* (in some languages, this is the more usual pattern). In the case of the formally asymmetrical pairs, we may confidently speak of the 'positive' and 'negative' terms of the opposition. Even with the doubly marked pairs there is a strong intuition of polarity: *accelerate* and *increase*, for instance, are felt to be positive, and *decelerate* and *decrease* are felt to be negative. The results of 'morphological experiments' reinforce this intuition. If we try to form opposite pairs conforming to the usual morphological pattern, we find that members of doubly marked pairs differ markedly in their plausibility as morphologically simple, positive terms: *accelerate*:*disaccelerate* are far more acceptable as opposites than *decelerate*:*disdecelerate*, and *increase*:*disincrease* are better than *decrease*:*disdecrease*.

The morphologically simple term in many of the asymmetrical pairs has an alternative partner which is also morphologically simple. The two alternatives are always close in meaning; sometimes they are almost identical: *unmarried*:*single*, *untrue*:*false*; sometimes there are differentiating nuances: *unsafe*:*dangerous*, *unclean*:*dirty*, *unkind*:*cruel*, *unhappy*:*sad*. It seems reasonable to assume that *dirty*, *false*, and so on have the same sort of relation to their partners as *unclean* and *untrue*; that is to say, we may regard them as being 'covertly' negative – i.e. negative in meaning, but without an overt negative affix.

Polarity can also be assigned fairly plausibly to most members of antonym pairs. For instance, relative to the scale over which *long* and *short* operate, it is *long* which is the positive term, as it represents a higher value: to make a *short* thing *long* one must add, not subtract, units of length. *Bad* is arguably negative, and *good* positive, with regard to the scale of merit: *badness* is not strictly the mere absence of merit – it is a positive property in its own right – but it is directionally identical to what a *short*-type opposite of *good* would be if it existed (there are some grounds for believing that *poor* fits this description).

There is a close relationship between polarity and impartiality. In pairs which manifest both properties it is invariably the positive term which either occurs itself in a weakly impartial question, or has a lexemically related strongly impartial unit. The overall picture can be tidied up if we extrapolate this relationship, and use facts concerning impartiality as direct evidence for polarity. For instance, the fact that *alive*, but not *dead*, can be used in weakly impartial questions may be taken as evidence that it is the positive term of the opposition; that is to say, *dead* must be conceived as meaning "not alive", rather than the converse.[2] (*Dead* and *alive* cannot, of course, be used as evidence for the relation between impartiality and polarity.)

11.3 **Linguistic polarity and natural polarity**

We have seen that there is an intimate relationship between what we shall henceforth refer to as †**linguistic polarity** and impartiality; put briefly, positive terms are associated with wider possibilities of impartial usage. But there is a profound question to be raised concerning the way aspects of experience are coded linguistically. Consider the matter of the extent of things. Why don't we have a positive concept of, say, COMPACTNESS – a scaled property of which *short* things would have a relative abundance, and *long* things a relative lack? Or, in the case of *dead* and *alive* (assuming we are correct in identifying *alive* as the positive term), why is the distinction coded this way, rather than in such a way that

247

dead emerged as the positive term? An examination of a range of examples suggests that several competing factors are responsible for determining the type of linguistic coding which comes about, and suggests further that these are arranged in a rank order of dominance, so that when several factors are in conflict it is the highest ranking one which predominates.

Let us begin with the simplest cases. Certain oppositions may be said to have a 'natural' polarity, in that in one of the states of affairs to be described some perceptually salient feature is present, and in the other state this property is absent. The 'absence' state is then a 'natural' negative, and its partner a natural positive, and one may postulate that in the majority of such cases the naturally negative state will be assigned a linguistically negative label. Take the case of *dead* and *alive*. Things which are *alive* possess many perceptually striking properties which *dead* things lack: movement, responsiveness to stimuli, and so on.[3] It is therefore normal that the state of being *dead* should have a linguistically negative label, and the state of being *alive* a linguistically positive one. In the case of *married* : *single/unmarried*, the most obvious difference between a married man and a single one is that the former has a wife (and in all likelihood children, too), while the latter is without these.[4] The designation of the state of matrimony by a linguistically positive term thus seems well-motivated. As a final illustration, consider *dress* : *undress*. The resulting states of these two verbs can most easily be designated as "with clothes" and "without clothes", and the position of the negative prefix is wholly explicable. If we had, instead, *strip* and *unstrip*, there would be an unexplained discrepancy between natural polarity and linguistic polarity (they certainly 'feel' most unnatural).

Perceptual salience is also an important determinant of natural polarity in the case of gradable concepts. It is presumably more natural to have a scale of LENGTH rather than one of SHORTNESS, SPEED rather than SLOWNESS, WEIGHT rather than LIGHTNESS, and so on, because these properties are more noteworthy, more attention-drawing. They are also, presumably, in some sense conceptually simpler: to conceive of a material, objective abundance in terms of a lack requires an effort of abstraction, and a more complex transformation of elementary perceptual data. Not surprisingly, in the majority of gradable opposites, linguistic polarity is congruent with natural polarity.

A different notion of natural polarity governs the class of reversive opposites. For these we need to define two concepts – 'normal action' and 'normal process' – which represent naturally positive polarity; the 'undoing' of either of these is naturally negative. We have seen that all reversives involve transitions between two states. For each pair of verbs, what we shall term an A-state and a B-state can be distinguished, whose characteristics are as follows: A-states require a relatively higher input of energy to bring about, they typically require effort to maintain in being, and they are typically more structured and more constrained; B-states, on the other hand, require less energy to bring about (indeed, they may well supervene spontaneously), they normally require no effort to maintain, and they are typically less structured and less constrained. In the most general terms, B-states are energy-states which are more highly favoured by the physical universe: A-states are generally more favoured by human beings, but require work to produce and maintain. Looked at from the point of view of thermodynamics, A-states are lower entropy states, and B-states are higher entropy states. More specifically, trousers tend to fall down, if left to themselves, rather than to rise (that is to say, spontaneous *undressing* is more likely than spontaneous *dressing*); screws tend to *unscrew* themselves, rather than to become tighter; suitcases tend to *unpack* themselves; rooms and handbag contents to *disarrange* themselves, and shoelaces to become *untied*; a horse-rider who pays insufficient attention will find himself *dismounting* somewhat precipitately; a *locked* door is part of a more structured and more tightly constrained system than an *unlocked* door. Now although the physical universe is slowly running itself down – i.e. is seeking always to increase entropy – it is vital for human civilisation, and indeed for all life, to work against this tendency. There is therefore a deep sense in which a (human) action which reverses entropy is more normal than one which assists the universe in its slide into chaos.[5] A normal process, on the other hand, simply represents the physical universe going about its normal business of increasing entropy. However, since all reversive pairs denote transitions between A-states and B-states, how do we tell which pairs involve natural actions and which natural processes? The answer is that in each reversive pair there is a relatively dependent term (pragmatic rather than logical dependence is the most relevant here) and a relatively independent term. For a pair denoting a normal action and its undoing, the change to an A-state is the independent one; for a pair denoting a natural process and its undoing, the change to a B-state is the independent one. Thus one cannot, in general, *undress* unless one has previously *dressed*, but since one is born naked, one can become *dressed* without having previously been *undressed*. Likewise, it is not normally possible to *unpack* a suitcase that has not been previously *packed*, but it is easy to pack one that has never been *unpacked*. On the other hand, for threads, *entangling* normally precedes

249

disentangling, and *rusting* precedes *de-rusting*. The nullification of either a normal action or a normal process is a naturally negative concept; this is reflected in the fact that, virtually without exception, it receives a linguistically negative label.

So far, we have only mentioned cases where natural polarity and linguistic polarity are congruent. Although this is most frequently the case, it is not always so. The most striking discrepancies are to be observed with privative antonyms. Consider, for example, *clean* and *dirty*. It is clear that *clean* is a natural negative: it denotes the absence of dirt. This dirt is often an obvious physical substance which has to be removed in the process of cleaning. The quantity of dirt present is the natural gradable property. Note also that 11 is more natural than 12:

11. Something is clean when there is no dirt present.
12. ? Something is dirty when there is no cleanness present.

There appears to be a tendency for natural scales to take as their positive direction the direction of infinite extendability, and if there is an end-point, for that to represent the negative end of the scale. So, for example, the scale of length has a natural end-point at zero length, and extends indefinitely in the other direction. In this respect, too, *clean* is a natural negative term, as it represents a kind of end-point. Note the parallelism between 13 and 14:

13. I'm half-way home.
    I'm nearly home.
    I'm home.
14. It's half-clean.
    It's nearly clean.
    It's clean.

But, linguistically, *clean* is the positive term of the opposition. This is shown by the existence of *unclean*, and by the fact that it occurs in the strongly impartial *How clean is it?* The pair *safe:dangerous* present a similar picture. *Safety* is the absence of *danger*:

15. When something is safe, there is an absence of danger.
16. ? When something is dangerous, there is an absence of safety.

Furthermore, *safety* has nothing like the attention-drawing qualities of *danger*, and is thus more likely to be perceived as the state in which something salient is absent. Yet *safe* is the linguistically positive term, which can carry a negative prefix (*unsafe*), and which has a strongly impartial use in *How safe is it?* An equally good case can be made that *accurate* is the natural negative in the pair *accurate*:*inaccurate*. *Accurate* is a natural absence term, as it denotes the absence of error; it represents zero on the most natural scale, namely, that grading the magnitude of the error. However, *accurate*, too, is linguistically positive. Is there any explanation for this lack of congruence between natural and linguistic polarity? All such cases have a property in common: naturally negative, but linguistically positive, terms are evaluatively positive, that is to say, they are terms of commendation, and their partners are terms of criticism. (This is not the same as saying that the qualities they denote are more highly valued than those denoted by their opposite partners. We may value happiness more highly than sadness, but to describe someone as *sad* is not to criticise him. *Happy* and *sad*, therefore, do not embody an evaluative polarity, as this is to be understood here. However, to describe something or someone as *dirty, dangerous, impure, dishonest, inaccurate*, etc. is to criticise, while to describe them as *clean, safe, pure, honest, accurate*, etc. is normally to commend.) It seems that evaluative polarity overrides natural polarity in the determination of linguistic polarity.[6]

Our account of the determinants of linguistic polarity is still incomplete. Consider the pairs *afraid*:*unafraid, spoilt*:*unspoilt, polluted*:*unpolluted*. In each of these pairs the linguistically negative term is evaluatively positive. Structurally, these pairs are similar to those discussed in the last paragraph: they are complementaries, with one gradable and one non-gradable term. They differ from the former type in that the natural zero term is linguistically negative, and the natural scale and the linguistic scale coincide. Do they have any property in common which might explain why in these cases evaluative polarity does not override natural polarity? One possible approach to this question is to look for a factor which is even more powerful than evaluative polarity, and is capable of overriding it. There is a candidate for such a factor. For each of our 'anomalous' pairs there is a peculiar restriction on the use of the linguistically negative term which is not found with other opposites. They may be used only in situations where the applicability of the linguistically positive term is strongly expected, or to be regarded as normal. For instance, one cannot use *unafraid* simply to denote lack of fear:

? I'm unafraid of breathing.

Unafraid is apt only in situations where it would be entirely normal to be *afraid*. Parallel constraints apply to the use of *unspoilt* and *unpolluted*. We may therefore postulate that when the meanings of a pair of opposites incorporate an explicit contrast of normality, the linguistically positive term is the one which embodies the notion of normality, whether or not an evaluative contrast is also present.

11.4 Logical polarity

There exists another conception of polarity, whose relationship with the types of polarity so far discussed is sometimes illuminating, sometimes puzzling. We shall call it †**logical polarity**, since it can be diagnosed by means of a test based on an analogy with logical negation. It is well-known that one negation cancels out another within its scope: for instance, the statement *John is dead* can be negated, giving *John is not dead*; if this, in turn, is negated, we end up with *It's not true that John is not dead*, which is logically equivalent to *John is dead*. This reversal of polarity when negation is applied to itself frequently enables us to discover which member of a pair of opposites is logically negative. Consider the pair *true* : *false*. It may appear to make little difference whether we consider that *true* should be understood to mean "not false", or *false* "not true": either of these would be adequate to account for the complementary relation between them. However, it is possible to find out which of these glosses is, in fact, correct:

> It's true that it's true ≡ It's true
> It's false that it's false ≡ It's true

Only in the case of *false* do we get the reversal of polarity which is characteristic of the negative term. To obtain full value from this test, one must not demand too much logical rigour: many terms can be made to yield a reversal of sorts, but only relatively few give a strict reversal of truth value in the way that *true* and *false* do. It can be taken as significant if there is merely a strengthening or intensification with one term, and a weakening, often somewhat paradoxical in nature, with the other:

> He's a good example of a good person.
> He's a bad example of a bad person. (reversal)

The following are further examples of the test in operation:

> He succeeded in succeeding.
> He failed to fail. (reversal)

Fail is the logically negative term.

> She obeyed my order to obey him.
> She disobeyed my order to disobey him. (reversal)

Disobey is the logically negative term.

> I love loving people.
> I hate hating people. (reversal)

Hate is the logically negative term.

> I am a friend of friendship.
> I am an enemy of enmity. (reversal)

Enemy is the logically negative term.

> I praise him for praising you.
> I criticise him for criticising you. (reversal)

Criticise is the logically negative term.

> A large measure of largeness.
> A small measure of smallness. (reversal)

Small is the logically negative term.

> It's long on length.
> It's short on shortness. (reversal)

Short is the logically negative term.

> It's heavy in respect of heaviness.
> It's light in respect of lightness. (reversal)

Light is the logically negative term.

Although some pairs remain refractory, with ingenuity this test can be applied to quite a wide range of opposites, even to some which at first sight seem unlikely candidates. *Married* and *single*, for instance, look rather unpromising, but, when expressed in the following way, the inherent negativity of *single* can be perceived:

> Mary is wedded to marriage. (i.e. 'married to the state of being married')
> Mary is unwedded to spinsterhood. (i.e. 'single with respect to the state of being single')

Or take *dress : undress: They undressed her of her state of undress*, though indubitably paradoxical, is nonetheless interpretable as meaning "They dressed her," and thus manifests a reversal that is not possible with *dress*.

For the majority of opposite pairs, linguistic polarity and logical polarity

253

are congruent, as indeed one might expect. The most interesting cases, however, are those where the two types of polarity do not fall together. In certain cases the discrepancy is illuminating, and explicable. Consider the case of *easy* and *difficult*. Linguistically, *difficult* is the positive term: we speak of the degree of *difficulty* of a task, and the question *How difficult is it?* is strongly impartial. Yet there is little doubt that *difficult* is logically negative:

> It's easy to make it easy.
> It's difficult to make it difficult. (reversal)

However, in this case linguistic polarity is probably congruent with natural polarity. It so happens that what is perceptually the most salient property is most easily conceptualised negatively. There is no doubt that obstacles encountered in the course of performing a task are more noticeable than facilitations; we are hardly aware of the easy parts of doing something, but the difficult parts loom large. The easiest way of conceptualising the property referred to by the pair *difficult*:*easy*, with a view to quantifying it, is to think in terms of the extent to which one cannot do something. This is essentially a negative notion. Another example is *near*:*far*. *Far* is linguistically positive: we commonly describe things as *not far*, but hardly ever as *not near* (*not* in *not far* is semantically akin to a negative prefix); the graded scale is one of *distance*, which is directionally identical to *far* (i.e. *greater distance* equals *further*); the strongly impartial question is *How far is it?* It is easy, however, to show that *far* is logically negative:

> X is near to everything near to Y.
> X is far from everything far from Y. (reversal)

Once again we must ask: why the discrepancy? The most likely answer, again, seems to be that linguistic polarity is following natural polarity. Greater spatial separation is perceptually more salient than lesser separation, just as long things are more noticeable than short things. Also, since there is a natural end-point to the scale of distance at the *near* end, whereas *far-ness* extends indefinitely, *near* makes a more satisfactory negative term. But the notion of distance, the most natural gradable property, is essentially a negative one: it is the degree of 'not-at-ness'.

The puzzling cases are those involving privative antonyms (e.g. *clean*:*dirty*, *accurate*:*inaccurate*, etc.) where, as we have seen, natural polarity is typically overruled by evaluative polarity. These fall into two groups. In one group, exemplified by *true*:*false*, *accurate*:*inaccurate*, *satisfactory*:*unsatisfactory*, logical polarity agrees with linguistic polarity:

It's true that it's true.
It's false that it's false. (reversal)

An accurate guess at an accurate measurement.
An inaccurate guess at an inaccurate measurement. (reversal)

A satisfactory example of satisfactory work.
An unsatisfactory example of unsatisfactory work. (reversal)

In all of these cases logical and linguistic polarity conflict with natural polarity: with regard to *accurate*:*inaccurate*, for example, one would expect the natural graded property to be 'distance from exactitude', i.e. inaccuracy. In the other group, logical polarity agrees with natural polarity, as against linguistic polarity. This group is exemplified by *clean*:*dirty*, *safe*:*dangerous*, *pure*:*impure*. The linguistically positive term of each of these pairs yields the tell-tale reversal, indicating that it is logically negative:

It's been cleaned of its cleanness.
It's safe from safety.
It's been purified of its purity.

The difference between these two groups with respect to the logical polarity of linguistically positive terms no doubt reflects a difference in their semantic nature, but it is at present unclear what this underlying difference is.

11.5 **Neutralisation and semantic markedness**

The term **neutralisation** refers to the non-appearance of a semantic contrast under certain circumstances, particularly when there is some reason for remarking on its absence.[7] Many instances of the non-appearance of a semantic contrast are not at all newsworthy. For instance, we do not say that the contrast between "male" and "female" is neutralised in *book*: at the very least, the term in which a particular contrast is said to be neutralised must be a superordinate of each of the terms (real or hypothetical) which realise, or would realise, the contrast. But even this is not enough to justify the use of the term *neutralisation*: we do not normally say, for instance, that the *dog/cat* contrast is neutralised in *animal*. There would be no point in this, as it is the function of *animal* to subsume a set of more specific terms: if the contrasts were still operative, we would end up with a duplicate set of specific terms.

There are two types of situation in which it is customary to speak of neutralisation. The first arises when a number of elements (usually two) stand jointly (but not singly) in a recognised relation to a single element.

So, for instance, the *doctor/dentist* contrast is neutralised in *patient*, and the *murderer/mugger* contrast is neutralised in *victim*. The existence of differentiation on one side of the opposition justifies us in regarding it as having been suppressed on the other side. The relations characteristic of proportional series may also give rise to neutralisation. Thus, the *ewe/ram* contrast may be said to be neutralised in *lamb*, there being no ovine parallels to *colt* and *filly*.

The other type of situation in which it is normal to speak of neutralisation is when a lexical unit which participates in an opposition (or set of oppositions) has a co-lexemic superordinate:

The strongly impartial occurrences of antonyms are a special case of this type of neutralisation: the contrast operative in *It's long/It's short* is neutralised in *How long is it?* It is important to be clear what this means. The *long* of *How long is it?* is a superordinate both of *long* and *short* in *It's* —: it therefore designates what they have in common, namely, the scale of LENGTH. This scale has an inherent directionality, so that *of greater length*, although it incorporates the neutralised sense of *long*, means "longer", rather than "shorter". The inherent directionality of the scale cannot be neutralised. If one were to postulate a co-extensive scale of SHORTH, designated by the nominalisation *shorth* (pronounced like *eighth*),[8] then *shorth* and *length* would not be synonymous, even though each would represent a neutralisation of the *It's long/It's short* distinction. In fact, at first sight, *of greater length* and *of greater shorth* would seem to manifest that very distinction. What is neutralised, however, in both *length* and in the hypothetical *shorth* is the "upper end of the scale"/"lower end of the scale" contrast. This line of argument leads inevitably to the conclusion that in both *longer* and *shorter* the *long/short* contrast is neutralised, again in spite of their clear oppositional difference of meaning. The difference in meaning between *longer* and *shorter*, in turn, seems to indicate that *shorter* operates over a scale of SHORTH. But this conflicts with the evidence given earlier (e.g. the fact that *How short is it?* and *twice as short* are committed) that there is no scale of SHORTH co-extensive with the scale of LENGTH. It is not at present clear how this conflict is to be resolved: perhaps our picture of polar antonyms operating over a single scale is incorrect; or perhaps *shorter* should be interpreted not as "of greater shorth" but – in spite of its morphological make-up – as "of lesser length" (intuitively this is not totally implausible).

Neutralisation is used to distinguish the **unmarked** term out of a set of contrasting terms: the unmarked item is the one with a co-lexemic sister-unit which is superordinate to the members of the contrasting set. In the case of a binary contrast, the second term is described as **marked**.[9] So, for instance, *animal* is the unmarked member of the set which includes *bird, fish, insect*, etc.; *dog* is the unmarked member, and *bitch* the marked member, in the *dog/bitch* contrast; and *heavy* is the unmarked, and *light* the marked member, of the *heavy/light* contrast.[10]

The impartial and committed units of an unmarked lexeme involved in a neutralised contrast may differ considerably in their frequency and distributional freedom.[11] In the case of *lion, dog* and *duck* it is the impartial units which have the greatest freedom of occurrence: they are the most likely to be operative in neutral contexts; and there is no restriction on using the superordinate unit to refer to a single member, or an unmixed group of members, of the marked category – *dog(s)*, for instance, may be used to refer to a bitch or group of bitches. The corresponding committed units are virtually restricted to contexts in which there is an explicit or implicit contrast with the unmarked term (e.g. *I prefer dogs to bitches, The lion and lioness watched the cubs playing*). In many cases it is the impartial units which are the more contextually restricted. This is true of *cow* and *hen*, for example. The impartial unit *cow*, for instance, occurs only in the plural; furthermore, it is doubtful whether a group of animals consisting exclusively of bulls may properly be referred to as cows (similarly with *cock* and *hen*), although such reference would be normal if the group contained both cows and bulls. The impartial unit of the lexeme *man* is even more restricted: it can only occur in generic usage – *Man is mortal, Men are mortal* (a mixed group of men and women cannot properly be referred to as men).

11.6 The nature of opposition

Opposition is a special case of incompatibility. *Long* and *short*, for instance, are incompatibles, since nothing can be at once *long* and *short* (relative to the same reference point); but obviously their relationship is different from that between *dog* and *cat*. We must now attempt to clarify the peculiar nature of opposites, and identify the characteristics which distinguish them from 'mere' incompatibles.

The first point to note is that not all lexical items are felt to have opposites. Ask someone for the opposite of *table*, or *gold*, or *triangle*, and

257

he will be unable to oblige. Some lexical items, it seems, are inherently non-opposable. The necessary absence of an opposite must be distinguished from an accidental absence. A competent speaker of English may be unable to supply opposites for *agile*, or *devout*, but this must not be confused with his inability to provide opposites for *brown* or *wistful*. In the case of *agile* and *devout*, the opposite concepts are easy enough to grasp, but there happen to be no lexical items in English to express them precisely. We may legitimately speak in such cases of a lexical 'gap': *agile* and *devout* form ready-made positive terms operating on scales of AGILITY and DEVOUTNESS, respectively, but the corresponding negative terms, expressing relative lack of these properties, are missing.[12] Notice that a term expressing a relative lack of some property, without a partner expressing a relative abundance, is inconceivable: if such a state of affairs happened to occur, speakers would merely re-conceptualise the scale so that the existing lexical item became positive.

In seeking to explain non-opposability, one cannot simply say that opposable notions belong to certain notional areas: both opposable and non-opposable terms may often be drawn from the same area. A good example of this is provided by colour terms. Here we find one exemplary pair of opposites in *black* and *white*; but *red*, *blue*, *green*, *yellow*, etc. have no opposites. A similar picture is presented by adjectives referring to emotional states: *happy* and *sad* are opposites, but *angry*, *disappointed*, *wistful*, *awed* and *amazed* are more like *red*, *yellow*, etc. (it is presumably no accident that we speak of 'emotional colour').

A quintessential property of true opposite pairs is an ineluctable 'twoness' in the relationship. *Black* and *white* form an exclusive natural twosome in a way in which no other pair of colour terms do. This binarity of opposites must be specified carefully.[13] It is immediately obvious that oppositeness cannot be completely accounted for by what might be termed 'mere binarity', that is, a dichotomous division that might easily, had history followed a different course, have been multiple. It is not enough, in other words, for some class to happen to have but two sub-classes, for terms denoting the latter to be thereby invested with the property of oppositeness, except in a very weak sense. Thus neither the division of flowering plants into *monocotyledons* and *dicotyledons*, nor of buses into *double-deckers* and *single-deckers*, yields anything but the feeblest of oppositions.

Some notion of an inherently binary contrast seems important for fully fledged opposites. Such a contrast would presumably be so constituted that neither member of a pair of lexical items manifesting it could conceivably have any other partner than the other member. An inherently binary contrast, in other words, would be one whose binarity was logically necessary. What sorts of contrast are inherently binary in this sense? Many relations based on the idea of a uni-dimensional scale or axis are inherently binary, and it may be that all inherently binary contrasts are describable in this way. For instance, a uni-dimensional axis can never have more than two extremes, so *top : bottom, front : back* and *full : empty* (and all antipodals) are inherently binary. Likewise, there are only two possible terms which are equi-distant from such extremes (barring synonyms), so that *usually* and *rarely*, for instance, which are equi-distant from *always* and *never*, respectively, stand (in that respect at least[14]) in an inherently binary relationship. Terms which are symmetrically disposed about the mid-point of an axis are inherently binary: *cool : warm, huge : tiny, fast : slow*. There are only two possible directions along a uni-dimensional axis: *up : down, rise : fall*. Terms which are reciprocally inter-definable in parallel ways define a minimal axis, and form an inherently binary set: the fact that *true* is equivalent to *not false*, and *false* to *not true* renders their relationship inherently binary (along with that of all complementary pairs). It seems impossible to find 'good' pairs of opposites for which a strong case cannot be made out that they display inherent binarity.

The notion of inherent binarity enables us to account for the fact that *black* has an opposite, but *yellow* has not. There is a uni-dimensional scale of neutral hue, whose extremes, *black* and *white*, constitute a naturally binary set. *Yellow* stands on no such scale, but belongs in a more complex colour space. One might postulate a scale of wave-length, but while this is objectively valid, it has no perceptual reality, since the extremes (within visible radiation) are *red* and *purple*, which are closer to one another perceptually than either is to such intermediate terms as *green* or *yellow*. Suppose, then, that we place the basic names of hues in a circle:[15]

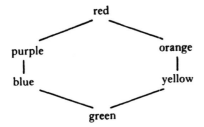

This shows the perceived relationships between the colours (as revealed, for instance, by the normality of the colour-terms in *X lies between Y and Z*). Do we not have opposites across the diameters of the circle, as

259

is arguably the case with the seasons? Some have argued that this is so for colours.[16] But it seems that in fact opposites are not constituted in this way, either with colours or seasons. Most native speakers do not feel that *purple* : *yellow*, *orange* : *blue* and *green* : *red* are opposites. As for the opposition between *summer* and *winter*, it needs no topological motivation : it is sufficiently accounted for by the fact that they are the *hottest* and *coldest* seasons, respectively; and *spring* and *autumn* are, respectively, the *beginning* and *end* of the growing season. If, in a suitable climate, a fifth season were introduced, say, a season of thaw, situated between *winter* and *spring*, the geometrical justification of the opposition between *summer* and *winter* would be destroyed, but neither their binary relationship, nor their status as opposites, would be affected.

There is still some essential element missing from our account of opposition – perhaps more than one. Although it is not possible to find good opposite pairs that do not express an inherently binary contrast, it is possible to find pairs expressing inherently binary contrasts which are not satisfactory opposites. Non-reversive indirect-converses are a case in point; other examples are the inherently binary sets generated by such definitions as "one day removed from Saturday", and "two months distant from March".

A clue to a possible essential ingredient of oppositeness comes from an examination of what other senses everyday non-technical terms for lexical opposites have. In most languages such terms are used in other, related senses; it may be that these embody deep intuitive insights into the nature of oppositeness. Three alternative senses are by far the most common, occurring either alone or in various combinations in different languages. The first is the static directional opposition exemplified in :

He sits opposite me at table.
We live on opposite sides of the river.

(Notice that in French the everyday word for lexical opposite, *contraire*, cannot be used in this sense.) The second is the dynamic directional opposition :

They were travelling in the opposite direction.

(In French one may speak of *le sens contraire*.) The third expresses the notion of antagonism, or confrontation. This cannot be exemplified from English, although the non-linguistic sense of *opposition* is not far off. In English, we would say *He's my opponent*, rather than *He's my opposite*;

but again, *opponent* and *opposite* are, of course, etymologically related. What all three related senses have in common is a directional opposition (even the third type, since antagonists prototypically face each other). Can we say, then, that a directional opposition, perhaps in an extended sense, underlies all opposites? Is this the key to the notion of opposition? It is surprising how many opposite pairs can be seen to embody a directional opposition. Obviously those treated in chapter 10 do. The same can be said for antonyms: *long* and *short* denote lengths *above* and *below* average, respectively. The hypothesis seems at first to run aground when we come to complementaries, which, as we have seen, reduce to simple negation. Yet, consider *present* and *absent*. The only possibility of change from either one of these is in the direction of the other: in a sense, therefore, they, too, 'face each other' from opposite ends of an axis. It could be that what is missing from *monocotyledon* : *dicotyledon* and *single-decker* : *double-decker* (also from pseudo-converses without a salient reversivity) is some form of directional opposition, rather than (or perhaps as well as) inherent binarity.

The suggestion so far is that a binary directional opposition is at the core of any pair of opposites. It could be argued, however, that the items which are 'one day removed from Saturday', namely, *Sunday* and *Friday*, embody a binary directional opposition, since one must travel in opposite directions along the time axis from *Saturday* in order to reach them. But these are not opposites. Why not? The answer is perhaps that although the binary directional relation to *Saturday* can be inferred from the meanings of *Friday* and *Sunday*, their meanings in no way highlight a mutual orientation towards *Saturday*. This might be expressed by saying that the directional binarity in *Friday* and *Sunday* is †**latent**; for a pair to be felt to be opposites, it must be †**patent**. Another illustration of the difference between latent and patent directional binarity is provided by the terms referring to boxers of different weight classes. Being a uni-dimensional scale, the scale of weight furnishes the possibility of several inherently binary contrasts of a directional sort, such as "top of the scale":"bottom of the scale", and "next to top of the scale":"next to bottom of the scale". These contrasts are realised by *heavy-weight* : *fly-weight* and *light heavy-weight* : *bantam-weight*, respectively. The first of these pairs may be felt by some to be weakly opposite, but surely not the second pair: intuitions will depend on how easily the latent information can be activated. These terms are not defined relatively, but in terms of actual weights. However, they could have been defined in such a way that the directional binarity was made patent: *maxi-weight* : *mini-weight*, and *sub-maxi-weight* : *sub-mini-weight*, for example, These coinages give a strong feeling of oppositeness, even though they are not in current use.

11.7 What makes a 'good' opposition?

It was proposed in the previous section that a binary directional opposition must form part of the meaning of any pair of opposites; furthermore, that part of their meaning must be at least to some degree patent. Presumably patency is a matter of degree, and the more patent a contained opposition is, the better examples of the category of opposites a pair of lexical items will be. Other factors contributing to the prototypicality of a pair of opposites can be identified. Three of these are worth singling out. The first is the ease with which a uni-dimensional scale can be conceptualised, on which the opposed terms may be symmetrically disposed. One of the reasons why *work* : *play* and *town* : *country*, for instance, are relatively weak opposites is the difficulty of establishing what the relevant dimension or axis is. The second factor is what might be termed the purity of the opposition, that is, what proportion of the meanings of the opposed terms is exhausted by the underlying opposition : the greater this proportion is, the stronger the felt opposition will be. This is why *father* and *mother* are weaker opposites than *man* and *woman*, which, in turn, are weaker than *male* and *female*; similarly, *giant* and *dwarf*, and *shout* and *whisper*, are less strongly opposed than *large* and *small*, and *loud* and *soft*. Finally, a good pair of opposites must be closely matched in respect of their non-propositional meaning: that is why, for instance, *tubby* and *emaciated* are not fully satisfactory opposites, although they incorporate a binary directional opposition.

Notes

11.1

    1. Cf. Lehrer (1974: 27).

11.2

    2. Wierzbicka (1980: 168–9) argues that *alive* should be analysed as "not dead":
It is "alive" which is the negative of "dead", not "dead" which is the negative of "alive". . . . One would say a sentence like "Bill is alive" only if one had reasons to suppose that someone thought Bill was dead. One can enter a room and announce "Bill is dead" without there having been any *previous statement* to the effect that Bill was alive. One can enter a room and announce "Bill is alive" only if there *has* been some previous statement to the effect that Bill is dead! (P. 168)
Without disputing Wierzbicka's account of the facts, one can legitimately ques-

tion her interpretation of them. This method of deciding on polarity would have the extraordinary result that *John is breathing* would have to be judged semantically negative, and *John is not breathing* semantically positive! Newsworthiness is not a reliable guide to polarity. Our account also contradicts McCawley (1972: 61) who claims that *alive* cannot be defined as "not dead", and *dead* cannot be defined as "not alive", on the grounds that not everything which is not dead (e.g. a piece of chalk) is necessarily alive. This line of argument would lead to the denial of the very possibility of complementarity, and would mean that, for instance, *untrue* could not be considered to mean "not true". It seems more fruitful to admit that complementarity is always accompanied by presuppositions of predicability.

11.3

3. It is presumably no accident that *dead* has a near-synonym *lifeless*. (This point may at first sight appear to be undermined by the existence of *deathless*. However, *deathless* is not a synonym of *alive*, but a hyponym; its linguistic negativity is predictable from the fact that it is normal for living things to die.)

4. The epithet *wifeless* would not be wholly inappropriate for an unmarried man; there is no term ending in -*less* which can be applied to a married man.

5. According to a resident of Peking interviewed on B.B.C.'s *Newsnight*, there is a Chinese proverb which translates as: *Water descends; Man ascends*. This expresses succinctly the point I am trying to make.

6. For the association between positive evaluation and the unmarked term of an opposition (for markedness see 11.5) see Zimmer (1964) and Boucher and Osgood (1969).

11.4 This section was inspired by Givón (1970).

11.5

7. This is somewhat vague, but I cannot find a stronger characterisation of the customary use of the term.

8. Notice that *shorth* would not be synonymous with *shortness*, which is committed.

9. There is a confusing variety of uses of the terms *marked* and *unmarked*. Lyons (1977: 305–6) distinguishes three distinct types of marking: formal marking (determined by the presence or absence of a formal 'mark', very often an affix – e.g. *dress* is unmarked, *undress* is marked); distributional marking (the item with the greatest freedom of occurrence is unmarked – e.g. *lion* is unmarked because, for instance, *male lion* is normal while *male lioness* is not); and semantic marking (the more specific term is marked). It should be noted that for Lyons it is lexemes which are marked or unmarked; for us, it is primarily the lexical units which form the terms of a particular opposition which are marked or unmarked (lexemes, as they are conceived here, do not, as such, have meanings). However, it would be a natural extension of our primary usage, with little danger of significant confusion, to speak of marked and unmarked lexemes. The markedness distinction is also sometimes applied to the specific and general units of the unmarked lexemes (Lyons comes close to this in calling *How big is it?* a marked question (1968: 466)). This is surely a different notion of markedness from the one which applies to the terms of an opposition, and seems likely to lead to confusion. We shall

use the terms *impartial* and *committed* to describe, respectively, the general and specific lexical items of an unmarked lexeme: that is to say, we shall describe, e.g., *dog* ("species") as impartial, and *dog* ("male of species") as committed with respect to the sex distinction.

10. A distinction should perhaps be made between cases where a member of a contrasting set of lexical units has a superordinate co-lexemic sister-unit (e.g. *animal* in *animal, bird, fish*, etc.), and cases of strict (excluding peripheral categories) and lax (including peripheral categories) units of a lexeme (e.g. *vegetable* (including *potato*) and *vegetable* (contrasting with *potato*). It is not clear that the notion of markedness is applicable to the latter case.

11. Lyons (1977: 309) discusses this type of variation in terms of degrees of semantic markedness. I am not sure that the notion of degree is applicable to our conception of semantic markedness.

10.6

12. There are, of course, near-opposites, and possibly pseudo-opposites, for these words. For instance, *clumsy* and *heavy-footed* have a near-antonymous relation to *agile* (*clumsy* is more general than *agile*, as it also stands in opposition to *dexterous*). For *devout*, we have the possibility of *impious*, and in the right context, *lax* (my feeling is that the former is an equipollent near-antonym, and the latter an overlapping pseudo-antonym). There is a type of 'missing' opposite intermediate between those whose meanings are difficult to conceive of and those whose meanings are easy to conceive of but happen not to be embodied in lexical items. In this type the opposite meanings are readily conceptualisable, but the lexical items are generally absent, which suggests that there is some motivation for the absence. Consider the words denoting various disabilities, disorders and imperfections in human beings: *blind, deaf, dumb, lame, bald, frigid, impotent, dyslexic*, etc. Some of these, such as *blind* (*sighted*) and *deaf* (*hearing*) now have established opposites, but the majority do not. They are all opposed to *normal*, of course, but this is so general that in many contexts it cannot be said to function fully adequately as an opposite, and a need is often felt for a more specific term ("normal in respect of X"): There was a mixed audience of bald and ? men. What should be used to fill the gap? *Haired?* – hardly!

13. Some linguists have espoused a much more thorough-going binarism, applying it to a wide range of linguistic structures. For binarism in semantics in particular, see Pottier (1974: 61ff).

14. Unfortunately for our purposes *usually* and *rarely* are not ideal opposites because *rarely* is gradable, while *usually* is not.

15. These six terms represent how the average English speaker would most probably divide the colour-spectrum (cf. Kay and McDaniel (1978: 610)).

16. E.g. Ogden (1932). Modern research (cf. Kay and McDaniel (1978)) suggests that there is a *physiological* opposition between green and red, and also between blue and yellow. For most speakers, however, this does not seem to lead to a *linguistic* opposition.

12
Synonymy

12.1 Absolute synonyms and the scale of synonymity

One variety of synonymy – cognitive synonymy – has already been introduced, in chapter 4, as one of the basic congruence relations. In this chapter, a broader conception of the notion of synonymy is developed, within which cognitive synonymy takes its place as one type, or degree; and the characteristics of all varieties of synonym are explored in some detail.

Let us take as the starting point for our discussion two robust semantic intuitions. The first is that certain pairs or groups of lexical items bear a special sort of semantic resemblance to one another. It is customary to call items having this special similarity synonyms; however, the intuitive class of synonyms is by no means exhausted by the notion of cognitive synonymy, as a glance at any dictionary of synonyms will confirm.[1] For instance, the Larousse *Synonymes* associates *nomade, forain* and *ambulant* together in one article as synonyms, but gives a distinct legal definition for each which makes clear that they are in no wise cognitive synonyms. Similarly, the *Dictionary of English Synonyms* gives *kill* as a synonym of *murder* (but, interestingly, not vice versa), and *strong* as a synonym of *powerful*: but again, cognitive synonymy is demonstrably absent (an accidental killing is not murder, and a strong car is not necessarily a powerful car). The second intuition is that some pairs of synonyms are 'more synonymous' than other pairs: *settee* and *sofa* are more synonymous than *die* and *kick the bucket*, which in turn are more synonymous than *boundary* and *frontier*, *breaker* and *roller*, or *brainy* and *shrewd*. (The items in each of these pairs occur in close association in *Roget's Thesaurus*; however, intuition might suggest that with the last pair we are approaching the borderline between synonymy and non-synonymy.) These two intuitions seem to point to something like a scale of synonymity. But before looking into this, let us try to obtain a clearer picture of the overall class of synonyms.

265

There is unfortunately no neat way of characterising synonyms. We shall attack the problem in two ways; first, in terms of necessary resemblances and permissible differences, and, second, contextually, by means of diagnostic frames. First of all, it is obvious that synonyms must have a significant degree of semantic overlap, as evidenced by common semantic traits. So, for example, *truthful* and *honest* fall within our broad class of synonyms, and have a relatively high semantic overlap, while *truthful* and *purple*, with virtually no traits in common, are about as far away from synonymy as one can get. However, it does not follow that the more semantic traits a pair of words share, the more synonymous they are. Consider the following pairs:

creature	philosophy
animal	tree
dog	cat
alsatian	spaniel

As we go down the list, the semantic overlap between the paired items increases. But, intuitively, they do not become more synonymous: *alsation* and *spaniel* are simply not synonyms. No matter how finely we further sub-divide the classes, provided we end up with satisfactorily disjunct sub-classes, we shall never reach synonymy. The key to this conundrum lies in the nature of the differentiating characteristics: synonyms must not only manifest a high degree of semantic overlap, they must also have a low degree of implicit contrastiveness. A major function of a term like *spaniel* is to exclude certain other closely related items, such as *alsation*, *collie*, etc. That is to say, the traits which distinguish *spaniel* from other members of what might be called its 'implicit contrast set' are, as it were, highlighted. In the case of *spaniel*, the other members of the contrast set are co-taxonyms; but this is not necessarily so in all cases – with *stallion*, for example, it would seem that the implicit contrast is more, or at least as much, with *mare* as with, say, *bull*. Furthermore, if the appropriateness of a term like *spaniel* with respect to some referent is denied (e.g. *That's not a spaniel*), there is at least an expectation that some other member of the implicit contrast set would be appropriate – in this case a dog of some other breed. Synonyms, however, are not like this. Although *truthful* and *honest* do not have identical meanings, in saying *John is honest* the difference with *John is truthful* is not being highlighted; nor, in saying *John is not honest*, is one implying that perhaps *truthful* would be more appropriate. Usually, denying one member of a pair of synonyms implicitly denies the other, too, unless there is some indication, either in the context, or, for instance, conveyed prosodically, that attention must be paid to nuances. In the following examples, a simple answer 'No' to the question would be inappropriate in the circumstances indicated:

1. A: Does this aeroplane have a motor?
   B: No. (odd if the aeroplane has an engine)
2. A: Has my husband been executed?
   B: No. (odd if A knows the man has been murdered)
3. A: Would you say that the candidate was pretty?
   B: No. (odd if the candidate is good-looking, or even handsome)

Synonyms, then, are lexical items whose senses are identical in respect of 'central' semantic traits, but differ, if at all, only in respect of what we may provisionally describe as 'minor' or 'peripheral' traits; an attempt will be made to characterise permissible differences between synonyms more precisely in 12.2 and 12.3.

Synonyms also characteristically occur together in certain types of expression. For instance, a synonym is often employed as an explanation, or clarification, of the meaning of another word. The relationship between the two words is frequently signalled by something like *that is to say*, or a particular variety of *or*:

He was cashiered, that is to say, dismissed.
This is an ounce, or snow leopard.

When synonyms are used contrastively, as they sometimes are, it is normal to signal the fact that it is the difference which must be attended to by some such expression as *more exactly*, or *or rather*:

He was murdered, or rather executed.
On the table there were a few grains or, more exactly, granules of the substance.

Notice that lexical items whose normal function is to contrast with one another do not co-occur normally with these 'nuance signallers':

? Arthur's got himself a dog – or more exactly, a cat.

Within the class of synonyms, as we have already noted, some pairs of items are more synonymous than others, and this raises the possibility

267

of a scale of synonymity of some kind. A scale needs at least one well-defined end-point; and if there is only one, it is more satisfactory for it to form the origin, or zero point, on the scale. With regard to degrees of synonymity, it seems that the point of semantic identity – i.e. absolute synonymy – can be established with some clarity (as we shall see in a moment); the notion of zero synonymity, on the other hand, is rather more diffuse. For one thing, it is probably not a unitary concept: *long*:*short* and *green*: *expensive* would presumably both count as examples of zero synonymity, but for different reasons. Furthermore, the dividing line between synonymy and non-synonymy is relatively vague in many cases. Where, in the following series, for instance, does synonymy end: *rap*:*tap*, *rap*: *knock*, *rap*:*thwack*, *rap*:*bang*, *rap*:*thud*? For these reasons it would seem better to make absolute synonymy the zero point on our scale; the scale will therefore be one of semantic difference rather than one of synonymy. (Given the fact that zero synonymity is not a unitary concept, perhaps the scale should be pictured as a series of concentric circles, with the origin at the centre, rather than as a line.)

According to the conception of word-meaning developed in this book, two lexical units would be absolute synonyms (i.e. would have identical meanings) if and only if all their contextual relations (as characterised in chapter 1) were identical.[2] It would, of course, be quite impracticable to prove that two items were absolute synonyms by this definition, because that would mean checking their relations in all conceivable contexts (it would also be theoretically impossible, if, as is probably the case, the number of possible contexts were infinite). However, the falsification of a claim of absolute synonymy is in principle very straightforward, since a single discrepancy in the pattern of contextual relations constitutes sufficient proof. It is convenient to conduct the search for absolute synonyms (or, more directly, the search for discrepancies between putative synonyms) in terms of the least specific of contextual relations, namely, relative normality. Furthermore, since it is inconceivable that two items should be equinormal in all contexts and differ in respect of some other contextual relation, and since, for our purposes, what is not reflected in differential contextual semantic relations is not meaning, it follows that equinormality in all contexts is the same as identity of meaning.

Let us now examine an illustrative sample of possible candidates for absolute synonymy. The following will serve: *begin*:*commence*, *munch*: *chew*, *hate*:*loathe*, *scandalous*:*outrageous*. As it happens, none of these pairs satisfies the criteria – for each, discriminating contexts can be found ('+' indicates "more normal", and '−' "less normal"):

4a. Johnny, tell Mummy when Playschool begins and she'll
    watch it with you.   (+)
 b. Johnny, tell Mummy when Playschool commences and
    she'll watch it with you.   (−)
5a. Arthur is always chewing gum.   (+)
 b. Arthur is always munching gum.   (−)
6a. I don't just hate him, I loathe him.   (+)
 b. I don't just loathe him, I hate him.   (−)
7a. That is a scandalous waste of money.   (+)
 b. That is an outrageous waste of money.   (−)

It is important in applying the test to make sure that any differences of normality have a semantic and not a syntactic origin. Since partial absolute synonymy is perfectly possible, only contexts in which both items are syntactically normal should be used (in so far as this can be ascertained). For instance, the difference in normality between 8 and 9 should not be taken as evidence for the non-synonymy of *hide* and *conceal*:

8. Where is he hiding? (normal)
9. Where is he concealing? (odd)

The fact that *hide* and *conceal* are not absolute synonyms can be demonstrated using only contexts where each is equally at home syntactically:

10a. Johnny, where have you hidden Daddy's slippers?   (+)
  b. Johnny, where have you concealed Daddy's slippers?   (−)

The problems concerning *nearly* and *almost* have already been discussed: but with these, too, without going beyond contexts where presumed syntactic differences are not operative, a purely semantic discrimination can be made:

11a. He looks almost Chinese   (+)
  b. He looks nearly Chinese.   (−)
12a. It was almost too horrible to look at.   (+)
  b. It was nearly too horrible to look at.   (−)

A normality difference between two word forms in a particular context is not acceptable evidence against absolute synonymy if one of the word forms is part of an idiom, i.e. an opaque or translucent sequence, because in that case it would not be a lexical item. So, for instance, the normality difference between *fast* and *rapid* in *John pulled a — one* is not relevant to arguments concerning the synonymity or otherwise of *fast* and *rapid*.

269

It is also important not to allow irrelevant senses of a word form to interfere with testing: the normality difference between 13a and b, for example, is not relevant to the question of whether *old* and *former* in 14a and b are absolute synonyms:

13a. Arthur's most recent car is an old one. (+)
   b. Arthur's most recent car is a former one. (−)
14a. He had more responsibility in his old job.
   b. He had more responsibility in his former job.

One thing becomes clear once we begin a serious quest for absolute synonyms, and that is that if they exist at all, they are extremely uncommon. Furthermore, it would seem reasonable to predict that if the relationship were to occur, it would be unstable. There is no obvious motivation for the existence of absolute synonyms in a language, and one would expect either that one of the items would fall into obsolescence, or that a difference in semantic function would develop. Students not infrequently suggest *sofa* and *settee* as absolute synonyms. It seems that as these terms are currently used, discriminating contexts are hard to find. But when I was a child, *sofa* was considered more 'elegant' than *settee*; however, several students have reported that for their parents *settee* was the more 'elegant' term. In view of this lability, the current relationship would appear unlikely to persist. It seems probable, and many semanticists have maintained,[3] that natural languages abhor absolute synonyms just as nature abhors a vacuum.

Absolute synonymy, then, is the end-point of our inverse scale of synonymity. Including this point, but extending some distance along the scale, is a region which represents propositional synonymy. Since there are synonyms which are not propositional synonyms (we shall call them plesionyms), the scale also extends beyond the limit of propositional synonymy, ultimately to shade into non-synonymy. Within each region of the scale, degree of synonymity varies continuously.

In the two sections which immediately follow, we shall examine the sorts of semantic difference between two lexical items that are compatible with propositional synonymy (section 2), and with plesionymy (section 3).

12.2 **Propositional synonyms**

Propositional synonymy was introduced briefly in chapter 4, It is obvious that, to be propositional synonyms, a pair of lexical items must have certain semantic properties in common. However, as we saw in the previous section, very few pairs of propositional synonyms are absolute synonyms; it follows from this that in the majority of cases a lexical item must, in some respects at least, be different in meaning from any of its propositional synonyms. In this section an attempt will be made to establish more clearly and explicitly the nature both of the semantic properties in respect of which propositional synonyms must be identical, and of those in respect of which they may differ.

Let us first make an important distinction between the two principal ways in which lexical meaning manifests itself. Consider the difference between 15a and b:

15a. I just felt a sudden sharp pain.
 b. Ouch!

There is a sense in which the content of the message conveyed by these two utterances is the same, or at least very similar; however, they differ in the way that the meaning is put across. We shall say that they differ in respect of †**semantic mode**; the meaning in 15a is in the **propositional mode**, while the meaning in 15b is in the **expressive mode**. The characteristics of propositional meaning depend partly on the propositional attitude expressed by the sentence in which it operates – that is to say, on whether it is a statement, question, command, exclamation, etc. In a statement it is the propositional meaning which determines the truth-conditions, either relative to a given state of affairs, or relative to other statements; it exercises this role at least partly by controlling the referential properties of referring expressions in the sentence. The role of propositional meaning in, for instance, questions, or commands, neither of which have truth-conditions, is different, though related: in questions, propositional meaning determines the range of utterances which constitute truthful answers; in commands, it determines the range of actions that count as compliance with or obedience to the command. Expressive meaning does not function in this way. Notice that 15a has truth-conditions, whereas 15b has not. At the risk of being thought presumptuous, one could challenge the veracity of 15a: *That's a lie – I gave you a double dose of Novocain*; it would make little sense to challenge 15b in this way. Expressive meaning carried by a lexical item in a statement plays no role in determining its truth-conditions. So, for instance, 16a and b have identical truth-conditions:

16a. Arthur has lost the key.
 b. Arthur has lost the blasted key.

However, if *blasted*, which carries only expressive meaning, is replaced

271

by *spare*, which carries propositional meaning, a statement with a different truth-condition is obtained:

17. Arthur has lost the spare key.

In parallel fashion, neither *blasted* nor *been and gone and* in 18 does anything to restrict the range of possible true answers to the question:

18. Who's been and gone and locked the blasted door?

Blasted has a similar lack of effect in 19b; any action which counted as compliance with 19a in a particular situation would necessarily also count as compliance with 19b (and vice versa):

19a. Shut that window!
  b. Shut that blasted window!

There are other differences between propositional meaning and expressive meaning. For instance, presented meaning is for the most part coded digitally – that is to say, it can vary only in discrete jumps; expressive meaning, on the other hand, at least in respect of intensity, can be varied continuously, and is therefore analogically coded. Suppose we want to grade the intensity of the pain in 15a: if we wish to do this in terms of propositional meaning, we have a set of discrete choices, and we must opt for one or another:

I felt a sudden sharp (very sharp/extremely sharp/...) pain.

The intensity of the pain expressed by 15b, however, can be varied with infinite subtlety by means of prosodic grading – i.e. by varying the loudness, starting pitch and pitch range of the intonation contour. (This phenomenon has already been met in connection with superlatives in chapter 9; superlatives all seem to have a component of expressive meaning.) Amenability to prosodic grading appears to be a close correlate of expressive meaning, at least in English. Another characteristic distinguishing expressive meaning from propositional meaning is that it is valid only for the utterer, at the time and place of utterance. This limitation it shares with, for instance, a smile, a frown, a gesture of impatience, or a dog's bark (all of which, as it happens, are also continuously gradable). The capacity of language to transcend the immediate context of utterance (sometimes referred to as the capacity for **displacement**), which enables me to talk about the pain I felt yesterday, or the pain Arthur will feel tomorrow in Australia, depends entirely on propositional meaning.

The relevance to propositional synonymy of the difference between propositional and expressive meaning is simple: the inherent meaning of a lexical item may be made up of either or both of these types of meaning; if two lexical items are propositional synonyms, then they must be identical in respect of propositional traits, but they may differ in respect of expressive traits. Let us now look briefly at the ways in which expressive meaning manifests itself in language.

There is a range of lexical items virtually all of whose meaning is expressive. The most obvious of these are the so-called 'expletives'. These can be exclamations:

Gosh! Wow! Hell's Bell's! Bother! Ace! I'll say!

or they may have a grammatical role within the sentence, usually of some kind of adjectival or adverbial modifier:

Get that damn dog off my seat.
You can blooming well put it back where you got it.

Words from taboo areas lend themselves readily to expletive use:

Holy shit! Balls! My arse! Piss off! Bugger me!

(Not a few non-taboo expletives are historically merely euphemistic alterations of taboo items: e.g. *Gosh* (*God*), *Heck* (*Hell*), *Gee whiz* (*Jesus*), etc.) Expletives are not, however, the only sorts of lexical item whose meaning is wholly of the expressive variety: consider *already, still* and *yet* in 20, 21 and 22:

20. He has already arrived.
21. He is still here.
22. He hasn't arrived yet.

None of these carries any propositional meaning, since 20, 21 and 22 are logically equivalent to 23, 24 and 25 respectively:

23. He has arrived.
24. He is here.
25. He has not arrived.

From this it follows that all three are propositionally synonymous with zero. It does not, of course, follow that they are meaningless: their meanings can interact both with each other, and with the meanings of other items, to produce semantic oddity:

? He is already still here.
? Has he only just arrived already?
? He has already finished – though I expected him to finish earlier.

273

Expressed meaning most characteristically conveys some sort of emotion or attitude – doubt, certainty, hope, expectation, surprise, contempt, disappointment, admiration, flippancy, seriousness, and so on. In appropriate contexts, *still*, *yet* and *already* can express emotion: 26, 27 and 28 would most likely express surprise:

26. Hasn't he arrived yet?
27. Has he arrived already?
28. Is he still here?

However, the meaning they express is not necessarily so distinctly emotive. Basically, what *still*, *already* and *yet* express in 29, 30 and 31 is an expectation, or set of expectations, on the part of the speaker:[4]

29. The shop should still be open when the meeting finishes.
30. We tried to contact him, but he had already left.
31. That stretch of line has not yet been electrified.

These sentences can be used to make statements of relative emotive neutrality. (The meaning carried by *still*, *already* and *yet* here is expressive, in spite of not expressing what would normally be described as an emotion; however, it does not appear to be prosodically gradable. Prosodic intensification is apparently possible for these items only when they carry a distinct emotive charge.)

Expressive traits and propositional traits may be simultaneously present in the meaning of a lexical item. This is true of words such as *daddy* and *mummy*; it is at least partly in respect of expressive meaning that these differ from *father* and *mother* (diminutive affixes often have a purely expressive function). *He's my daddy* can be challenged with *No, he's not*, but that impinges only on the propositional meaning (i.e. "He's my father"), and does not call into question the genuineness of the expressive meaning. Other examples of words with 'mixed' meanings are *paw* (in the sense of "hand"), *mug* (in the sense of "face") and *blubber* (in the sense of "weep").

It is possible that expressive meaning is even more important than has been so far suggested; it is arguable that communication would be impossible without it. Every communicative utterance must transmit as part of its meaning an indication of intended propositional attitude. Without this, an utterance would be communicatively dead – it would resemble a proposition 'entertained' by a logician. The expression of propositional attitude has the effect of, as it were, energising a proposition. Propositional attitude may be signalled by a specific lexical item:[5]

I promise to be faithful.
I warn you not to go.

or by word order:

He is here.
Is he here?

or it may be indicated prosodically. But whatever its bearer is, there are good reasons for believing that it is conveyed via the expressive mode. Take as an example a simple question such as *What is she wearing?* The interrogative sense of this shows a number of typical expressive characteristics. First, it is tied to the utterer and to the time and place of utterance. (Notice that interrogativity is not restricted to the expressive mode: in *Arthur asked John what Mary was wearing* it appears as a propositional trait of *asked* – furthermore, it is 'displaced'.) Second, it is prosodically gradable: *What IS she wearing?* Finally, it cannot be directly challenged: one cannot reply to *What is she wearing?* with *That's untrue – it was you who bought it for her* (meaning that the interrogativity is false, since the questioner already knows the answer). It is significant, too, that expressive meaning carried by lexical items in, say, a question, does not fall within the scope of the interrogativity in the way that propositional meaning in a question does, but interacts with it and modifies its quality. For instance, the expressive meaning carried by *already* in *Have they arrived already?* is not part of what is being asked; what it does is change the quality of the interrogativity, so that *Have they arrived already?* is not quite the same kind of question as *Have they arrived?*

Some lexical items have an expressive capacity which is not in evidence in all contexts of use – unlike the examples considered so far – yet it does not seem satisfactory to regard them as ambiguous. Among such elements two types are distinguishable. First, there are those which, although capable of quite neutral employment, can also be invested with emotive expressive meaning, usually prosodically. For instance, *baby* in 32a and b is emotively cool:

32a. Mother and baby are progressing satisfactorily.
  b. The baby was born prematurely.

But *baby* can be invested with tremendous emotion:

33. Oh, look – a baby! Isn't he adorable?

In contrast, *infant* and *neonate* are incapable of expressive use, although their propositional content is very close to that of *baby*. While it is perhaps not satisfactory to say that *baby* is inherently expressive, the difference between it and *infant* in respect of expressive potential must be considered inherent. The second type of element with latent expressive capacity is slightly different. Like those of the first type, such elements are capable of emotively neutral use; but whereas the former need to be charged with emotion prosodically, the latter are not so responsive to this, but seem to pick up expressive traits from the context, and, as it were, focus and amplify them. Compare, first of all, 34a and b:

34a. I want you to go on taking these tablets, Miss Smith.
  b. I want you to continue taking these tablets, Miss Smith.

There is little difference between these other than perhaps in respect of evoked meaning due to difference of register; neither *go on* nor *continue* here carries a significant burden of expressive meaning. Compare 34a and b, however, with 35a and b, and 36a and b:

35a. He went on complaining about it for hours afterwards.
  b. He continued complaining about it for hours afterwards.
36a. I can tell you, it went on for quite some time.
  b. I can tell you, it continued for quite some time.

Again there is a register effect; but in addition, *go on* seems to amplify the expressiveness implicit in the utterances, while *continue*, if anything, damps it down. As another example of the same phenomenon, consider *issue* and *put out* (in the relevant senses). Sentences 37a and b differ only slightly, in the manner of 34a and b:

37a. We shall be putting out a detailed statement later today.
  b. We shall be issuing a detailed statement later today.

but there is a much greater difference between 38a and b:

38a. Public opinion has been seriously misled by the stream of lies and half-truths the management has been putting out over the last few months.
  b. Public opinion has been seriously misled by the stream of lies and half-truths the management has been issuing over the last few months.

It seems that lexical items characteristic of informal style are more likely to be 'expressive amplifiers' than items belonging to more formal styles. There seems also to be a correlation between what might be termed 'lexical eccentricity' (i.e. idioms – including phrasal verbs, frozen metaphors, bound collocants like *foot* in *foot the bill*, etc.) and expressiveness.

Lexical items differing only in respect of inherent expressive traits, or potential expressivity – *jolly* and *very*, *father* and *daddy*, *cat* and *pussy*, *infant* and *baby*, *go on* and *continue* – are propositional synonyms. It must be remembered that although emotion and attitude are typically conveyed via the expressive mode, this is not necessarily the case. One may convey one's sadness by saying *I feel sad*; this utilises the propositional channel and constitutes a statement which may be false. (It is possible that this sentence is ambiguous between an expression of sadness and a description of one's emotional state. If so, my remarks apply only to the latter interpretation.)[6] It is fairly common to find pairs of words whose meanings differ only in that they express different evaluative judgements on their designated referents (or one expresses a judgement while the other is neutral): *horse, nag*; *car, banger*; *a smart alec, a clever chap*; *mean, careful with one's money*, etc. These evaluative traits undoubtedly belong to the semantic area that is typical of the expressive channel, and some of the evaluative meaning may well be expressive. However, according to our criteria, none of the pairs of items just mentioned are propositional synonyms, since they yield sentences with different truth-conditions. It follows that the evaluative traits must be at least partly propositional in nature:

A: Arthur tried to sell me an old nag.
B: No, he didn't – it was a perfectly good horse.
A: I hear Arthur's very mean.
B: No, he isn't – he's just careful with his money.
A: Arthur's a smart alec.
B: No, he isn't – but he is clever.

Propositional and expressive meanings are the most important types of meaning in language, and we can think of them as what a speaker principally utilises and directly manipulates in order to convey his intended message. There are other aspects of the meanings of words, however, whose primary sphere of operation is not the interface between speakers' intentions and language, but the interactions amongst linguistic items constituting a discourse. The primary function of these semantic properties is not so much to encode message components directly (although they may do this secondarily) as to place restrictions on what linguistic items can occur together normally within the same sentence, or within the same discourse. In normal utterances, these restrictions have the effect of adding informational redundancy to the message, and cohesiveness to the discourse (thereby facilitating the hearer's task of decoding); the restrictions can also, however, be deliberately flouted, giving rise to oddness, which may, for instance, act as a signal that an utterance is not to be interpreted literally. These semantic properties will be dealt with under two headings: (i) presupposed meaning and (ii) evoked meaning.[7] Let us begin with the presupposed meaning.

The expression *presupposed meaning* is used here in a pre-theoretical sense to refer to semantic traits which are, as it were, taken for granted in the use of an expression, or lexical item, but not actually asserted, denied, questioned, or whatever, in the utterance in which they appear. Particular presuppositions (i.e. presupposed traits) can be regularly and characteristically associated with specific lexical items – hence their interest to us. For instance, the use of the verb *drink* takes for granted the existence of an actual or potential 'sufferer' of the act of drinking, which has the property of being liquid. Thus, *Arthur drank it*, *Did Arthur drink it?*, *Arthur didn't drink it* and *Drink it, Arthur!* in normal use all presuppose that *it* refers to a liquid, that is to say, someone eavesdropping on a conversation in which any of these sentences occurred would be able to conclude with some confidence that *it* referred to some sort of liquid (barring metaphorical usage). It is this constancy of inferability, irrespective of whether the sentence containing *drink* functions as an assertion, denial, or question, etc., that qualifies the trait "liquid" to count as a presupposition of *drink*.

The main effect of the presupposed semantic traits of a lexical item is to place restrictions on its normal syntagmatic companions; we therefore refer to such traits as semantic co-occurrence restrictions (these were introduced in 4.12). It is necessary to distinguish two types of semantic co-occurrence restriction. First, there are those which are a logically inescapable concomitant of the propositional traits of a lexical item. Consider the verb *die*; this imposes semantic constraints on the nature of its grammatical subject:

> Arthur died.
> The aspidistra died.
> ? The spoon died.
> ? Arthur's exam results died.

The only things that can without oddness be said to die are those which are (a) organic, (b) alive (and possibly also (c) mortal: ? *The angel died*). The semantic traits "organic", "alive" and "mortal" are logical prerequisites of the meaning of *die* – the notion of dying is inconceivable in their absence. We shall refer to semantic co-occurrence restrictions which are logically necessary as **selectional restrictions**. Now consider the lexical item *kick the bucket*. This has the same selectional restrictions as *die*, but it imposes further semantic requirements on its subject:

> Arthur kicked the bucket.
> (?) The hamster kicked the bucket.
> ? The aspidistra kicked the bucket.

Unlike *die*, *kick the bucket* (in its idiomatic sense) is fully normal only with a human subject. But this additional restriction does not arise logically out of the meaning of *kick the bucket*. The propositional meaning of *kick the bucket* is not "die in a characteristically human way", but simply "die"; the restriction to human subjects is semantically arbitrary.[8] We shall call arbitrary co-occurrence restrictions of this type **collocational restrictions**.

A logical relationship between collocational restrictions and cognitive synonymy will be established by definition: we shall define collocational restrictions as co-occurrence restrictions that are irrelevant to truth-conditions – that is to say, those in respect of which lexical items may differ and still be propositional synonyms. This is not entirely straightforward, as the diagnosis of propositional synonymy where collocational differences are involved requires judgements concerning the truth-conditions of odd sentences. Consider how the following questions would normally be answered in the circumstances specified in brackets:

> 39. Is there something wrong with the engine of your lawn-mower?
>   (There is something wrong with the (electric) motor.)
> 40. Is Arthur the one with beer-foam on his moustache?
>   (Arthur is the one with beer-froth on his moustache.)
> 41. Have you grilled the bread?
>   (You have toasted the bread.)
> 42. Has the aspidistra kicked the bucket?
>   (The aspidistra has died.)

He would be a pedant indeed who could answer these questions with an unequivocal 'No.' The only possible cooperative response would surely be either 'Yes,' or something like 'You can't say that, you have to say XYZ – but the answer to your question is "yes".' On the strength of our reluctance to brand sentences like *The lawn-mower engine is faulty* as false (even though odd), when it is true that the lawn-mower motor is faulty, we shall classify *engine* and *motor* as propositional synonyms; also, for parallel reasons, *grill* and *toast*, *froth* and *foam*, and *kick the bucket* and *die*.

279

Selectional restrictions, being logically necessary, are inseparable from the propositional traits that presuppose them, and can therefore hardly be said to have a distinct function in an utterance (although they have the effect of contributing to informational redundancy). Collocational restrictions, on the other hand, are not logically necessary, so it is legitimate to ask what they bring to an utterance. Generally speaking, they are not primarily there to encode part of the message: in the majority of occurrences, presupposed traits (whether collocational or selectional) are duplicated by propositional traits carried by the lexical items within their scope. For instance, in *My grandfather passed away yesterday*, *passed away* imposes collocational restrictions on its grammatical subject, requiring it to be human. But *passed away* is not the primary carrier of the trait "human": this role is performed by *grandfather*, of which "human" is an inherent propositional trait. Even in a sentence such as *He passed away yesterday*, it is not *passed away* which is the hearer's principal indication that the subject is human; in most circumstances of use of this sentence, the referent of *he* would be already known to the addressee, and the information derivable from *passed away* that 'he' was human would be, in that sense, redundant. We can observe the role of collocational restrictions by comparing 43 and 44:

43. My grandfather passed away yesterday.
44. My grandfather died yesterday.

(*Die* carries the same propositional traits as *pass away*, but lacks its collocational restrictions.) Setting aside the difference of register between *die* and *pass away*, it can be seen that these two sentences have the same message-conveying potential. The only difference between them is that 43 displays the greater semantic cohesion, in that its subject is more predictable from the rest of the sentence. Both selectional restrictions and collocational restrictions can be given a more active semiotic role. Presupposed meaning can, for instance, be used to 'leak' information:

A: What's John going to give me for my birthday?
B: I'm sworn to secrecy – but I advise you not to drink it all at once.

Or co-occurrence restrictions can be deliberately flouted for metaphoric effect:

Arthur's parrot's just passed away.

Collocational restrictions vary in the degree to which they can be speci-

280

fied in terms of required semantic traits. When fully specifiable, they may be described as †**systematic collocational restrictions**. In most such cases (but not all), the restrictions behave as presuppositions of the selecting item. We have already met *kick the bucket* and *pass away*, which require a human subject. *Grill* and *toast* probably belong to this category, too. They denote the same action or process from the point of view of the agent, but different patients are involved. Grilling is a method of cooking, whereas toasting is not: things that get toasted are normally already cooked, whereas items for grilling are raw. Hence our hypothetical eavesdropper, on hearing *Are you going to grill them or fry them?*, would be able to form some opinion concerning the likely nature of the referents of *them*. In cases where most of a lexical item's collocants display certain semantic properties, so that its use sets up an expectation of a certain type of collocant, but there are exceptions to the general tendency, we may speak of †**semi-systematic collocational restrictions**. For instance, a *customer* typically acquires something material in exchange for money; a *client*, on the other hand, typically receives a less tangible professional or technical service. Hence bakers, butchers, shoe-shops and newsagents have customers, while architects, solicitors and advertising agencies have clients. But the people who use the services of a bank, surprisingly, can be called its customers. (The collocational restrictions of *client* are systematic.)

The collocational ranges of some lexical items can only be described by listing permissible collocants. Such items will be described as having †**idiosyncratic collocational restrictions**. As a possible set of cognitive synonyms which differ in respect of idiosyncratic collocational restrictions, consider the following:

	unblemished	spotless	flawless	immaculate	impeccable
performance	−	−	+	+	+
argument	−	−	+	−	?
complexion	?	?	+	−	−
behaviour	−	−	−	−	+
kitchen	−	+	−	+	−
record	+	+	−	?	+
reputation	?	+	−	?	?
taste	−	−	?	?	+
order	−	−	?	+	+
credentials	−	−	−	−	+

The judgements recorded above represent my own intuitions. I can discern no semantic motivation for the collocational patterns. The propositional synonyms *umpire* and *referee* also exemplify idiosyncratic collocational preferences. The collocational restrictions of items like *umpire* and *referee* cannot, of course, give rise to presuppositions. Indeed, it is debatable whether idiosyncratic restrictions are a matter of semantics at all.[9]

Like presupposed meaning, what we shall call †**evoked meaning** primarily contributes to discourse cohesion, and only secondarily has a direct communicative role. Again like presupposed meaning, it does not affect the truth-value of containing sentences, and thus provides a further potential source of variation among propositional synonyms. The possibility of evoked meaning is a consequence of the existence of different dialects and registers within a language. Let us first look at dialect. We shall not concern ourselves with the intricacies of the notion of dialect: we shall take the simple view that dialects are varieties of a language that have a high degree of mutual intelligibility, and are characteristic of distinguishable groups of users. Dialectal variation can be classified as geographical, temporal, or social; it must be borne in mind, however, that these dimensions of variation are not rigidly separable, since, for instance, certain regional variants may be more or less restricted to older, or lower class, speakers. As far as we are concerned, a word belonging to one dialect is relevant to the description of another dialect only to the extent that it is reasonably familiar to speakers of the latter, and at the same time recognised as being characteristic of speakers of the former. For example, the Scots words *glen*, *loch*, *wee* and *dram* are probably familiar to most speakers of English outside Scotland and recognised as Scottish; on the other hand, the word *flesher* (=*butcher*), which not infrequently crops up in discussions of synonymy, is of dubious relevance for a description of standard English because of its unfamiliarity. For a different reason, a word like *tartan* is probably not relevant in this connection, either; although most speakers would doubtless associate it with Scotland and things Scottish, it is a normal item of standard English, and is not particularly distinctive of speakers of Scottish English.

There is no reason in principle why a lexical item in one dialect should not be a virtually exact translation equivalent of a different lexical item in another dialect: such equivalence may well be uncommon, but there is no need to imagine any centrifugal tendency, as with absolute synonyms within one dialect. However, even if two particular items could be shown to have exactly parallel sets of contextual relations in their respective 'home' dialects, they would still not be absolute synonyms in either one of the dialects, but only propositional synonyms. This is because a displaced item has the power of evoking images and associations of its 'home' surroundings, which can interact in complex ways with the new environment, and this is sufficient to differentiate the 'foreign' item semantically from its native synonym.

Among dialectal synonyms, those of the geographical variety are perhaps of minor significance. There is no shortage of examples – *autumn*:*fall*, *lift*:*elevator*, *glen*:*valley*, *wee*:*small* – but they do not loom large in the linguistic experience of most speakers. Much more important (alas!) are synonyms drawn from different social dialects: the consequences of choice from among these, especially for anyone aspiring to move from one social class to another, may go well beyond the relatively innocuous evocation of geographical and cultural associations linked with geographical variants. Most language-users are extremely sensitive to this dimension of variation. When I was a boy, the room in the house where washing-up and cooking were done was called the *scullery*. As my father progressed in his profession, and his salary and social standing improved, this room became first the *kitchen*, and then the *kitchenette*. Concurrently, the *settee* became the *sofa*, *serviettes* metamorphosed into *napkins*, and one stopped going to the *lavatory* (or, more commonly, the *lav*) and went to the *toilet* instead. [10] Among certain social groups whose members identify themselves at least partly by the use of a distinctive 'slang', the temporal dimension of variation is as important as, and interacts with, the social dimension, in that it is vital, if someone wishes to maintain his status in the group, not to use out-dated terminology. Since slangs typically have a very rapid lexical turnover, this criterion discriminates sharply between 'insiders' and 'outsiders'. However, longer term lexical changes, like the replacement of *wireless* by *radio*, and *swimming-bath* by *swimming-pool*, create dialectal synonyms (characteristic of dialects spoken by different generations) whose overall significance is of the same order as that of geographical variants.

Whereas dialects are language varieties associated with different characteristics of users (e.g. age, class and regional affiliation), registers are varieties of language used by a single speaker, which are considered appropriate to different occasions and situations of use. One analysis of register, which will suffice for our purposes, distinguishes three interacting dimensions of variation: **field, mode** and **style**. [11] *Field* refers to the topic or field of discourse: there are lexical (and grammatical) characteristics of, for instance, legal discourse, scientific discourse, advertising language, sales talk, political speeches, football commentaries, cooking recipes, and so on. Obviously some of the lexical differences among these fields of discourse are due to the fact that different referents constitute typical foci of attention: one is more likely to encounter *flour*, *eggs* and *bake* in a cooking recipe than in a revivalist sermon; and no doubt *sin, Hell* and *repent* are more likely in the latter. But it is by no means rare for the same referent to have different names on different occasions. If the names differ only in respect of the fields of discourse in which they typically appear, then they will be propositional synonyms. So, for example, *matrimony* may be regarded as a field-specific synonym (most frequently encountered in legal and religious contexts) of one of the senses of *marriage* ("state of being married"); *wedlock* overlaps with *matrimony*, but is perhaps more likely to be heard in church than in a court of law. By way of contrast, *boobs* is used non-pejoratively in the dress-designing trade to refer to what in other circumstances might be called *breasts* (*boobs* is also used non-technically as a colloquialism not far removed semantically from *tits*; whether this constitutes true ambiguity or not is an interesting question).

The second dimension of register is mode, which is concerned with the manner of transmission of a linguistic message – whether, for instance, it is written, spoken, telegraphed, or whatever. Again there are possibilities of synonymy, such as, for instance, *about* : *concerning* : *re*; *re* is characteristic not only of written languages as opposed to spoken language, but, more specifically, of business correspondence – that is to say, it is marked for field as well as mode. Field and mode variants resemble dialectal variants in that they can be regarded as semantically neutral (in the relevant respect) when they occur in their normal contexts, but become alive with associations (i.e. evoked meaning) when transported to alien environments:

Oh look! A neonate! Isn't he lovely?

A neonate is just a new-born baby, but the word is redolent of the research laboratory and the clinic, and these associations jar with the general tenor of the utterance.

Style refers to language characteristics which mark different relations between the participants in a linguistic exchange. These may depend on a number of factors – roles defined by the situation (e.g. interviewer and interviewee), how familiar the participants are with each other, what their relative social positions are, whether they are mutually hostile, indifferent, or friendly, and so on. To some extent, this may be regarded as the formal–informal dimension; but, in reality, it is much more complex than this. Style is of particular interest to us because it is this dimension of variation which spawns the most spectacular proliferation of cognitive synonyms. The multiplication of synonyms is most marked in the case of words referring to areas of experience which have a high emotive significance, such as (in our culture) death, sex, excretory functions, money, religion, power relations, and so on. For referents in these areas we typically find a range of subtly differentiated terms, which allows an utterance to be finely tuned to its context:

(a) *kick the bucket, buy it, snuff it, cop it, pop off, peg out, expire, perish, die, pass away, decease,* etc.

(b) *fuck, screw, shaft, bang, ball, lay, have it off with, make, score with, bed, go to bed with, sleep with, make love with, have sex with, have intercourse with, be intimate with, perform coitus with,* etc.

(c) *piss, pee, piddle, wee-wee, have a slash, spend a penny, point Percy at the porcelain, pass water, urinate,* etc.

(d) *arse-licker, bootlicker, toady, yes-man, sycophant,* etc.

(Some of these items may be differentiated in respect of field as well as style – it is virtually impossible to separate these two factors completely.) Style variants are undoubtedly capable of carrying evoked meaning, but they also differ in a more positive way. They are not semantically passive, even in their most normal contexts; they actually, in a sense, express aspects of situations, and can therefore help to create them. For instance, a speaker can establish a relation of intimacy with a hearer merely by choosing one lexical item rather than another in the course of a conversation. For this reason, at least some of the semantic properties of style variants are probably better treated as aspects of expressive meaning, rather than evoked meaning.

12.3 **Plesionyms**

†**Plesionyms** are distinguished from cognitive synonyms by the fact that they yield sentences with different truth-conditions: two sentences which differ only in respect of plesionyms in parallel syntactic positions are not mutually entailing, although if the lexical items are in a hyponymous relation there may well be unilateral entailment. There is always one member of a plesionymous pair which it is possible to assert, without paradox, while simultaneously denying the other member:

It wasn't foggy last Friday – just misty.

You did not thrash us at badminton – but I admit you beat us.

He is by no means fearless, but he's extremely brave

It wasn't a tap I heard – more of a rap.

She isn't pretty, but in her way she is quite handsome.

He was not murdered, he was legally executed.

The loch where we were fishing is not a lake – it's open to the sea.

Lexical semantics

The line between plesionymy and propositional synonymy can be drawn with some precision. However, the limits of plesionymy in the opposite direction along the scale of synonymity are more difficult to specify; as the semantic distance between lexical items increases, plesionymy shades imperceptibly into non-synonymy. We shall rely on the discriminatory powers of *not exactly* and *more exactly*, which match fairly well our intuitions as to what is lexicographically appropriate. *Not exactly* and *more exactly* seem to be selectively tuned to differences of presented meaning, as they do not collocate normally with propositional synonyms:

> ? He kicked the bucket – or, more exactly, he died.
> A: Is that your daddy?
> B: ? Not exactly – it's my father.

Propositional synonyms apart, *more exactly* and *not exactly* collocate normally with pairs of lexical items whose semantic differences are relatively unimportant:

> A: Was there a fog that day?
> B: Not exactly – more of a mist.
> We stopped by the side of a lake – or, more exactly, a loch, since there was an opening to the sea.
> He was executed – murdered, more exactly.

If, however, the differences exceed a certain level of significance, then the result is odd:

> ? My father's a policeman – or, more exactly, a butcher.
> ? Our dog – or, more exactly, our cat – died yesterday.
> ? We bought a mare – or, more exactly, a stallion.

It should be noted that *more exactly* is normally used to cancel a minor semantic trait and introduce a correction; the two lexical items should therefore be of the same level of specificity:

> ? He was murdered – or, more exactly, he was killed.
> He was executed – or, more exactly, he was murdered.

If one of the lexical items is a hyponym of the other, only *not exactly* will collocate normally, and then only if it qualifies the hyponym:

> A: Was he killed?
> B: ? Not exactly – he was murdered.
> A: Was he murdered?
> B: Not exactly – but he WAS killed.

It is rather difficult to give a principled account of plesionymy. The following proposals have obvious shortcomings, but it is hoped that they may at least help to clarify the problems.

As a beginning, let us draw a distinction between †**subordinate semantic traits** and †**capital traits**. Subordinate traits are those which have a role within the meaning of a word analogous to that of a modifier in a syntactic construction (e.g. *red* in *a red hat*, and *quickly* in *ran quickly*); capital traits are those which play a part analogous to that of the head in a construction (e.g. *hat* in *a red hat*, and *ran* in *ran quickly*). Which traits of a lexical item are subordinate and which are capital can usually be determined by reference to the relative naturalness of paraphrases. For instance, *stallion* is propositionally synonymous with both *male horse* and *equine male*,[12] but there can be little disagreement as to which is the more natural; the indications are, therefore, that "male" is a subordinate semantic trait of *stallion*. Similarly, *nag* is more naturally glossed as "worthless horse" than "equine object of disrespect" (or whatever); so "worthless" is a subordinate trait. This method of diagnosis would lead us to identify "walk" as the capital trait of *stroll*, "laugh" of *guffaw*, "wave" of *breaker* and *roller*, and "good-looking" of *pretty* and *handsome*. It seems reasonable to seek a connection between the relation of plesionymy and the status of differentiating traits: a pair of lexical items would seem, on the face of it, to be more likely to be plesionyms if they differ only in respect of subordinate traits. There may well be a tendency for this to be so, but there is no simple correlation. It seems that the relative saliency of subordinate and capital traits is quite variable, and it is not at present clear to what extent this variation is systematic (in the sense of being predictable from other semantic properties). The pairs *pretty*:*handsome*, *mare*:*stallion* and *murder*:*execute* exemplify the sort of variation that can be observed. Consider first the pair *pretty*:*handsome*. These exemplify the expected relation between the status of traits and synonymy, or the lack of it: that is to say, they are identical in respect of capital traits, differing only in respect of subordinate traits; and they are plesionyms. The second pair, *mare*:*stallion*, resemble *pretty*:*handsome* in that they are identical in respect of capital traits and different in respect of subordinate traits. However, unlike *pretty*:*handsome*, they are not plesionyms – in fact, they are more like opposites. It appears that the subordinate traits in *mare*:*stallion* have been, as it were, promoted to equal status (as far as determination of synonymy is concerned) with the capital traits. Notice, however, that this promotion is not accompanied by a simultaneous demotion of the capital traits, since, for instance, *stallion* and *bull* (which have the same subordinate traits but different capital traits) are non-synonymous. *Murder* and *execute* exemplify a third possibility. If the arguments in chapter 6, that *murder* belongs to the taxonomy of crimes and *execute* to the taxonomy of punishments, is correct, then this pair have the same subordinate traits but different capital traits. In this they resemble *bull* and *stallion*. Unlike the latter pair, however, they are plesionyms. This suggests that not only have their subordinate traits been highlighted or promoted, but their capital traits have been demoted, a suggestion which is strengthened by the observation that *murder* : *rape* and *execute* : *imprison* – which have the same capital traits but different subordinate traits – are non-synonymous. Highlighted subordinate traits together with back-grounded capital traits seem to be characteristic of items in taxonomies; highlighted subordinate traits without concomitant backgrounding of capital traits may be characteristic of impure opposites, or, since *hand-some* : *pretty* could perhaps also be claimed to encapsulate the "male" / "female" opposition, of impure opposites in which the pure opposition is not too deeply embedded.

We have already noted that plesionymy shades gradually into non-synonymy; it would therefore be a step forward if we could identify scales of variation of specific properties along which neighbouring lexical items would be plesionyms, and distant ones non-synonyms, with possibly an indeterminate zone in between. Examples of this state of affairs can be found among lexical strings of the type discussed in chapter 8; adjacent items in a string tend to be perceived as synonyms, (provided they are not of opposite polarity), whereas non-adjacent items are generally felt to be non-synonymous. For instance, *fog* and *mist*, and *mist* and *haze*, are plesionyms, but *fog* and *haze* are not; *mound* and *hillock*, *hillock* and *hill*, and *hill* and *mountain* are probably all plesionymous pairs, but not so *mound* and *mountain*, or even *hill* and *mound*, or *hillock* and *mountain*; *giggle* and *laugh* are plesionyms, but not *giggle* and *guffaw* – and so on. The notion of 'semantic distance' can be tentatively extended to items which vary in respect of more than one property (although the more axes of variation there are, the more difficult it is to say precisely what is meant by 'distance'). For instance, *rap* and *tap* are para-synonyms, as are *thud* and *thump*, and possibly also *rattle* and *clatter*; however, *tap* and *thump* are too far apart for synonymy, as are *thud* and *rattle*. Another scale of variable semantic distance is the 'to some extent' scale: certain lexical items, although strictly incompatibles, nonetheless have a certain type of resemblance:

A parish priest is to some extent a teacher.

A professional footballer is to some extent an entertainer.

A teacher is to some extent an actor.[13]

Many items related in this way are too far apart semantically to count as plesionyms:

? My brother is a priest – or, more exactly, a social worker.

But if they are close enough, they qualify:

My brother is a teacher – or, more exactly, a coach.

12.4 Congruence relations and synonymy

The congruence relations described in chapter 4 are applicable – with certain reservations – to both cognitive synonymy and plesionymy. The application to plesionymy is the more straightforward. Since they differ in respect of criterial traits, a pair of plesionyms must, strictly speaking, be incompatibles, compatibles, or hyponym and superordinate. (Of course if they are criterially congruent, then they are no longer plesionyms, but cognitive synonyms.) Whatever the strict nature of the semantic contrast, its communicative significance is diminished relative to what it would be if the contrasting items were not plesionyms; it therefore seems justifiable to give congruence relations within synonymy special names. We shall therefore speak of †**micro-relations**:

micro-incompatibility:	*roller : breaker,*	*execute : murder*
	priest : pastor,	*cashier : unfrock*
	pretty : handsome,	*orchestra : band*
micro-compatibility:	*review : article,*	*letter : note*
	brainy : cunning	
micro-hyponymy:	*roller : wave*	*execute : kill*
	pretty : good-looking	*cashier : sack*
	fearless : brave	

Congruence relations do not apply in precisely the same way to cognitive synonyms. Because cognitive synonyms have identical criterial traits, and hence identical logical properties, we cannot use entailment relations to define incompatibility, hyponymy, and so on. However, there undoubtedly do exist relations analogous to these. Take the case of cognitive synonyms which differ only in their ranges of normal collocation. We can define the (more specific) sense relation between the members of such a pair in terms of the relationship between their respective ranges of normal occurrence. The two ranges may be disjunct (e.g. *addled : rancid*), giving a relationship analogous to incompatibility; or they may overlap (e.g. *engine* : *motor*), giving a relationship analogous to compatibility; or the range of normal collocation of one member may be included in that of the other (e.g. *lively* : *spritely*), giving a relationship analogous to hyponymy. Items with identical collocational ranges, provided there were no other differences, would, of course, be absolute synonyms. Similar relationships can in principle be established for cognitive synonyms differing in other respects. To bring out the parallelism with incompatibility, hyponymy, etc., and at the same time to emphasise the relative insignificance of the differentiating traits, we may speak of †**nano-incompatibles, †nano-compatibles, †nano-hyponyms** and †**nano-superordinates.**

It was suggested in 12.1 that propositional synonyms are 'more synonymous' than plesionyms, which, in turn, are 'more synonymous' than non-synonyms. Among propositional synonyms, full congruence, in general, gives the closest relationship, followed by inclusion, then overlap, and, finally, disjunction. Within plesionymy a similar order of degree of synonymity applies, except that fully congruent items actually belong to the more synonymous larger category of propositional synonyms. Within the whole class of cognitive synonyms, or the whole class of plesionyms, the correlation between degree of synonymity and congruence type is not perfect, because semantic traits differ in their differentiating power. Within a group of items which are all synonyms of one another of the same type, however, the correlation is perfect. It sometimes happens, in a set of items consisting of a superordinate and two or more mutually incompatible hyponyms, that the superordinate is close enough to each of its hyponyms to be considered a plesionym, but the hyponyms, because of their disjunct relation, are too distant to be plesionyms of each other. This appears to be the case with *horse* : *stallion* : *mare*. By our criteria, *horse* and *stallion* are plesionyms, as are *horse* and *mare*, whereas *mare* and *stallion*, because of the highlighted sex difference, are not.

12.5 'Absolute', 'propositional' and 'plesio-' relations outside synonymy

The categories of 'absolute', 'propositional' and 'plesio-', which we have utilised for the description of different types of synonymy, can in principle be extended to all lexical relations, although it appears that, outside of synonymy, 'plesio-' relations are of little interest. Absolute synonymy was shown to be a somewhat rare phenomenon; but whereas there is reason to believe that absolute synonymy is in some sense unnatural, and very probably unstable, there is no reason why a language should 'abhor' absolute antonymy or absolute hyponymy. However, it is easier to define absolute synonymy than it is to define other absolute relations. Any difference of meaning whatsoever disqualifies a pair of lexical items from being absolute synonyms; but a hyponym and a superordinate, for instance, or a pair of antonyms must obviously display some differences of meaning. So we need to specify what differences of meaning are permissible for absolute relations, and what are impermissible. One way of doing this is to use propositional synonymy as a model, and say that, for instance, X is an absolute hyponym of Y if (i) X is a hyponym of Y, and (ii) X does not differ in meaning from Y in any of the ways that non-absolute cognitive synonyms may differ. That is to say, they must not differ in respect of register or dialect (relatively unproblematical); they must not differ in respect of expressive meaning (also relatively unproblematical); and they must not differ collocationally. This last criterion is more difficult, since items with different criterial traits will inevitably differ in their patterns of co-occurrence. What is to be outlawed from absolute relations is a difference of co-occurrence not sanctioned by differences in criterial traits. This is easy to state, but in practice might present problems. Nonetheless, a pretty convincing case could probably be made for considering, say, *dog* to be an absolute hyponym of *animal*, and *long* an absolute antonym of *short*. Generally speaking, if X is an absolute R of Y, then anything that is a propositional synonym of X will be a propositional R of Y. Thus, for instance, *clean* and *dirty* are absolute antonyms; *mucky* is a propositional synonym of *dirty*, so *clean* and *mucky* are propositional antonyms.

With synonymy, our survey of the systematic aspects of word-meanings comes to a conclusion: the majority of important topics have been at least touched on, though a definitive account of any one of them, even at the descriptive level, still lies in the future. It should be borne in mind, however, that the present investigation has been severely circumscribed by the search for structure and system in the vocabulary: a great deal that is important about the meanings of words – to lay users of language, at any rate – is particular and idiosyncratic. The contextual approach employed in this book is capable of yielding much valuable information about the individual semantic properties of words – but that path has not been pursued here.

Notes

La synonymie est la relation sémantique qui a fair couler le plus d'encre, relation que le sens commun estime claire, mais que les logiciens ne cessent de proclamer crucifiante.

Tutescu (1975: 108)

Lexical semantics

12.1

1. I am using the term *synonymy* in something like its traditional sense; most linguistic semanticists would restrict its use to what is here called cognitive synonymy.
2. I owe this definition to Haas. Lyons (1981: 50–1) proposes a different classification of synonyms:

   (i) synonyms are *fully* synonymous if, and only if, *all their meanings* are identical;
   (ii) synonyms are *totally* synonymous if, and only if, they are synonymous *in all contexts*;
   (iii) synonyms are *completely* synonymous if, and only if, they are identical *on all (relevant) dimensions of meaning*.

   (p. 50)

   Lyons defines absolute synonyms as expressions that are fully, totally and completely synonymous, and partial synonyms as expressions which (if I understand him correctly) satisfy at least one, but not all three, of the above criteria. He also has a category of near-synonyms, which are 'more or less similar, but not identical' in meaning, and insists strongly on the distinction between near-synonymy and partial synonymy.

   Presumably *identical* in (i) and *synonymous* in (ii) are to be understood in the sense of *completely synonymous* as in (iii). Although Lyons insists that near-synonymy is not the same as partial synonymy, it should be noted that by his definitions near-synonyms qualify as incomplete synonyms, and therefore as partial synonyms (though, of course, they represent only one variety). Definition (ii) appears, in practice, to make unacknowledged use of the notion of normality: otherwise Lyons's statement (p. 52) that *large* 'cannot be substituted for *big* in *You are making a big mistake*' is difficult to interpret.

   The definition of absolute synonymy suggested here is effectively not very different from a conflation of Lyons's (ii) and (iii), except that:

   (a) Lyons's definition (iii) leaves open the question of how many dimensions of meaning there are, and how to determine whether two words are identical on any particular dimension. The Haasian definition does not require prior identification of dimensions of meaning, and points to a method of testing potential candidates for absolute synonymy which relies on a single basic intuition.

   (b) Lyons's separation of total and complete synonymy is to allow for the possibility that two words might be completely synonymous, but not have identical distributions, due to differences in collocational restrictions. Although it is not immediately obvious, this is allowed for in the definition adopted here, since differences in normality not having a semantic origin are to be discounted (see also note 9 below). (Lyons defines synonymy in terms of lexemes: his definition (i) is therefore not applicable to lexical units.)
3. See, for instance, Soll (1966: 95), Gauger (1972), Baldinger (1980: 239, note 42).

12.2

4. I do not believe that *still*, *yet*, *already*, etc. necessarily introduce anything as strong as a presupposition (although a strong expectation may be difficult in practice to distinguish from a presupposition).
5. *Promise* and *warn* in these sentences do more than signal propositional attitudes: they belong to the class of performative verbs (see Austin (1962) and

Searle (1969)), that is, verbs whose mere utterance (in appropriate circumstances) can count as the carrying out of an act.

6. It is also possible that *I feel sad* is simultaneously expressive and propositional, or it may even be indeterminate – i.e. something superordinate to both.

7. This account of possible differences between propositional synonyms is not necessarily exhaustive. I am not sure, for instance, whether I ought to have included *ring up* and *telephone* (v.), which differ only in respect of the possibility of contextual *versus* indefinite deletion of the direct object (see Allerton (1982: 134–5)). In *John is ringing up now*, the definite object is latent (contextually deleted), whereas in *You can't see Mary just at the moment, she's telephoning*, the direct object can remain unidentified. Nor am I sure about *suitable : appropriate* and *right : correct*:

> He gave a suitable answer.
> ? He gave the suitable answer.
> He gave an appropriate answer.
> He gave the appropriate answer.
>
> ? He gave a right answer.
> He gave the right answer.
> He gave a correct answer.
> He gave the correct answer.

Perhaps this is a matter of grammatical, as opposed to semantic, collocational restrictions? (My attention was drawn to these examples by Patrick Griffiths.) I have deliberately excluded lexical converses, though it has been suggested – Kastovsky (1981) – that they should be regarded as propositional synonyms, differing only in thematic meaning (i.e. in respect of which participant's point of view is encoded). It is, of course, important to emphasise the equivalence of, for instance, *John is in front of Bill* and *Bill is behind John*; but the difference between *John is in front of Bill* and *John is behind Bill* is equally important, and it is this which has decided where our treatment of lexical converses should be located.

8. Cf. Palmer (1976: 97).

9. Nor, being non-systematic, are they syntactic; they are probably best simply described as lexical (cf. Allerton (1984)). The existence of semantically arbitrary collocational restrictions may at first sight seem to invalidate the definition given earlier of absolute synonymy. However, that definition specifies that absolute synonyms must be identical *in respect of semantic normality* in all contexts. In 1.2 it was stated that meaning expresses itself ultimately in patterns of association of open set elements. It is true that *flawless*, say, collocates with a characteristic group of open set elements. But the regularity of patterning goes no deeper than this, because the collocants of *flawless* have no aspects of further patterning with open set elements that (a) unite them into a group (i.e. they form a group *only* in respect of collocability with *flawless*), and (b) distinguish them from the collocants of *unblemished, impeccable*, etc. This would not be the case if the patterns of collocation were semantically motivated. In principle, therefore, idiosyncratic collocational restrictions can be discounted in testing for absolute synonymy.

10. It is interesting that *lavatory*, according to Nancy Mitford (1956), is (or was) also the upper-class word. It is not uncommon for the upper and lower classes to be jointly distinguished, in terms of lexical usage, from the genteel middle classes.

11. See Halliday, McIntosh and Strevens (1964: 87–94). Hudson (1980: 49) suggests *tenor* instead of *style*, to avoid confusion with the everyday meanings of *style*.

12.3

12. But see the remarks in ch. 6, note 2 on *gelding*.
13. The relationship in these sentences is unilateral:

? A teacher is to some extent a parish priest.
? An entertainer is to some extent a footballer.
? An actor is to some extent a teacher.

At present it is not clear what semantic properties are essential to this type of relation, nor what factors govern the directionality of the relation. (For some discussion see Lakoff (1973).)

REFERENCES

Allerton, D. J. (1975) Deletion and pro-form reduction. *Journal of Linguistics 11*, 213–37
    (1979) *Essentials of Grammatical Theory*. London: Routledge & Kegan Paul
    (1982) *Valency and the English Verb*. London: Academic Press
    (1984) Three (or four) levels of word cooccurrence restriction. *Lingua 63*, 17–40
Allerton, D. J., Carney, E. & Holdcroft, D. (1979) *Function and Context in Linguistic Analysis*. Cambridge University Press
Allwood, J., Anderson, L.-G. & Dahl, Ö. (1977) *Logic in Linguistics*. Cambridge University Press
Alston, W. P. (1964) *Philosophy of Language*. Englewood Cliffs, N.J.: Prentice-Hall
Anderson, E. S. (1978) Lexical universals of body-part terminology. In J. H. Greenberg, C. H. Ferguson & E. A. Moravscik (eds.), *Universals of Human Language, Vol. 3. Word Structure*. Stanford University Press, pp. 335–68
Austin, J. L. (1962) *How to Do Things with Words*. Oxford: Clarendon Press
Bach, E. & Harms, R. T. (eds.) (1968) *Universals in Linguistic Theory*. New York: Holt Rinehart
Backhouse, A. E. (1981) Japanese verbs of dress. *Journal of Linguistics 17*, 17–30
Baldinger, K. (1980) *Semantic Theory: Towards a Modern Semantics*, translated by W. C. Brown and edited by R. Wright. Oxford: Basil Blackwell
Bar-Hillel, Y. (1955) Idioms. In W. N. Locke & A. D. Booth (eds.), *Machine Translation of Languages*. Cambridge, Mass.: MIT Press (with Wiley, New York), pp. 183–93
Bauer, L. (1983) *English Word-formation*. Cambridge University Press
Bazell, C. E., Catford, J. C., Halliday, M. A. K. & Robins, R. H. (1966) *In Memory of J. R. Firth*. London: Longman
Bendix, E. M. (1966) *Componential Analysis of General Vocabulary*. The Hague: Mouton. Also published as part 2 of *International Journal of American Linguistics, 32*, 2, and publication 41 of Indiana University Research Center in Anthropology, Folklore and Linguistics
Berlin, B. (1978) Ethnobiological classification. In E. H. Rosch & B. Lloyd (eds.), *Cognition and Categorisation*. Hillsdale, N.J.: Lawrence Erlbaum Associates
Berlin, B., Breedlove, D. E. & Raven, P. H. (1973) General principles of classification and nomenclature in folk biology. *American Anthropologist 75*, 214–42
Berlin, B. & Kay, P. (1969) *Basic Color Terms: Their Universality and Evolution*. Berkeley: University of California Press
Bever, T. G. & Rosenbaum, P. S. (1971) Some lexical structures and their empirical validity. In D. D. Steinberg & L. A. Jakobovits (eds.), *Semantics: An Interdisciplinary Reader in Philosophy and Psychology*. Cambridge University Press, pp. 586–600
Bierwisch, M. (1967) Some semantic universals of German adjectives. *Foundations of Language 3*, 1–36
    (1969) On certain problems of semantic representation. *Foundations of Language 5*, 153–84

Lexical semantics

(1970a) On classifying semantic features. In M. Bierwisch & K. E. Heidolph (eds.), *Progress in Linguistics*. The Hague: Mouton

(1970b) Selektionsbeschränkungen und Voraussetzungen. *Linguistische Arbeitsberichte 3*, 8–22, Karl-Marx Universität, Leipzig

Black, M. (1962) *Models and Metaphors: Studies in Language and Philosophy*. Ithaca, N.Y.: Cornell University Press

Bolinger, D. (1965) The atomisation of meaning. *Language 41*, 555–73

(1972) *Degree Words*. The Hague: Mouton

(1980) *Language: The Loaded Weapon*. London: Longman

Boucher, T. & Osgood, C. E. (1969) The Polyanna hypothesis. *Journal of Verbal Learning and Verbal Behaviour 8*, 1–8

Brooke-Rose, C. (1958) *A Grammar of Metaphor*. London: Secker & Warburg

Brown, C. H. (1976) General principles of human anatomical partonomy and speculations on the growth of partonomic nomenclature. *American Ethnologist 3*, 3, 400–24

Brown, C. H., Kolar, J., Torrey, B. J., Truong-Quang, T. & Volkman, P. (1976) Some general principles of biological and non-biological folk classification. *American Ethnologist 3*, 73–85

Brown, R. W. (1958) How shall a thing be called? *Psychological Review 65*, 14–21. Reprinted in R. C. Oldfield & J. W. Marshall (eds.), *Language*. Harmondsworth: Penguin

Brown, R. W. & Lenneberg, E. H. (1954) A study in language and cognition. *Journal of Abnormal and Social Psychology 49*, 454–62

Bunge, M. (1969) The metaphysics, epistemology and methodology of levels. In L. W. Whyte, A. G. Wilson & D. Wilson (eds.), *Hierarchical Structures*. New York: Elsevier

Carnap, R. (1952) Meaning postulates. *Philosophical Studies 3*, 65–73

Chaffin, R. & Hermann, D. J. (1984) The similarity and diversity of semantic relations. *Memory and cognition 12*, 134–41

Chaffin, R. & Winston, M. The semantics of part–whole relations: an empirical taxonomy. Unpublished MS

Channell, J. (1980) More on approximations – a reply. *Journal of Pragmatics 4*, 5, 461–76

Chomsky, A. N. (1965) *Aspects of the Theory of Syntax*. Cambridge, Mass.: MIT Press

Clark, H. H. & Clark, E. V. (1977) *Psychology and Language: An Introduction to Psycholinguistics*. New York: Harcourt Brace Jovanovich

Cole, P. & Morgan, J. L. (eds.) (1975) *Syntax and Semantics, Vol. 3: Speech Acts*. New York: Academic Press

Cole, P. & Sadock, J. M. (eds.) (1977) *Syntax and Semantics, Vol. 8: Grammatical Relations*. New York: Academic Press

Coleman, L. & Kay, P. (1981) Prototype semantics: the English word "lie". *Language 57*, 26–44

Cook, W. A. (1978) *Introduction to Tagmemic Analysis*. Washington, D.C.: Georgetown University Press

Coseriu, E. (1967) Lexikalische Solidaritäten. *Poetica 1*, 293–303

(1968) Les structures lexématiques. In W. Th. Elwert (ed.), *Probleme der Semantik*. Supplement 1 (N.S.) to *Zeitschrift für Französische Sprache und Literatur)*, Wiesbaden, pp. 3–16

(1975) Vers une typologie des champs lexicaux. *Cahiers de Lexicologie 27*, 30–51

(1976) Die Funktionelle Betrachtung des Wortschatzes. In *Probleme der Lexicologie und Lexicographie*, Sprache der Gegenwart 39. Düsseldorf: Pädagogischer Verlag Schwann, pp. 7–25

Cowie, A. P. (1981a) Introduction to *Applied Linguistics 2*, 203–6

(1981b) The treatment of collocations and idioms in learners' dictionaries. *Applied Linguistics 2*, 223–35

(1982) Polysemy and the structure of lexical fields. *Nottingham Linguistic Circular 11.2*, 51–64

Cowie, A. P., Mackin, R. & McCaig, I. R. (1983) *Oxford Dictionary of Current Idiomatic English*, vol. 2. London: Oxford University Press

Cruse, D. A. (1975) Hyponymy and lexical hierarchies. *Archivum Linguisticum* (N.S.) 6, 26–31

(1976) Three classes of antonym in English. *Lingua 38*, 281–92

(1977) The pragmatics of lexical specificity. *Journal of Linguistics 13*, 153–64

(1979a) On the transitivity of the part–whole relation. *Journal of Linguistics 15*, 29–38

(1979b) Reversives. *Linguistics 17*, 957–66

(1980) Antonyms and gradable complementaries. In D. Kastovsky, 1980a, pp. 14–25

(1982) On lexical ambiguity. *Nottingham Linguistic Circular 11.2*, 65–80

(1983) Review of A. Wierzbicka, *Lingua Mentalis: The Semantics of Natural Language*. *Journal of Linguistics 19*, 265–72

(1984) Review article on J. F. Ross, *Portraying Analogy*. *Journal of Linguistics 20*, 351–9

Dahl, Ö. (1979) Review article on J. Lyons, *Semantics*, 1977. *Language 55*, 1, 199–206

Davidson, D. & Harman, G. (eds.) (1972) *Semantics of Natural Language*. Dordrecht: Reidel

Dowty, D. (1979) *Word Meaning in Montague Grammar*. Dordrecht: Reidel

Ducháček, O. (1965) Sur quelques problèmes de l'antonymie. *Cahiers de Lexicologie 6*, 55–66

Fillmore, C. J. (1968) The case for case. In Bach & Harms, 1968, pp. 1–88

(1971) Some problems for case grammar. In R. J. O'Brien (ed.), *Report of the 22nd Annual Round Table Meeting on Linguistics and Language Studies*. Washington, D.C.: Georgetown University Press, pp. 35–56

(1972) Subjects, speakers and roles. In Davidson & Harman, 1972, pp. 1–24

(1977) The case for case reopened. In Cole & Sadock, 1977, pp. 59–81

Fillmore, C. J. & Langendoen, D. T. (eds.) (1971) *Studies in Linguistic Semantics*. New York: Holt, Rinehart and Winston

Firth, J. R. (1957) Modes of meaning. In J. R. Firth, *Papers in Linguistics 1934–1951*. London: Oxford University Press

Fitter, F., Fitter, A. & Blamey, M. (1974) *The Wild Flowers of Britain and Northern Europe*. London: Collins

Fraser, B. (1970) Idioms within a transformational grammar. *Foundations of Language* 6, 22–42

Gauger, H.-M. (1972) Zum Probleme der Synonymie. *Tübinger Beiträge zur Linguistik* 9, Tübingen

Geckeler, H. (1971) *Strukturelle Semantik und Wortfeldtheorie*. Munich: Fink

(1980) Die Antonymie in Lexikon. In Kastovsky, 1980a, pp. 42–65

Givón, T. (1970) Notes on the semantic structure of English adjectives. *Language 46*, 816–37

Greenberg, J. (1966) *Language Universals*. Janua Linguarum, Series Minor, 59. The Hague: Mouton

Grice, H. P. (1975) Logic and conversation. In Cole & Morgan, 1975, pp. 41–58

Gruber, J. S. (1976) *Lexical Structures in Syntax and Semantics*. Amsterdam: North Holland

Haas, W. (1962) The theory of translation. *Philosophy 37*, 208–28. Reprinted in G. H. R. Parkinson (ed.), *The Theory of Meaning*. Oxford University Press, 1968, pp. 86–108.

(1964) Semantic value. In *Proceedings of the IXth International Congress of Linguists* (Cambridge, Mass., 1962). The Hague: Mouton, pp. 1066–72

(1973) Review article on J. Lyons, *Introduction to Theoretical Linguistics*. *Journal of Linguistics 9*, 71–113

(1975) Syntax and semantics of ordinary language II. *Proceedings of the Aristotelian Society, Supplementary Volume 49*, 147–69

(1985) Function and structure in linguistic descriptions. In R. Dirven & V. Fried (eds.), *Functionalism in Linguistics*. Amsterdam: J. Benjamins

Halliday, M. A. K. (1966) Lexis as a linguistic level. In Bazell *et al.*, 1966, pp. 148–62

Halliday, M. A. K., McIntosh, A. & Strevens, P. (1964) *The Linguistic Sciences and Language Teaching*. London: Longman

Harris, Z. S. (1951) *Structural Linguistics*. Chicago and London: University of Chicago Press

Healey, A. (1968) English idioms. *Kivung (Journal of the Linguistics Society of Papua New Guinea) 1*, 2, 71–108

Hjelmslev, L. (1961) *Prolegomena to a Theory of Language*, translated by F. J. Whitfield. Madison: University of Wisconsin Press

Hoenigswald, H. M. (1965) Review of J. Lyons, *Structural Semantics. Journal of Linguistics 1*, 191–6

Hoppenbrouwers, G. A. J., Seuren, P. A. M. & Weijters, A. J. M. M. (forthcoming) *Meaning and the Lexicon*. Proceedings of the Second International Colloquium on the Interdisciplinary Study of Meaning in Natural Language, Kleve, 1983

Howard, P. (1985) *A Word in Your Ear*. Harmondsworth: Penguin

Hudson, R. A. (1980) *Sociolinguistics*. Cambridge University Press

Hunn, E. S. (1983) The utilitarian factor in folk biological classification. *American Anthropologist 84*, 830–47

Kastovsky, D. (ed.) (1980a) *Perspektiven der Lexikalischen Semantik*. Beiträge zum Wuppertaler Semantikkolloquium vom 2–3 Dezember 1979. Bonn: Bouvier Verlag Herbert Grundmann

(1980b) Selectional restrictions and lexical solidarities. In Kastovsky, 1980a, pp. 70–92

(1981) Interaction of syntax and the lexicon: lexical converses. To appear in J. Esser & A. Hubler (eds.), *Festschrift Vilem Fried*. Tübingen: Narr (*Tübingen Beiträge zur Linguistik, 149*)

(1982) "Privative opposition" and lexical semantics. *Studia Anglica Posnaniensia 14*, 29–45

Katz, J. J. & Fodor, J. A. (1963) The structure of a semantic theory. *Language 39*, 170–210. Reprinted in J. A. Fodor & J. J. Katz (eds.), *The Structure of Language: Readings in the Philosophy of Language*. Englewood Cliffs, N.J.: Prentice-Hall, 1964, pp. 479–518

Kay, P. (1971) Taxonomy and semantic contrast. *Language 47*, 866–87

Kay, P. & McDaniel, C. K. (1978) The linguistic significance of the meanings of basic color terms. *Language 54*, 610–46

Kempson, R. M. (1973) Review of Fillmore & Langendoen, *Studies in Linguistic Semantics*, 1971. *Journal of Linguistics 9*, 120–40

(1977) *Semantic Theory*. Cambridge University Press

Kempson, R. M. & Cormack, A. (1981) Ambiguity and quantification. *Linguistics and Philosophy 4*, 259–310

Kimball, J. (ed.) (1975) *Syntax and Semantics*, vol. 4. New York and London: Academic Press

Kooij, J. (1971) *Ambiguity in Natural Language*. Amsterdam: North Holland

Kripke, S. (1972) Naming and necessity. In Davidson & Harman, pp. 253–355. Also published separately: *Naming and Necessity*. Oxford: Basil Blackwell, 1980

Lakoff, G. (1971) Presupposition and relative well-formedness. In Steinberg & Jakobovits, 1971, pp. 329–40

(1973) Hedges: a study in meaning criteria and the logic of fuzzy concepts. *Journal of Philosophical Logic 2*, 4, 458–508

Lamb, S. M. (1964) The sememic approach to structural semantics. In A. K. Romney

& R. G. D'Andrade (eds.), *Transcultural Studies of Cognition*, pp. 57–78. Special
publication of *American Anthropologist 66*, 3, pt. 2

Lantz, De Lee & Stefflre, V. (1972) Language and cognition revisited. In P. Adams (ed.),
Language in Thinking. Harmondsworth: Penguin, pp. 236–54

Leech, G. N. (1974) *Semantics*. Harmondsworth: Penguin

   (1983) *Principles of Pragmatics*. London: Longman

Lehrer, A. J. (1974) *Semantic Fields and Lexical Structure*. Amsterdam: North Holland

   (1985) Markedness and antonymy. *Journal of Linguistics 21*, 397–429

Lehrer, A. J. & Lehrer, K. (1982) Antonymy. *Linguistics and Philosophy 5*, 483–501

Lenneberg, E. H. (1961) Color naming, color recognition, color discrimination: a re-
appraisal. *Perceptual and Motor Skills 12*, 375–92

Levin, S. R. (1977) *The Semantics of Metaphor*. Baltimore and London: The Johns Hopkins
University Press

Levinson, S. C. (1983) *Pragmatics*. Cambridge University Press

Ljung, M. (1974) Some remarks on antonymy. *Language 50*, 74–88

Long, T. H. & Summers, D. (1979) *Longman Dictionary of English Idioms*. London: Longman

Lutzeier, P. R. (1981) *Wort und Feld*. Tübingen: Max Niemeyer Verlag

   (1983) The relevance of semantic relations between words for the notion of lexical field.
Theoretical Linguistics 10, 147–78

Lyons, J. (1963) *Structural Semantics*. Oxford: Blackwell

   (1968) *Introduction to Theoretical Linguistics*. Cambridge University Press

   (1977) *Semantics*. Cambridge University Press

   (1981) *Language, Meaning and Context*. London: Fontana

McCawley, J. (1972) *Logical and Syntactic Arguments for Semantic Structures*. Reproduced
by the Indiana University Linguistics Club

Mackin, R. (1978) On collocations: words shall be known by the company they keep. In
Strevens, 1978, pp. 149–65

Makkai, A. (1972) *Idiom Structure in English*. The Hague: Mouton

Malkiel, Y. (1959) Studies in irreversible binomials. *Lingua 8*, 113–60. Reprinted in Malkiel,
1968, pp. 311–56

   (1968) *Essays on Linguistic Themes*. Oxford: Blackwell

Marsh-Stefanovska, P. J. (1982) 'A Contrastive Study of Some Morphologically Related
Opposites in English and Macedonian'. Unpublished M.A. dissertation, University of
Manchester

Martin, R. (1976) *Inférence, Antonymie et Paraphrase*. Paris: Klincksieck

Matthews, P. H. (1974) *Morphology*. Cambridge University Press

   (1979) *Generative Grammar and Linguistic Competence*. London: George Allen & Unwin

   (1981) *Syntax*. Cambridge University Press

Mervis, C. B. & Roth, E. M. (1980) The internal structure of basic and non-basic color
categories. *Language 57*, 384–405

Miller, G. A. & Johnson-Laird, P. N. (1976) *Language and Perception*. Cambridge, Mass.:
Harvard University Press; Cambridge, England: Cambridge University Press

Mitchell, T. F. (1971) Linguistic "goings-on": collocations and other lexical matters arising
on the syntagmatic record. *Archivum Linguisticum 2* (N.S.), 35–69

Mitford N. (ed.) (1956) *Noblesse Oblige*. London: Hamish Hamilton

Mooij, J. A. A. (1976) *A Study of Metaphor*. Amsterdam: North Holland

Moore, T. & Carling, C. (1982) *Understanding Language: Towards a Post-Chomskyan
Linguistics*. London: Macmillan

Murdoch, Iris (1969) *The Nice and the Good*. Harmondsworth: Penguin

Newmeyer, F. J. (1974) The regularity of idiom behaviour. *Lingua 34*, 326–42

Nida, E. (1975) *Componential Analysis of Meaning*. The Hague: Mouton

Lexical semantics

Nunberg, G. (1979) The non-uniqueness of semantic solutions: polysemy. *Linguistics and Philosophy 3*, 143–84

Ogden, C. K. (1932) *Opposition*. London. Reprinted, with a new introduction by I. A. Richards. Bloomington, Ind.: Indiana University Press, 1968

Palmer, F. R. (1976) *Semantics: A New Introduction*. Cambridge University Press

Pohl, J. (1966) Les Antonymes: Economie et Conscience Linguistiques. In Y. Lebrun (ed.), *Recherches Linguistiques en Belgiques*. Wetteren: Universa

(1970) Remarques sur les Antonymes. In D. Cohen (ed.), *Mélanges Marcel Cohen*. The Hague: Mouton

Pottier, B. (1974) *Linguistique Générale*. Paris: Klincksieck

Pulman, S. G. (1983) *Word Meaning and Belief*. London: Croom Helm

Rhodes, R. (forthcoming) Lexical taxonomies. To appear in Hoppenbrouwers, Seuren & Weijters, forthcoming

Richards, I. A. (1965) *The Philosophy of Rhetoric*. New York: Oxford University Press

Robertson, M. (ed.) *Keats: Poems Published in 1820*. Oxford: Clarendon Press

Roget, P. M. (1852) *Thesaurus of English Words and Phrases*. London. Abridged and revised, with additions by J. L. Roget & S. R. Roget. Harmondsworth: Penguin, 1953

Rohdenburg, G. (forthcoming) Unmarked and marked terms in English. To appear in Hoppenbrouwers, Seuren & Weijters, forthcoming

Rosch, E. H. (1973) Natural categories. *Cognitive Psychology 4*, 328–50

(1978) Principles of categorisation. In E. Rosch & B. Lloyd (eds.), *Cognition and Categorisation*. Hillsdale, N.J.: Lawrence Erlbaum Associates

Rosch, E. H. & Mervis, C. (1975) Family resemblances: studies in the internal structure of categories. *Cognitive Psychology 7*, 573–605

Rosch, E., Mervis, C., Gray, W., Johnson, D. & Boyes-Braem, P. (1976) Basic objects in natural categories. *Cognitive Psychology 8*, 382–439

Ross, A. S. C. (1956) U and non-U: an essay in sociological linguistics. In Mitford, 1956

Ross, J. F. (1981) *Portraying Analogy*. Cambridge Studies in Philosophy. Cambridge University Press

Sampson, G. (1979) The indivisibility of words. *Journal of Linguistics 15*, 39–47

Sapir, E. (1944) On grading: a study in semantics. *Philosophy of Science 2*, 93–116. Reprinted in Sapir, 1949

(1949) *Selected Writings in Language, Culture and Personality*, edited by D. G. Mandelbaum. Berkeley: University of California Press

Schwartz, S. P. (1979) Natural kind terms. *Cognition 7*, 301–15

(1980) Natural kinds and nominal kinds. *Mind 89*, 182–95

Searle, J. R. (1969) *Speech Acts*. Cambridge University Press

Sebeok, T. A. (ed.) *Current Trends in Linguistics*, vol. 3. The Hague: Mouton

Soll, L. (1966) Synonymie und Bedeutungsgleichheit. *Germanisch-romanische Monatsschrift 16*, 90–9

Stebbing, L. S. (1952) *A Modern Elementary Logic*. London: Methuen

Steinberg, D. D. & Jakobovits, L. A. (eds.) (1971) *Semantics: An Interdisciplinary Reader in Philosophy, Linguistics and Psychology*. Cambridge University Press

Strawson, P. F. (1952) *Introduction to Logical Theory*. London: Methuen

Strevens, P. (ed.) (1978) *In Honour of A. S. Hornby*. Oxford: Oxford University Press

Tarski, A. (1965) *Introduction to Logic*. New York: Oxford University Press

Trier, J. (1934) Das Sprachliche Feld. Eine Auseinandersetzung. *Neue Jahrbücher für Wissenschaft und Jugendbildung 10*, 428–49

Trubetzkoy, N. S. (1969) *Principles of Phonology*, translated by C. A. M. Baltaxe from *Grundzüge der Phonologie*. Göttingen: Vandenhoek & Ruprecht, 1958. Berkeley: University of California Press

Tuțescu, M. (1975) *Précis de Sémantique Française*. Paris: Klincksieck

References

Ullmann, S. (1962) *Semantics: An Introduction to the Science of Meaning*. Oxford: Basil Blackwell

van Overbeke, M. (1975) Antonymie et gradation. *La Linguistique 11*, 135–54

Van Valen, L. (1964) An analysis of some taxonomic concepts. In J. R. Gregg & F. T. C. Harris (eds.), *Form and Strategy in Science*. Dordrecht: Reidel

Vendler, Z. (1967) *Linguistics in Philosophy*. Ithaca, N.Y.: Cornell University Press

Wachtel, T. (1980) Pragmatic approximations. *Journal of Pragmatics 4*, 201–11

Warczyk, A. (1981) Antonymie, négation ou opposition? *La Linguistique 17*, 29–48

Weinreich, U. (1966) Explorations in semantic theory. In Sebeok, 1966, pp. 395–477

(1969) Problems in the analysis of idioms. In J. Puhvel (ed.), *Substance and Structure of Language*. Berkeley and Los Angeles: University of California Press, pp. 23–81

Werth, P. (ed.) (1981) *Conversation and Discourse: Structure and Interpretation*. London: Croom Helm

Wierzbicka, A. (1980) *Lingua Mentalis: The Semantics of Natural Language*. Sydney: Academic Press

Wilson, D. & Sperber, D. (1981) On Grice's theory of conversation. In Werth, 1981, pp. 152–77

Zikri, M. S. (1979) A Comparative Study of Lexical Relations in English and Arabic. Unpublished Ph.D. thesis, University of Manchester

Zimmer, K. E. (1964) *Affixal Negation in English and Other Languages*. Supplement to *Word 20*, 2, Monograph 5. New York: Linguistic Circle of New York

Zwicky, A. & Sadock, J. (1975) Ambiguity tests and how to fail them. In Kimball, 1975, pp. 1–36

SUBJECT INDEX

abnormality (semantic), 11–15, 21, 110–19, 111, 123, 209, 259; dissonance, 12, 21, 100–9, 111; improbability, 13, 21, 111; pleonasm, 12, 21, 100–9, 123; zeugma, 13, 21, 209, 259
absolute, cognitive and plesio-relations (except synonymy), 290–1; absolute *v*. cognitive antonymy, 291; absolute *v*. cognitive hyponymy, 291
absolute meaning, 21
absolute synonymy, 21, 268–70
accomplishments, 174
achievements, 174
actions, 174
activities, 174
affinity and disaffinity (semantic), 16–18
affixes, derivational, 77; inflectional, 77
allomorphs, 45
ambiguity, 49–68, 83, 85, 121; direct tests for, 58–66: difficulties with, 62–6, identity test, 62–3, incomplete contextual conditioning, 58–60, independent maximisation, 60–1, 82, *Yes/No* test, 60–1, 82, 83, zeugma test, 61–2, 63–6; and establishment of senses, 69–70; indirect tests for, 54–7: different opposites, 55, different paronymic relations, 55–6, different synonyms, 55; non-lexical type, 66–8; and proportional series, 85, 121; quasi-syntactic type, 67–8; of scope, 67–8; and sense-spectra, 83; unit-type variety, 50, 63
ambiguous *v*. general word forms, 51–2
amplifiers, expressive, 276
analogues, lexical, 125–6
antagonism between senses, 61–6
antipodals, 224–5, 242
antonyms, antonymy, 204–20, 244–6, 291; cognitive *v*. absolute types, 291; contrastive aspects of, 218–20; definition of, 204, 221; equipollent type, 208–14; gradability of, 204; implicit comparativity of, 206; and implicit superlatives, 216–17;

and inherentness, 214–16; overlapping type, 208–14; pivotal region of underlying scale, 205; polar type, 208–14; privative type, 208–14; pseudo-comparatives *v*. true comparatives, 206; in questions, 208–14; semantic correlates of group membership, 208, 218–20; and stative verbs, 217–18; sub-types of, 206–14; and underlying scale, 204–6
arbitrary units of communication, 46
asymmetric relations, 113
asyntactic idioms, 38
attachments, 167–8, 180

backgrounding of semantic traits, 53
base (and paronym), 130
basic vocabulary items, 146, 156
binarism, 264
binarity, inherent, 109, 257–62; contingent, 258–9; latent *v*. patent, 261
binomials, irreversible, 39–40, 47
but-test, 17, 123

canonical semantic traits, 18–19, 124, 155
capital semantic traits, 287–9
categorisers, semantic, 32–4
catenary relations, 113
chains, lexical, 187–92; cycles, 190; helices, 189–92
classemes, 134
class-member relation, 176
closed proportional series, 121
closed set items, 3, 20
collection-member relation, 176
collocational restrictions, 48, 81, 107; and cognitive synonymy, 279–82; idiosyncratic type, 281; and informational redundancy, 280; semi-systematic type, 281; systematic type, 281
collocational uniqueness and the recurrent contrast test, 29–32
collocations, 29–32, 40–1, 48; bound type, 41; and idioms, 40–1; semantic cohesion of, 40

co-meronymy, 159–60
commitedness, 209, 264
comparatives of antonyms, 206; pseudo-comparatives, 206; true comparatives, 206
compatibles, compatibility, 92–3; contingent type, 93; strict type, 93
complementaries, complementarity, 198–204; and counteractives, 202; degrees of complementarity, 200–1; and gradability, 202–4; and interactives, 201–2; and presupposition, 262–3; pseudo-complementaries, 242; and reversives, 201; and satisfactives, 202
components (semantic), 22; and proportional series, 134
compositionality, 45
congruence relations, 86–8
congruence variants, 86–8, 95–6; congruent relations, 95; hypo-relations, 95; in meronyms, 163–4; in opposites, 240–2; in proportional series, 126–7; semi-relations, 95; super-relations, 95 in synonymy, 289–91
congruent relations, 95
consistency in proportional series, 122
constituent, semantic, 24–32; discontinuous type, 31; minimal type, 25–6; peripheral types, 29–32
context, extra-linguistic *v.* linguistic, 1
contextual approach, 1–21
contextual modulation, 52–3
contextual relations, 16
contextual selection, 52–3
contextually deleted elements, 110
contingent ordering in lexical chains, 191–2
continuum of criteriality, 18–19
contradiction, 15
contrariety, 15
contrast (semantic), recurrent, 15
contrastive aspects of antonymy, 218–20
conventional implicature, 221
convergence in meronomies, 170
converses, 231–40; and comparatives of antonyms, 243; congruence variants of, 95–6, 240–2, 243; hypo-converses, 95, semi-converses, 243, super-converses, 96, 240; direct *v.* indirect types, 234; four-place types, 237–9; indirect types, 233–40; as opposites, 239–40; three-place types, 237–9
conversion, 135
'Cooperative Principle', 81
corrigibility, as test for syntactic deviance, 2–3, 20
co-taxonomy, 137, 145, 150–2; and incompatibility (in taxonomies), 150–2
counteractives, 202

counterparts, 225
covert categories, 148–9
creativity, lexical, 50, 81
creativity, syntactic, 50
criterial semantic traits, 16–18
criteriality as continuum, 18–19
crossed interpretation, 62, 63, 64, 68
cycles, lexical, 190

data of semantics, 8–10
dead metaphors, 41–5; and foreign learners, 44; and idioms, 41–5; and lexical forms, 77; and translation, 42–4
deep case, 111
degree-terms, 192–5
deictic elements, deixis, 196
delimitation of lexical units; paradigmatic, 49–74; syntactic, 74–80; syntagmatic, 23–48
demotion of semantic traits, 52–3
derivational affixes, 77
derived words, 77
determining and determined elements, 110
deviance: normalisation by contextual manipulation, 7–8; normalisation by substitution, 3–6; semantic *v.* syntactic, 1–8
diagnostic frames, 13–14
differentiable relations, 115–17
direct criteria for ambiguity, 58–66, 82
directional opposites, 223–43; antipodals, 224–5; converses, 231–40; counterparts, 225; directions, 223–4; restitutives, 228; reversives, 226–31
directions, 223–4
disaffinity (semantic), 16–18
discontinuous semantic constituents, 31
displacement, 272
dissonance (semantic), 12, 21, 100–9, 111

elicitors, phonetic, 35
encapsulation, 105, 111, 123
endocentric constructions, 104
endonyms, endonymy, 123, 124–33 (passim)
entailment, 14, 15; mutual, 15; unilateral, 15
entropy and reversivity, 248–50
equipollent antonyms, 208–14
equipollent oppositions, 221
establishment of senses, 68–71; and ambiguity tests, 69–70
evaluation and polarity, 251
evoked meaning, 110, 282–5; and cognitive synonymy, 282–5; and dialect, 282–3; and register, 283–5
excluded semantic traits, 16–18
exclusive reference, 156
exonym, 123, 124–33 (*passim*)

Subject index

expected semantic traits, 16–18
expressive amplifiers, 276
expressive meaning, 45, 110, 271–7; and
continuous gradability, 272; and
displacement, 272; and expletives, 273;
expressive amplifiers, 276; expressive
paradox, 17; potentially expressive items,
275–6; *v.* propositional meaning, 271–7;
and prosodic grading, 272
expressive mode, 271
expressive paradox, 17

facultative relations, 162, 178–9
false paronymy, 132
features (of events, states, etc.), 175
features (semantic), 22
felicity conditions, 220
field (register), 283–4
field (semantic), 21
folk-taxonomies, 145
formal scatter, 111
frozen metaphors, *see* dead metaphors
functional domain of parts, 165–6
fundamentum divisionis, 134

gaps, lexical, 149, 171; in meronomies, 171;
in taxonomies, 149
general (*v.* ambiguous) word forms, 51, 52
general *v.* idiosyncratic restrictions, 111
generality *v.* vagueness, 81
generic level of taxonomy, 146, 153–5
gradability of antonyms, 204; of
complementaries, 202–4
grade-terms, 192–5
gradual oppositions, 221
group-member relation, 175–6

head, semantic, 103
head, syntactic, 47
head-complement constructions, 103
head-modifier constructions, 103
hetero-paronymy, 131
hierarchies, 112–18, 136–56, 157–81,
181–95; branching *v.* non-branching,
112–13, 181–7; labelled part–whole type,
160; levels of, 117–19, 181–7;
meronomies, 157–81; non-branching
type, 181–95; origin of, 114; relation of
difference of, 113; relation of dominance
of, 113; taxonomies, 136–56
highlighting of semantic traits, 53
holo-meronyms, holo-meronymy, 165, 182;
and grammatical hierarchies, 182
holonyms, 162–5; facultative *v.* canonical,
162; hypo-holonym, 163; locating
holonym, 164; super-holonym, 164
homonymous lexical form, 80
hyponyms, hyponymy, 21, 88–92, 124, 137,

139, 291; cognitive *v.* absolute, 291; and
direction of entailment, 88–91; and
endonymy, 124; hyponym and
superordinate, 88–9, 109; and taxonymy,
137, 139
hypo-relations, 95, 131, 163, 240–2;
-antonyms, 240–2; -holonyms, 163;
-opposites, 240–2; -paronyms, 131;
-reversives, 241

iconic units of communication, 46
identity test for ambiguity, 62, 63, 82
idiomaticity, 46
idioms, 37–45, 46, 47, 132, 135; asyntactic
type, 38; circularity of traditional
definition of, 37 and collocations, 40–1;
and dead metaphors, 41–5; and foreign
learners, 44; and intensification, 47;
modifiability of elements of, 38, 47; and
paronymy, 132; predictability of
properties of, 39, 47; syntactic restrictions
of, 38; and translation, 42–4
idiosyncratic collocational restrictions, 281
impartiality, 208–14, 244–6, 247, 264;
strong *v.* weak types, 244–6
implicit superlatives, 216–17, 218
improbability, 13, 21, 111
inappropriateness, 107, 111
inclusive reference, 156
incompatibility, 21, 93–5, 109, 150–2; and
co-taxonymy, 150–2; and oppositeness,
109
incongruity, 107
inconsistency in proportional series, 122
independent reversives, 228–30
indicators, semantic, 32–4, 39; full type, 33,
39; partial type, 34, 39
indirect tests for ambiguity, 54–6, 81; for
generality, 57
inflectional affixes, 77
inherent binarity, 109, 257–62
inherent *v.* contextual semantic features,
111
inherent ordering in lexical chains, 191–2
inherentness and antonymy, 214–16
integral parts, 167–8
interactives, 201–2
intersecting taxonomies, 152–3
intransitive relations, 114
intuitions as semantic data, 9–15
irreversible binomials, 39–40, 47

labelled part–whole hierarchies, 160
latent binarity, 261
latent elements, latency, 104, 110, 127
lax proportional series, 127–8
levels, hierarchical, 117–18, 145–56, 170–1,
181–7; of meronomies, 170–1, 181–7;

substantive type, 118; of taxonomies, 145–56, 181–7; technical type, 118
lexemes, 49–50, 80, 81, 83; finite enumerability of, 49; and polysemy, 80
lexical analogues, 125–6
lexical chains, 187–92; helical type, 189–92; inherent *v.* contingent ordering in, 191–2
lexical configurations, 112–35; and lexical fields, 134
lexical creativity, 50
lexical cycles, 190
lexical fields, 134
lexical form, 77
lexical hierarchies, 136–95; meronomies, 156–80; non-branching types, 181–95; taxonomies, 136–56
lexical relations, introduction to, 84–111; low-level types, 84–6; paradigmatic *v.* syntagmatic types, 86, 106–9; syntagmatic types, 100–9, 110
lexical siblings, 125–6
lexical solidarities, 110
lexical units, 23–48, 49–74, 74–80, 81, 83; and Kempson's lexemes, 81; paradigmatic delimitation of, 49–74; primary type, 79; re-definition of, 77; secondary type, 79; and sense, 49; and sense-spectra, 83; syntagmatic delimitation of, 23–48; syntactic delimitation of, 74–80
linguistic meaning, 21
linguistic polarity, 246–7, 248–52, 254–5; and logical polarity, 254–5; and natural polarity, 248–52
linkage, 52–3, 81
local meronyms, 164
local senses, 74, 79, 83
locating holonyms, 164

marked term of opposition, 257, 263–4
'Maxim of Quantity', 156
meaning *v.* grammar, 1–8
meaning postulates, 22
meaning, types of: absolute, 21; evoked, 110, 282–5; expressive, 45, 110, 271–7; linguistic, 21; pragmatic, 22; presupposed, 104–7, 110–11; propositional, 45, 271–7; semantic, 22
meaning of a word, 15–20; and encyclopaedic facts, 19; and pragmatics, 19
measure terms, units of measure, 185–6, 193
meronomies, 157–79; convergence in, 170; gaps in, 171; levels in, 170–1; land taxonomies, 177–9; type constancy in, 168–9
meronyms, meronymy, 95, 124, 160–5; 167–8, 172–7, 182; close relatives of,

172–7: class-member relation, 176, collection-member relation, 176, event-feature relation, 175, group-member relation, 175–6, process (etc.)-phase relation, 174, substance-particle relation, 177; definitions of, 160–5; and endonymy, 124; facultative *v.* canonical types, 162; holo-meronyms, 165, 182; hypo-meronyms, 164; local meronyms, 164; non-concrete meronyms, 172–5: events, 173–4, places, 172–3; para-meronyms, 163; super-meronyms, 163; transitivity of meronymy, 167–8
metaphor, 41–5, 48; dead metaphor, 41–5
micro-relations, 289; -compatibility, 289; -hyponymy, 289; -incompatibility, 289
mode (register), 284
mode (semantic), 271
modulation by context, 52–3
morpheme, 36, 45
mutual entailment, 15

nano-relations, 290; -compatibility, 290; -hyponymy, 290; -incompatibility, 290
natural kind terms, 140–3, 155
neutralisation, 255–7
nominal kind terms, 140–3, 155
non-branching lexical hierarchies, 181–95; chains, helices and cycles, 187–92; derivation from branching type, 181–7; ranks, grades and degrees, 192–5
non-convergence in hierarchies, 134
non-interruptibility of word, 36
normalisation of deviance, 3–8; by contextual manipulation, 7–8; by substitution, 3–6
normality and polarity, 251–2
normality (semantic), 11–12, 20

object-material relation, 177
onomatopoeia, 34, 46
opacity, semantic, 39–40; degrees of, 39–40
open proportional series, 120
open set items, 3, 20, 46
oppositeness, opposition, 197–8, 257–62; and binarity, 258–62; and directional opposition, 260–2; good opposites, 262; and mere incompatibility, 257; opposable and non-opposable notions, 258
opposites, lexical, 197–264; antipodals, 224–5; antonyms, 204–20; complementaries, 198–204; congruence variants, 240–2; converses, 231–40; counteractives, 202; counterparts, 225; directional types, 223–43; directions, 223–4; hypo-opposites, 240–2; interactives, 201–2; pseudo-congruent opposites, 242; pseudo-opposites, 240–2;

opposites (*cont.*)
  restitutives, 228; reversives, 226–31;
  satisfactives, 202; super-opposites, 240–2
opposition, types of (Prague School), 221
origin, of hierarchy, 114
overlapping antonyms, 208–14
overspecification, 153–5

paradigmatic delimitation of lexical units,
  49–74
paradox, 17, 107; expressive type, 107
para-relations, 99–100, 145, 163;
  -hyponymy, 99, 145: and para-taxonomy,
  145; -incompatibility, 99–100;
  -meronymy, 163; -taxonymy, 145
paronymic relations, 55
paronyms, paronymy, 81, 130–3; base and
  paronym, 130; false paronyms, 132;
  hetero-paronymy, 131; hypo-paronyms,
  131; super-paronyms, 131; zero-derived
  paronyms, 132–3
partial relations, 96–7
partonomies, 180
parts, 157–60, 158–9, 165–6, 167–8, 169;
  autonomy of, 158–9; determinate
  function of, 159; functional domain of,
  165–6; integral parts *v.* attachments,
  167–8; non-arbitrary boundaries of,
  158–9; *v.* pieces, 157–8; segmental type,
  169; systemic type, 169
part–whole hierarchy, labelled, 160
passive selection of senses, 69
patent binarity, 261
peripheral categories, 148–9
philonyms, 106
phonaesthesia, 35, 46
phonetic elicitors, 35
pieces *v.* parts, 157–60
pivotal region of antonym scale, 205
pleonasm, 12, 21, 100–9, 123
plesionyms, 285–9; and micro-relations, 289
polar antonyms, 208–14, 248
polarity, 246–55, 262–3; and evaluation,
  251, 263; linguistic polarity, 246–7;
  logical polarity, 252–5; natural polarity,
  248–52; and normality, 251–2; and
  privative antonyms, 250–1; and
  reversives, 248–50
polysemy, 80
possible semantic traits, 16–18
pragmatic implication, 21
pragmatic meaning, 19, 22
presupposed meaning, presupposition,
  104–7, 110–11, 262–3, 278–82; and
  cognitive synonymy, 278–82; and
  collocational restrictions, 279–81; and
  complementarity, 262–3; and selectional
  restrictions, 279–81

primary lexical units, 79
privative antonyms, 208–14, 250–1; polarity
  of, 250–1
privative opposition, 221
processes, 174
productive output as semantic data, 8–9
productive selection of senses, 69
promotion of semantic traits, 52–3
proper nouns, 140, 183, 185, 186, 196
proportional series, 118–35; and ambiguity,
  85, 121; cells in, 118; closed *v.* open
  types, 120–1; congruence mis-match in,
  126–7; consistency *v.* inconsistency in,
  122; quasi-series, 129–33; and semantic
  components/features, 134; strict *v.* lax
  types, 127–8
propositional *v.* absolute and plesio-
  relations, 290–1
propositional antonyms, 291
propositional hyponyms, 291
propositional meaning, 45, 271–7; *v.*
  expressive meaning, 271–7
propositional mode, 271
propositional synonymy, 21, 88, 111,
  270–85, 290, 293; and collocational
  restrictions, 279–82; and evaluative
  meaning, 277; and evoked meaning,
  282–5; and expressive meaning, 271–7;
  and nano-relations, 290; and presupposed
  meaning, 278–82
prototypes, 22
prototypical features, 22
prototypical taxonomic categories, 148–9
pseudo-comparatives of antonyms, 206
pseudo-relations, 98–9, 240–2;
  -complementaries, 242; -opposites,
  240–2; -synonyms, 98–9, 242
pun test (=zeugma test) for ambiguity,
  61–2, 63–6

quasi-proportional series, 129–33
quasi-relations, 97, 149–50; in taxonomies,
  149–50
quasi-syntactic ambiguity, 67–8
quasi-syntactic differences between partial
  synonyms, 97

rank-terms, 192–5
recurrent semantic contrast, 15, 26–9,
  29–32, 40–1; and collocational
  uniqueness, 29–32; and syntactically
  determined elements, 29, 31–2; as test for
  semantic constituency, 26–9, 40–1
recursiveness of sense-creating rules, 81
reduction (syntactic), 102
register, 100, 110, 282–5; field, 283–4;
  mode, 284; style, 284–5

relation of difference of hierarchy, 113
relation of dominance of hierarchy, 113, 134
relations, contextual, 16
relations, lexical, introduction to, 84–111
relations, logical, 113–16
reproductive distinctiveness, 45
restitutives, 228
reversible verbs, 229
reversives, 201, 226–31, 240–2, 248–50; and
    antonym groups, 230; congruence
    variants of, 240–2; and entropy, 248–50;
    independent type, 228–30; polarity of,
    248–50
rigid designators, 141–2, 155
root, lexical, as basis for lexical semantics,
    46

satisfactives, 202
scope ambiguity, 67–8
secondary lexical units, 79
segmental parts, 169
selection of senses by context, 52, 53, 69;
    passive type, 69; productive type, 69
selectional restrictions, 107, 110, 111, 278
selector and selectee, 104
semantic affinity and disaffinity, 16–18
semantic categorisers, 32–4
semantic constituents, 24–32, 40;
    discontinuous type, 31; minimal type, 25,
    26; peripheral types, 29–32
semantic deviance, tests for, 4–8
semantic features/components, 22
semantic field (Haasian), 21
semantic field and sense-spectra, 73
semantic head, 103
semantic indicators, 32–4, 39; full type, 33,
    39; partial type, 34, 39
semantic meaning, 22
semantic mode, 271
semantic opacity, 39–40; degrees of, 39–40
semantic proportion, 15
semantic role, 111
semantic tallies, 32–4; pure and impure
    types, 33
semantic traits, 16–20, 52–3, 287–9;
    backgrounding of, 53; canonical type, 19;
    capital type, 287–9; criterial type, 16;
    demotion of, 52–3; excluded type, 16;
    expected type, 16; highlighting of, 53;
    possible type, 16; promotion of, 52–3;
    subordinate type, 287–9; unexpected
    type, 16
semantic transfer rules, 83
semantic transparency, 37
semantics as experimental science, 8–9; as
    observational science, 8–9
semes, 134
semi-relations, 95

semi-systematic collocational restrictions,
    281
senses of lexical units, 49, 80–1; discreteness
    of, 80–1
sense-spectra, 71–4, 83, 164; as lexical units,
    73; local senses on, 74, 83; and
    meronymy, 164; metaphorical type, 73–4;
    non-metaphorical type, 74; and semantic
    fields, 73
siblings, lexical, 125–6
sound symbolism, 35, 46
stative verbs as antonyms, 217–18
stem (lexical), 77, 83
stock and attachment, 167–8
strict proportional series, 127–8
strong impartiality, 204–6
style (register), 284–5
subordinate semantic traits, 287–9
substance–particle relation, 177
substantive levels of hierarchy, 118
superlatives, implicit, 216–17, 218
superordinate, 89
super-relations, 95, 131, 163–4, 240–2;
    -antonyms, 240; -converses, 240;
    -holonyms, 164; -meronyms, 163;
    -opposites, 240–2; -paronyms, 131
symmetric relations, 113
synonymity, scale of, 265–6, 268, 270
synonyms, synonymy, 21, 111, 265–94;
    absolute type, 21, 268–70;
    characterisation of class, 266–7;
    propositional type, 21, 111, 270–85; and
    congruence relations, 289–91; Lyons's
    classification of, 292; plesionyms, 285–9
syntactic delimitation of lexical units, 74–80
syntactic deviance, tests for, 4–8
syntactically determined semantic
    constituents, 29, 31–2
syntagmatic delimitation of lexical units,
    23–48
syntagmatic lexical relations, 100–9, 110
systematic collocational restrictions, 281
systemic parts, 169

tallies, semantic, 32–4; pure and impure
    types, 33
tautonyms, 106
taxonomies, 136–56, 177–9; covert
    categories in, 148–9; gaps in, 149; generic
    level in, 146, 153–5; intersection between,
    152–3; levels in, 145–55; and
    meronomies, 177–9; natural (folk) v.
    scientific types, 145–6; peripheral
    categories in, 148–9; prototypical
    categories in, 148–9; quasi-relations in,
    149–50
taxonyms, taxonymy, 120, 137–45, 155; and
    classification of living things, 144; and the

taxonyms (*cont.*)
good category principle, 143–4; and hyponymy, 137, 139, 155; and natural kind terms, 140–3; and nominal kind terms, 143; parataxonymy, 145; and 'type' readings, 141
trait, semantic, *see* semantic trait
transfer features, 111
transitive relations, 114
transitivity of hyponymy, 165; of meronymy, 167–8; of "piece of" relation, 158; of taxonymy, 165
transparency, semantic, 37
true comparatives of antonyms, 206
typical features, 22

underspecification, 153–5
unexpected semantic traits, 16–18
unilateral entailment, 15
units of measure, measure terms, 185–6, 193

unit-type ambiguity, 50, 63, 78
unmarked term of opposition, 257, 263–4; and positive evaluation, 263

vagueness, 81; and generality, 81; use of term by others, 81; *vague v. well-defined*, 81

weak impartiality, 244–6
words, 15–20, 35–6, 38–9, 77; derived type, 77; and idioms, 38–9; meanings of, 15–20; non-interruptibility of, 36; as syntactic units, 35–6

xenonyms, 106

Yes/No test for ambiguity, 60–1, 82, 83

zero-derived paronyms, 132–3
zeugma, 13, 21, 209, 259

AUTHOR INDEX

Allerton, D. J., 20, 45, 48, 83, 110, 111, 293
Allerton, D. J., Carney, E. & Holdcroft, D., 20
Allwood, J., Anderson, L.-G. & Dahl, Ö., 21
Alston, W. P., 81
Anderson, E. S., 180
Anderson, L.-G., see Allwood, J.
Aristotle, 81
Austin, J. L., 220, 292

Backhouse, A. E., 243
Baldinger, K., 292
Bar-Hillel, Y., 46
Baudelaire, 242
Bauer, L., 134
Bendix, E. M., 22
Berlin, B., 156
Berlin, B., Breedlove, D. E. & Raven, P. H., 156
Berlin, B. & Kay, P., 156
Bever, T. G. & Rosenbaum, P. S., 134
Bierwisch, M., 22, 111, 220
Black, M., 48
Blamey, M., see Fitter, F.
Bolinger, D., 22, 46, 220, 221
Boucher, T. & Osgood, C. E., 263
Breedlove, D. E., see Berlin, B.
Brooke-Rose, C., 48
Brown, C. H., 180
Brown, C. H., Kolar, J., Torrey, B. J., Truong-Quang, T. & Volkman, P., 156
Brown, R., 156
Bunge, M., 134

Carling, C., see Moore, T.
Carnap, R., 22
Carney, E., see Allerton, D. J.
Chaffin, R. & Hermann, D. J., 180
Chaffin, R. & Winston, M., 180
Channell, J., 82
Chomsky, A. N., 81, 110

Coleman, L. & Kay, P., 22
Collinge, N. E., 81
Cook, W. A., 195
Cormack, A., see Kempson, R. M.
Coseriu, E., 22, 110, 134, 180, 221
Cowie, A. P., 45, 46, 48, 81
Cowie, A. P., Mackin, R. & McCaig, I. R., 45
Cruse, D. A., 22, 81, 155, 156, 180, 220, 221, 242

Dahl, Ö., 180, see also Allwood, J.
Dowty, D., 180
Ducháček, O., 220

Fillmore, C. J., 111
Firth, J. R., 21
Fitter, A., see Fitter, F.
Fitter, F., Fitter, A. & Blamey, M., 196
Fodor, J. A., see Katz, J. J.
Fraser, B., 46

Gauger, H.-M., 292
Geckeler, H., 22, 134, 180, 220
Givón, T., 263
Grice, H. P., 81, 156, 221
Griffiths, P., 293
Gruber, J. S., 111

Haas, W., 20, 21, 45, 46, 222, 292
Halliday, M. A. K., 111
Halliday, M. A. K., McIntosh, A. & Strevens, P., 294
Harris, A. S., 45
Healey, A., 46
Hermann, D. J., see Chaffin, R.
Hjelmslev, L., 22, 134
Hoenigswald, H. M., 109
Holdcroft, D., see Allerton, D. J.
Howard, P., 20
Hudson, R. A., 294
Hunn, E. S., 156

Author index

Johnson-Laird, P. N., *see* Miller, G. A.

Kastovsky, D., 110, 111, 221, 293
Katz, J. J. & Fodor, J. A., 22, 110
Kay, P., 134, *see also* Berlin, B. and Coleman, L.
Kay, P. & McDaniel, C. K., 264
Keats, 12, 225
Kempson, R. M., 81, 82, 83, 110
Kempson, R. M. & Cormack, A., 82
Kolar, J., *see* Brown, C. H.
Kooij, J., 82
Kripke, S., 155

Lakoff, G., 294
Lamb, S., 134
Leech, G. N., 22, 81, 83, 110
Lehrer, A. J., 110, 134, 156, 196, 220, 221, 262
Lehrer, A. J. & Lehrer, K., 220, 221
Lehrer, K., *see* Lehrer, A. J.
Levin, S. R., 48
Levinson, S. C., 22, 81, 110, 196, 220, 221
Ljung, M., 220
Long, T. H. & Summers, D., 48
Lutzeier, P. R., 134, 180
Lyons, J., 20, 21, 22, 45, 46, 81, 82, 83, 109, 110, 111, 134, 155, 180, 196, 220, 221, 242, 263, 264, 292

McCaig, I. R., *see* Cowie, A. P.
McCawley, J., 242, 263
McDaniel, C. K., *see* Kay, P.
McIntosh, A., *see* Halliday, M. A. K.
Mackin, R., 21, 48, *see also* Cowie, A. P.
Makkai, A., 46
Malkiel, Y., 47
Marsh-Stefanovska, P. J., 222
Martin, R., 220
Matthews, P. H., 45, 81, 83, 110, 243
Mervis, C., *see* Rosch, E. H.
Miller, G. A. & Johnson-Laird, P. N., 109, 134
Mitchell, T. F., 46, 48
Mitford, N., 293
Mooij, J. J. A., 48
Moore, T. & Carling, C., 22, 81
Murdoch, I., 12

Newmeyer, F. J., 47
Nida, E., 22
Nunberg, G., 82

Ogden, C. K., 220, 264
Osgood, C. E., *see* Boucher, T.

Palmer, F. R., 293
Plato, 81
Pohl, J., 220
Pottier, B., 22, 134, 264
Pulman, S. G., 22, 155, 156

Raven, P. H., *see* Berlin, B.
Rhodes, R., 156
Richards, I. A., 48
Roget, P. M., 265
Rohdenburg, G., 156
Rosch, E. H., 22, 156
Rosch, E. H. & Mervis, C., 156
Rosch, E. H. *et al.*, 156
Rosenbaum, P. S., *see* Bever, T. G.
Ross, J. F., 21, 81

Sadock, J., *see* Zwicky, A.
Sampson, G., 22
Sapir, E., 220, 221
Schwartz, S. P., 155
Searle, J. R., 293
Söll, L., 292
Sperber, D., *see* Wilson, D.
Stebbing, L. S., 134
Strawson, P. F., 21
Strevens, P. *see* Halliday, M. A. K.
Summers, D., *see* Long, T. H.

Tarski, A., 134
Torrey, B. J., *see* Brown, C. H.
Trier, J., 134
Trubetzkoy, N. S., 221
Truong-Quang, T., *see* Brown, C. H.
Tuţescu, M., 291

Ullmann, S., 46, 48

van Overbeke, M., 220
van Valen, L., 134
Vendler, Z., 180
Volkman, P., *see* Brown, C. H.

Wachtel, T., 82
Warczyk, A., 220
Weinreich, U., 46, 111
Wierzbicka, A., 22, 262, 263
Wilson, D. & Sperber, D., 81
Winston, M. *see* Chaffin, R.
Wolstenholme, D., 48

Zikri, M. S., 222
Zimmer, K. E., 221, 263
Zwicky, A. & Sadock, J., 82

310

Printed in the United Kingdom by
Lightning Source UK Ltd., Milton Keynes
139484UK00001B/40/A